The Savannas

The Savannas

Biogeography and Geobotany

MONICA M. COLE

Department of Geography
Royal Holloway and Bedford New College
University of London

1986

ACADEMIC PRESS
Harcourt Brace Jovanovich, Publishers
London · Orlando · San Diego · New York
Austin · Boston · Sydney · Tokyo · Toronto

ACADEMIC PRESS INC. (LONDON) LTD.
24–28 Oval Road, London NW1 7DX

United States Edition published by
ACADEMIC PRESS, INC.
Orlando, Florida 32887

British Library Cataloguing in Publication Data

Cole, Monica, M.
The Savannas: biogeography and geobotany.
1. Savanna ecology
I. Title
574.5′2643   QH541.5.P7

ISBN 0-12-179520-9

Phototypeset by
Dobbie Typesetting Service, Plymouth, Devon

Printed in Great Britain by
Galliard (Printers) Ltd., Great Yarmouth

Preface

Savanna vegetation of varying physiognomy and floristic composition covers very large areas between the tropical rain forests and the mid-latitude deserts in the southern continents. Derived from an Amerindian word that was first used in the sixteenth century to describe treeless grasslands in the West Indies, the term savanna has since been used to describe the mixed tree and grass type of vegetation found in all tropical latitudes. In the individual continents it has been applied to different forms of vegetation. In some areas local terms have been introduced for distinctive structural types, in others the term savanna has been used for grasslands derived from forest by the deliberate use of fire.

Differing usage of the term savanna has been accompanied by differing views on the factors influencing its distribution with some authors stressing either climatic or pedological or anthropological factors, or a combination of these, and others citing the interplay of many factors, including geomorphology, geology and the role of man.

The form and composition of the savanna vegetation reflect the interrelationships between the evolution and migration of plant species on the one hand and the interplay of environmental factors that produces habitats that vary spatially and are subject to continuous temporal change on the other. The precise relationships that determine the nature and composition of the vegetation in any area are complex. The relative importance of individual environmental factors varies from place to place.

This book attempts to provide a framework within which the relationships between the distribution of the major categories of savanna vegetation, the vegetation associations and the plant communities within them and the environmental conditions can be understood, and the precise relationships between the vegetation and the interplay of individual environmental parameters can be investigated and evaluated. In these aims and objectives the book differs from other published works that concentrate on the dynamics and functions of the ecosystem and on human ecology.

Constraints of space have necessitated selection of areas for detailed study. Attention has been concentrated on the core areas of distribution of savanna woodlands in Zambia, of savanna parklands in South Africa and of low tree and shrub savannas in South West Africa/Namibia and Botswana. More space has been accorded to the savannas of Africa than to those of Australia and South America because they exhibit the greatest variety of form and composition and the most complex relationships to landscape evolution following the break-up of Gondwanaland, of which Africa formed the central part.

In the text reference is made to places that could not be shown on accompanying maps and diagrams and in some instances the reader will need to consult the large-scale maps of individual countries. Within the constraints of space, both in the text and in the selection of illustrations, the author has endeavoured to provide as wide, representative and detailed coverage as possible. In the interest of simplicity no accents have been used in place names or authors' names.

Monica M. Cole
April 1986

Acknowledgements

This book is the result of some thirty years of investigation during which the author has enjoyed the encouragement and support of colleagues in the Universities of the Witwatersrand, Keele and London, and of friends and former students in the Universities of Queensland, Melbourne, Sydney and Adelaide. Some field studies have been supported by students and assistants on research projects sponsored by the UK Natural Environment Research Council, the former Ministry of Technology and the Department of Industry and by geologists and field personnel of mining companies. In many countries research has been facilitated by the hospitality and help of farmers and officers of research organizations, government departments and international agencies. To all these people and organizations, too numerous to name, the author records her gratitude.

The final manuscript has been typed by Mesdames Pat Adams, Rosemary Dawe, Mary Hodges and Liz Carey. Hitherto unpublished maps and diagrams have been drafted by Mr Ron Halfhide and Misses Claire Wastie and Susannah Hall. To all these people the author extends her warm thanks.

Contents

List of illustrations

1   Introduction

Tropical savannas cover some 23 million km^2 between the equatorial rain forests and the mid-latitude deserts and semi-deserts. They clothe about 20% of the earth's land surface, 65% of Africa, 60% of Australia, 45% of South America and about 10% of India and Southeast Asia. The areas they occupy embrace the greater part of the world's undeveloped and underdeveloped lands. Despite the vast extent, wildlife resources and present and potential importance of these areas for domestic stock and crop production, however, the relationships between the tropical savanna vegetation and environmental conditions are less well understood than those of most other ecosystems (Huntley and Walker 1982).

Although there is no commonly agreed definition of the word savanna (Bourliere 1983), there is increasing consensus that, characteristically, savanna vegetation comprises a continuous grass stratum usually with trees and/or shrubs exhibiting similar structural and functional characteristics. It includes plant communities of diverse floristic composition and varying physiognomy from pure grasslands, parklands and low tree and shrub savannas to open deciduous woodlands, thicket and scrub (Chapter 2). In some areas gradational floristic and physiognomic changes mark the transition from one type of savanna to another; in others the changes are abrupt and the boundaries are sharp. Invariably the boundary between savanna and tropical forest is well defined and abrupt, the change to forest being marked by the disappearance of grasses and the presence of evergreen and semi-deciduous tree species whose morphology and physiology contrast with those of the savanna species.

The tropical savannas are characteristic of areas with a strongly seasonal summer rainfall regime and a dry period lasting from four to seven or eight months in the cooler season. The distinctive categories of savanna occupy similar soils and are associated with similar distinctive landforms in each continent, where characteristic savanna landscapes may be recognized.

The diverse floristic composition and differing physiognomic forms of savanna vegetation have promoted differing definitions and classifications of the savannas, usually elaborated for particular continents or regions in which their authors conducted their research (Chapter 2). The complex distribution patterns of the savannas as a whole and of the distinctive types of vegetation within them have generated conflicting views on the relative importance of the factors influencing their distribution and aroused controversy over their status and origin (Chapter 3). The divergent views arose partly from studies being conducted in isolation in one continent or one region and partly from inadequate scientific research. In the last two decades, however, research in different fields undertaken singly or collaboratively by biogeographers, ecologists and palynologists, zoologists, ornithologists and entomologists, pedologists and geomorphologists, agronomists, foresters and wildlife conservationists has contributed to the elucidation of some of the

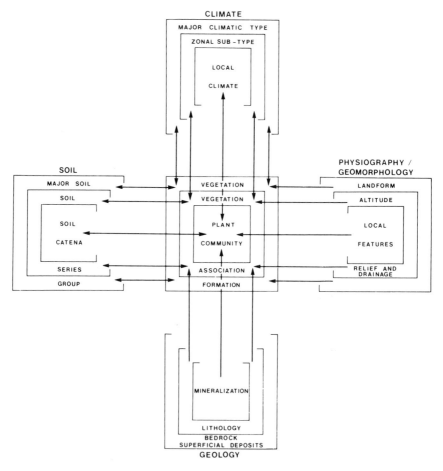

Figure 1.1. Interrelationships between vegetation communities, climate, soils, physiography/geomorphology and geology at differing levels of classification.

problems; exchanges of information and experiences between scientists in different continents have promoted effective comparison of similar environments and facilitated understanding of comparable problems. Hence an objective assessment of the relative importance of the factors influencing the distribution and origin of the savannas is now possible.

Like all types of vegetation the savannas reflect the interplay of changing sets of environmental conditions in space and time (Figure 1.1). Their floristic composition is in part a legacy of the past and their present distribution, while closely related to current climatic and edaphic conditions, has been influenced by climatic changes over geological time, by the long-term geomorphological evolution of the landscape and by the short-term effects of grazing, fire and man's cultural practices. The influences of these interacting interrelated factors on the present form, composition and distribution of the savannas are examined in this book.

2 Definition, morphology and classificiation of savanna vegetation

An understanding of the problems that have beset the formulation of an agreed definition of savannas requires consideration of the origin, historical and present use of the term. The formulation of an acceptable global classification of the discrete forms of vegetation to which the term is applied requires consideration of both their physiognomy and their floristic composition. The former reflects the interplay of current climatic and edaphic conditions and the influences of fire, grazing animals and man's cultural practices. The floristic composition is the legacy of evolutionary changes that have been influenced by major climatic changes, geological events and geomorphological processes operating over a very long period of time. Some families, genera and species of savanna plants are descended from floras of Cretaceous or Tertiary age; others evolved later. Some have widespread distributions; others are restricted to a few areas. Most savanna species exhibit characteristic morphological and physiological features that are adaptive to the environmental conditions. Some display different physiognomic forms under differing climatic and edaphic regimes whereas others do not vary.

Today, as in the past, the form and composition of the savanna vegetation is constantly changing both spatially and temporally in response to constantly changing environmental conditions. At any given time the vegetation is in a state of dynamic equilibrium with the environment. Definition and classification must have regard to this and be sufficiently flexible to accommodate the distinctive types of savanna vegetation that are found in each continent.

DEFINITIONS OF SAVANNA

The term savanna is believed to originate from an Amerindian work which, in a work on the Indies published in 1535, was used by Oviedo y Valdes to describe 'land which is without trees but with much grass either tall or short'. Subsequently Grisebach (1872), Drude (1890) and Schimper (1903) extended its use to include grasslands with trees and thereafter the term was used to describe the mixed tree and grass types of vegetation found in all tropical latitudes.

The term savanna has been applied to different forms of vegetation in different continents. In addition to grasslands with variable tree and shrub components, in all continents, forms of savanna woodland that have been influenced to varying degrees by fire are included. In some countries savanna is used also for grasslands that have been derived from tropical forest by the deliberate and repeated use of fire. In many countries local terms are used for distinctive types of savanna.

In tropical America the term savanna is used for any grassland, with or without trees, natural or man made. This accords with the definition proposed by Beard, namely 'a plant formation of tropical America comprising a virtually continuous ecologically dominant stratum of more or less xeromorphic herbs, of which grasses and sedges are the principal components, with scattered shrubs, trees or palms sometimes present' (Beard 1953). Thus defined, the term embraces the tropical grasslands and palm-studded grasslands of the Llanos of the Orinoco basin of Venezuela. It includes also the physiognomic forms of vegetation known as cerradao, cerrados, campos cerrados, campos sujos and campos limpos that form a continuum from woodlands with a grassland ground layer to pure grasslands in Brazil and occur over smaller areas in Venezuela, Guyana and Surinam, and in some of the Caribbean islands. In Brazil the dry types of vegetation, known as caatingas, that vary from thorny woodland in the more humid areas of the Agreste to low tree, shrub and succulent vegetation in the arid areas of the Sertao are not normally regarded as savanna, but they and their counterparts in Venezuela are comparable with the low tree and shrub communities in Africa and Australia that are regarded as savanna.

In central and southern Africa savanna is used for open deciduous woodlands, including those locally known as miombo, that are composed of fairly tall, mesophyllous trees and a well defined grass stratum, for parklike vegetation comprising grasslands studded with microphyllous trees of low to medium height, for grasslands with scattered clumps of trees or bushes, for treeless grasslands of tall perennial mesophytic grasses and of short annual grasses mixed with perennial grasses with narrow rolled leaves, and for open forms of vegetation composed of scattered low growing microphyllous trees and shrubs and a ground layer of perennial and annual grasses. The term bushveld is used locally for the parklike forms of savanna which together with the low tree and shrub forms are regarded as the most typical savannas.

In Australia the term savanna has been used for the open woodlands of fairly tall mesophyllous trees and a well defined grass layer, for open tree-studded grasslands with a parklike appearance and for open forms of vegetation composed of small trees and shrubs and a grass layer of annual and perennial grasses. The open grasslands, distinguished as tussock grasslands and hummock grasslands, have been excluded although they interdigitate with the other forms of savanna and are composed of the same grass species.

In Asia, forms of vegetation resembling the deciduous mesophyllous woodlands and thorny microphyllous parklands of Africa are regarded as savannas that have been derived from deciduous forests by cutting, burning, grazing and cultivation extending over many centuries.

Although the term savanna has been applied to different types of vegetation in the different continents, with the emphasis on grasslands in South America, on parklands and low tree and shrub in Africa, and on open woodlands and shrublands in Australia and Asia, there is now a convergence of views to include those forms of vegetation that occur between the equatorial rain forests and the mid-latitude deserts and have a continuous grass stratum that is either treeless or studded by trees and shrubs of variable height and density. There is agreement that the various forms of tropical savannas share structural and functional characteristics that enable them to withstand seasonal drought, that they exhibit distinctive seasonal rhythms of growth and productivity and that they are dynamic. Although some aspects of savanna physiognomy and some morphological features of characteristic species are attributed to fire, opinions differ over the extent to which this has influenced the overall structure of the vegetation or the role that it has played in its creation.

Since, in different continents and countries, vegetation of differing physiognomy and floristic composition is included in the tropical savannas, a classification that accommodates all the different types is needed. For this, some knowledge of the morphological features and physiological responses of the characteristic species is essential.

MORPHOLOGICAL FEATURES AND PHYSIOLOGICAL RESPONSES OF SAVANNA VEGETATION PLANTS

The floristic composition of savanna vegetation varies greatly between the continents. Morphological features vary between species and physiological responses differ in accordance with plant/soil moisture relationships which are dependent on both climatic and edaphic conditions. It is therefore perhaps not surprising that whereas there are physiognomic resemblances between the discrete categories of savanna in each continent, the species share some common morphological features and physiological responses but also show striking differences. The latter are manifest particularly in the tree and shrub strata of the savanna woodlands, parklands and low tree and shrub savannas.

The dominant grasses in the grass stratum of all savanna areas are now known to belong to the C4 group, i.e. those exhibiting the C4 photosynthetic pathway (Kortshack *et al.* 1965, Hatch and Slack 1966, Huntley 1982, Medina 1982a, Nix 1983), which is favoured by high light intensity, high temperatures and high evaporation rates. Physiologically the savanna grasses differ from those of temperate lands and of semi-deciduous tropical forests which belong to the C3 group. Within the savannas aspartic acid-forming C4 grasses predominate in the drier areas where there is a higher nitrogen availability in the soils, whereas malate-forming C4 grasses predominate in the moister areas. These characteristics of savanna grasses are most important for identifying tropical savannas and for discriminating different categories of vegetation within them. The characteristic savanna grasses have a tussock form that is produced by seasonal aerial shoots arising from perennating underground structures or rhizomes that are relatively close to the surface. The leaves show varying degrees of scleromorphy and the apical buds are frequently protected by old leaf sheaths. In the drier areas of Australia some grass species are resinous, this feature being characteristic of *Aristida contorta*, commonly called the Kerosene grass, and most highly developed in the *Triodia* and *Plectrachne* species known locally as spinifex. These two latter genera form hummocks and rings, growth features that are absent from the African and South American savanna grasses.

The trees and shrubs of the savanna woodland display a variety of leaf form with marked contrasts between the continents. The leaves of most tree species are scleromorphic, a result of abundant mechanical tissue and, especially in South America, of the deposition of silica. In Brazil the leaves of the characteristic cerrados trees — *Kielmeyera* spp., *Vochysia* spp., *Salvertia convallariodora*, *Caryocar brasiliensis* — are large, coriaceous or leathery (see Figure 2.3). Those of *Curatella americana*, due to the deposition of silica on their underside, are sandpapery, whereas those of *Aspidosperma tomentosa* are hairy. The less common leguminous tree species, however, have smaller pinnate leaves. In Africa the leaves of the characteristic *Brachystegia*, *Isoberlinia* and *Julbernardia* spp. trees are mesophyllous and pinnate and less sclerophyllous than those of the typical South American species. Those of the less common *Uapaca* spp. however are larger and coriaceous. In Australia the dominant *Eucalyptus* spp. have drooping sclerophyllous and strongly resinous leaves of medium size. Thus whereas sclerophyllous leaves of medium to large size are characteristic of savanna woodlands, the different species in the different continents exhibit a variety of different forms and characteristics.

The leaves of the tree and shrub species of the drier savannas in the different continents likewise exhibit similarities and contrasts. In Africa and South America, respectively, the characteristic *Acacia* and *Caesalpinia* species have microphyllous pinnate leaves (Figure 2.1) whereas in Australia the *Eucalyptus* trees have mesophyllous leaves and the *Acacia* trees and shrubs are leafless, the function of photosynthesis being performed by expanded stems or phyllodes. Thorns are a characteristic feature of tree and shrub species of Africa (Figure 2.1) and South America and are variously regarded as evolutionary developments representing reduced leaves effecting water economy in drought periods or as a defensive mechanism against browsing herbivores. Many species in the drier types of African savannas, however, are not spinescent while this feature is virtually absent from Australia.

Figure 2.1. Branch of *Acacia giraffae* tree showing large leathery seed pods, microphyllous pinnate leaves and thorns. Near Witvlei, South West Africa.

Whereas the trees and shrubs of the savanna woodlands and low tree and shrub forms of savannas have leaves of contrasting character, those of the parklike savannas, particularly of Africa and Australia, are similar. This is due to the presence of common genera which include *Adansonia* (the Baobab), *Terminalia* and the related *Piliostigma* and *Bauhinia* genera.

Contorted trunks and branches and the development of thick corky barks are characteristic features of the trees of the South American cerrados, but not of the African and Australian savanna woodlands. These features have been attributed to the effects of fire but recent work indicates that tortuosity results from the death of apical meristems after each period of leaf formation and the development of adventitious buds from the vascular cambium of older branches during the next growth season (Laboriau *et al.* 1964, Sarmiento and Monasterio 1983). This is regarded as an adaptive response to seasonal drought that is also effective against recurrent fires.

Comparative experimental work on *Caryocar brasiliense* grown from seed under normal field conditions and under irrigation has shown that the loss of shoots following leaf production that causes tortuosity is an adaptive response to seasonal drought, for it does not occur under irrigation (Labouriau *et al.* 1964). It is an effective defence against recurrent fires but is not a response to such events. It seems probable that possession of a thick corky bark is a further morphological feature that enables plants primarily to withstand drought and secondarily the effects of fire.

The characteristic trees and shrubs of the savanna woodlands of Africa, Australia and South America are able to regenerate from rootstocks or xylopodia after the destruction of aerial parts by fire or drought. The *Brachystegia, Isoberlinia* and *Julbernardia* species of Africa and the *Eucalyptus* species of Australia are characterized by ligno tubers that begin to develop at the seedling stage. This suggests a morphological feature that enables the species to survive under conditions of recurrent drought rather than in response to recurrent fire, although it also enables plants to withstand the latter. The varied forms of xylopodia developed by cerrados plants (Rawitscher *et al.* 1943, Rawitscher and Rachid 1946, Rachid 1947) are similarly effective organs for drought resistance. The extensive root systems that characterize many savanna trees and shrubs enable them to exploit the water and mineral resources of a great volume of soil (Sarmiento and Monasterio 1983). Cerrado trees can develop enormous root systems in deep soils, tap roots of *Andira humilis* being found at depths of 18 m in Brazil (Rawitscher *et al.* 1943) and lateral roots of several tree species in the Venezuelan llanos extending for 20 m or more (Foldats and Rutkiss 1969). Some of the *Acacia* species develop deep tap roots, those of *A. tortilis* having been found at 30 m in mine shafts. On the other hand *Terminalia sericea* and some of the *Combretum* species develop extensive shallow lateral root systems. The differing root systems of different tree and shrub species enable them to survive under differing climatic and edaphic conditions and to exploit the water and mineral resources of different depths of soil. They also enable them to grow in a stratum of grasses with which they do not compete.

Belonging to many different families, genera and species, savanna trees and shrubs exhibit a great variety of flowers and of fruits and seeds. In the drier areas of Africa species like *Rhigozum brevispinosum* and *Catopractes alexandrii* (Chapter 10) as well as the *Acacia* spp. develop delicate showy flowers that are attractive to pollinators during the dry season (Figure 2.2). These are short lived but the seeds develop within thick leathery casings that provide effective protection from desiccation. The seeds are shed after the first rains when conditions for germination are optimal. Thick seed pods are

Figure 2.2. *Rhigozum brevispinosum* showing delicate showy yellow flowers, microphyllous leaves and thorns, Ghanzi area, Botswana.

characteristic of the *Brachystegia*, *Julbernardia* and *Isoberlinia* tree species of Africa, and of the *Acacias* of both Africa and Australia (Figure 2.1). The seeds of the cerrado species are likewise contained in thick casings, a characteristic feature of many savanna species enabling them to withstand drought. The seeds of the winged fruits of *Combretum* and *Terminalia* species are well protected, as are those of the Australian *Eucalyptus* spp. which are enclosed by an operculum. Effective protection against drought and explosive or winged mechanisms for seed dispersal are well developed in many species.

Within different categories of savanna individual species display varying physiological responses to climatic and edaphic conditions. Most of the trees and shrubs of the savanna woodlands, parklands and low tree and shrub savannas of Africa, South America and Asia shed their leaves for periods that vary with the length of the dry season. Most flower and produce new leaves before the rainy season. In South America, however, some of the cerrados tree species, notably *Curatella americana*, shed their old leaves and produce new ones simultaneously so that they are virtually evergreen. The *Eucalyptus* and *Acacia* species of Australia are evergreen although they produce new flushes of growth after rains. In all continents and in all types of savanna the physiological responses of individual species are related both to their morphological features and to the environmental conditions that influence moisture and nutrient availability. The phenology of individual species depends on this interface between morphology and environment and hence varies greatly.

From the above outline it is evident that some of the morphological features and physiological responses of the characteristic species furnish important criteria for defining savannas and classifying individual categories. Thus the identification of C4 grasses and the distinction between the aspartic acid formers of the drier areas and malate formers of the wetter areas are important. Among the trees and shrubs, in addition to differences of spacing and height, distinctions between mesophyllous and microphyllous leaves and between the length of the leafless period are important. Root characteristics, notably the presence of ligno tubers or xylopodia, distinguish savanna woodland trees; variations in the root systems of the trees or shrubs in the drier areas, however, indicate that these are less important than other classificatory criteria although locally important as a reflection of edaphic conditions.

CLASSIFICATIONS OF SAVANNAS

Several attempts, using differing criteria, have been made to classify vegetation on a global basis. While satisfactorily identifying some of the major vegetation formations, the classifications have limitations in universal application and most have generally failed to discriminate the major categories of tropical savannas.

A satisfactory classification of savanna vegetation must accommodate the types of vegetation for which the term is used in each continent. It must have regard to the differing levels of ecological detail available for different areas and be capable of representation at different mapping scales.

For different continents, countries and regions knowledge of savanna ecology varies from outline information on physiognomy and characteristic species at one extreme to detailed phytosociological data and measurements of structure and life form, biomass and productivity at the other. Because of differences in the species composition of the vegetation between the continents, a global classification must be based, at the primary level, on physiognomy. Such a classification is suitable for relatively small-scale maps depicting the different types of savanna vegetation of the individual continents. Within the country or region, however, a floristic classification of the vegetation is often more meaningful than a structural one for the composition of the vegetation reflects the interplay of many more environmental factors and of variations in their relative importance from place to place. Such a classification is suitable for large-scale maps of the vegetation associations and plant communities within the different types of savanna vegetation.

Alternative approaches

Of the vegetation classifications based on structure and life-form, those of Dansereau (1951, 1957, 1958) and Dansereau and Arros (1959), variously modified to meet local needs, have been most widely used. The original schemes based on five categories of life-form, with seven categories of leaf shape and size, four of leaf texture and four of function combined with considerations of the height of erect woody plants and herbs and percentage cover, produced one category of savanna vegetation (Table 2.1). This was purely a structural formation that was independent of floristic composition and could occur in any climate or on any soil. It was unrepresentative however of any of the distinctive forms of tropical savanna vegetation, although it approached that of the parklike savannas of Africa.

The woodland formation discriminated by the classification, on the other hand, resembled the savanna woodland types of Africa and Australia and the campos cerrados of Brazil and Venezuela; and the steppe formation resembled the vegetation of small trees and shrubs with an incomplete grass cover that characterizes large areas of savanna in the drier areas of Africa and Australia. Recently, a modified form of Dansereau's classification has been successfully used to distinguish variants within the parklike savanna of the Transvaal Bushveld Basin in Africa (van der Meulen and Westfall 1980) (Chapter 9).

For the International Biological Programme, Fosberg (1967) formulated an alternative classification that used the horizontal spacing between plants as a primary discriminant, height as a secondary criterion and function, i.e. evergreen or deciduous and predominant life-form based on the characteristics of leaf size (megaphyllous, mesophyllous and microphyllous) shape (needle or broad leaf) and texture (sclerophyllous, succulent, etc.), as tertiary

Table 2.1. *Vegetation formation classes of Dansereau (1957)*

Formation class	Stratification		Cover value (%)	Cover description
Woodland	Woody plants	>8 m	25–60	(i–c)
Savannas	Woody plants	2–10 m	10–25	(i–p)
	Herbaceous plants	0–2 m	25–100	(i–c)
Steppe	Woody plants	0.1–2 m	0–25	(b–i)
	Herbaceous plants	0–2 m	10–50	(i–p)

c continuous; i interrupted; p scattered; b sparse.
Note: Herbaceous is used here to include all non woody plants: herbs, grasses, bryoids, etc.

criteria. This classification discriminated tall savanna and low savanna within the category of closed vegetation in which the plants, whether trees, shrubs or herbs, are predominantly touching or overlapping; it identified steppe savanna within the open vegetation in which the distance between plants is greater than their diameter. The final classification elaborated many vegetational units into one of which, by using the key, a given plant community could be accommodated. The complex nomenclature, however, detracted from recognition of the major categories of savanna vegetation. Some classes, like shrub steppe savanna, despite the antithesis of terminology, are meaningful but they may be readily identified within a simpler low tree and shrub savanna category.

The classification formulated by Kuchler (1949) which is based first on the foliage, form and function, secondly on the density or spacing of plants and thirdly on height using a letter coding, effectively describes the physiognomy of most forms of vegetation (Table 2.2). In this classification the layer having the most extensive coverage within the vegetation is stated first. This, however, requires a subjective decision so the campos cerrados of Brazil could be classified as SlGc or GcSl and the comparable savanna woodlands of Africa and Australia as SmGt, SlGt, SmGl, etc.

The very different and unique classification formulated by Raunkiaer (1907, 1916) used one feature that summarizes the physiognomy and functional behaviour of individual plant species. This is the height above ground of the

Table 2.2. Criteria for classification of vegetation according to A. W. Kuchler

Function and form of foliage	Density or spacing of plants	Height
B broad leaf evergreen	c continuous	*Woody vegetation*
D broad leaf deciduous	i interrupted	+ tall
E evergreen needleleaf	p scattered	over 25 m
N deciduous needleleaf	b sparse	m medium
S semi-deciduous		10–25 m
M mixed		l low
O without leaves		less than 10 m
G graminoid		s scrub
H herbaceous		z dwarf scrub
L lichens and mosses		
		Grasses and herbs
		t tall
		over 2 m
		m medium
		0.5–2 m
		l low
		less than 0.5 m

Table 2.3. Criteria for the classification of vegetation according to C. Raunkiaer

Classes	Height	Position of perennating buds
Phanerophytes	0.5–25 + m	On branches
mega-phanerophytes	over 25 m	exposed to
meso-phanerophytes	10–25 m	prevailing
micro-phanerophytes	2–10 m	meteorological
mano-phanerophytes	0.5–2 m	conditions
Chamaephytes	0.0–0.5 m	In the air a little above ground level
Hemi-cryptophytes	Aerial shoots survive only for growing season Biennial and perennial plants	In the surface layers of the soil
Geophytes	Aerial parts ephemeral	Beneath soil in underground stem or rootstock, e.g. bulbs, rhizomes, tubers
Therophytes	Annuals and ephemerals that survive the unfavourable period in the form of seeds	

Note: Qualifying descriptions cover whether buds are naked or protected by scales, whether hemi-cryptophytes have caespitose or rosette leaves, etc.

perennating buds that carry the special growing tissues in which all new cells are produced (Table 2.3). It equates to the degree of protection needed to ensure survival during extremes of temperature and aridity. The classification of all species present in an area into the Raunkiaer categories yields a life-form spectrum that characterizes the vegetation. It has been used effectively to distinguish differences in the low tree and shrub savannas in different parts of Botswana (Chapter 10). Since the classification takes account of both the life-form and the floristic composition of the vegetation it is more informative than other classifications, but its use requires prior recognition of the distinctive physionomic and floristic units in the vegetation, and the recording and classification of vast quantities of data. While, given these prerequisites, the classification could effectively discriminate and define the various categories of savanna vegetation, it is impracticable. Moreover, for mapping purposes, the life-form spectra would have to be translated into structural units.

None of the systems proposed for classifying vegetation on a global basis are entirely satisfactory for the savannas. Alternative systems have been used with varying degrees of success in individual continents. A structural classification based on selected criteria was used for the vegetation map of Australia (Williams 1955). The criteria used for defining the vegetation forms were:

(1) four divisions of life form: trees (+ 8 m high), tall shrubs (2–8 m), low shrubs (– 2 m) and herbs (especially grasses).

(2) density or coverage of dominants in three divisions: very dense (spacing less than twice the diameter of the canopy), mid-dense (spacing greater than twice the diameter of the canopy) and open.

Sub-forms were recognized on the basis of leaf texture of the dominants, i.e. mesomorphic or sclerophyllous; and whether the dominants are single stemmed or multi-stemmed, unistoreyed or multi-storeyed. The classification distinguishes savanna woodland, tree and low tree savanna and shrub savanna; it separates the tropical grasslands as tussock grasslands and hummock grasslands and it introduced categories of low-layered forest and low-layered woodland that occur within the savanna belt. The low-layered forest accommodates the vegetation dominated by *Acacia harpophylla* (the brigalow) which, however, varies so greatly in height and density as to occur as layered forest, low-layered forest, low-layered woodland and savanna woodland. The low-layered woodlands include those dominated by *Acacia cambagei* (gidgea), *Callitris glauca* (pine) and *Acacia aneura* (mulga). The interdigitation of the distributions of the various categories of savanna recognized in the classification precludes their separate mapping on a continental scale and for the map of Australia necessitated a compromise representation of alternating stripes of the colours assigned to each category.

The vegetation map of Africa south of the Tropic of Cancer prepared by Keay *et al.* (1959b) under the auspices of the Association pour l'Etude Taxonomique de la Flore d'Afrique Tropicale was based on structure and used the names for the physiognomic types recommended by a meeting of specialists in Phytogeography held at Yangambi in the Congo in 1955. These included dry deciduous forest, woodland, savanna and steppe for types occurring within the savanna belt. A fundamental and controversial distinction was made between savanna and steppe and the classification of the mixed tree and grass types of vegetation was based first on the nature of the herbaceous layer—i.e. savanna or steppe—and then on the density of the woody vegetation. Both terms were used for physiognomic types ranging from purely herbaceous vegetation to open woodland. The term savanna was used for 'vegetation in which perennial mesophytic grasses (e.g. *Hyparrhenia* spp.) at least 80 cm high, with flat, basal and cauline leaves, play an important part' whereas 'steppe' was used for 'vegetation in which annual plants are often abundant between the widely spaced perennial herbs; perennial grasses present have narrow, rolled or folded, mainly basal leaves and are usually less than 80 cm high'. The adoption of this classification provoked some difficulties. The complex distribution patterns of the diverse vegetation types led to such classes as 'dry deciduous forest (and savanna)' and 'woodlands, savannas (and steppes)'. The latter class was subdivided into 'relatively moist types' and 'relatively dry types'. The second of these included savanna grasslands with broad leaved *Combretum* and *Terminalia* trees, *Colophospernum mopane* woodlands and grasslands with microphyllous *Acacia* trees, each of which are distinctive vegetation types, both physiognomically and floristically. Comparable problems arose from the grouping of diverse vegetation types in the other classes.

Proposed classification

None of the foregoing classifications are entirely satisfactory. A more flexible classification, based primarily on physiognomy and secondly on floristic composition is needed. Accordingly the simple classification outlined in Table 2.4 (Cole 1963b) is followed in this book. The distinctive savanna types of Africa and Australia that fall into each category of this classification are given in Table 2.5. Not every type is included in the table but where cited in the text its savanna type category is stated. Vegetation types of intermediate character, often representing depauperate legacies of woodlands that flourished when the climate was wetter than today, are indicated as intermediate types.

Table 2.4. Proposed savanna terminology (Cole 1963b)

Savanna woodland
Deciduous and semi-deciduous woodland of tall trees (more than 8 m high) and tall mesophytic grasses (more than 80 cm high); the spacing of the trees more than the diameter of canopy

Savanna parkland
Tall mesophytic grassland (grasses 40–80 cm high) with scattered deciduous trees (less than 8 m high)

Savanna grassland
Tall tropical grassland without trees or shrubs

Low tree and shrub savanna
Communities of widely spaced low-growing perennial grasses (less than 80 cm high) with abundant annuals and studded with widely spaced, low-growing trees and shrubs often less than 2 m high

Thicket and scrub
Communities of trees and shrubs without stratification

South America has been omitted from the tables. Generally there is greater comparability between the savanna vegetation of Africa and Australia than of either with South America (Figures 2.3 to 2.17; 5.2, 10.1, 18.1 and 18.2). In both Africa and Australia the five categories of savanna vegetation are distinct from one another both physiognomically and floristically. By contrast in South America there is a continuum — locally distinguished as cerradao, cerrados, campos cerrados, campos sujos, campos limpos — with the same species throughout. The cerradao, cerrados and campos cerrados are savanna woodlands comparable with those of Africa and Australia. The campos limpos are comparable with the watershed savanna grasslands of Africa and Australia. The only area with a savanna parkland type of vegetation is the High Pantanal. Typical low tree and shrub savannas are absent from South America where the semi-arid terrain carries a thorny and succulent vegetation in which grasses are poorly represented.

The proposed classification accords with the two-fold division of savanna types recognized as moist/dystrophic savanna and arid eutrophic savanna by specialists at the Symposium on Dynamic Change in Savanna Ecosystems held in Pretoria, at Nylsvlei Research Station and in the Kruger National Park, South Africa, in 1979. This placed the savanna woodlands and associated grasslands of seasonally waterlogged terrain (including the Llanos of Venezuela) in the moist/dystrophic savanna category and the savanna parklands and associated grasslands, the low tree and shrub savannas and the succulent thorny vegetation of the Sertao of Brazil in the arid/eutrophic category. Under this classification the problematic *Burkea africana–Terminalia* woodlands and the *Colophospermum mopane* woodlands were satisfactorily included in the moist/dystrophic and arid/eutrophic categories respectively.

The categories of savanna vegetation recognized in the proposed classification identify the major physiognomic types and separate units whose tree and shrub components have contrasting morphological features. They also distinguish the main categories of grasses (Figure 2.18) as was demonstrated by Johnson at the Symposium on the Management of Savanna Resources held in Brisbane in 1984.

Within the five broad savanna categories indicated in Table 2.4 it is possible to accommodate the vegetation associations and plant communities that have been described and mapped by various authors for different countries and regions in Africa and Australia. Within the classification for each continent it is also possible to accommodate quantitative information on changes in vegetation physiognomy and function in particular areas obtained from phytosociological data classified according to the Dansereau, Kuchler and Raunkiaer systems suitably amended for local conditions.

Table 2.5. A proposed classification for the savanna vegetation

| | AFRICA | | | AUSTRALIA | | |
| | | | | | Authority | |
Proposed classification	Vegetation association	Authority R. W. J. Keay et al.	Vegetation association	R. J. Williams	T. G. Wood
Savanna woodland	Brachystegia-Isoberlinia-Julbernardia woodlands	Woodlands, savannas (and steppes)	Eucalyptus woodlands	Woodland	Savanna woodland
	Cryptosepalum low forest and woodland	woodlands, savannas (and steppes)			
	Baikiaea plurijuga woodlands	Dry deciduous forest and savanna	Callitris glauca woodland	Low-layered woodland	Savanna woodland
	Colophospermum mopane woodlands	Woodlands, savannas (and steppes)	Acacia harpophylla woodlands	Low-layered forest	Savanna woodland or savanna
Savanna parkland	Acacia-Terminalia-Piliostigma-Combretum grasslands	Woodlands, savannas (and steppes)	Acacia-Bauhinia-Terminalia grasslands	Tree and low tree savanna or included in tussock grassland	Savanna
Savanna grasslands	Hyparrhenia-Themeda-Setaria-Echinochloa grasslands Trichoptery grasslands	Swamps	Astrebla-Iseilima-Dichanthium grasslands	Tussock grasslands	Savanna

	Chrysopogon-Aristida-Cenchrus grasslands with Acacia and Commiphora spp. Stipagrostis uniplumis grasslands with Acacia-Grewia spp.	Wooded steppe with abundant Acacia and Commiphora	Triodia associations with Acacia and Eucalyptus spp.	Tree and low tree savanna	Desert steppe
Low tree and shrub savanna	Chrysopogon-Aristida-Cenchrus grasslands with Acacia and Commiphora spp. Stipagrostis uniplumis grasslands with Acacia-Grewia spp.				
Thicket and scrub	Acacia-Commiphora thickets Colophospermum mopane scrub	Thicket	Acacia aneura scrub Acacia harpophylla scrub	Low-layered woodland	Mulga scrub
Intermediate types	Burkea africana woodland Terminalia sericea woodland Terminalia prunioides woodland Combretum imberbe woodland	Woodlands, savannas (and steppe)	Acacia shirleyi scrub Acacia cambagei scrub	Low-layered woodland	

Figure 2.3. Typical campos cerrados/savanna woodland on level plateau near Lagoa Santa, Minas Gerais, Brazil. *Salvertia convallariodora* (top right), *Kielmeyera coriacea* (centre right), *Qualea grandiflora* (centre left).

Figure 2.4. Savanna woodland characterized by *Brachystegia boehmii* and *Isoberlinia paniculata* trees on the lateritic plateau near Kafwala, Kafue National Park, Zambia.

Figure 2.5. Savanna woodland dominated by *Eucalyptus racemosa* trees and *Heteropogon contortus* grass on lateritic plateau near valley of Lagoons station, Queensland, Australia.

Figure 2.6. Open savanna woodland with small *Protea* sp. trees grading to watershed savanna grassland on the mid-Tertiary peneplain, with near surface laterite, south of Choma, Zambia.

Figure 2.7. Open savanna woodland with *Grevillea* and *Hakea* spp. trees, grading to watershed savanna grassland where laterite is near surface on the mid-Tertiary peneplain of the Lake Galilee plateau, Queensland, Australia.

Figure 2.8. Dry savanna woodland dominated by *Colophospermum mopane* trees on alkaline black clay soils near Buleya, Zambezi valley, Zambia.

Figure 2.9. Savanna woodland dominated by *Acacia harpophylla* trees on alkaline black clay soils near Bollen, Queensland, Australia.

Figure 2.10. Relatively open dry savanna woodland with giant baobab tree, *Adansonia digitata*, Zambezi valley near the Victoria Falls, Zambia.

Figure 2.11. Open savanna woodland or parkland of *Acacia* and *Terminalia* spp. trees and *Adansonia gregorii* (baobab, left) on reddish brown loams, Victoria river valley, Northern Territory, Australia.

Figure 2.12. Savanna parkland with *Acacia albida* and *A. woodii* trees on brown clay loams at margins of the Kafue Flats, Zambia.

Figure 2.13. Savanna parkland of *Acacia homalophylla* (boree) trees and *Astrebla pectinata* grass on dark brown clay loams near tributary of Bulloo river, Whynot station, west of Quilpie, Queensland, Australia. From Cole (1982a) with permission from Springer-Verlag, Heidelberg.

Figure 2.14. Savanna parkland characterized by *Diospyros acida*, *Acacia*, and *Piliostigma* spp. trees and *Hyparrhenia filipendula* grass on dark brown to black clay loams derived from limestone near Chunga camp, Kafue National Park, Zambia.

Figure 2.15. Savanna parkland of *Bauhinia cunninghamii* (right and left) and *Terminalia grandiflora* trees (centre) and *Sorghum plumosum*, *Aristida fallax* and *Dichanthium fecundum* grasses on dark brown loams derived from basalt, south of Katherine, Northern Territory, Australia.

Figure 2.16. Flood plain grassland of *Oryza*, *Themeda* and *Eriachne* spp. studded with compass termite mounds along the Finniss river, Northern Territory, Australia. Trees in background on low lateritic residual.

Figure 2.17. Thicket and scrub of the caatinga dominated by *Caesalpinia pyramidalis*, between Cipo and Jeremboa, Bahia, Brazil.

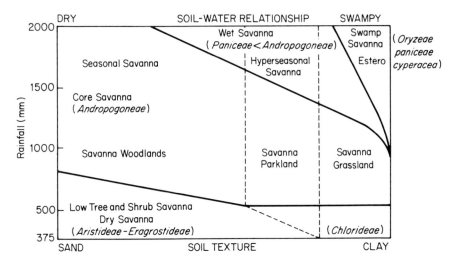

Figure 2.18. Relationships between savanna types and savanna grasses and rainfall, soil water and soil texture (according to R. W. Johnson, pers. comm.).

3   Environmental influences on the distribution of savanna vegetation

Views on the relative importance of factors influencing the distribution of savanna vegetation have varied according to the scale and the area of study and have changed over the years as more specific information has become available from more detailed research.

THE VIEWS OF DIFFERENT WRITERS

Before 1960 the distribution of savanna vegetation was variously explained by different writers who stressed the influence of either climate, pedological or anthropogenic factors, or a combination of these factors. Writers who investigated the thinly peopled South American savannas were impressed by the influence of physical environmental factors whereas those working in Asia and Africa, particularly the more densely peopled areas of West Africa, concluded that much of the savanna was a degraded form of vegetation replacing forest that had been cut and burnt by man.

Investigations of the Australian savannas were focused primarily on reconnaissance studies of the physical environment for the assessment of potential for agricultural development. Their main objective was the recognition of land systems, each characterized by particular combinations of vegetation, soils, relief, geomorphology and geology. Authors recorded the incidence of fire, and described the roles of geological events and climatic changes on landscape evolution but they did not evaluate the influences of these or other factors on the present day vegetation.

Writers favouring climatic influences over the world distribution of savannas emphasized the importance of rainfall periodicity and of moisture deficiency during the cooler dry season of the year. Thus Grisebach (1872), Schimper (1903), Hayek (1926) and Bews (1929) all attributed the grassy savannas directly to alternating wet and dry seasons. Later Troll reiterated the climatic relationships basing his views on the similarity of life-forms in the vegetation formations of comparable climatic regions. Those conducting detailed studies over smaller areas, however, found such broad relationships inadequate. As early as 1892 Warming, in his classic work on the vegetation around Lagoa Santa in Minas Gerais, Brazil, associated the campos cerrados with a seasonal climate combined with special soil conditions which he believed caused a periodic deficiency of moisture. Trapnell (Trapnell 1943; Trapnell and Clothier 1937; Trapnell *et al.* 1950) in his publications on Northern Rhodesia, now Zambia, gave due weight to climatic influences but stressed the close association between vegetation and soil and even suggested that 'physiographic factors are perhaps the greatest importance in determining the distribution of soil and vegetation types'. Here, however, he was concerned primarily with the coincidence of physiographic regions and climatic regimes.

Writers who regarded pedological factors of greatest importance based their arguments either on mineral deficiencies in the soil, or on defective subsoil drainage. In Brazil, Jones (1930) and Waibel (1948) believed that certain geological formations developed poor soils capable of supporting only a savanna vegetation. Beard (1949, 1953), who investigated numerous localities in northern tropical America, Bennett and Allison (1928) in Cuba and Charter (1941) in British Honduras, on the other hand, associated savannas with more or less flat areas with impeded soil drainage caused by the presence of an impermeable layer in the soil. Henkel (1931) reached a similar conclusion for Rhodesia, now Zimbabwe, commenting on the inability of forest trees to become established in areas subject to periodic waterlogging. Later Ferri and Lamberti (1960) recognized a similar relationship for the campos cerrados covering the tabuleiros (coastal plateaux) of Pernambuco.

Views that conflicted with those regarding savanna vegetation as a product of the physical environment were expressed by many writers, notably Aubreville (1938, 1949) in his works on Africa and Brazil, Christoffel (1939) writing on the Gran Sabana of Venezuela, Phillips (1930) on South and East Africa and Stebbing (1937), Keay (1949, 1951, 1952, 1953) and Clayton (1958a) on West Africa. These writers considered that savannas were fire induced, having replaced forest which was cut and burnt by man to make way for cultivation or to improve the grazing. Others cited lightning strike as an initiation of fire, particularly in areas remote from man's activities. Some writers, however, regarded fire as an accessory rather than a primary factor. Thus Pulle (1906, 1938), Ijzerman (1931) and Lanjouw (1936) considered that profound leaching of the soil in Surinam produced a poor low forest which was readily fired and thereby converted into savanna. In Zambia several authorities have commented on the ease and rapidity with which fire sweeps through the dry grass cover of the chipya vegetation characteristic of the light humic loams in the north east of the country. In

Brazil, Rawitscher (1948), Ferri (1944, 1955), Ferri and Coutinho (1958) and Ferri and Lamberti (1960) distinguished between those campos cerrados considered to be natural or climax and those created by felling the forest trees and burning the ground vegetation.

The author's studies in Africa and Brazil led her, in 1956, to question the adequacy of the views then held to explain the distribution of the savanna vegetation (Cole 1956). She focused attention on the dynamic nature of vegetation and drew attention to the roles of geomorphology and climatic change in bringing about the current distributions of vegetation types. Subsequently she demonstrated their importance in Brazil (Cole 1960a) and in Zambia (Cole 1963a) and alluded to their role in Australia (Cole 1962, 1963b, 1965, 1967). The publication of her views virtually coincided with that of King's *Morphology of the Earth* (1962) elaborating the extensive pediplaned surfaces with which she associated the savanna vegetation in the southern continents.

After 1960 detailed studies of smaller areas made possible critical assessment of the precise roles of interacting factors on savanna distributions. Studies of the savanna vegetation in an ecosystem context were undertaken in an attempt to resolve the conflicting views of those stressing the role of the physical environment on the one hand and those attaching most importance to anthropogenic forces on the other (Eden 1964).

Soil profile studies together with precise measurements of soil moisture conditions elucidated the critical role of soil moisture/plant relationships in the Rupununi savanna of Guyana and confirmed the results of similar work involving also studies of ground water movements in Brazil (Ferri 1961a,b,c, Ferri and Coutinho 1958, Ferri and Lamberti 1960) and Venezuela (Sarmiento and Monasterio 1969). In the Rupununi savannas Eden could find no evidence to suggest that the savannas had been derived from forest; and whilst accepting that grass fires might influence the composition of the vegetation he noted that when fire extended into the forest in dry years, regeneration by forest species occurred during subsequent wet years.

Detailed studies over relatively small and widely separated areas in Australia characterized respectively by savanna woodland, savanna grassland and low tree and shrub savanna confirmed the exacting control of the physical environment and revealed the great sensitivity of plant communities to habitat conditions, notably the mineral nutrient status of the soil as well as soil moisture regimes (Nicholls *et al.* 1964–65, Cole 1962, 1965, 1967, 1971a,b, 1973, 1977, Cole *et al.* 1974, 1977). Similar studies undertaken in South West Africa, Namibia and Botswana, South Africa and Rhodesia/Zimbabwe between 1967 and 1970 and in Brazil and Venezuela between 1964 and 1965 revealed similar relationships (Cole 1965, 1980, Cole and Brown 1976, Cole and le Roex 1978, Boshoff 1978, Mason 1975).

Since 1960 studies of the savanna/forest boundary have contributed to an understanding of the relationships between the savanna vegetation and environmental factors. Following such studies in Venezuela in 1964 the author concluded that the boundary between savanna and forest will occur where strongly contrasting conditions brought about by one or a combination of several environmental factors obtain and that 'water relations are vital' (quoted by Hills 1965). This view was endorsed by studies of soils and vegetation in the savanna/forest boundary zone of the northeastern Mato Grosso of Brazil during the Royal Geographical Society's 1967–69 expedition. There the most important factor was soil texture; related primarily to bedrock geology this exerted a critical influence on soil moisture relationships (Askew *et al.* 1970b). The role of fire as an influence over the forest/savanna boundary was dismissed. In West Africa, the stronghold of the protagonists of the controlling influences of man and fire, studies made by Morgan and Moss in western Nigeria established the stability of the forest/savanna boundary over a ten year period despite increasing population density and increased cultivation and demonstrated not only the overriding influence of physical environmental features, particularly soils, on vegetation distribution but also the control exerted by vegetation/soil conditions on the type of agriculture practised by the African farmers (Moss and Morgan 1970).

While evidence has been accumulating to support the overriding importance of fundamental influences of factors of the physical environment rather than of fire on the distribution of savanna vegetation, palynological studies in Colombia, Venezuela and Guyana (van der Hammen 1963, van der Hammen and Gonzalez 1960, 1965; Wijmstra and van der Hammen 1966) have established the historically great age of some savannas, revealed fluctuations in the occurrence of forest and savanna over Recent geological time and suggested connections between vegetation distributions and geomorphology. Since 1971 further information on the past as well as present distributions of savanna vegetation has become available from interpretations of the false colour imagery acquired by the earth resources satellites Landsat 1, 2 and 3 (Cole 1977, 1982a,b, 1984; Cole and Edmiston 1980; Cole and Owen-Jones 1977). For some areas the imagery from repetitive passes of the satellites has yielded information on the seasonal, annual and historic changes in the vegetation cover and thrown light on geological events and geomorphological processes, thereby assisting an understanding of the relationships between vegetation and environmental parameters over time.

In recent years greater understanding of the tropical savannas has resulted from studies of biomass and productivity, plant physiology, the role of large herbivores, small animals and micro-organisms on the functioning of the ecosystem and on both protection from and the controlled use of fire on savanna resilience and stability that has been undertaken from research stations in several countries (Huntley and Walker 1982, Bourliere 1983). Further understanding has come from this interchange of information between scientists during international symposia and follow-on field investigations of the savannas in Venezuela in 1964, South Africa in 1979, and Australia in 1984.

With the information that is now available a new perspective of the factors influencing the distribution of the savanna vegetation both in space and time is possible. Werger (1978) has recently emphasized the interrelationships between vegetation and many environmental factors, any one of which may have greater impact in one area than in another. The author accords with and extends this view. She regards the distribution of the savanna vegetation, and that of the physiognomic types of vegetation associations and plant communities within it as the expression of the interplay of all the environmental factors that, over time, have been and are subject to continuous change in response to the geomorphological evolution of the landscape, geological events and major climatic changes.

Overlying the impacts of these factors are those caused by grazing animals, decomposer fauna, fire and man's cultural practices, which must be regarded as secondary rather than primary influences.

THE PHYSICAL ENVIRONMENT OF THE SAVANNA LANDS

While the various forms of savanna vegetation are the present expression of the interplay of many environmental factors over space and time, prior consideration of individual factors assists an understanding of their relative importance within this interplay in specific areas.

Climate

The physical environment of the savanna lands is unified by a seasonal but predictable rainfall regime which provides moisture during the period most favourable for plant growth in the warmer part of the year but causes moisture deficiencies and plant stress during the dry cooler season. This climatic feature distinguishes the savanna environment from that of the tropical forests where all season rainfall provides moisture for uninterrupted year-long growth and from the deserts where low and erratic rainfall causes such extreme conditions of water deficit that only plants able to restrict or suspend growth, store water or complete their life cycle in the brief periods after rains can survive.

Within the savanna belts that, in both hemispheres, extend over some 15–20° of latitude between the Tropics and the Equator, there are considerable climatic variations. The annual rainfall generally decreases with increasing latitude from about 2000 mm at the margin of the tropical forests, to about 250 mm at the desert margins. At the same time the length of the dry season increases from three or four months to eight or nine months and becomes more clearly defined and severe. Temperatures vary with latitude, altitude and exposure. The range between the daily maxima and nightly minima increases towards the desert margins where frost on winter nights, particularly in hollows, may severely limit tree growth. Generally speaking the mean monthly temperatures for the warmest months vary from 25–30°C near the margins of the tropical forests to 30–35°C near the desert margins. In the same direction those for the coolest month vary from 13–18°C to 8–13°C. Particularly near the desert margins, low winter temperatures may restrict distribution of some sensitive trees and shrubs. Throughout the savanna zones clear skies and high levels of solar radiation favour photosynthesis, plant growth and biomass yields. The limiting factors are those imposed by unfavourable soil water balance or water deficit caused by drought and by inadequate or excessive drainage.

The soil water balance is influenced by evapotranspiration. For the savanna zones the daily potential evapotranspiration rates have been estimated to range from 2–4 mm during the wet season and from 4–10 mm during the dry season, with annual totals varying from 1000–1500 mm or even 2000 mm according to the length of the dry season (Thornthwaite 1948, Papadakis 1961). Total potential evapotranspiration exceeds the annual rainfall in many areas. Everywhere seasonal water deficit is a characteristic feature of areas with savanna vegetation, its severity varying with the length and intensity of the dry period and with edaphic conditions.

The length of the effective growing season and growth index values are important influences on savanna vegetation. Growth index values, calculated by interfacing plant response to major light, temperature and moisture regimes, are available only for Australia. There the gradients show a broad relationship between high values and the distribution of the C4 grasses typical of savanna vegetation (Fitzpatrick and Nix 1970, Nix 1983). This relationship confirms the importance of climatic influences on savanna vegetation since the C4 photosynthetic pathway is favoured by high light intensity, high temperatures and high evaporation rates. The C4 grasses are excluded by low light intensity from closed canopy forests of C3 tree species and occur in the continuously humid tropical environments only where unfavourable edaphic conditions inhibit tree growth (Sarmiento and Monasterio 1975, Monasterio and Sarmiento 1976). The C4 grasses are also excluded from cooler areas with lower evaporation rates where C3 grasses dominate. The distinction between tropical savannas dominated by C4 grasses and other types of grassland vegetation dominated by C3 grasses has also been recognized in tropical South America (Medina 1982a) and Africa (Huntley 1982). There, although growth index values are not available, the climatic data suggests that similar combinations of high light intensity, high temperatures and high evaporation rates produce gradients comparable with those in Australia. The combination of climatic factors that determine the distribution of the C4 grasses exert a fundamental influence over the distribution of the savannas as a whole, but they do not explain the distributions of the several physiognomic categories of savanna vegetation or the contrasts in their floristic composition.

Soils and soil classification

Soils of strongly contrasting colour, profile characteristics, texture, moisture holding capacity and base status occur within the savanna zones. These have been given different names by different authors using different criteria in

Table 3.1. Interrelationships of rocks, vegetation and soil types in Young's (1976) and the FAO-UNESCO (1974) classification schemes and some comparisons with the USDA (1975) classification scheme

	Young's (1976) classification scheme		FAO-UNESCO classification scheme		USDA (1975) classification scheme
Vegetation	Felsic to intermediate rocks	Basic rocks	Felsic to inter-mediate rocks	Basic rocks	No sub-divisions according to rock type
Rain forest	Leached ferrallitic soils	Leached ferrisols	Ferralsols		Oxisols
Forest/ savanna boundary	Weakly ferrallitic soils		Ferralsols		Oxisols
	Ferruginous soils	Ferrisols	Acrisols	Dystric nitosols	Ultisols
Savanna	Weathered ferrallitic soils		Ferralsols		Oxisols
		Eutrophic brown soils		Eutric nitosols	
	Ferruginous soils		Acrisols Luvisols		Ultisols Alfisols

From Montgomery and Askew in Bourliere 1983.

global and continental classifications. The most widespread soil types are the highly leached generally sandy, lateritic soils and the base rich montmorillonitic black clay soils identified in the early pedological publications (Prescott and Pendleton 1952, Mohr and van Baren 1954). Later, several different classifications, each based on the profile characteristics, accorded new diagnostic names to these and other soil types occurring within the savannas and adjacent rain forests (Table 3.1) (d'Hoore 1964, FAO UNESCO 1974, USDA 1975, Young 1976). In these classifications, adopted for soils maps of Africa and of the world, the highly leached lateritic soils are designated as ferrallitic soils, ferralsols or oxisols and the montmorillonitic soils are termed vertisols. Massive or indurated laterite, renamed plinithite in the USDA classification, is present in the weathered ferrallitic soils. Less leached soils with an argillic textural or a structural B horizon or both are termed ferruginous soils or acrisols and luvisols, and ultisols and alfisols by different authors. The clay fraction of these soils, like that of the ferrallitic soils, is dominated by kaolinite and hydrous oxides of iron and aluminium. The ferruginous soils are usually characterized by the presence of iron oxide concretions rather than massive laterite. The moderately nutrient rich and the nutrient rich dark red and brown soils that develop over basic rocks and are more freely draining than the montmorillonitic black clays or vertisols are respectively differentiated as ferrisols or dystric nitosols or as eutrophic brown soils or eutric nitosols (Table 3.1). In Australia, however, a different terminology was developed (Northcote 1965, 1968, Stace *et al.* 1968, Stephens 1962, Stewart 1956) and widely used in studies of savannas areas. This distinguished strongly leached lateritic podzolic soils and other podzolic types that could be equated to the ferrallitic soils, a range of soils with profiles dominated by sesquioxides and including krasnozems and red and yellow earths equivalent to the ferruginous soils; and groups of mildly leached dark soils including montmorillonitic black earths equivalent to vertisols and of mildly leached brown soils including types comparable with the ferrisols and eutrophic brown soils or nitosols of the other classifications.

The different terminologies that have been used in soil classifications at different times and in different continents complicate considerations of the relationship between the different categories of savanna vegetation and soil conditions and necessitate cross referencing of soil nomenclature.

For plant growth, the most important soil properties are texture, structure, moisture holding capacity and drainage, nutrient status, organic matter content and pH. Recent authors on savanna soils, using the terminology of Young's soil classification, have therefore distinguished the soils mainly on the basis of their drainage characteristics for what have been termed the moist seasonal savannas and dry seasonal savannas within seasonal climatic zones, and for savannas in non seasonal climatic zones (Montgomery and Askew

1983). Of the well drained soils, ferruginous soils and weathered ferrallitic soils are recognized as common within both the moist seasonal and dry seasonal savannas, weakly ferrallitic soils as common in the former; within the dry seasonal savanna eutrophic brown soils and ferrisols are recognized over basic rocks and the presence of vertisols is noted. However the last is included within the category of hydromorphic soils which include, within the moist savannas, the gleys characteristic of the large depressions or dambos in the plateau surface of Zambia and the ground water laterites that are widespread in level upland areas of Ghana, along valleys on the plateau of Zimbabwe and on the Llanos of Venezuela.

Another recent author has identified distinctions between non calcareous and calcareous soils within the savanna zone and between the dystrophic, mesotrophic and eutrophic varients in the former categories as of the most importance for savanna vegetation (Huntley 1982, following MacVicar 1977). The dystrophic soils are so highly leached that the total exchangeable Ca, MgK Na expressed in ml per 100 g clay is less that 5. The lateritic or ferrallitic soils are of this nature. The eutrophic soils have been subject to little or no leaching so that the total exchangeable Ca, Mg, K and Na expressed as ml per 100 g clay exceeds 15. The black clay soils or vertisols and eutrophic brown soils or nitosols are in this category. Mesotrophic soils that fall between the two extremes include some of the ferruginous soils of Africa and podzolic soils of Australia. Contrasting with the non calcareous soils, the calcareous soils contain free calcium carbonate or calcium magnesium carbonate and are base saturated.

The distribution of the moist and arid savannas of Africa is recognized as being related to the base status of the major soil types (Huntley 1982). On a broad regional basis the savanna woodlands or moist savannas occupy the dystrophic and some mesotrophic non calcareous ferrallitic soils with which laterite is usually associated whereas the drier types of savanna woodland, savanna parkland and low tree and shrub savannas occupy the arid eutrophic non calcareous soils and the calcareous soils with which calcrete is frequently associated. Moist savanna woodland species occur within the arid savannas where dystrophic acidic sands overlie crystalline rocks or sandstones (Rutherford 1972, Coetzee *et al.* 1976) and species of the dry savannas extend into the moist savanna woodlands on base rich substrates provided by termitaria (Cole 1963b, White 1965, Fanshawe 1968, Malaisse 1978, Huntley 1982, see also Chapter 8). Comparable broad relationships may be recognized also in Australia and tropical South America.

The differing soil classifications and the selection by different authors of differing criteria for discriminating the soils of the savannas outlined above emphasize the problems posed in seeking an understanding of pedogenesis and in identifying the relationships between vegetation and soils in savannas.

While some broad relationships have been recognized, in reality the distribution of both vegetation communities and soil types are complex, for they are related in turn to climate, physiography and geology and to the geomorphological evolution of the landscape.

Geomorphology, geology and soil development

In each continent the savanna lands are characterized by similar sequences of land forms that represent the legacy of the long-term geomorphological evolution of the landscape under the interacting influences of changing climatic conditions and geological events.

In the higher rainfall zones monotonously level plateaux, occasionally surmounted by residual hills, characterize extensive areas. They terminate in abrupt escarpments and belts of dissected country that descend to lower and sometimes equally level plateaux or plains. Near the escarpments these plains are studded with flat topped mesas and residual hills representing outliers of the higher surfaces. The lower surfaces extend into the drier zones of the savanna lands, where they may be mantled by wind blown sand. The detailed relief of the surfaces varies with the stage of erosion and the underlying geology. The most pronounced features generally occur in the hilly escarpment zone at the contact between distinctive surfaces. With increasing distance from this zone the relief becomes more subdued and ultimately remarkably level. Over basalts, soft sedimentary rocks, superficial sands and alluvium the mature surface is usually level to gently undulating. Over exposed granite or gneiss it is studded with tors and whaleback and bornhardt inselberge (see Twidale 1981); and, where resistant volcanic and meta volcanic, sedimentary and meta sedimentary rocks, notably rhyolites, quartzites, syenites and calc silicates occur, the surface is broken by steep sided hills and ranges.

In individual continents and individual areas, two, three, four or more surfaces of differing elevation related to one another in steplike fashion with an intervening belt of hilly terrain, may be present. In each continent however, there are marked contrasts between the monotonous level terrain of the higher plateaux in the higher rainfall zones and the more varied terrain in the drier country.

In each continent the higher plateaux are usually underlain by lateritic material that in places has become indurated on exposure to the atmosphere. This outcrops in the cliff features of the peripheral escarpments, termed cuirasses in Africa, 'breakaways' in Australia, and caps the outlying mesas. Resident relics of it form a coarse gravel layer over individual hills and a veneer of fine gravel over adjacent plains. The lower surfaces are frequently underlain by calcrete whose thickness may exceed 30 m in the drier areas where it may be mantled by deep aeolian sand.

The level plateaux are considered by some authors to represent planation surfaces formed by either peneplanation or pediplanation processes (see King 1962, 1967, Cole 1960a, 1961, 1963a,b, 1982a) and by others to result from stripping following deep weathering (Thomas 1974, Twidale 1981). In some areas, notably in the varied terrain below the higher plateaux, drainage patterns that are unrelated to present relief or geology provide evidence of drainage superimposition from a previous surface developed over younger rocks that have been removed by erosion (see Wellington 1955). This drainage superimposition may be associated with the exposure of lithologies of differing resistance and/or the resurrection of ancient landscapes as in the Transvaal plateau basin of South Africa (see Chapter 9). In other areas complex landscape features are associated with differential warping followed by accelerated erosion, as in northern Australia (see Chapter 16) and in Zambia (see Chapter 8). Although different authors have advocated the role of one process rather than another in geomorphology, the evidence indicates that at different times and in different places all the processes cited above have been involved in fashioning the present landscapes and that they have influenced both soil development and vegetation distributions.

Until the Cretaceous period South America, Africa, India and Australia all formed part of the old continent of Gondwanaland. Many of the features of the landscape, the soils and the vegetation of the savannas date from that time. Gondwanaland began to break up in Jurassic times and the parts that now constitute India and the southern continents began to drift apart from the Cretaceous onwards. This drifting, further earth movements in the Tertiary and succeeding periods, and major climatic changes in the Pleistocene caused changes in the geomorphological evolution of the landscape, in soil development and in the plant cover. The legacies of all these events and changing processes are manifest in the savanna landscapes today.

In the three southern continents the widespread distribution of laterite in layers beneath the higher plateaux, as cappings over the Mesozoic rocks of outlying mesas and as gravel veneers over both residual hill features and the adjacent plains in the lower terrain supports the theory that it is a legacy of deep weathering processes under hot wet climatic conditions during the Cretaceous and early Tertiary periods when tropical forests were widespread over the components of Gondwanaland. At that time the deep weathering processes produced ferrallitic or lateritic soil profiles that, below the surface A horizon, were characterized by ferruginous B horizons passing downwards into a mottled zone and thence a kaolinitic pallid zone overlying weathered bedrock. Such profiles are well displayed in several localities in eastern Queensland, Australia today, e.g. in the cliffs along the coast at Redcliffe

Figure 3.1. Lateritic profile, Little Red Bluff, Australia. (From Cole 1965, with permission of Bedford College.)

and Woody Point, on the Binjour plateau; and in the Little Red Bluff south of Charters Towers (Figure 3.1). Under subsequently drier climatic conditions and with exposure at surface following erosion, the ferruginous horizons became indurated laterite and the pallid zone was re-silicified to form duricrust (Figures 3.2 and 3.3).

The impact of the deep weathering processes differed over different bedrock types. Over granites and gneisses, which underlie may savanna areas, they penetrated the joints and fractures, disintegrated the softer matrix and detached the more resistant material as blocks, thereby preparing the way for tor formation and later exposure of whaleback and bornhardt inselberge once the mantle of weathered material was removed (see Figure 7.3). Over basalts, shales and bedded limestones they caused uniform rotting to great depths whereas over resistant metamorphic rocks, especially quartzites, their effects were minimal.

The break-up of Gondwanaland and the Tertiary earth movements were followed by the onset of drier conditions which led to the breakdown of the forest cover. At the same time continental uplift initiated planation processes that progressively stripped the mantle of weathered material formed by the earlier deep weathering processes. The resultant landforms — namely plateaux terminating in steep escarpments and belts of dissected country, outlying mesas and, over granite and gneiss, tors surrounded by pediments — suggest that erosion was achieved by pediplanation processes. Where erosion proceeded to the removal of whole geological units the drainage became

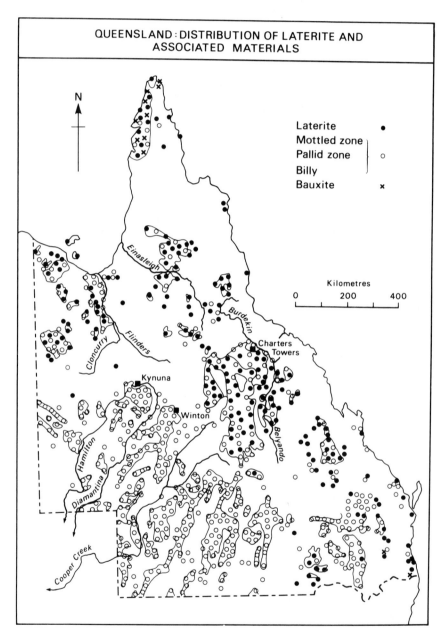

Figure 3.2. Distribution of laterite and associated materials (after Connah and Hubble in Hill and Denmead 1960).

Figure 3.3. Residual laterite in savanna grasslands near Kynuna, Australia.

Figure 3.4. Black cracking clay soil, Kynuna, Australia.

Figure 3.5. Impala in savanna parkland of the Kruger National Park, South Africa.

superimposed and, over contrasting lithologies, ancient landscapes were resurrected (see Chapter 9). These processes were particularly active in areas subject to crustal warping. Where, during the fluctuating climatic conditions that characterized the Pleistocene period, aridity caused the complete breakdown of the plant cover, the A horizon soil material above the lateritic B horizon was removed and redeposited in the form of sand plains in nearby areas. The sequence of landscape features that characterize the savanna lands (see Figures 5.19, 7.2, 7.3 and 14.2) were thus created primarily by pediplanation processes acting over surfaces mantled by deeply weathered material as the climatic conditions changed from constantly hot wet to seasonally hot wet or to hot and arid and as the continents experienced periodic uplift and crustal warping.

The soils of the savanna lands are the products of pedogenesis that has been influenced by past and present atmospheric and soil climatic conditions, and by geomorphological processes acting upon different parent materials weathered from different types of bedrock and superficial deposits. The legacy of palaeo conditions is perhaps more important in the savanna lands than elsewhere. It is partly responsible for the complex, repetitive distributional patterns of different soil types with which are associated the distinctive types of savanna vegetation.

Both the nature and distribution of the major soil types that occur within the savanna belts are related to the landscape features (see Figure 7.3). Some soils are the legacies of past climatic conditions, others are influenced mainly by current climate, by relief and climate and by bedrock geology.

In broad outline weathered ferrallitic and lateritic soils are typical of the planation surfaces of the higher plateaux in the higher rainfall areas; there laterite occurs at or near the surface in the peripheral zones where the ferruginous zone has become indurated on exposure. Ferruginous soils with podzolic characteristics, namely an argillic B horizon beneath a leached A horizon, occur over the dissected terrain marking the junction between planation surfaces. On the intermediate and lower planation surfaces montmorillonitic or margallitic black cracking clay soils or vertisols occur over base rich rocks and alluvium over the flat surfaces, and grey and brown loams of heavy texture have developed over lightly dissected terrain over rocks with good internal drainage. Arid red earths characterize the drier country near the desert margins.

The main soil types cited differ greatly in their profile characteristics, in their physical features and chemical composition. The weathered ferrallitic soils are highly leached and deficient in soil nutrients. Being the residual legacy of former wetter climatic epochs they are old and exhausted, and because of the absence of slope the surface layers are not readily removed by the agents of normal healthy erosion. Thus soil renewal through replacement of material weathered from the underlying bedrock proceeds slowly if at all. The soils vary in depth from several centimetres to one or two metres and in texture from sands to sandy clays. In some areas soils in the accepted sense are lacking and the surface is covered only by surficial accumulations of sands, gravels and ferruginous concentrations. In the extreme case the ferruginous concretionary B horizon of the old profile is at or near the surface and comprises indurated laterite. A product of a fluctuating water table, this ferruginous horizon, particularly where indurated, impedes drainage so that during the alternating wet and dry seasons the surface soils are subject to alternating waterlogging and drought. Where these soils prevail only shallow rooted species able to tolerate these conditions and deeprooted species able to tap the ground water (which usually occurs at a depth of 10–20 m) are able to survive. In both cases the species must be able to withstand the low nutrient status of the soils.

The ferruginous soils occur in the dissected belts of country below the margins marking the edge of the higher planation surfaces. They are characteristically over acid crystalline basement rocks. Because the drainage conditions are better than over the plateaux and because the renewal of parent material proceeds normally the profiles, usually 100–200 cm deep, display eluvial and illuvial horizons, the former a leached sandy clay loam and the latter a clay. The surface soils are grey or red in colour and of sandy texture. They have some reserves of weatherable minerals and although the clays are kaolinitic the exchange capacity is higher than in the ferrallitic soils. In some areas of Zambia, Zimbabwe and Botswana the presence of stone lines in the profiles suggests that the soils are polygenetic and have been re-worked from the materials of pre-existing profiles. Where the dissected zones between planation surfaces are underlain by limestone or basalt with good internal drainage, reddish brown clays or clayloams with a high base status occur, notably in Zambia (see Chapter 8) and eastern Queensland, Australia (Chapter 17). Formerly called krasnozems, now renamed ultisols or nitosols, these soils are more favourable for plant growth.

The montmorillonitic or margallitic black cracking clay soils or vertisols present different problems for plant growth. Developed over base rich rocks they have a high nutrient status but their self mulching characteristics, occasioned by the propensity of the montmorillonite clay to swell and puff after rains and to crack deeply on drying out, imposes severe strains on plant roots (Figure 3.4). The grey and brown loams, developed where slight dissection results in better drainage conditions, are more favourable although calcrete nodules or a calcrete layer may be present at depth.

The arid red earths that characterize the semi-arid terrain comprise unleached skeletal soils without profile differentiation and usually less than 100 cm deep. They have a sandy to sandy clay loam texture; over residual hills their composition is closely related to bedrock type but in level terrain they may contain an admixture of aeolian sand and they are frequently underlain by massive calcrete.

While, as indicated, the main soil types are associated with particular landscape features, in detail soil distributions are complex, being influenced by differences in the geological bedrock producing the parent material and by major and minor changes of relief and drainage that respectively cause an interdigitation of major soil types and catenary sequences within them. Thus while ferruginous light sandy soils are characteristic of granite parent materials, where drainage is poor near stream courses in level terrain sodic soils occur. Soils with low calcium and high magnesium ratios cover serpentinite bedrock. Coarse nutrient deficient skeletal sandy or stony soils occur over quartzites whereas base rich clays have formed over shales and diabases.

The physical environment of the savanna lands thus presents a sequence of landscape features with interrelated climatic, geomorphological, geological and soil conditions that have evolved over a long period of time. In outline the distributions of the various forms of savanna vegetation ar related to these features as depicted in simplified form for Africa in Figure 7.3. Within this framework the distributions of individual vegetation associations are occasioned mainly by variations in the soils and geology, and modified by the activities of man and grazing animals.

THE INFLUENCE OF PHYSICAL FACTORS ON THE BROAD-SCALE DISTRIBUTION OF SAVANNA VEGETATION

On a global basis, in undisturbed natural terrain, the change from tropical forest to savanna occurs where the availability of moisture and nutrients throughout the year is inadequate to sustain closed forests with well developed shrub layers. The savanna vegetation is composed of an open stratum of trees and/or shrubs and a ground layer of grasses. The height and spacing of these components, which determine the categories of savanna cited above, is influenced mainly by soil moisture conditions, while the composition of the vegetation units within each category varies with nutrient status. Within given climatic limits both soil moisture and nutrient availability depend on parent material which may be related to bedrock geology or to superficial deposits such as wind blown sand, alluvium and colluvium or to weathering products such as laterite and calcrete. Consequently the various categories of savanna vegetation and the vegetation associations and plant communities within them exhibit complex distributions which reflect their relationships to edaphic conditions. In turn these are related to the geomorphological evolution of the landscape and the extent to which bedrock geology has been exposed from beneath weathering products or mantled by superficial materials.

On a continental basis the savanna woodlands extend from the margins of the tropical forests where the annual rainfall averages 1500 mm and the period of drought and relatively low temperatures in winter becomes marked, into areas with only about 500 mm of rainfall concentrated in the summer half year. Here the low tree and shrub savannas begin and extend to the desert margins where the annual rainfall averages less than 250 mm and is highly erratic in occurrence. Grasslands and parklands occur throughout the savanna belt, occurring under specific edaphic conditions within areas of savanna woodland and low tree and shrub savanna. In some areas all categories of savanna occur in juxtaposition.

Most of the savanna woodlands are associated with old planation surfaces (see Figures 5.19, 7.2 and 14.2) and are believed to represent a legacy of the vegetation which flourished during the Tertiary and even earlier geological periods when under hot wet climatic conditions laterization processes were active (Cole 1960, 1963, 1964). Subsequently, in drier epochs, under increasing competition for available moisture and nutrients many species were unable to survive: as the vegetative cover deteriorated the top A horizon material of the lateritic soil profile was removed and redeposited at the margins of the lateritic plateaux to form the sandplains which today support distinctive tree and shrub or shrub communities as, for example, in southwestern Queensland and east of Geraldton in Western Australia, in western Zambia and in parts of the Kalahari in southern Africa. Under the drier climatic conditions and with the removal of the A horizon of the soil the ferruginous B horizon became indurated to laterite or plinthite (USDA 1960). Planation surfaces characterized by such a layer at or near the surface support many of the present day savanna woodlands. The most extensive surfaces date from the Tertiary period and these carry the core areas of the savanna woodlands. Some, however, date from the Cretaceous or even the Jurassic and Rhaetic, the latter notably in Brazil (Chapter 5, Cole 1960a); others are post-Tertiary. Following the continental uplift which initiated each erosion cycle responsible for cutting these planation surfaces, dissection has proceeded at their margins. This has exposed bedrock and led to the redistribution of lateritic gravel, particularly along river beds where, in some cases, precipitation from iron rich waters emanating from the planation surfaces has cemented it to form ground water laterite (see Figures 6.8 and 8.24). Savanna woodlands extend onto areas of exposed bedrock, areas underlain by groundwater laterite and areas where redistributed laterite gravel mantles black soils plains characterized by savanna grassland (see Figure 16.6). In most cases, however, their composition changes with changes in the edaphic conditions over each type of terrain. Over the planation surfaces their composition also varies with differences in the age of the surface and in the soil and drainage conditions.

The low tree and shrub savannas typically cover younger and lower-lying planation surfaces cut across bedrock which is only thinly mantled by residual arid red earth soils (see Figure 10.1). When residual hills of outcropping bedrock rise above these surfaces taller trees occur. Where relict lateritic plateaux of the older planation surfaces occur within the low tree and shrub savannas they carry savanna woodland as near Tucano in eastern Brazil (Cole 1960a) and north of Cloncurry in Australia (Nicholls *et al*. 1964–65). Where there are shallow depressions or pans in which accumulating sediments have weathered to soils of heavy texture savanna grasslands occur. Where considerable thicknesses of calcrete and wind blown sand mask bedrock the low tree and shrub savannas show marked changes of form and composition.

The savanna grasslands cover three categories of terrain, in each of which the soil conditions are inimical to tree growth. Firstly they occupy the extensive plains characterized by dark brown or black cracking clay soils which have developed over Cambrian limestones and later sediments on the Barkly Tableland of Australia, over Cretaceous and later sediments in the Great Artesian basin of Australia (Figures 16.4) and over Quaternary sediments in the Orinoco valley of Venezuela. Secondly savanna grasslands occupy valleys floored by alluvium and again characterized by black cracking clays, in Tanzania, Zambia (Figure 8.10) (Cole 1963a,b), Zimbabwe and Botswana, Brazil and Venezuela and in northern Australia (Figure 2.16). Thirdly savanna grasslands occur over the central core areas of the old lateritized planation surfaces where, under extreme conditions of seasonally alternating waterlogging and drought, the savanna woodland trees become smaller and less frequent and eventually disappear. In each continent different grass species characterize the savanna grasslands of each type of terrain.

The savanna parklands occur over rolling terrain where dark brown loams have formed over base rich relatively porous bedrock such as limestone, basalt or pyroxenite or over alluvium (see Figures 2.12 and 2.13). In Africa they occupy the better drained terrain where limestones of the Katanga system have been exposed around the margins of the Kafue Flats and Lukango swamps in Zambia (Figure 8.14), those parts of the South African Lowveld and Bushveld underlain by pyroxenite or basalt, and the plains floored by Stormberg basalt northwest of Ghanzi in Botswana (Figure 10.23). In Brazil they occupy the High Pantanal and in Australia they cover those areas underlain by Proterozoic limestone and/or alluvium in the valleys of the Victoria and Roper rivers in the Northern Territory, the rolling basaltic country around Peak Downs and Springsure in eastern Queensland and parts of the Great Artesian Basin (see Figures 17.2 and 17.4). In most areas their distribution is closely linked to that of the savanna grasslands of the plains and flood plains, the vegetation changing to parkland where, by virtue of slope or dissection or bedrock type, more freely drained soils permit tree growth.

The last category of savanna, namely scrub, is of relatively limited extent, occurring particularly where redistributed lateritic material mantles the surface exposed in the later erosion cycles. In Australia it includes the stands of *Acacia cambagei* and *A. shirleyii* which occur alike within the savanna grassland and low tree and shrub savanna zones.

The trees that dominate the savanna woodlands belong to different genera in each continent (Figures 2.3, 2.4 and 2.5) but in the most central areas of the oldest planation surfaces in Africa and Australia members of the floristically old Proteaceae family are present — *Protea* and *Faurea* spp. in Africa, *Banksia*, *Grevillea* and *Hakea* spp. in Australia (Figures 2.6 and 2.7). *Acacia* spp. dominate the low tree and shrub savannas of Africa whereas *Eucalyptus* and/or *Acacia* spp. do so in Australia, but in each continent they are accompanied by other genera which, under certain conditions, become dominant. The savanna parklands of Africa and Australia are floristically most similar being characterized by *Acacia*, *Piliostigma* and *Terminalia* trees in Africa, by *Acacia*, *Bauhinia* and *Terminalia* trees in Australia and in both by the occasional baobab, *Adansonia digitata* in Africa and *A. gregorii* in Australia (Figures 2.10 to 2.15). Floristically the composition of the savannas vegetation of South America is distinct from that of Africa and Australia.

THE INFLUENCE OF BIOTIC FACTORS ON THE DISTRIBUTION OF SAVANNAS

Great faunal contrasts exist between the savannas of Africa, Australia and tropical South America. Whereas those of eastern and southern Africa sustain large herds of a great variety of wild herbivores, and also their carnivorous predators, only kangaroos and wallabies occur in large numbers in Australia and the mammalian fauna of the South Amerian savannas is virtually restricted to small numbers of deer on the dry open grasslands of central and southern Brazil, and bigger colonies of the large rodent, capybara, in the Pantanal of Brazil and on the esteros of Venezuela.

The reptilian and avifaunas of Africa are also richer than those of the other continents while invertebrates are more numerous and more active in the ecosystem (see Barbault 1983, Fry 1983).

In addition to the wild fauna the savannas support large numbers of domestic herbivores. In Australia and South American and in some parts of Africa these today outnumber the wild herbivores.

The evolution of wild herbivores

The faunal differences between the southern continents emanate from the break-up of Gondwanaland and relate to the differing environmental conditions in each continent following that event. In Africa oscillations between forest, moist and arid savannas that were associated with climatic changes in the Tertiary and Pleistocene favoured the evolution, speciation and radiation of ungulates and of other faunal groups. In South America and Australia isolation and periods of aridity were unfavourable.

In Africa the Proboscidea, which includes the elephant, and the Perissodactyla, which includes rhinoceros and zebra, predominated from the Eocene to the Miocene (Sinclair 1983). In the Oligocene the Artiodactyla, which includes the pig, hippopotamus and giraffe families, and the very large Bovidae family, which includes buffalo and antelopes, evolved and the Bovidae developed the ruminant stomach capable of digesting cellulose from coarse plant material. This gave them an advantage which enabled them to diversify when alternating expansion and contraction of forest, moist and dry savannas, associated with climatic changes in the Pliocene and Pleistocene, provided stimuli for speciation and opportunities for radiation and the occupation of new niches.

Today there are 78 species of antelopes and buffalo whose distributions reflect these changes. Additionally there are two species of giraffe, two species of hippopotamus and three species of pig that evolved during the same period. Most species have overlapping distributions within the concentric belt of savannas that girdle the tropical forests of the Congo basin and West Africa, but three separate races of hartebeest occur in the Sahel, Tanzania and South Africa, and three different species of oryx have isolated distributions in areas that were dry refuges when the forest vegetation expanded in the wetter periods of the Pleistocene — namely the gemsbok in Namibia, beisa oryx in the northeastern Horn of Africa and the scimitar horned oryx in the Sahara. Today, as in the past, the variety, numbers and distributions of the different species of wild herbivores are related to the nature, quality and variety of the food supply which distinguishes the savannas of Africa from those of the other continents (see p. 378).

In South America the first ungulates appeared in the Cretaceous and reached their maximum diversity in the early Miocene. However, due to aridity, they decreased in the late Miocene and Pliocene. Following the land connection with North America in the Pliocene, mammals belonging to seven orders and including mastodons, horses, tapirs, camelids, peccaries and deer moved into South America. Most, however, disappeared in the Pleistocene, probably because the grazing degenerated as a consequence of unfavourable climate, so that today only small numbers of deer occur in the savannas.

The bovids never reached South America, where only the cariomorph rodents, notably the large capybara, occupy the herbivore niche.

Australia has remained isolated since the break-up of Gondwanaland and its fauna of large wild herbivores is restricted to kangaroos and wallabies. These in fact have their centre of speciation and have achieved their largest populations in the savanna woodlands (see Newsome 1983). The distribution of species appears to be related to vegetation and climate since the antilopine kangaroo is confined to the northern savanna woodlands, the wallaroo occupies a belt farther south, and the grey kangaroo is confined to the eastern savanna woodlands, whereas the red kangaroo has a wider distribution in the drier areas. Different species of wallaby show similar distributions. The break in the distributions of both kangaroo and wallaby species to the south of the Gulf of Carpentaria is notable. It coincides with the northward extension of the belt of *Astrebla* dominated savanna grasslands and with drier conditions.

The fauna of the Asian savannas is impoverished. Like that of South America it was formerly richer, with herds of cervids, bovids, rhinoceros and elephant. Under acute human population pressures these have been almost wiped out by hunting so that today large wild herbivorous mammals occur only in a few protected areas in savanna woodlands and flood plains.

The distribution of wild herbivores

While hunting has reduced the wild faunas of the savannas to differing degrees in different continents, studies of the vegetation indicate that the diversity and abundance of wild herbivores in Africa, their uniformity in Australia and paucity in South America are related fundamentally to differences in the nature and nutrient properties of the grazing and browse. In Africa the great extent of low tree and shrub savannas and of savanna parkland characterized by sweet grasses, a high proportion of which are aspartic acid-formers, associated with soils of high nitrogen availability, is undoubtably responsible for the great wealth of wild herbivores. These grasses retain their high nutritive properties throughout the year. They support the large herds of impala, kudu, common waterbuck, red hartebeest which, with black rhinoceros and with gemsbok, springbok and zebra in the most arid areas, are virtually confined to them (Figures 3.5 and 3.6). Elephant, giraffe, buffalo, wildebeest and eland also attain their highest densities in these areas. Here the shrubs and trees, notably *Grewia* and *Acacia* spp., afford valuable browse with high contents of calcium and phosphorus (see pp. 237–243); here *Sclerocarya caffra* yields palatable fruits on which, when fermenting, elephants get drunk. The *Brachystegia–Isoberlinia* savanna woodlands, by contrast, provide herbage of greater bulk during the rainy season but it is

Figure 3.6. Zebra at the contact of low tree and shrub savanna and savanna grassland Etosha pan, South West Africa (note outcropping calcrete in foreground).

Figure 3.7. Wild descendants of introduced water buffalo on the Marrakai plains, Northern Territory, Australia.

Figure 3.8. *Brachystegia longifolia–Julbernardia paniculata* woodland used for making charcoal (foreground), Chati Forest Reserve near Kitwe, Zambia.

less nutritious and becomes harsh and unpalatable during the dry period. These areas are occupied by smaller numbers of sable antelope, roan antelope, waterbuck and reedbuck. Significantly, the largest concentrations of wild game occur in areas where there is a juxtaposition of differing types of savanna—each of which provides grazing and browse at different periods of the year. This sustains the migrations of game that are such a characteristic feature of areas like the Serengeti plains of Tanzania and the northern Kalahari, Etosha pan and Okavango area of southern Africa.

Comparably favourable grazing and browse for wild herbivores are absent from the South American and Australian savannas. There are few grasses in the arid savanna of South America and many of the shrubs are unpalatable. The herbage of the savanna woodlands is poorer than that of Africa and the savanna grasslands are subject to periodic inundation. In Australia the characteristic *Triodia* spp. grasses of the low tree and shrub savannas are sclerophyllous, resinous and unpalatable; sweet grazing is confined to local pockets of *Astrebla* and *Dichanthium* spp. grassland on heavy soils derived from alluvium. None of the *Eucalyptus* spp. trees and few of the phyllodinous *Acacia* trees and shrubs afford good browse. Before European settlement, however, the savanna woodlands and grasslands of Australia sustained large numbers of kangaroos and wallabies. These continue to survive, despite regular shooting to reduce their numbers since they compete for grazing with large herds of domestic cattle.

The introduction of domestic herbivores

The abundance of grasses that favoured the development of wild herbivores in the savannas also favoured domestic herbivores, notably cattle, sheep and goats when they were introduced into the southern continents. Introductions began with the waves of nomadic people entering Africa from southwestern Asia from 7000 BP onwards. They were followed centuries later when Europeans settled in the three continents. Impacts differed. In Africa, prior to European occupation, introductions occurred over a very long period as migrating peoples followed the dry savanna zones of northern and eastern Africa, avoiding the savanna woodlands where tse-tse flies act as vectors for trypanosomaisis (see Cumming 1982). With European settlement, however, large herds of cattle were rapidly built up in the savanna grasslands and savanna woodlands of South America and Australia where this disease does not occur. In Africa, due to the prevalence of tse-tse fly in the savanna woodlands, the drier savannas continued to be the main cattle rearing areas whereas in the other continents they were relatively less important.

Where grazed on the native vegetation, introduced herbivores have become part of the ecosystem. On large ranching properties in northern Australia cattle share the grazing with kangaroos and wallabies and on the Marrakai Plains of the Northern Territory also with the wild descendants of water buffalo introduced in the last century (Figure 3.7). In Africa cattle graze with lechwee and puku on the Kafue Flats and in South West Africa/Namibia with herds of springbok and with kudu. When settlement is closer or cattle are raised on introduced pastures, however, their impact is a part of man's cultural practices.

The conservation of wildlife

During the present century recognition of the value of wildlife resources, and of the threats to its continued existence posed by increasing herds of domestic stock and growing population pressures, has led to the setting aside of large areas as National Parks, where the native fauna is protected against hunting and competition from introduced species. Most of these parks are in Africa, where they have provided opportunities for studying the interrelationships between vegetation and fauna.

The interrelationships between vegetation and fauna

Bcause of the contrasts in the herbivorous fauna between the continents the interrelationships between vegetation and fauna must have differed greatly before the introduction of domestic herbivores by nomadic people and European settlers just as they do now.

It is generally accepted that plants and animals follow parallel interrelated lines of evolution and it is argued that the dominant spinescence in the plants of the arid low tree and shrub savannas of South America and Africa represents a defensive characteristic that is related respectively to the past and continuing high diversity and abundance of herbivores in these continents. The virtual absence of spinescence in species of the low tree and shrub savannas of Australia and the moist savanna woodlands in all continents is considered to favour this view against that regarding spinescence as related to water economy for which some authors believe that there is little physiological evidence (Huntley 1982). However, in Africa the wild herbivores nevertheless browse the spinescent species as well as such favoured shrubs as the *Grewia* spp. which lack thorns and are eaten also by domestic cattle and goats. The spread of introduced spinescent species in some overgrazed savanna grasslands and parklands in Queensland does not necessarily support a correlation between spinescence and grazing, as suggested by Huntley, for in these areas edaphic changes related to geomorphological processes favour the spread of shrubs (Chapter 17). The reasons for the development of thorns by some species remains uncertain but their possession may represent a morphological development that enables species to outcompete thornless species primarily under conditions of drought and secondarily under heavy browsing.

Available evidence indicates that the interrelationships between the wild herbivores and the vegetation are such as to maintain the stability of the ecosystem. This is particularly so in Africa where different wild game species favour different plant species and plants at different stages of growth. Thus lechwe, puku and waterbuck prefer the aquatic grasses, where accessible, of periodically flooded areas like the Kafue Flats of Zambia, whereas other antelopes prefer *Themeda triandra*, *Sporobolus pyramidalis*, *Bothriochloa radicans* or *Schmidtia pappaphoroides*. Buffalo prefer grass leaves of more than 10 cm in length whereas wildebeeste favour shorter grasses (Sinclair 1983). Different preferences lead to successional grazing. On the Serengeti plains, for example, when the short grasses of the ridge tops dry out, buffalo and zebra move down the catena, followed by topi, wildebeest and Thomsons gazelle, the larger animals making the grazing at the lower levels more favourable for the smaller animals by removing the coarser material (Bell 1970, 1971). Comparable movements have been observed in the *Acacia woodlands* of Tanzania (Lamprey 1963) and in the *Colophospermum mopane* woodlands of Zambia (Jarman 1972) where in the dry season waterbuck, zebra and warthog first leave the ridge tops for the flood plains and are followed in turn by impala and elephant which are mixed grazers/browsers and lastly by kudu, predominantly a browser. Even in areas where large increases in some species, such as elephant in the Tsavo national park, lead to large-scale destruction of trees, it appears likely that this prepares the way for occupation by other species, whose grazing habits enable trees to regenerate so that long-term stability is maintained by self regulatory processes.

Grazing by domestic cattle imposes a more severe strain on the vegetation for there is a greater concentration on the most palatable grass species. On cattle ranches in southern Africa the keeping of springbok and kudu and the introduction of goats to browse the shrubs represent attempts to reduce this. However there is little evidence to suggest that large-scale ranching has fundamentally changed the savanna vegetation in the southern continents. Rather it is in accord with very resilient forms of vegetation. On the other hand, however, overstocking and overgrazing has devastated the savannas of West Africa and India.

The interrelationships between the vegetation and other faunal elements are important for the functioning of the savanna ecosystem. The distribution of carnivores is related to that of herbivores with large predators like lions, leopards, cheetahs, jackals, hyaenas and wild dogs being important in Africa, and tigers in Asia. The distribution of the avifauna, which is rich in species in the savannas, is dependent on food supplies. The large running birds, the ostrich of Africa and emu of Australia, occupy the plains grasslands. The berry eaters like the barbets of Africa and the seed eaters like the weaver finches of Africa and parrots of Australia have most influence on the vegetation. In Australia the parrots, like rodents, will built up very large populations in wet years of high seed production but decline in dry years so that numbers are self regulating and stable. Rodents are numerous in the savannas. The burrowing forms influence soil conditions, but only the giant capybara of South America has an important effect on the vegetation, its role resembling that of the ungulates of Africa and kangaroos of Australia.

Reptiles and invertebrates have important roles as primary and secondary consumers and as decomposers within the savanna ecosystem. The savanna grasslands are the breeding grounds for grasshoppers and locusts whose impact, however, is on the crops of neighbouring lands. The activities of termites, however, have a direct influence on the soils and vegetation of the savannas. Some species build very large mounds (Figures 2.16, 8.7, 8.13 and 8.15) and in so doing bring up from depth soil and weathered parent material which may be of different composition from the surrounding surface soil. Because of their differing soil composition and freer drainage large termite mounds may support trees and shrubs of different species from adjacent areas and act as the vehicles of vegetational change (Chapter 8).

Overall the interrelationships between the vegetation and the wild and domestic fauna of the savannas indicate functional stability. While wild herbivores may influence the physiognomy of the vegetation and the morphology of some species they are unlikely to have influenced the distribution of the various forms of savannas. Rather their distributions and movements accord with the nutritive properties of the grazing and browse of each type of savanna, which in turn are related to the physical environment wherein lies the fundamental dynamism of change.

THE ROLES OF FIRE
AND OF MAN'S CULTURAL PRACTICES

The effects of fire on savanna vegetation and its role in savanna ecosystems are controversial. In the savanna woodlands fire is a regular occurrence, caused by lightning strike or by man in order to drive out wild game during hunting, to destroy dry grass and stimulate the growth of new shoots for grazing animals and to clear felled brushwood in preparation for cultivation. In the savanna parklands and low tree and shrub savannas fire is both rare and unwelcome. The distinction in the occurrence of fire between the different categories of savanna vegetation is fundamental to an understanding of its role.

In the savanna woodlands the large amount of inflammable dry grass in the dry season constitutes a fire hazard. In the author's experience fire quickly destroys this dry material, passes quickly over the surface and causes little or no damage to living plant material. As indicated in Chapter 5 those features of the vegetation that have been considered to result from or be the effects of fire — tortuosity, deciduous branches and regrowth from adventitious buds on old branches and roots, ligno tubers and xylopodia — are morphological features enabling plants primarily to withstand drought, although by the same token they also enable them to be fire resistant. Fire, in fact, serves the valuable function of removing the dead grass and litter. The trees and shrubs are remarkably resilient and regenerate from rootstocks if their aerial parts are destroyed and the removal of dead grass and litter stimulates the production of new shoots by the perennial grasses. Fire therefore acts as a stabilizing influence rather than as a destructive force in the savanna woodlands.

Several authors have demonstrated that protection from fire leads to the regeneration of forest species and extension of forest into savanna woodland areas in Africa and Brazil (Trapnell 1959, Trapnell *et al.* 1976, Lawton 1964, Ferri 1973). The experiments near Kitwe in Zambia and at Emas, near Pirassununga in the state of Sao Paulo, Brazil, however, have been conducted at the forest/savanna woodland boundary in areas of relatively fertile well drained soils over sloping or dissected terrain at the periphery of plateaux. Under such conditions forest rather than savanna woodland would be the climax vegetation and as dissection proceeds in current geomorphological cycles the forest would extend at the expense of savanna. Here a distinction must be made between fire induced savanna woodlands over dissected terrain in boundary zones and the typical core savanna woodlands of the level plateaux. Recognition of this distinction is important also in West Africa where research on forest outliers in Nigeria has discounted the role of fire and demonstrated that the distributions of forest and savanna accord with differing edaphic conditions which are acknowledged in differing agricultural practices (Moss and Morgan 1970, see Chapter 12).

The infrequency of fire in the dry types of savanna woodland, in parklands and low tree and shrub savannas is related to the lesser production of dry grass material resulting from the fact that the grasses grow more slowly in the rainy season and retain their nutritive properties throughout the dry season. There is less inflammable material, the cover is less dense and the value of the grazing makes fire unwelcome. Moreover, notwithstanding the lower rainfall, the heavier soils characteristic of the dry savanna woodlands and savanna parklands retain moisture for longer periods than those of the savanna woodlands, thereby reducing fire risks. In some areas of low tree and shrub savanna, notably over light sandy soils, fires may be started by carelessness or deliberately, but their impact is short lived, studies of sequential Landsat imagery showing that vegetation returns to its prefire state within two or three years.

Overall the evidence indicates that while fire is a factor within savanna ecosystems, its influence on vegetation is to maintain stability except at the savanna woodland/forest boundary where its deliberate use may extend savanna and protection from it encourage the regeneration of forest.

Man influences the vegetation by cutting trees for house-building, fencing and fuel, by using fire for hunting and stimulating new grass growth for domestic stock and by clearing land for cultivation. The impact has differed in the separate categories of savanna and between the continents. It has been greatest in Asia and Africa, particularly West Africa (Chapters 12 and 13), most widespread in the savanna woodlands, but in favoured localities most severe in the savanna parklands.

In Asia and Africa the savanna woodlands have provided timber and fuel and have been used for shifting cultivation on a land rotation of variable length for centuries. It is believed that man's activities have fundamentally changed the vegetation in India and West Africa (Chapters 12 and 13). In Zambia, however, for which the chitamene system of shifting agriculture has been fully documented (Trapnell 1953, Trapnell and Clothier 1957; Figure 3.8), the length of the rotation has been related to the quality of the soils which is expressed in the floristic composition of the vegetation. In the long term the latter has probably not changed greatly as a consequence of periodic cultivation. The impact of the cutting of timber, fencing and fuel, however, has been severe in some areas, particularly on and near the Copperbelt. In Australia and South America man's impact on the savanna woodlands has been mainly associated with cattle ranching activities. In Australia his attempts to reduce tree growth and increase grass coverage have demonstrated the remarkable resilience of savanna vegetation, particularly in the woodlands of *Eucalyptus populnea* in eastern Queensland where these trees sucker vigorously after any disturbance.

Man's greatest impact on savanna vegetation has been in the savanna parklands where large areas have been cleared for crop production, particularly for maize production in central southern Africa and for sorghum and sunflower production in eastern Queensland in Australia. Where water is available for irrigation smaller areas of low tree and shrub savannas with favourable alluvial soils have been cleared for horticulture, particularly in the South African Lowveld.

Compared with other ecosystems, that of the savannas appears to be relatively stable. Savanna vegetation of every category survives in each continent despite the occurrence of fire and disturbance by man. The palaentological and palynological records indicate that these forms of vegetation have been in existence for a very long time (van der Hammen 1983). This indicates fundamental relationships with physical environmental factors, and a harmony with biotic influences that accord vegetational stability which has been modified but not radically changed by fire or by man.

4   The savannas of South America

Since the term 'savanna' originates from an Amerindian word that was used to describe 'land without trees but with much grass either tall or short', it is understandable that in tropical America it is used today for any grassland with or without trees, natural or man made. This usage generally follows the definition of Beard (1953), while in Guyana the term is applied also to areas of herbaceous swamp from which grasses as well as trees may be absent.

The forms of grassy vegetation that grade from woodland to pure grassland and are known as cerradao, campos cerrados, campos sujos and campos limpos in Brazil are normally regarded as savannas both there and in Venezuela, Colombia, Guyana, Surinam, French Guiana and the Caribbean islands where comparable types occur. Physiognomically similar vegetation comprising a grass stratum with scattered pine trees that covers hilly terrain in the central American republics from Costa Rica to Guatemala is of more doubtful status. Pine trees are unknown in the acknowledged savannas of tropical America. Research in the pine-studded grassland of Honduras and Costa Rica has established that this vegetation has been derived from mesophytic forest by burning, clearing and cultivation and that on abandonment of agriculture it is colonized by forest species and reverts to forest (Johannessen 1963, Taylor 1963, Budowski 1956).

In other areas the pine trees intermingle with the typical cerrado tree species, *Byrsonima crassifolia* and *Curatella americana*. However, whereas the characteristic cerrado species of the typical savanna woodlands have evolved from the flora that occupied Gondwanaland before the supercontinent broke up and the sections drifted apart to form separate southern continents, the *Pinus* species originated in North America and entered Central America only when the Tertiary orogeny produced the Western Cordilleras linking North and South America. Their migration pathways over hilly terrain would be consistent with their becoming constituents of tropical forests rather than of savanna woodlands which are usually found over level plateau surfaces. For the above reasons the pine-studded grasslands are excluded from further consideration in this text.

The dry types of vegetation that occur in northeastern Brazil, where they are known as caatinga, and in northern Venezuela, are not normally regarded as savanna in those countries, but they are comparable with vegetation types in central and southern Africa that are regarded as typical savannas. For this reason and because elucidation of the distributional relationships between them and the grassy savannas is essential for an understanding of the distributions of the latter, they are considered here.

In Brazil periodically inundated and swamp grasslands, that occupy relatively small areas along flat valley floors, are known as pantanal. The same name is used for the large area of seasonally inundated vegetation along the Parana–Paraguay river system. Comparable areas are known as esteros in Venezuela. The pantanal grasslands of the valleys are comparable with those occupying the dambos of Africa, while the complex mosaic of savanna grasslands and woodlands, caatinga and forest that characterizes the seasonally inundated Pantanal along the Parana–Paraguay river system is comparable with the similar mosaics along seasonally flooded sections of the Zambezi in Barotseland in western Zambia (Chapter 8), in the Okavango inland delta area of Botswana (Chapter 11) and along the many streams in the Channel Country of western Queensland in Australia (Chapter 19).

The main area of distribution of savanna woodlands and associated watershed grasslands in South America is over the centre of the Brazilian plateau; outlying areas occur within the tropical forest belt along the east coast of Brazil, and north of the Amazon basin in Venezuela, Guyana, Surinam and French Guinana, in the Brazilian state of Amapa, and in the Caribbean islands of Cuba, Dominica and Hispaniola.

Smaller patches of imperfectly known savanna woodlands occupy interfluves within the Amazon basin providing 'stepping stones' between the core area in central Brazil and the northern outliers. The savanna woodlands in central Brazil are floristically very rich but the northern and eastern outliers contain few tree species. The imperfectly known patches in Venezuelan Amazonas appear to have more species than the more remote outliers, including some of tropical and African and Asian affinity indicative of a Gondwana origin. Throughout their extent the savanna woodlands and associated watershed grasslands of tropical America occupy level plateau surfaces with either impoverished lateritic soils or nutrient deficient sands derived from sandstone bedrock.

The main area of lowland savanna grasslands is in the Llanos of the Orinoco basin of Venezuela and the adjacent territory of Colombia. Smaller areas occur, however, within the savanna woodlands where along the valley sides or plateau edges the water table is near the surface for most of the year.

The core area of caatinga vegetation is in the area known as the drought polygon of northeast Brazil, but outliers occur on dry sites within the

Pantanal. Physiognomically comparable but floristically distinctive forms of dry thorn savanna occupy the Unare basin in Venezuela and cover smaller areas in other Caribbean states.

In South America the distribution of the various forms of savanna and their relationships to environmental factors, although complex, are simpler than in either Africa or Australia. In South America the savanna woodlands are of more uniform composition throughout their range and there is a continuum from woodland through low tree and shrub communities largely composed of the same species to savanna grassland. The distributions of these communities display a comparatively simple relationship to old planation surfaces with relict lateritic soils. For all these reasons the South American savannas are considered first. Attention is focused particularly on those areas in which the author has conducted field investigations and on the core areas of distribution of each type of savanna. Information on other savanna areas in South America is available elsewhere (Sarmiento 1983).

5 The savanna woodlands, savanna grasslands and low tree and shrub savannas of Brazil

Vegetation with the physiognomic characteristics of savanna is described by the local names of cerradao, campos cerrados or cerrados, campos sujos, campos limpos, pantanal and caatinga in Brazil. The first three have a distinctive and well defined grass dominated ground layer with trees and shrubs of variable but generally low stature distributed at varying densities to produce woodland, parkland and low tree and shrub savanna. The cerradao and campos cerrados have been classified as semi-deciduous tropical woodlands and the campos sujos and campos limpos as tall grass savannas. In both physiognomy and floristic composition there is, however, a continuous sequence or continuum from fairly dense woodland (cerradao) through open woodland (campo cerrado) and low tree and shrub savanna (campo sujo) to open grassland (campo limpo) with some species present in all types (Cole 1960a, Goodland 1971a). In this the grassy savannas of Brazil differ from those of Africa and Australia where the boundaries between the distinctive categories are sharp. The pantanal is dominantly a moist to wet grassland in places studded with scattered trees giving a parklike appearance. The caatinga includes the tropical deciduous thorny xerophytic woodland of the area known locally as the Agreste and the low thorny and succulent vegetation exhibiting characteristics of low tree and shrub savanna in the Sertao. Grasses are poorly represented in the caatinga vegetation which, however, resembles some forms of savanna vegetation around the periphery of the Kalahari and in the Bushveld and Lowveld of southern Africa.

Both the cerrado and caatinga types of vegetation have been studied periodically in different areas for over a century. The increasing information that has become available, particularly from detailed studies of the campos cerrados around the new capital, Brasilia, on the Serra do Roncador in northeast Mato Grosso (Eiten 1972, 1975, 1978, 1982, Brown *et al.* 1970,

Ratter *et al.* 1973) and in the state of Sao Paulo (Ferri 1964, 1971, 1973, Labouriau 1966) has led to a recognition that current vegetation distributions are the result of the interplay of many environmental factors in space and time. Regionally the relative importance of individual factors may vary but everywhere the vegetation is in delicate balance with the environment and will change with a change in any one factor.

THE VIEWS OF SUCCESSIVE WRITERS ON THE DISTRIBUTION AND ORIGIN OF THE SAVANNA VEGETATION OF BRAZIL AND NEIGHBOURING TERRITORIES

The early writers attributed the distribution of the savanna vegetation of Brazil and its neighbouring territories either to climatic or pedological or biotic factors, or to a combination of these factors. Most of those favouring climatic influences stressed the importance of a seasonal rainfall regime and associated the distribution of the grassy savannas with alternating wet and dry seasons; but Warming (1892) in his studies of the campos cerrados around Lagoa Santa in Minas Gerais linked the influence of a seasonal climate with specific soil conditions that he believed caused a periodic deficiency of moisture.

Most writers favouring the dominant influence of pedological factors cited mineral deficiencies in the soils and Jones (1930) and Waibel (1948) suggested that poor soils capable of supporting only a savanna vegetation developed over certain geological formations. Others argued that profound leaching resulted in impoverished soils supporting a poor low forest that was readily fired and thereby converted to savanna. These views contrasted with those of writers on northern tropical America who associated savannas with flat areas with impeded soil drainage caused by an impermeable layer within the soil profile (Bennett and Allison 1928, Charter 1941, Beard 1953). Clearly the emphasis attached to particular characteristics depended on the area of study.

Contrasting views from those regarding the savanna vegetation of Brazil as a product of the physical environment were expressed by Rawitscher (1948) and Ferri (1955) who, from studies made near the forest/savanna boundary in Sao Paulo state, concluded that the campos cerrados were fire induced, having replaced forest that had been burnt by man. In this they accorded with the views of writers on the savannas of West, South and East Africa.

Since none of these views, taken alone or in combination, satisfactorily explained the distribution of the savanna vegetation of Brazil, in 1956 the author, recognizing the dynamic nature of vegetation, examined the distribution of the savanna vegetation, in relation not only to climatic, edaphic and biotic influences operative today, but also to landscape evolution and climatic change. She found close relationships between vegetation distributions, landforms and geomorphological processes and formulated a simple model showing these relationships (Cole 1960a). The validity of the model has been largely confirmed by the results of studies made in 1967–69 in the Serra do Roncador area, northeastern Mato Grosso by several investigators under Royal Society/Royal Geographical Society sponsorship working in collaboration with the National Research Council of Brazil (Askew *et al.*, 1970a,b, Brown *et al.* 1970). It has also been supported by the investigations into the levels of major elements, notably calcium, potassium, phosphorus and aluminium in the tissues of typical campo cerrado tree species (Arens 1958, 1963, Lopes and Cox 1971, 1977, Goodland 1971b, Goodland and Pollard 1973).

THE SAVANNA WOODLANDS AND ASSOCIATED GRASSLANDS OF BRAZIL

The cerradao and the campos cerrados constitute forms of savanna woodland comparable with those characterized by *Brachystegia*, *Isoberlinia* and *Julbernardia* spp. trees in Africa and by *Eucalyptus* spp. trees in Australia. The campos limpos are equivalent to the watershed savanna grasslands and the campos sujos represent the transitional type. The latter may contain small trees and shrubs of *Roupala montana*, Proteaceae, the family characteristic of the transitional zone between savanna woodlands and watershed savanna grasslands in both Africa and Australia.

The physiognomy and composition of the savanna woodlands and associated savanna grasslands

The campos cerrados form the characteristic savanna woodlands of Brazil. 'Campo' means literally an 'open field' and 'cerrado' is the Portuguese for 'closed'. The combination campo cerrado aptly describes vegetation comprising a mixture of tall grasses and low contorted trees whose canopy is closed by the touching crowns and interlocking branches of relatively closely spaced trees but is sufficiently open for light to penetrate to the ground through which movement is relatively easy (Figures 2.3 and 5.1).

The characteristic trees of the campos cerrados are only four to eight metres high so that the woodland is of lower stature than the comparable forms in Africa and Australia. Both trunks and branches are highly contorted and have thick corky barks that are often deeply fissured. Frequently the end branches do not taper and often both flower and leaf buds arise directly from

Figure 5.1. Campos cerrados savanna woodland near Brasilia.

the branches with little or no stem. In the possession of these features, once regarded as adaptations to resist fire and now known to be adaptations to seasonal drought, the savanna woodland trees of Brazil differ from their counterparts in Africa and Australia.

Most of the common trees have very large leaves which in some species like the pau santo, *Kielmeyera coriacea*, pau de arara, *Salvertia convallariodora* and peroba de campo, *Aspidosperma tomentosum*, are borne in rosette-like clusters at the tips of the branches. The leaves of the first two, like those of the pequi, *Caryocar brasiliensis*, pau terra, *Qualea* and *Vochysia* spp., and murici, *Byrsonima coccolobifolia* and *B. crassifolia* are hard, coriaceous or leathery and stiff. Their surface is smooth or asperous. The peroba de campo, *Aspidosperma tomentosum*, however, has excessively tomentose leaves of large size arranged in rosette-like clusters at the tips of the branches. In many species the veins stand out as hard ridges on the underside of the leaves while in the lixiero, *Curatella americana*, the undersides of the leaves have a sandpapery texture that is due to the presence of silica. Contrasting with these species, the leguminous trees of which *Stryphnodendron barbatimao* and *Dimorphandra mollis* are common in some areas, have small, thin, pinnate leaves while the mangaba, *Hancornia speciosa*, found in the wetter areas, has small hard evergreen leaves. Due to the structure of the leaf tissue and the thick cuticle the leaves of all these trees have a greyish green colour.

The trees retain their foliage into the dry season when they continue to transpire freely (Ferri 1944, 1955, Rachid 1947, Rawitscher 1948). The trees may lose their leaves for a very short period—sometimes only a few days—at the end of winter, but they do not shed them simultaneously and the vegetation is only semi-deciduous or brevi-deciduous. In this respect the campos cerrados differ from the deciduous caatinga and from the thorn savanna of Africa but resemble the savanna woodlands characterized respectively by trees of the *Brachystegia, Isoberlinia* and *Julbernardia* genera in Africa and by *Eucalyptus* spp. in Australia. Most of the cerrado trees produce flushes of new leaves when temperatures begin to rise before the end of the dry season. Like those of the *Brachystegia, Isoberlinia* and *Julbernardia* spp. in Africa which display a similar seasonal response, the new leaves are often bright reddish in colour. The leaf retention and continued transpiration of the cerrado trees during the dry season and the appearance of new leaves before the summer rains appears to be related to deep rooting systems that enable the trees to tap ground water and to the development of underground perennating structures, ligno tubers or xylopodia that store food and water. In these features the cerrado trees resemble the *Boscia* spp. trees in the low savanna woodlands in parts of western Botswana (see p. 236) and the *Brachysteigia, Isoberlinia* and *Julbernardia* spp. trees of Zambia and the adjacent territories respectively.

The sclerophyllous leaves of the typical cerrados tree and shrub species were formerly regarded as an adaptation to drought. This view was challenged when the apparent adequacy of ground water supplies enabling the species to transpire freely during the dry season was recognized (Rachid 1947, Rawitscher 1948). Later work suggested a connection between scleromorphy and mineral deficiencies in the soils that limit growth and produce an accumulation of carbohydrates leading to the deposition of cellulose, thick cuticle and sclerenchyma, i.e. the scleromorphic characters (Arens 1963). More recent work has shown that the cerrado species have internal strategies that enable them to thrive in soils with high aluminium levels that would be lethal to most plants. These strategies include both aluminium accumulation and aluminium exclusion. The former has been found in 20% of cerrado tree species and is most marked in *Salvertia convallariodora* whose leaves have been found to contain over 20 000 ppm. Aluminium exclusion is associated with higher uptakes of other minerals, notably calcium and potassium (Goodland and Pollard 1973).

The grass stratum of the campos cerrados is comprised of perennial tufted narrow-leaved species. The most common grasses are *Tristachya chrysothrix* and *Aristida pallens* but other species of *Aristida, Melinis minutiflora* and species of *Paspalum, Panicum* and *Andropogon* may also be present, some of them entering from areas cleared for grazing or cultivation.

Where the campos cerrados cover large areas over the centre of the Brazilian plateau the flora is very rich, comprising hundreds of species (Eiten 1963, 1978). With distance from the core area of distribution, however, the number of species decreases and few are present in isolated outliers. Most of the

Figure 5.2. Cerradao near the periphery of the high chapada between Carmo de Paranaibo and Lagoa Formosa, Minas Gerais. Altitude about 1000 m.

Figure 5.3. Campos cerrados savanna woodland grading to campos sujos on the high windswept plateau between Carmo de Paranaibo and Lagoa Formosa, Minas Gerais. Altitude about 1000 m.

Figure 5.4. Campos cerrados, grading to campos sujos and campos limpos on the level peneplaned or pediplaned surface studded with inselberge, near Feira de Santana, Bahia. Surface ascribed to Velhas cycle by L. C. King. The willowy trees are *Hancornia speciosa*.

species do not occur in other types of vegetation and most display the characteristic responses and adaptations to seasonal drought and poor soils cited above. All these features suggest that the campos cerrados represent climax vegetation whose species and species characteristics have evolved over a long period of time. Despite the rich flora, unlike the savanna woodlands of Africa and Australia, the cerrados contain no discernible vegetation associations. Instead its composition is infinitely variable — a feature that may be related to the greater environmental uniformity associated with lesser dissection of the old planation surfaces and lesser exposure of bedrock in Brazil compared with Africa and Australia.

In one direction the campos cerrados grade into cerradao (Figure 5.2), a higher denser form of woodland within which discrete vegetation associations have been recognized in northeastern Mato Grosso. The cerradao is usually composed of the same species as the campo cerrado but the trees attain a height of 10 to 15 metres. Tree species characteristic of the drier forms of mata or forest may also be present, notably *Bowdichia virgiloides* and species of *Hymenaea*, *Piptadenia* and *Machaerium*, all belonging to the Leguminosae family, and respectively having the common names of sucupira de mata, jatoba, angico and jacaranda.

In the opposite direction the campo cerrado grades into the campo sujo, meaning 'dirty grassland', consisting of grassland with scattered shrubs and small trees, frequently species of *Kielmeyera* and *Roupala* that are seldom more than two or three metres high (Figures 5.3 and 5.4). As the trees and shrubs decrease in numbers and species and in stature the campo sujo passes into campo limpo, or 'clean grassland', which is usually dominated by *Aristida* species.

The distribution of the savanna woodlands and associated savanna grasslands of Brazil

The main area of savanna woodlands and associated savanna grasslands is over the high interior plateaux or chapadoes of the Mato Grosso, Goias and Minas Gerais. There all types are represented with campos limpos usually occupying the centres of the plateaux and being succeeded in turn by campos sujos and campos cerrados towards their periphery. Outliers of campos cerrados, however, occur on the coastal taboleiros of Bahia, Sergipe, Alagoas and Pernambuco, as well as north of the Amazon in Amapa and the various Caribbean territories (Figure 5.5). The distribution of campos cerrados is thus discontinuous, with great stretches of forest clothing the intervening areas. Over the interior the savanna is unbroken over vast areas but in the eastern coastal belt it is interrupted by numerous ribbons of forest extending inland along valleys from the mata zone of the littoral. In both areas,

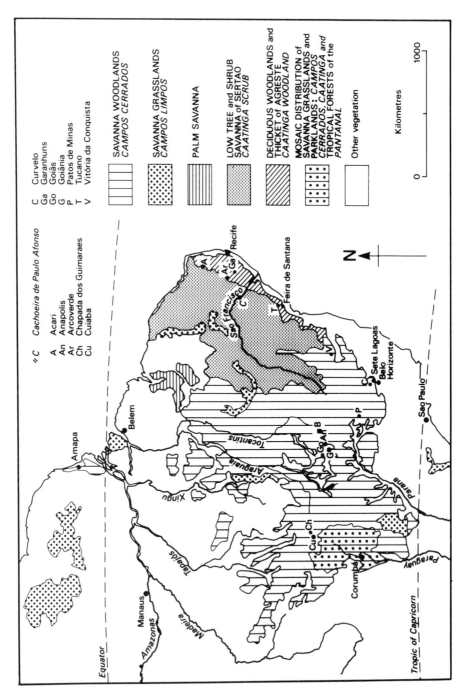

Figure 5.5. Distribution of major categories of savanna vegetation types, Brazil.

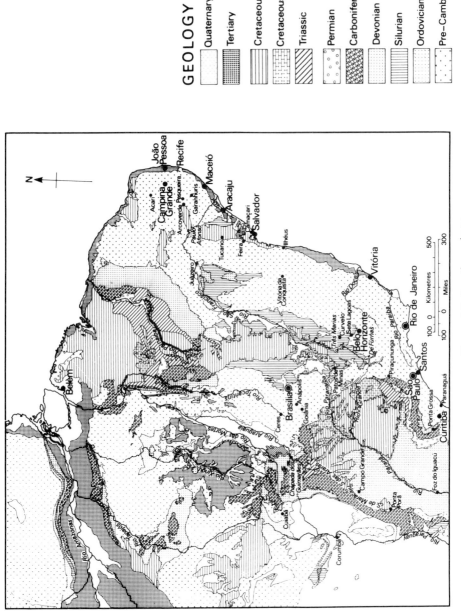

GEOLOGY

Quaternary
Tertiary
Cretaceous
Cretaceous/Jurassic
Triassic
Permian
Carboniferous
Devonian
Silurian
Ordovician/Cambrian
Pre–Cambrian

Figure 5.6. Brazil, geology.

however, it covers level plateau surfaces that represent planation surfaces, either peneplains or more probably pediplains, and either formed over more or less horizontally disposed Cretaceous to Tertiary sedimentary rocks or cut across folded Precambrian to Palaeozoic sedimentaries and ancient crystalline rocks (Figure 5.6). In the areas studied by the author the campos cerrados do not normally occur over sloping terrain, giving way to a dry type of forest both along the valleys cut into the plateaux and the dissected terrain at the periphery of the plateaux. The change from savanna to forest is invariably abrupt. There is rarely any transition zone where savanna and forest species are intermixed and in some areas the boundary is actually linear. In the area of the Serro do Roncador studied by the Royal Society/Royal Geographical Society sponsored group of investigators, campos cerrados, campos limpos and a dry type of forest occur on both level plateaux and on gently sloping terrain that, according to the direction of the drainage either northwestwards to the Xingu or eastwards to the Araguaia, is subject to differing degrees of dissection. In the watershed area that has been subjected to crustal tilting (Brown *et al.* 1970) or warping the relationships between vegetation distributions and environmental factors, as on the Congo–Zambezi watershed in Zambia, likewise affected by crustal warping (see p. 129), reflect conditions of ecological tension wherein the boundary between savanna and forest, under the influence of current geomorphological processes, is in a state of flux.

Relationships between the distribution of the savanna woodlands and associated savanna grasslands and the physical environment

The influence of climatic factors   Over the high plateaux of central Brazil where the savanna woodlands and associated savanna grasslands—the cerradao, cerrados, campos cerrados, campos sujos and campos limpos— have their main and by far the largest areas of distribution, the tropical climate is characterized by seasonal temperature and rainfall regimes. The summers are hot and rainy; the winters relatively cool and dry. The annual rainfall varies from about 200 mm at the margins of the Amazon Lowlands to about 750 mm in the east near the boundary with the caatinga. Over most of the central plateau it averages between 1100 and 1600 mm concentrated in the period October to April. There is a well defined dry season of about five months duration from May to September when, as the temperature reaches the daily maximum, the relative humidity may drop to 30%. As the temperature falls, however, the atmosphere becomes quite moist and dew often falls at night. In most years some rainfall occurs in July and August. Temperatures show mean maxima of around 30°C and mean minima of around 26°C during the rainy season when the mean daily range is usually less than 12°C. In the early part of the dry winter period temperatures usually vary between daily maxima around 27.5°C and nightly minima of 18°C but they may fall to 7°C. The daily variation of temperature is greater than the seasonal variation and the diurnal range is greater in the cooler dry season than in the summer wet season. The highest temperatures normally occur before the rains in September and October when the diurnal variations are most extreme. Except at moderate altitudes in Sao Paulo State at the southern edge of the campos cerrados frosts are practically unknown. Strong winds, however, are a characteristic feature of the winter season and combined with low temperatures and drought may be unfavourable for tree growth. They are felt most sensibly on the highest and least broken plateaux where, significantly, campos cerrados grade through campos sujos to campos limpos. The presence of relatively dry types of mata or forest within the main savanna woodland zone and the fact that the trees of the cerrados flush into new leaf during the dry season, however, cast doubt on the overriding influence of climatic factors over the distribution of the latter vegetation type. Patches of mata clothe the undulating volcanic terrain near Patos de Minas which lies within and rises slightly above the main campos cerrados belt of Minas Gerais; mata also covers the dissected hilly country between Goiania and Anapolis within the savanna belt of Goias (Faissol 1952). On the taboleiros along the east coast campos cerrados occur in a zone where the temperatures are high throughout the year and the rainfall is certainly adequate and sufficiently well distributed to support forest. Here other factors must be responsible for the occurrence of savanna woodlands and savanna grasslands. On the Serra do Roncador in northeastern Mato Grosso, where during investigations made by the 1968 Royal Society/Royal Geographical Society expedition 1372 mm of rainfall fell in 148 days, almost all between January and April and between October and December, Askew *et al.* (1970) believe that the occurrence of a broad belt of dry forest between the equatorial rain forests and the campos cerrados indicates the important influence of climatic factors on the forest/savanna boundary. There, the regional boundary between campos cerrados and cerrados and the dry forest coincides with differences in soil texture related to lithological variations in parent rock, but it is believed to be determined by differences of soil moisture status occasioned by these textural differences. More strongly than in the core area of campos cerrados distribution on the Brazilian plateau, in this vegetational tension zone the boundary between savanna and forest will occur where there are strongly contrasting conditions caused by sharp differences in one or a combination of several of the environmental factors. Water relations may be critical but they are influenced by the interplay of many climatic, edaphic and geomorphological factors.

The influence of pedological factors The general association of savanna woodlands and grasslands with level planation surfaces and of mata or forest with sloping or dissected terrain suggests that their distributions may be influenced by soil and ground water conditions.

On the plateaux the soils, for the most part derived from sandstone, are generally freely drained, sandy and infertile; varying in colour from grey to red, they lack humus and have been leached of their more readily soluble minerals; they contain concentrations of iron and aluminium. These highly weathered and leached soils fall within the category of dystrophic soils; they vary in depth from a few millimetres to several metres and usually lack any marked horizon differentiation. Usually called latosols in Brazil, they represent the equivalent of the ferrallitic soils or ferrasols characteristic of the savanna woodlands of Africa. In some areas soils in the accepted sense are lacking and the surface is covered only by surficial accumulations of sand, gravel and pebbles and by deposits of ferruginous concretions. The last mentioned may form a lateritic iron pan known in Brazil as canga. This may occur at surface or below variable thicknesses of sand. The sandy soils have a poor moisture retaining capacity; rainwater rapidly soaks through them but the hardpan arrests its further downward percolation and causes poor drainage conditions. Shallow lakes may even form over the surface after rain. Under such conditions only shallow-rooted plants able to withstand alternating waterlogging and drought, and deep-rooted species able to penetrate the hardpan and draw upon the ground water (which usually occurs at a depth of 10 to 20 metres below the surface) are able to survive. Ability to draw upon the ground water enables the cerrado trees to retain their leaves and transpire freely throughout the dry season (Rawitscher 1948, Rawitscher *et al.* 1943), whereas inability to do so, combined with intolerance of alternating waterlogging and drought, precludes the forest trees species from the level plateaux.

The characteristic features of the plateau soils are due to the fact that they are senile. Because of the absence of slope the exhausted surface layers are not readily removed by the agents of normal healthy erosion, and soil renewal through replacement by material weathered from the parent rock proceeds extremely slowly if at all. Consequently with continued leaching the soils become progressively poorer and the hardpan more sharply defined and more fully developed. However, where there is some slope, as in a valley or over dissected terrain, there is a healthy balance between soil removal and soil renewal, a higher level of fertility is maintained and the soils have a good moisture retaining capacity and are well drained. Moreover, the ground water table occurs at shallower depth. Under such conditions forest trees are able to establish themselves. Thus the sudden change from savanna on the plateaux to mata in the valleys and over dissected country is readily explained by the soil character and pedogenesis, and by ground water conditions.

The importance of the influence of soil and drainage conditions on the vegetation on the plateaux is emphasized by the occurrence of cerradao or mata where the soils have a higher nutrient status and/or better moisture relationships as in declivities or baixadas, on the slopes of valleys and over igneous bedrock. The denser form of the campo cerrado, approaching cerradao in the environs of Brasilia occurs over deep red to reddish brown latosols. Around Curvelo in Minas Gerais abrupt changes from campos cerrados to cerradao take place where changes of surface configuration are matched by changes from grey to red sandy soils (Figure 5.7). At Lagoa Santa in the same state comparable changes from campos cerrados to deciduous forest with *Astronium uncendeuva, Cedrela fissilis,* and *Piptadenia macrocarpa* (Warming 1892, Alvim and Araujo 1952) occur over limestone bedrock producing soils with a high pH, particularly in the vicinity of moist or water-bearing sinkholes. Similar changes occur on soils of calcareous origin in Goias. Near Patos de Minas the campos cerrados gives way to forest with *Bowdichia virgiloides, Hymenaea courbaril* and *Piptadenia macrocarpa* trees where the level plateau underlain by Triassic sandstones gives way to gently undulating country over volcanic tuffs that yield dark brown soils of high nutrient status. A similar abrupt change occurs over gabbros and diorite bedrock in the Mato Grosso de Goias west of Goiania and Anapolis.

These observable relationships between vegetation distributions and pedological conditions are supported by the results of major element analysis of soils and plant tissues which show that the physiognomic gradient in the cerrados vegetation types is marked by a fertility gradient (Goodland 1971b, Goodland and Pollard 1973). Within the Triangulo Mineiro of Minas Gerais campo sujo occupies soils with the lowest levels of phosphorus, nitrogen and potassium; it grades into campo cerrado on slightly less infertile soils; this in turn thickens to cerradao where the levels are somewhat higher although still too low for most trees of the mata (Goodland and Pollard 1973). Significant negative correlations between aluminium and the critical nutrients, calcium together with magnesium and potassium in this area, indicate that aluminium toxicity occurs in the senile dystrophic latosols of this area; the cerrado plants are extraordinarily tolerant of such conditions. As cited earlier most have nutrient strategies that either accumulate or exclude the metal. Aluminium-accumulating plants are rare in the world's flora and their prevalence in the campos cerrados seems to confirm the importance of pedological influences on the distribution of this vegetation.

On the Serra do Roncador vegetation/soil relationships differ in some respects from those found within the core area of campos cerrados distribution over the centre of the Brazilian plateau. Both campos cerrados and dry forest occur on dystrophic soils; the dry forest generally occupies the more subdued relief associated with the less active streams draining to the

Figure 5.7. Campos cerrados (foreground) changing abruptly to cerradao (background) where a change of relief from level to gently sloping is marked by a change from grey sandy to red sandy soils.

Figure 5.8. Caating scrub near Arcoverde, Sertao. Creeping cactus (foreground) is *Pilocereus gounellei*.

Figure 5.9. High caatinga forest near Garanhuns, Pernambuca. The trees are *Caesalpinia pyramidalis* and the tall cactus (background left) is *Gereus squamosus*.

Xingu river whereas campos cerrados cover the more dissected relief associated with the more actively downcutting Araguaia river system, but both types of vegetation transgress the divide (Askew *et al.* 1970b). Near the regional vegetational boundary the soils under forest are of finer texture than those under campos cerrados, being sandy clay loams instead of sands or loamy sands; to the south campos cerrados occur also on clay soils and to the north dry forests occupy a range of soil textural types other than very sandy soils. However, whereas campos cerrados occupies soils that have only a thin litter layer of relatively undecomposed plant debris, the soils supporting dry forest contain decomposed organic matter which has been incorporated into the soil fabric to promote a granular or sub-angular blocky structure (Askew *et al.* 1970a,b). These differences may partly be attributable to the nature of the vegetation the soils support, but overall it would appear that dry forest is restricted to the soils of higher nutrient status and greater moisture availability.

The role of fire   Some Brazilian botanists, notably Rawitscher (1942, 1944) and Ferri (1955, 1973), have attributed to fire a major role in the formation and distribution of the campos cerrados. Most areas show some evidence of fire and the cerrado trees and shrubs exhibit morphological features that could be interpreted as adaptations to resist fire. While fire undoubtedly affects the vegetation, it is no longer regarded as a determinant of the distribution of the campos cerrados, which is now acknowledged to be governed fundamentally by the interplay of physical environmental factors.

Rawitscher and Ferri carried out most of their work in the mata/campo cerrado boundary zone at Emas near Piracununga in the State of Sao Paulo where there was a tendency for cerrado species to invade areas of forest that were burnt. With studies of the vegetation in the remote scantily populated interior of Minas Gerais, Goias and the Mato Grosso, which is the core area of campos cerrados distribution, the fundamental role of physical environmental factors have come to be appreciated (Cole 1960a,b, Brown *et al.* 1970, Ratter *et al.* 1973). Here fire has been used by Amerindians during hunting but its impact in a given area has been sporadic and infrequent. Where lightning has struck trees there is no evidence of it causing a fire. Here therefore fire could not account for the nature or distribution of campos cerrados. Moreover, if an area of forest within a forest region is burnt today it is not replaced by campo cerrado but by the pioneer species of the forest.

The campos cerrados constitute a homogeneous type of vegetation composed of distinct species with well defined characteristics; this clearly recognizable type of vegetation covers vast tracts of country. Both in its core area in central Brazil and in the outlying areas along the east coast and again north of Amazon, its character and composition are broadly the same. This uniformity between areas so widely separated from one another makes any contention that the campo cerrado is fire induced extremely improbable. Moreover it is difficult to see how the seeds of the typical cerrado species could be carried thousands of miles across densely forested country to the numerous areas in which campos cerrados are found today.

THE NATURE OF THE CAATINGA AND ITS RELATIONSHIP TO THE PHYSICAL ENVIRONMENT

The caatinga vegetation is very different from the campos cerrados and related types of vegetation. It consists of thorny trees and shrubs that lose their leaves during the dry season (Ferri 1953a,b, 1955, Ferri and Labouriau 1952), of spiny succulents and of low-growing herbs that come up after rain (da Cunha 1940). It occupies the hot, arid northeast of Brazil where its distribution is governed mainly by the duration and intensity of drought. Outlying patches, however, occur in the pantanal and caatinga species are prominent on the restingas—the old sand dunes and sand spits along the east coast.

Within the main caatinga zone differences of relief, rainfall, ground water conditions and soils are associated with differences in the nature and composition of the vegetation. Thus the extensive level peneplains that are cut across ancient crystalline rocks and are characterized by stony surfaces with little or no soil carry only the low scrub of the Sertao (Figure 5.8). This consists of thorny jurema trees (*Mimosa* spp.), the giant creeping cactus xique xique (*Pilocereus gounellei*), small jointed cacti called quipa (*Opuntia* spp.), and various thorny euphorbias, small cacti and bromelias. By contrast the undulating surface of the less arid Agreste appears originally to have carried high caatinga forest but, as a result of centuries of occupation and cultivation, little—and that most probably secondary growth—remains today. The caatinga forest (Figure 5.9) is dominated by the caatingueria tree (*Caesalpinia pyramidalis*) associated with giant cacti, especially the mandacaru (*Cereus jamacuaru*) and faxeiro (*Cereus squamosus*) and numerous low-growing opuntias and euphorbias. All the trees shed their leaves during the dry season (see Figure 2.17) and even during the rainy period severely restrict their transpiration during the middle of the day (Ferri 1953a,b, 1955, Ferri and Labouriau 1952). On the slopes of the serras, however, the higher rainfall and more humid atmosphere, combined with better soils and more favourable ground water conditions, supports a more luxuriant growth in which evergreen brauna (*Quebrachia brasiliensis*), joazeiro (*Zizyphus joazeiro*) and imbuzeiro (*Spondias tuberosa*) trees are present. The last-mentioned, however, possesses underground water storage organs that enable it to withstand drought. Along the dry watercourses, in both the Sertao and the Agreste galleries of caraibeira

Figure 5.10. Evergreen *Capparis* sp. trees following dry watercourse in the Sertao between Pocoes and Jequie, Bahia, contrasting with the leafless caatinga in the dry winter season.

Figure 5.11. Aerial view of the Pantanal showing forest restricted to the higher drier sites and grassland on the flooded areas.

Figure 5.12. Relationships between vegetation and geomorphology between Sao Gortardo and Carmo de Paranaibo, Minas Gerais.

(*Tabebuia caraiba*), oiticica (*Licania rigida*) and ico (*Capparis* spp.) trees that likewise retain their leaves throughout the year, reflect the presence of ground water within reach of their roots (Figure 5.10).

The low vegetation of the Sertao may be likened to the low tree and shrub savannas and the caatinga forests to the thickets of Africa where species of *Zizyphus* and *Capparis* are also present, and *Zizyphus mucronata* is regarded as a good indicator of ground water.

THE PANTANAL

The pantanal (Figure 5.11) is a complex mosaic of savanna grasslands and woodlands, caatinga forest and mata. It embraces the extensive flat lands bordering the Paraguay river and its tributaries that are flooded for several months each year between December and May. Only isolated hills and low ridges a few metres above the level of the water remain dry. In this environment, subject to alternations of long periods of drought and of inundation, differences of soil and degree of inundation are responsible for a variety of vegetation types. Characteristic are grasslands composed of Angola grass (*Panicum spectabile*), capim mimosa verdadeiro (*Paratheria prostrata*), capim mimosa vermelho (*Setaria geniculata*), capim de bezerro (*Paspalum repens*) and capim araguaia (*Paspalum fasciculatum*). These are studded with clumps of trees, usually the cerrado species ipe roxa (*Tecoma aurea*), ipe amarelo (*T. caraiba*) and *Curatella americana* which grow near termite nests around which sediments accumulate, providing pockets of soil that are protected against the flood waters. Away from the rivers, in the areas above the level of the normal floods, the clumps of trees become more numerous as the transition is made from the low to the high pantanal. The latter grades to campo cerrado where complete freedom from flood is associated with an apparently random distribution of trees. On the higher levees adjacent to the main river there are patches of tropical forest with Chacoan affinities and on dry stony ground caatinga forest is characteristic. The pantanal is thus a complex in which the several types of savanna and the tropical forest are all represented.

THE ORIGIN OF THE SAVANNA VEGETATION

In seeking an understanding both of the present distribution of the savannas and of the manner in which this distribution has come about, attention must be directed to the role of dynamic change in the vegetation and to its relationship with the geomorphological evolution of the landscape.

Historical plant geography and the role of dynamic change

In studying the historical plant geography of tropical Brazil, the present distributional relationships between the grassy savannas, the caatinga and the mata are of fundamental importance. Here the discontinuous nature of the distribution of both the grassy savannas and the caatinga is of outstanding significance, the former having its main centre over the interior plateaux and outlying areas in the pantanal, along the east coast and north of the Amazon basin. By contrast, except where cleared by man, the mata has a continuous distribution occupying the Amazon basin, occurring along the coasts and extending in finger-like projections up the valleys towards the interior.

Equally important are the distributional relationships between the grassy savannas and the mata and between the caatinga scrub and caatinga forest. Here the coincidence of the grassy savannas with high-level plateaux and the abrupt change to mata over the dissected country at their periphery, and along the valleys cutting back into them, is notable. So likewise is the occurrence of caatinga scrub over the low-lying peneplains, whereas caatinga forest occurs on the slopes of the serras rising above them and again over the dissected country at their periphery.

The distributional relationship between the grassy savannas and the caatinga is likewise significant. It is most clearly seen in Bahia where the two types of vegetation interdigitate in a number of localities. In the south, near Vitoria da Conquista, campo cerrado covers the higher plateaux whereas caatinga occupies the lower ground. Farther north, near Tucano, 'islands' of campo cerrado occur over the small taboleiros of Cretaceous to Tertiary rocks that rise above the extensive caatinga-covered pediplains cut across ancient crystalline rocks below. Both types of vegetation cover level terrain but the campo cerrado occupies the higher surfaces. Throughout the state of Bahia either caatinga forest or a dry scrubby type of mata covers the escarpments separating the level plateaux and likewise the slopes of the serras rising above them, while ribbons of tall, evergreen trees follow the watercourses and provide a connecting link with the mata along the coast.

The distributional relationships between the grassy savannas, caatinga and mata suggest that all three vegetation formations are in a state of flux. Near the limits of their distribution their composition is subject to dynamic change, with any modification of the local environmental conditions leading to the extension of one type and the recession of another. The relative age of the three formations is uncertain. From a study of its character and composition and of all the factors influencing its distribution, however, it seems clear that the campo cerrado is composed of species belonging to an ancient flora and that it represents a type of vegetation that was once more widespread. Formerly its distribution was continuous. Today only remnants survive with the large tract in central Brazil representing the centre or core area, and the outliers in eastern Brazil and north of the Amazon impoverished relict communities. By contrast the mata and the caatinga appear to be of more recent origin. Their gradual extension has been responsible for the gradual recession of the campo cerrado and other types of grassy savanna. The key to the changes that have occurred lies in the geomorphological evolution of the landscape, in geological events and climatic changes.

Vegetation distribution and geomorphology

Of outstanding significance again is the fact that the grassy savannas cover the high-level plateaus, whereas mata occupies the valleys and the dissected country in the more humid parts of Brazil; and that caatinga scrub characterizes the low-lying level terrain of the arid northeast, whereas caatinga forest or even dry mata covers the slopes of the serras and campo cerrado occurs on the higher taboleiros.

Everywhere the plateaux represent peneplains or pediplains, the end product of an old cycle of erosion. By contrast the hilly lands represent dissection in a new cycle. As this proceeds the level plateaus are being consumed. Over much of the northern part of Brazil the surface features appear to result from the processes of pediplanation propounded by L. C. King, with dissection proceeding by headward erosion up the valleys and by scarp recession at the margins of the plateaus. As this proceeds the level terrain is replaced by sloping ground, soils are renewed and the drainage improved and the microclimatic conditions are ameliorated. So in the more humid parts of tropical Brazil as the plateaux recede the conditions become more favourable for pioneer forest species which invade the campos cerrados. This occurs as soon as the level surface gives way to a sloping one. The cerradao may represent a transitional stage which, however, is usually short-lived. In the light of this sequence the sharp boundary between campo cerrado and mata, the occurrence of both types of vegetation in the same climatic zone in the eastern coastal belt, the presence of campos cerrados over the tongue of country forming the watershed between the Rio Sao Francisco and the Rio Grande, and the occurrence of the greatest tract of grassy savanna over the highest and most extensive plateaus in central Brazil are all readily explained. For under the current cycle of erosion dissection is most vigorous in the coastal areas. As it proceeds from the coast inland, so the mata extends up the river valleys towards the interior. At the same time, however, as scarp recession and pediplanation proceed, the younger and lower pediplains are growing at the expense of the older ones and are advancing towards the interior. As they do so the vegetation formations extend landwards in sympathy with them. In northeast Brazil the growth of the younger and lower pediplains is bringing about an extension of the area subject to acute aridity. Consequently there the caatinga is advancing at the expense of the campos cerrados.

The relationship propounded between the distribution of the major vegetation formations and the geomorphological evolution of the landscape may be demonstrated by more detailed reference to some of the areas subjected to close study. Of the level surfaces involved, some of those in the area east of the Goias/Minas Gerais border have been dated by L. C. King (1957), and others farther west have been studied by Brazilian geomorphologists. In all areas, the dating ascribed to the level peneplains or pediplains lends support to the contention that, according to whether the climate is humid or arid, either the mata or the caatinga is advancing at the expense of the grassy savannas.

The relationship between vegetation and geomorphology is very striking in Minas Gerais, where campo cerrado covers the level chapadoes which form the watershed between the Rio Sao Francisco and the Rio Grande and gives way to forest in the belts of hilly country at their periphery and along the valleys cutting back into them (Figure 5.12). Developed over Cretaceous sandstones the surfaces of these chapadoes have been ascribed to a Gondwana (Jurassic) cycle of erosion by L. C. King, who considers, further, that the valleys and the belts of hilly country have been and are being fashioned in later cycles which he dates as post-Gondwana (mid-Cretaceous) and Velhas (later Tertiary). Erosion in this later cycle has almost completely consumed the surface of an intermediate Sul-Americana cycle (Miocene or mid-Tertiary) and has uncovered Silurian schists which, given an adequate slope weather to soils capable of supporting mata. In this region the mata is clearly advancing at the expense of the campo cerrado as the older peneplains or pediplains are being destroyed.

In Goias and the Mato Grosso, where the grassy savannas achieve their greatest extent, their distribution is coincident with the level chapadoes which Brazilian geomorphologists believe represent an erosion surface of post-Rhaetic but pre-Cretaceous age. In Goias this surface, called by them the Pratinha surface, truncates highly inclined rocks dating back to the Precambrian period. Standing at an average elevation of 1000–1300 m it may be the equivalent of King's Gondwana surface farther east. Between Goiania and Anapolis it is in the process of active dissection. Here the relationship between the vegetation and geomorphology is very striking, for everywhere the level remnants of the Pratinha surface carry some form of grassy savanna, whereas along the valleys of the rivers cutting into it the vegetation changes abruptly to mata (Figure 5.13). As in Minas Gerais, here also the mata is clearly advancing at the expense of the campos cerrados.

The most convincing relationship between the distribution of savanna and mata and the geomorphological evolution of the landscape, however, occurs

Figure 5.13. Relationships between vegetation and geomorphology between Goiania and Anapolis. *Kielmeyera* sp. tree frames the picture.

Figure 5.14. View across campos cerrados-covered Cuiaba surface cut across Precambrian phyllites and gneisses representing a pre-Devonian peneplain now in the process of dissection in a current cycle of erosion. Sao Vicente escarpment of Devonian sandstone leads up to the Chapada de Guimaraes whose level surface is of post-Rhaetic but pre-Cretaceous age.

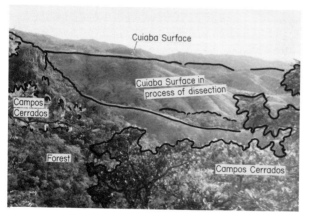

Figure 5.15. Dissected slopes of the Cuiaba surface immediately below the Sao Vicente escarpment, east of Cuiaba, Mato Grosso. Forest is extending from valleys and up slopes as erosion proceeds, whereas campos cerrados covers the peneplaned surface from which the photograph was taken.

in the western part of the Mato Grosso where grassy savannas cover two extensive peneplaned surfaces separated from one another by a wooded escarpment which, in places, is some 700 m from foot to crest. The two peneplains are cut across rocks of very different character and which are characterized by soils of somewhat different composition. The higher of the peneplains is the Chapada de Guimaraes, east of Cuiaba. Developed over Devonian sandstones and shales, it has been tentatively correlated with the Pratinha surface of Goias and Minas Gerais. Standing at an average elevation of about 1000 m it carries a savanna vegetation that grades from campos cerrados at its periphery to campos limpos in the centre. The vast extent of the Chapada de Guimaraes is due to the preservation of the peneplain over a wide area. It is, however, being consumed in a current erosion cycle and, significantly, near Sao Jose de Serra, where it forms the watershed between the Amazon and Paraguay drainage, belts of mata may be seen following the valleys of the headstreams of these great rivers eating back into the plateau surface. Westwards the Chapada de Guimaraes is separated by the Sao Vicente escarpment from the lower Cuiaba peneplain which is cut across highly inclined Precambrian phyllites and gneisses. This has an average elevation of 250 m and, since horizontally disposed Devonian sandstone may be seen overlying it in the Sao Vicente escarpment, it has been dated as pre-Devonian. The present surface may, therefore, represent an exhumed pre-Devonian peneplain that has been exposed as a result of pediplanation in a post-Pratinha erosion cycle and may correspond to one of the later cycles recognized by King in Minas Gerais. Like the Pratinha surface of the Chapada de Guimaraes, the Cuiaba peneplain is also being dissected in a current erosion cycle. Where it is preserved the vegetation is typical campos cerrados, but along the valleys and up the slopes fashioned in the current erosion cycle there is a change to mata (Figures 5.14 and 5.15). The Sao Vicente escarpment also is forest-clad. Here again, then, the evidence points to an extension of the mata at the expense of the grassy savannas.

In the environs of the Serra do Roncador in northeastern Mato Grosso vegetation/soil/geomorphology relationships are more complex. The Serra do Roncador is a plateau between the headwaters of the Xingu and Araguaia rivers (Brown 1970). It is underlain mainly by sandstones of Carboniferous and Cretaceous age whilst the flanking basins are floored by Tertiary and Quaternary sediments.

The plateau which slopes gently northwards and eastwards is believed to have originated as a planation surface in Jurassic or more probably Tertiary times but today it is dissected to varying degrees by streams draining to the Xingu and Araguaia. The drainage divide is asymmetrical with gradients to the Araguaia being three times those to the Xingu. Sharp contrasts of relief, stream patterns and profiles distinguish the areas drained by the two river systems. The northwestern area drained by the Rio Suia Missu to the Xingu is crossed by few streams and has a subdued relief. The eastern and southern area draining to the Araguaia is dissected by innumerable incised and actively downcutting streams. The smaller headwater channels of both systems appear to be unstable compared with the main channel of the Siua Missu (Thornes 1970).

The campos cerrados/dry forest boundary straddles the Serra do Roncador. Vegetation distributions are clearly related to relief and drainage features. Dry forest is virtually uninterrupted over the subdued relief in the northwest, its distribution being broken only by swampy gallery forest and thicket along the Rio Suia Missu. By contrast complex patterns of cerrados and cerradao over the interfluves and of swampy gallery forest, valley forest, deciduous seasonal forest and grassland along the floors and slopes of the valleys characterize the dissected area to the southeast; both cerradao and campos cerrados occupy the gently convex slopes but only grassland is found in the seepage zones associated either with outcrop of indurated laterite or with the contact of sandstone and underlying shale. Characteristically, belts of grassland occupy the wet zone parallelling the streams where they separate the campos cerrados and the gallery forests in a manner similar to that seen in the dambos of Africa. In some wet areas islands of cerrado tree species occupy the drier sites accorded by termite mounds.

At first sight the relationships between savanna and forest, relief and geomorphology on the Serra do Roncador appear to depart from the norm. In fact they resemble those found along the Congo/Zambezi watershed in Africa and at the northern edge of the Barkly Tableland in Australia where topographic, edaphic and vegetational adjustments are taking place following crustal warping. On the Serra do Roncador the relief and drainage features cited earlier, the prominent scarp extending around the sources of the eastward draining streams and the distribution of laterite on their valley sides suggest that a westward sloping planation surface, probably of Tertiary age formerly extended over the whole area. As postulated by Brown (1970) subsequent eastward tilting consonant with the present day regional slope of the plateau may have led to river incision, the creation of an asymmetrical divide and the progressive capture of the Xingu headwaters by tributaries of the Araguaia but more probably differential warping, comparable with that in central and southern Africa and in northern Australia, postdated the Tertiary planation. Accompanied by flexing in the vicinity of the present watershed and unequal relative depression of the drainage systems on either side, it would have initiated the same geomorphological processes. Such warping would explain the convexities of slope in the terrain, the instability in the headwater channels, the stepped valleys, the exposure of laterite in the valley sides and the incision into shale bedrock by the eastward flowing streams. It would also accord with the presence of Tertiary and Quaternary sediments in the drainage basins and the suboutcrop of rocks of Carboniferous and Cretaceous age underlying the Serra do Roncador.

Vegetation distributions may now be explained within a geomorphological context. Cerrados types of vegetation originally extended over the higher parts of the planation surface which was characterized by dystrophic soils. They possibly extended into the area now occupied by dry forest. As on the Congo/Zambezi watershed in Zambia the differential warping promoted the erosion of the dystrophic soils in the areas subject to uplift and favoured the formation of more humic soils in the relatively depressed areas. As this occurred swamp gallery and valley forest came to occupy the valleys and the campos cerrados retreated. Where valley incision exposed either indurated laterite or the contact between sandstone and underlying shale, water seepage zones developed. As the cerrado trees succumbed to the wet conditions these zones became occupied by grassland. Where in the course of time mesophytic soils formed in the more mature valleys, deciduous seasonal forest developed.

Thus in the vicinity of the Serra do Roncador the present distributions of savanna woodlands and grasslands are related to the interplay of climatic and edaphic factors under the influences of dynamic geomorphological processes triggered by differential warping of an old planation surface.

In eastern Brazil both the vegetational distributions and the multiplicity of erosion cycles are most complex. In the arid northeast, caatinga covers the extensive level peneplains or pediplains that, cutting across Archaean granites, (Figure 5.16), are believed by King to have been fashioned in a post-Tertiary or Quaternary cycle to which he has given the name Paraguacu. He believes this cycle to be more advanced in eastern Brazil and particularly in Bahia than elsewhere. Within the caatinga relicts of campos cerrados occupy the last remnants of higher taboleiros belonging to Velhas and earlier cycles. Thus the tongue of campos cerrados near Vitoria da Conquista covers surfaces dated by King as belonging to the post-Gondwana and Sul-Americana cycles, whereas the surrounding caatinga covers the Velhas and Paraguacu surfaces. All these surfaces are cut across Archaean granites. Further north near Tucano 'islands' of campo cerrado occur in a 'sea' of caatinga. Here the campos cerrados cover small taboleiros that are built of Cretaceous sandstones and represent the last remnants of the Velhas surface which is being consumed in the Paraguacu cycle. Near the coast, however, where the climate is humid, the onslaught of the Paraguacu cycle is bringing about the extension of mata up the valleys of the rivers cutting back into the coastal taboleiros. The latter, built of Tertiary sandstones and characterized by infertile sandy soils and poor drainage, carry campos cerrados (Figure 5.17). Where the rivers have cut right back through the taboleiros their valleys are followed by ribbons of forest extending into the caatinga zone. Everywhere the slopes of the

Figure 5.16. Caatinga scrub on lower peneplaned surface near Acari, Sertao. *Pilocereus gounellii* in left foreground.

Figure 5.17. Contact between campos cerrados on ill-drained level taboleiro with sandy soils derived from Tertiary sandstone (foreground) and forest along river valley cutting into the plateau. Near Olinda, north of Recife, Bahia.

Figure 5.18. Pantanal along Rio Sao Francisco between Moema and Melo Viana, Minas Gerais. Campos sujos in foreground.

taboleiros and of the serras representing the remnants of earlier erosion surfaces are clothed either with high caatinga forest or with a dry type of mata. The distribution of the various types of vegetation in eastern Brazil, although more complex than in the centre of the country, is thus seen to be related to the geomorphological features in a most convincing way. Figure 5.19 is an attempt to show this relationship in diagrammatic form.

Evidence of a sequence from grassy savanna to mata and caatinga under conditions that are the reverse of those over the plateaux is found in the pantanal where river deposition is creating new land. There the newest and wettest areas carry pure grassland, which grades to grassland with scattered clumps of cerrado trees on the older flat lands where floods are less frequent, and is replaced either by mata or by caatinga, depending on the soil, where natural levees built well above flood level provide well-drained sites. In a similar way along the east coast the ill-drained river flats are occupied by grassland and sedge swamp, whereas mata occurs on the levees and caatinga species are found on the restingas. In the pantanal the rise from the low to the high pantanal suggests that continental uplift has occurred in the past and that the reduction in the extent and degree of inundation following such uplift has been responsible for vegetational change bringing about the gradual replacement of wet grassland and sedge swamp by campos cerrados. Such uplift would accord with King's views on pediplanation.

The role of geology

The absence of readily identifiable vegetation associations within the cerrado vegetation, as cited earlier, is related to the remarkably uniform edaphic conditions over vast areas. These are due, firstly to the extent and degree of preservation of old planation surfaces with relict lateritic soils, and secondly to the predominance of sandstone in the geological formations underlying the savanna areas. Compared with Africa and Australia where the destruction of the old planation surfaces with the concomitant removal of relict soils and exposure of underlying bedrock is more advanced, geology exerts a lesser influence over the distribution of plant communities in the savannas of Brazil and indeed of South America as a whole. However, as in Venezuela (Chapter 6) distinctive plant communities covered the iron ore bodies within the savanna woodlands of Minas Gerais while anomalous vegetation occupied the area of toxic ground over the porphyry copper deposit at Caraiba southeast of Joazeiro in the caatinga of northeast Brazil (Cole 1965).

The role of plant succession

Within the campos cerrados and the caatinga there are shallow depressions that carry a distinctive vegetation. In its upper reaches on the campos

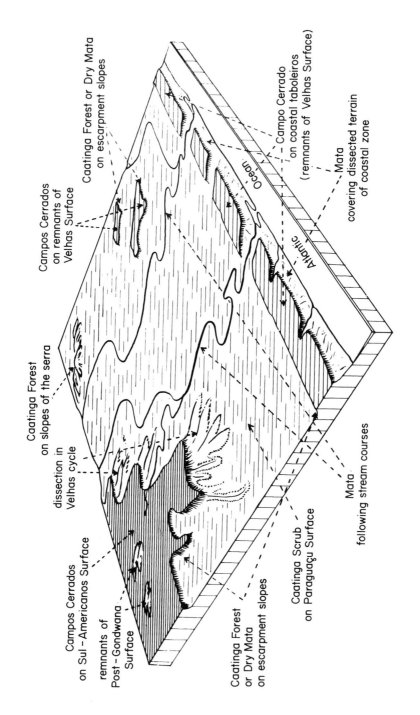

Campos Cerrados
on remnants of
Velhas Surface

Caatinga Forest or Dry Mata
on escarpment slopes

Campo Cerrado
on coastal taboleiros
(remnants of Velhas Surface)

Mata
covering dissected terrain
of coastal zone

Ocean

Atlantic

Caatinga Forest
on slopes of the serra
dissection in
Velhas cycle

Campos Cerrados
on Sul-Americanos Surface
remnants of
Post-Gondwana
Surface

Caatinga Forest
or Dry Mata
on escarpment slopes

Caatinga Scrub
on Paraguaçu Surface

Mata
following stream courses

Figure 5.19. Block diagram showing relationships between vegetation and geomorphology in Brazil.

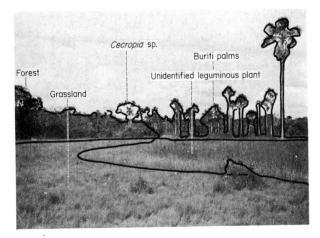

Figure 5.20. Hydrosere in depression in level chapada between Anapolis and Ceres, Goias. Unidentified legume and buriti palm, *Mauritia vinifera* occupy wettest central area and sedges and grasses the drier margin of the depression. Campos cerrados cover adjacent areas of plateau but give way to forest on slopes (background). *Cecropia* sp. forest pioneer, at edge of swamp.

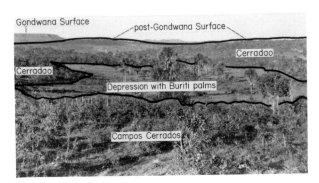

Figure 5.21. Stand of buriti palm, *Mauritia vinifera*, in a depression in the post Gondwana surface of the Chapada north of Presidente Olegario, Minas Gerais. Campos cerrados on level plateau (foreground and on horizon), cerradao on the sloping terrain.

Figure 5.22. Stand of carnauba palms, *Copernicia cerifera*, in a slight depression where the water table is near surface, in the Sertao between Serrinha and Caldas de Jorro, Bahia.

cerrados-covered chapada in Minas Gerais, the Sao Francisco river, for example, is bordered by a broad flat valley that carries a vegetation of grasses and sedges known locally as pantanal (Figure 5.19). Similar stretches of pantanal occupy flats within the campos cerrados-covered Cuiaba peneplain. The vegetation of these areas in undoubtedly seral, a contention that is supported by the succession found around open bodies of water on the Tocantins plateau between Annapolis and Ceres in the state of Goias, on the chapada near Presidente Olegario in Minas Gerais (Figures 5.20 and 5.21) and again on the high pantanal in the state of the Mato Grosso. Here an unidentified leguminous plant and the buriti palm (*Mauritia vinifera*) occupy the wettest areas, whereas the drier margins are covered with sedges and grasses. As the swamp dries out the buriti palms die off, as was evident near Ceres at the time of the author's studies. In the caatinga zone the shallow depressions occupied by stands of carnauba palm (*Copernicia cerifera*) are comparable (Figure 5.22). The vegetation of flats and depressions of this nature is clearly seral. Unless the macro-environmental conditions change it will in time be succeeded by the vegetation characteristic of the surrounding area.

CONCLUSIONS

The distributions of the savanna woodlands and grasslands, the caatinga and the mata or dry forest may thus be explained in terms of the ages of their respective floras, the geomorphological evolution of the landscape and the response of individual species to the interplay of climatic and edaphic factors, the latter controlled by geomorphology. The exact distribution at any given period of time is related to the stage in the cycle of erosion, with the campos cerrados representing an edaphic climax on the level plateaux and the mata a climatic climax on those lands that due to current dissection are well drained and have good soils. In a similar way, the caatinga scrub of the Sertao is an edaphic climax and the high caatinga forest a climatic climax. The pantanal is seral. The situation, however, is dynamic. The surface features are being continuously modified by erosion and deposition and the climate and soil conditions are subject to slight but progressive change. Successional and migrational changes are continually occurring in the vegetation with a general tendency for an extension of forest and caatinga at the expense of the campos cerrados/savanna woodlands and the savanna grasslands. At any time, however, man may upset the equilibrium and by the use of fire and the grazing of stock he may halt or reverse the progression. At any time, too, changes of climate or earth movements may upset the prevailing tendencies as they have undoubtedly done in the past, as can be deduced from pollen records from other parts of South America that indicate oscillations between cerrados and mata (van der Hammen 1963, 1972, 1974, 1983, van der Hammen and Gonzalez 1960, 1965, Wijmstra and van der Hammen 1966, Gonzalez *et al.* 1965). Periods of increased dissection, either associated with a moister climate or following continental uplift, will favour the extension of forest, whereas increased aridity will lead to the spread of the caatinga. Long periods of stability, resulting in the formation of vast planation surfaces mantled by excessively weathered soils of low nutrient status, will favour grassy savanna in the wetter areas and caatinga shrub in the more arid ones.

6 The savanna woodlands, savanna grasslands and low tree and shrub savannas of northern tropical America

North of the Amazon basin the savanna vegetation of Venezuela, Guyana, Surinam and the adjacent parts of Brazil displays broad similarities to but also significant contrasts with that over the Brazilian plateau.

The grassy savannas have a broadly similar physiognomy to those of central Brazil but most take the form of treeless grasslands or very open campos cerrados/savanna woodlands; there is virtually no development of cerradao

Figure 6.1. Very open savanna woodlands/campos cerrados with small *Curatella americana* and *Byrsonima crassifolia* trees and *Trachypogon* and *Axonopus* spp. grasses on sandy soils on Tertiary planation surface between Anaco and Sao Tome. Abrupt transition to savanna grassland in background.

Figure 6.2. *Mauritia minor* palm savanna on level terrain between dry woodland (background) and the esteros of the Lower Llanos. Between Paraguacu and Santa Marie de Epire.

and the campos cerrados usually gives way abruptly to open grass-lands without an intervening zone of low trees and shrubs comparable with the campos sujos of Brazil (Figure 6.1). The grass layer is usually dominated by *Trachypogon montufari*, associated with *Axonopus* spp. and other *Trachypogon* spp.; the most common trees are *Curatella americana* and *Byrsonima crassifolia*, but *Bowdichia virgiloides* is prominent in some areas and *Byrsonima coccolobifolia* and *Roupala acuminata* may also be present. These tree species occur also in the Brazilian savannas where, however, more species are present. On the other hand there are many grass and herb species in the Venezuela savannas. In some areas species with forest or tall woodland affinities are present, while in the Llanos of Venezuela a distinctive palm savanna characterized by *Mauritia minor* occurs at the periphery of the grasslands of the seasonally inundated 'esteros' and in some instances between them and areas supporting a dry type of woodland (Figure 6.2).

The dry types of vegetation contrast with those of Brazil. They comprise fairly tall dry forest physiognomically similar to the Caatinga forest and also low forms of savanna woodland or low tree and shrub savanna. The former is comprised mainly of *Caesalpinia granadillio*, *C. corialia*, *Acacia* spp. (notably *A. farnesiana*), *Capparis* spp. (notably *C. odorotissima*) trees and *Pereskia guamacho*, taxonomically the earliest cactus. *Ceiba pentandra*, *Tabebuia chrysantha*, a *Copaifera* sp., and *Pterocarpus vernalis* may be present and species of humid forest affinity occasionally occur. The lower forms are characterized by *Prosopis juliflora* (the mesquite), *Croton* spp., as well as *Pereskia guamacho, Leimaiicereus sessius, Opuntia* spp. and *Jatropha* spp. Grasses are poorly represented.

The dry types of savanna vegetation in Venezuela resemble the dry savanna woodlands and some of the savanna parklands in Africa (see Chapter 9) rather than the low tree and shrub savannas of either Africa or Australia. *Pterocarpus* species occur in the dry forests of both Venezuela and Africa and palm savannas occur on sites with comparable soils. The large *Cereus* and *Pilocereus* spp. *Cactaceae* that are characteristic of the Brazilian Sertao are absent from the low tree or shrub savannas in Venezuela.

The contrasts between the savanna vegetation of Brazil and that north of the Amazon basin result from differing environmental conditions that stem from differing geological and geomorphological evolution.

THE DISTRIBUTION OF THE GRASSY SAVANNAS

Savanna grasslands cover some $150\,000\ km^2$ in the lower Llanos of the Orinoco basin where Quaternary materials mantle Tertiary and older sediments (Figures 6.3 and 6.4). These valley grasslands in some ways resemble those covering the plains south of the Gulf of Carpentaria in Australia, which are likewise underlain by Tertiary and Quaternary materials.

Northwards, in the slightly more elevated upper Llanos, the savanna grasslands give way to campos cerrados/savanna woodlands where ground water laterite outcrops or is near surface, and over laterite-capped mesas and plateaux of Tertiary sediments that represent relics of the formerly more extensive end-Tertiary planation surface (McConnell 1968) (Figure 6.5). These plateau relics are widespread near Jusepin, between El Tigre and Pariaguan and north of Calabozo. They compare with the laterite capped Mesozoic residuals on the plains of northern Australia (Chapter 16).

In the lower Llanos the distribution of the savanna grasslands is broken by tropical forest galleries along the rivers and by patches of tropical forests, locally called 'morichals', on humic gley soils in slight declivities where the surface is very gently undulating. The distribution of the campos cerrados/savanna woodlands virtually coincides with the end-Tertiary planation surface. Where this is being consumed by erosion the campos cerrados give way abruptly to dry savanna woodland over the dissected peripheral slopes and to dry types of savanna parkland or low tree and shrub savanna over the level terrain of the lower surface below, fashioned in a later erosion cycle. The changes are clearly displayed between Jusepin and La Ceiba and between El Tigre and El Sombrero (Figure 6.10).

South of the Llanos numerous small patches of savanna grassland and campos cerrados/savanna woodlands occur within the tropical forests along

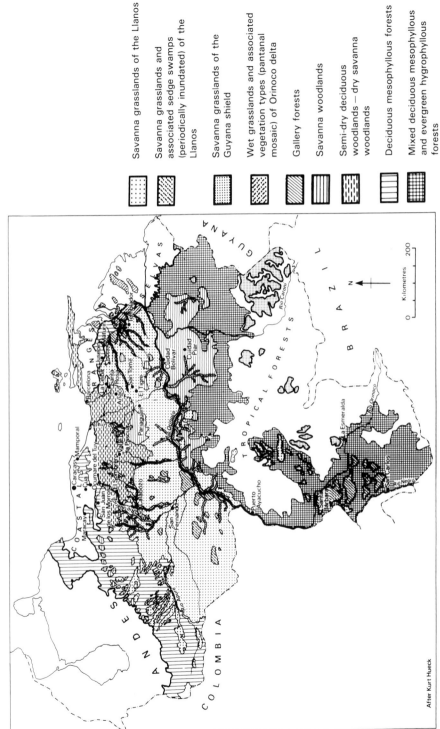

Savanna grasslands of the Llanos

Savanna grasslands and associated sedge swamps (periodically inundated) of the Llanos

Savanna grasslands of the Guyana shield

Wet grasslands and associated vegetation types (pantanal mosaic) of Orinoco delta

Gallery forests

Savanna woodlands

Semi-dry deciduous woodlands – dry savanna woodlands

Deciduous mesophyllous forests

Mixed deciduous mesophyllous and evergreen hygrophyllous forests

Figure 6.3. Distribution of main types of vegetation in Venezuela.

After Kurt Hueck

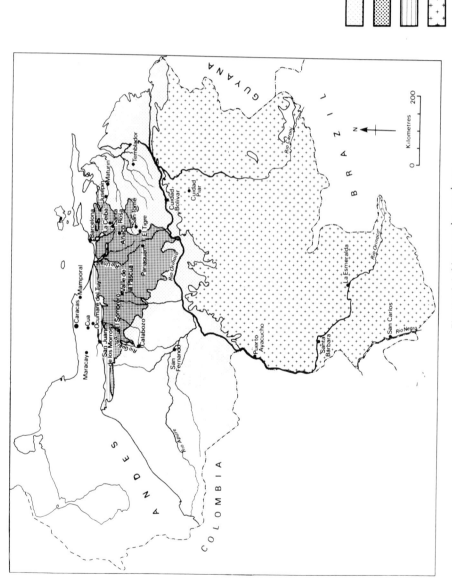

Figure 6.4. Venezuela, geology.

Quaternary

Tertiary

Cretaceous

Pre–Cambrian

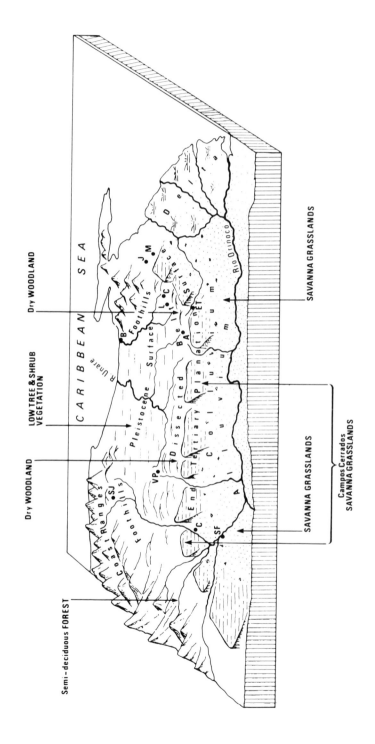

Figure 6.5. Relationships between vegetation, soils and geomorphology in northern Venezuela. A Anaco, B Barcelona, C Calabozo, ET El Tigre, J Jusepin, L La Ceiba, M Maturin, SF San Fernando, SJ San Juan de los Morros, VP Valle de Pascua.

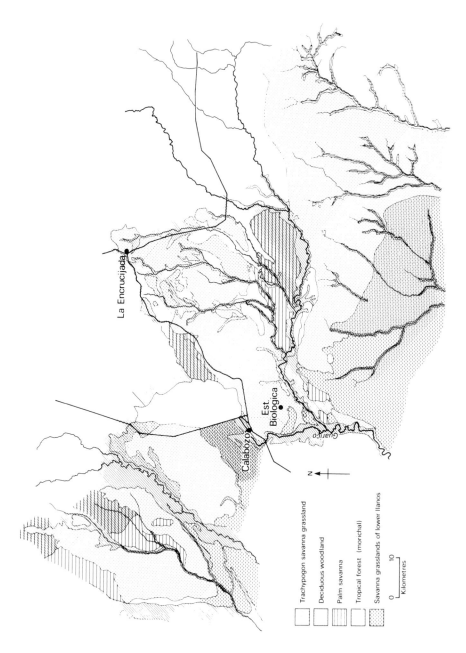

Figure 6.6. Distribution of vegetation types in the Llanos of Venezuela.

the upper Orinoco and Rio Negro valleys, while larger areas occur, again within the tropical forest belt, in the southern part of the Guyana Precambrian Shield. Here savannas occupy plateau surfaces within the Pakaraima mountains, including those related to flat-lying Roraima sandstones and dolerite sills and those related to the 700–800 m planation surface. These savannas transgress the Venezuela–Guyana border. At a lower level — between 100 and 150 m — the Rio Branco–Rupununi savannas extend across the Brazil–Guyana border. The savannas of the Guyana Shield, unlike those of the Orinoco valley, cover watershed areas.

Overall there are fundamental differences between the savannas of central Brazil and those north of the Amazon. Whereas those of central Brazil are mainly campos cerrados/savanna woodlands occupying a plateau area, those north of the Amazon are predominantly savanna grasslands occupying a major drainage basin. Whereas the grassy savannas of Central Brazil occupy old planation surfaces, with the exception of the campos cerrados/savanna woodlands on the relicts of planation surfaces in the Llanos and on the Guyana Shield, the grassy savannas of Venezuela occupy depositional surfaces.

The island distribution of campos cerrados/savanna woodlands and associated grasslands on residual relicts of planation surfaces north of the Amazon suggests that they are outliers of a formerly continuous distribution centred on the planation surfaces on the Brazilian plateau, whereas the savanna grasslands of the Llanos developed later following deposition in the Orinoco basin.

RELATIONSHIPS BETWEEN THE DISTRIBUTIONS OF THE GRASSY SAVANNAS AND THE PHYSICAL ENVIRONMENT

The influence of climatic factors

As elsewhere, the savannas of northern tropical America occur where the climate is characterized by consistently high temperatures and a marked dry period. The length and severity of the dry season varies between the individual savanna areas, but everywhere only plant species that can tap ground water or can evade the moisture stress by deciduosity or dormancy can survive the dry period.

In the Orinoco basin the distribution of the savanna grasslands and associated campos cerrados/savanna woodlands virtually coincides with the area receiving 1300–1400 mm of rainfall concentrated in the April–November period and experiencing mean monthly temperatures that vary between 23.2°C and 15.9°C at Calaboza and between 26.6°C and 29.2°C at San Fernando de Apure. North and east of Calabozo the grassy savannas give way abruptly to dry types of savanna woodland and parkland where the rainfall averages only 800–1000 mm concentrated in five to six months of the year, resulting in an intervening period of severe moisture stress. Northwest and south of San Fernando de Apure where the annual rainfall is heavier — between 1400 and 2000 mm with a wet season lasting eight to nine months — the vegetation changes to deciduous or semi-deciduous forest with some islands of grassy savanna.

In the Rio Branco–Rupununi savannas temperatures are similar to those in the Orinoco basin; the average annual rainfall is higher — 1621 mm at St Ignatius — but 83% falls in the April–August period so that the dry period is longer. The rainy season is longer in the forest areas to the south, where Manaos receives 1850 mm over eight months, and also to the north and east where the Guyana coastlands experience a second rainy period in December and January. The Rio Branco–Rupununi savannas are surrounded by forest and the relationship of the boundary to the length of the dry period is not clear.

The rainfall regime in the outlying savanna areas along the upper Orinoco is uncertain. Puerto Ayacucho receives an average of 2041 mm and experiences four dry months but San Carlos on the Rio Negro has an average fall of 3521 mm fairly evenly distributed throughout the year. The patches of savanna begin well to the north of San Carlos and their distribution may be partly related to the incidence of a dry period causing conditions of moisture stress for forest trees; but their 'island' distribution within forested areas experiencing the same rainfall regime suggests that other factors may be more important.

Throughout northern tropical America the complex and often inter-digitating distributions of the various forms of grassy savannas, dry woodlands, parklands and low tree and shrub communities and tropical forests indicate that factors other than climatic ones are influencing the vegetation.

The influence of relief, soils, geomorphology and geology

The savanna grasslands and the campos cerrados/savanna woodlands characteristically occupy level surfaces and give way either to dry woodland or to semi-deciduous tropical forest over dissected terrain. The very extensive savanna grasslands, associated savanna woodlands and patches of tropical forest occupying the infilled Orinoco Basin, however, must be distinguished from the smaller savanna woodlands and associated savanna grasslands occupying the end-Tertiary and earlier planation surfaces within the Guyana Shield. The relationships between the vegetation and the interrelated influences of climate, relief, soils, geomorphology and geology will be examined by reference to specific areas in each.

THE SAVANNAS OF THE ORINOCO BASIN

In the Orinoco basin there is a simple two-fold division between the campos cerrados/savanna woodlands and associated savanna types of the Upper Llanos and the savanna grasslands and associated vegetation types of the Lower Llanos but within each the actual distribution of the several types of vegetation is quite complex (Figures 6.3 and 6.6).

The Calabozo-San Fernando de Apure area

In the western Llanos the Biological Station of Los Llanos southeast of Calabozo has provided opportunities for the study of the savanna vegetation. The station is located near the western limit of the relatively dry savanna grasslands and associated campos cerrados/savanna woodlands of the Upper Llanos. San Fernando de Apure lies in the centre of the wet, periodically inundated swamp grasslands of the Lower Llanos. In both areas the grasslands are interrupted by small patches of tropical forest and dry woodland.

Some 50 miles north of Calabozo small islands of campos cerrados/savanna woodlands with *Curatella americana* and *Bowdichia virgiloides* trees occupying lateritic soils on relicts of the end-Tertiary planation surface occur within dry savanna woodlands. Larger areas of campos cerrados occur near Calabozo where indurated laterite outcrops in level to gently undulating terrain (Figure 6.8). This laterite, known locally as arrecife, has been regarded as a ground water laterite formed where the pebbly material of an ancient river terrace of Pliocene or early Pleistocene age has been cemented by iron-rich waters. In places the laterite outcrops but elsewhere it is at a variable depth below the surface, being covered by reddish yellow sandy loam on the higher ground in the northern part of the Biological Station and by yellow finer sandy loam on the lower ground in the south. The laterite is underlain by mottled clay. Sarmiento and Monasterio (1969), however, have suggested that the laterite is an ancient cuirass that was folded when the old fluvial terrace was uplifted and is now exposed where erosion has bared the upfolds.

The composition of the grasslands at Calabozo varies in response to soil differences, that in turn are related to geomorphology (Sarmiento and Monasterio 1969). Where the laterite is exposed the savanna is open and woody elements are infrequent. Some species, notably *Bulbostylis conifera*, *Polycarpaea corymbosa* and *Tephrosia tenella*, that are rare on deeper soils, are common, while others of wider ecological range are more abundant. The species cited belong to genera that are common on similar sites in Africa and Australia. On the yellow sandy loam soils in the south *Trachypogon vestitus* is a dominant grass whereas it is absent from the coarser reddish yellow sandy loams in the north. In both areas *Eragrostis maypurensis* occurs

Figure 6.7. Section exposing indurated laterite on the Tertiary planation surface at its contact with the Pleistocene surface below (background) between Jusepin and La Ceiba. A bed of Quaternary pebbles overlies the laterite.

Figure 6.8. Open campos cerrados with scattered *Curatella americana* and *Bowdichia virgiloides* trees in a grassland of *Trachypogon* and *Aristida* spp. over relict plateau of Tertiary planation surface with outcropping ground water laterite called arrecife north of Calabozo.

Figure 6.9. Savanna grassland with scattered *Bowdichia virgiloides* trees on the Pliocene planation surface between El Tigre and Pariaguan. Sandy clay over laterite exposed in pit opened for road metal.

where there is less than 30 cm of soil above the laterite layer whereas a great variety of grasses, and notably *Hyptis* spp., occur on the deeper soils. Stands of trees that include *Cassia moschata* and *Pterocarpus vernalis* that belong to the neighbouring forests occur only on the deeper soils where the grasses *Paspalum plicatum* and *Aristida capillacea* replace the dominant grasses of the savanna grasslands and campos cerrados/savanna woodlands.

Studies of the rooting habits of the trees of the campos cerrados/savanna woodlands have shown that *Curatella americana, Byrsonima crassifolia* and *Bowdichia virgilioides* develop extensive surface root systems because their thicker roots are unable to penetrate the lateritic conglomerate, arrecife. In some cases the roots of a tree of 6 m in height may be over 15 m long. Inability to penetrate the laterite layer is doubtless a restricting factor for other tree species that are found only on the deeper soils.

On the Lower Llanos differences of soils, micro-relief and degree of inundation are responsible for differences in the nature and composition of the vegetation. A palm savanna characterized by *Mauritia minor* borders the swamp grasslands of the esteros in the same way as that dominated by the *Pandanus* palm borders the swamp grasslands of the Marrakai Plains in northern Australia. Galleries of tropical forest follow the better drained soils of the levees bordering the major rivers and stands of *Copernicia tectorum* occupy heavy clay soils in areas that are flooded annually.

The Jusepin-la Ceiba–Sao Tome–Temblador area

Similar relationships between the vegetation, the soils and geomorphology are evident in the eastern section of the Llanos.

East of a line running from Jusepin to la Ceiba and thence to Santa Rosa and Pariaguan open campos cerrados/savanna woodlands with *Curatella americana* trees characterize the infertile sandy soils of the flat topped mesas and level plateaux that represent remnants of the old Pliocene planation surface (Figure 6.9). Near Pariaguan *Byrsonima crassifolia, B. coccolobifolia, Bowdichia virgilioides* and *Roupala acuminata* trees are also present. Dry forests cover the dissected country bordering the mesas and plateaux on their northwestern margins but give way to dry woodland on the level Pleistocene planation surface which has cut into the Pliocene surface from the north and west (Figure 6.10). Within this area palm savannas occupy the clay soils of the lower areas (Figure 6.2).

Most of the area to the east of a line from Maturin to Cuidad Bolivar is covered by savanna grasslands whose nature and composition, as near Calabozo, are related to soils, micro-relief and geomorphology. On the Lower Llanos grasslands of *Trachypogon montufari* associated with *Axonopus canescens, Andropogon bicornis*, other grass species and a variety of legumes

Figure 6.10. Dissected edge of Pliocene planation surface exposing the kaolinitic zone of the laterite profile. Change from open campos cerrados savanna woodlands and grasslands on the Tertiary surface to dry deciduous woodland on the dissected Pleistocene surface between El Tigre and Valle de Pascua.

Figure 6.11. Savanna grasslands with scattered *Curatella americana* trees over the level 300 m planation surface below Cerro Bolivar (right) whose slopes carry tropical forests.

Figure 6.12. Campos cerrados savanna woodland over the 300 m planation surface near Cerro Altimira. Indurated laterite outcrops at its edge.

occupy the acidic grey sandy soils of the better drained areas but give way to swamp savannas dominated by the sedge *Rhyncosphora globosa* in the northern areas. Declivities where humic gley soils have formed carry patches of tropical forest which appear to be extending.

The Upper Orinoco-Rio Negro area

Studies of the La Esmeralda and Santa Barbara savannas in southern Venezuela have revealed broadly similar relationships between vegetation, soils and geomorphology to those on the Llanos, but the occurrence of savanna grasslands and of semi-deciduous forest on adjacent free draining sites suggest that climatic changes since the Pleistocene may have had a controlling influence (Eden 1974).

Santa Barbara and La Esmeralda receive a similar average annual rainfall of 2700–2900 mm and experience brief dry periods in November and January–February (Tate and Hitchcock 1930), these being slightly longer at Santa Barbara. In both localities the savannas occupy a lowland plain of similar elevation, 110 m at Santa Barbara and 120 m at La Esmeralda. At La Esmeralda a few low hills and ridges of outcropping or sub-outcropping schist and quartzite rise above the lowland plain. The hills are flanked by spreads of colluvium producing gentle slopes that decline into broad alluvial depressions and flats. The free-draining upper slopes carry sandy latosolic soils whereas the lower, poorly drained areas are characterized by ground water laterites and humic gley soils. At Santa Barbara the lowland plain is underlain by granite which frequently outcrops on the upper slopes and local summit areas. Gentle colluvial slopes decline from these areas into ill-drained depressions. Indurated laterite is exposed on the summit and upper slope areas where derived lateritic gravel also occurs. Most soils, however, are developed from highly weathered granitic regolith and, as at La Esmeralda, grade from free-draining latosols on the upper slopes to ground water laterites and humic gleys in the bottomlands. The latosols, however, are of heavier texture than those at La Esmeralda, consisting mainly of sandy loams to sandy clays with iron concretions in their profiles. In both areas all the soils are acid and infertile with a low cation exchange capacity and low base saturation.

Both at La Esmeralda and Santa Barbara the ill-drained areas support a herbaceous savanna of grasses and sedges, dominated by *Paspalum* spp. and *Rhynchospora* sp. and associated with *Andropogon virgatus*, *Leptocoryphium lanatum* and *Sileria hirtella* at La Esmeralda and with *Mesosetum* spp. at Santa Barbara. In both areas stands of *Mauritia* sp. palms occur in perennially wet swamps while at Santa Barbara small woody shrubs of *Byrsonima verbascifolia* may occur on the lower slopes.

An open, low savanna woodland comprising *Byrsonima crassifolia* trees, accompanied at Santa Barbara by *Platycarpum orinocense* and *Curatella americana* trees and a grass stratum dominated by *Trachypogon montufari* is characteristic of the freely draining sites at both La Esmeralda and Santa Barbara. At the first mentioned, however, except on quartzite ridges where *Byrsonima crassifolia* is joined by other tree species, notably *Trattinickia burserifolia* and *Anaxagorea brevipes*, the trees rarely exceed 2 m in height whereas at Santa Barbara *Byrsonima crassifolia* usually exceeds 4 m and *Platycarpum orinocense*, which favours laterite and granite outcrops, may reach 8–10 m. *Leptocoryphium lanatum*, *Paspalum carinatum* and *Bulbostylis conifers* occur in the herbaceous layer in both areas, together with *Mesosetum* spp. and *Axonopus aureus* at Santa Barbara and *Panicum caricoides* at La Esmeralda, being more frequent on recently burnt sites.

Semi-deciduous to evergreen forests form galleries along the drainage lines at Santa Barbara and occur also, adjacent to open savanna woodland, on freely drained sites with latosols. At La Esmeralda they occupy humic gley soils.

The occurrence of the semi-deciduous to evergreen forests on both wet and dry sites, on humic gley and on latosolic soils question the influence of soil on its distribution. The sharpness of the boundary between savanna and forest and the sparseness of the people, both now and in prehistoric times, discount the possibility of fire having created the savanna by the destruction of forest although it may assist in their maintenance against the invasion of forest trees. The disjunct distribution of the islands of savanna at La Esmeralda and Santa Barbara within the major zone of tropical forest and their floristic affinities with the savannas of Guyana, Surinam and Brazil suggest that these islands represent relict communities from an earlier drier environment that have been fire maintained against invasion by forest (Eden 1974). While the evidence indicates an ancient origin for the savannas their present distributions appear to be directly influenced by soil and drainage conditions that, in turn, are related to the geomorphological evolution of the landscape and to the interplay of geological events and climatic changes.

THE SAVANNAS OF THE GUYANA SHIELD

Numerous areas of savanna interrupt the tropical forests of the Guyana Shield. Here attention will be focused on two areas where detailed studies have been made, namely the Cerro Bolivar area and the Rupununi area.

The Cuidad Bolivar–Cerro Bolivar area

Southwest of the Orinoco delta the country is characterized by three distinct planation surfaces that each carry savanna vegetation. These are separated by scarp slopes and cut into by drainage lines carrying forest vegetation. In the Cerro Bolivar area remarkable changes of vegetation occuring over iron orebodies emphasize the influence of bedrock geology and of the related edaphic conditions.

South of Puerto Ordaz campos cerrados/savanna woodlands and grasslands with *Curatella americana* and *Byrsonima* spp. trees cover the poorly drained sandy soils derived from Quaternary sediments deposited on the end-Tertiary planation surface. Southwards forests surround tors and whalebacks of outcropping Precambrian granite and clothe the slopes of the cerros, but campos cerrados/savanna woodlands cover the level terrain (Figure 6.11). Near Cuidad Piar savanna grasslands cover the planation surface forming the watershed between drainage to the Rios Caroni and Aro. This has an elevation of 200–350 m and has been dated as mid- to late Tertiary. Where outcropping indurated laterite or canga produces a more freely draining surface, 300 m high, campos cerrados/savanna woodland with *Curatella americana*, *Byrsonima crassifolia* and *B. coccolobifolia* is found (Figure 6.12). Where erosion has removed the laterite and is currently dissecting the old surface savanna grasslands cover the interfluves and galleries of tropical forest follow the rivers.

In the area around Cuidad Piar Precambrian banded ironstones, disposed in a series of anticlinoria and synclinoria, produce a number of ridges characterized by steep sides and accordant summit levels. In favourable synclinal structures leaching has removed the silica and concentrated the iron in the banded ironstones to produce iron orebodies grading over 60% iron at Cerro Bolivar, Cerro Altimira and San Isidro. These occur over the tops and slopes of the hills. Savanna grasslands and campos cerrados/savanna woodlands cover the summit bevels that represent the remains of the 700–800 m planation surface dated as late Cretaceous. Tropical forests clothe the sides of the ranges where dark reddish brown loams have weathered from banded ironstone and gneissic bedrock. The vegetation, however, changes abruptly and dramatically to a dry scrub characterized by small *Clusia* affin. *renggerioides* and *C. schomburgkiana* trees, *Myrcia* affin. *acuminata* and *M. parvifolia* shrubs, cacti and bromeliads over the iron orebodies. The change is caused by edaphic aridity related to weathering processes over the orebodies. Leaching and hydration produce a surface iron rich crust with loose fines of pure haematite below. As the fines settle, the crust collapses to form a cavernous surface whose extreme aridity can sustain only drought resistant plants. On the flanks below some of the orebodies, notably those at Cerro Altimira and San Isidro, rubble eroded from the orebodies has been deposited and recemented as canga to form level to gently sloping terrace-like features. These are covered by campos cerrados/savanna woodland with *Curatella americana* and *Byrsonima* spp. trees.

The Rio Branco-Rupunini savannas

The Rio Branco–Rupununi savannas within the Guyana Precambrian Shield cover level terrain that has a similar altitude — between 90 and 150 m — and is believed to form part of the same planation surface as that covered by campos cerrados/savanna woodlands and savanna grasslands of the Orinoco Basin.

Numerous studies have been made of the northern Rupununi savanna (Bleackley 1962, Eden 1964, 1970, Goodland 1964, 1966a). This covers the lowland area between the Kanuku mountains which rise steeply to some 1000 m to the south and the Pacaraima mountains rising abruptly to over 300 m in the north. Whereas the mountains are built of Precambrian igneous and metamorphic rocks the lowland comprises a southern belt of gently sloping gravel ridges and outwash slopes dissected by the headstreams of the Rio Branco and a northern shallow trough infilled by recent alluvium; the latter extends to the Ireng river and to the foot of the Pacaraima mountains. The lowland is considered to form part of a planation surface named the Rupununi surface and provisionally dated as end-Tertiary (McConnell 1962) by reference to the comparable Pliocene surface in the Orinoco basin. The belt of gravel ridges and outwash slopes, with an elevation of 110–140 m compares with the Upper Llanos and the alluvial trough at 90–100 m with the Lower Llanos.

The northern part of the lowland trough forms a low and ill-defined watershed between drainage to the Amazon via the Rio Branco and to the Essequibo via the Rupununi river. Formerly the whole area drained eastwards by the proto Berbice whose headwaters, however, were captured by those of the Rio Branco at the close of Tertiary times (McConnell 1959, 1968). Today the headstreams of the Rio Branco are incised into the Rupununi planation surface — at St Igantius the Takutu river bed is 30–40 cm below the level of the floodplain (Eden 1970) — but at the height of the rains they cannot carry the high surface run-off, back up, overflow their banks and flood large areas of the lowland trough.

The soils, like those of the Llanos, are derived from colluvial and alluvial materials deposited over the planed surface, vary with the micro-relief and drainage conditions and are everywhere highly leached, acid and deficient in plant nutrients. On the more elevated free-draining areas yellowish red latosolic soils occur over areas of ironstone gravels that represent the degraded and redistributed residue of a formerly extensive layer of laterite, outcrops of which occur in places. Downslope heavier brown sandy loams have developed over sheetwash colluvium. Depressions within the area of ironstone gravels and associated deposits are characterized by ground water laterite. In the lowland trough that is subject to flooding or waterlogging each rainy season, extensive areas of ground water laterite and low-humic gley soils occur.

The relationships between the vegetation, soils and geomorphology are similar to those in the Llanos. Thus campos cerrados/savanna woodlands cover the more elevated freely draining areas, grade into campos sujos low tree and shrub savanna downslope and give way to savanna grassland in the seasonally flooded or waterlogged areas. The campos cerrados/savanna woodlands are characterized by *Curatella americana, Byrsonima* spp., and *Bowdichia virgiliodes* trees, sometimes accompanied by *Randia* and *Roupala* spp. The herbaceous vegetation is characterized by *Trachypogon plumosus, Andropogon, Aristida, Mesosetum* and *Paspalum* spp. Both types of savanna are floristically similar to those of the Llanos.

Field observations have led Eden (1964, 1970) to conclude that the distribution of both savanna types in the Rupununi area are influenced primarily by soil and soil moisture conditions. Only herbaceous savanna is found where the land is flooded or waterlogged for one to three months each year and the ground water levels fall to 3–5 m during the dry season. The campos cerrados tree species that extend their roots deep to tap ground water in the dry season cannot withstand the waterlogging and malaeration in the hydromorphic zones in the rainy season. Trees disappear where gleyed soil horizons occur within 25–50 cm of the surface. At the same time, *Trachypogon plumosus*, the characteristic grass of the campos cerrados/savanna woodlands gives way to the sedges *Rhynchospora barbata* and *Fimbristylis ferruginea*. Within the more elevated areas Eden found that the gradation from campos cerrados to campos sujos coincided with a change from soils derived from ironstone gravels to those derived from colluvium and was partly associated with soil compaction, possibly associated with burning.

THE INFLUENCE OF FIRE ON THE DISTRIBUTION OF THE GRASSY SAVANNAS

All the grassy savannas in northern tropical America are burnt at varying intervals during the dry period. In each the campos cerrados/savanna woodland tree species exhibit the same fire resistant characteristics as in Brazil. Controlled burning experiments on the Estacion Biologica de los Llanos, Calabozo, suggest that fire may be responsible for some changes in both the herbaceous and woody layers of savanna vegetation, may keep the savanna open and discourage invasion by forest species (Eden 1967, Sarmiento and Monasterio 1975) but field observations both in the Llanos and in the other savanna areas indicate that the various forms of savanna vegetation have not been derived from forest as a result of burning (Eden 1964, 1970, 1974).

In the savanna grasslands with clumps of trees on the Alto Llano at Calabozo, following four fire-free years there was little change in either the density or the composition of the grass cover but organic debris had accumulated. After this period burning, intensified by the dry organic matter, halved the cover, modified the proportions of individual grasses species and led to an increase in pioneering sedges. In the tree clumps *Curatella americana*, *Byrsonima crassifolia* and *Bowdichia virgiliodes*, the only tree species present before fire was controlled, still formed 91% of those present after four fire-free years but they were accompanied by nine other species, notably *Randia aculeata*, which, however, were killed in the subsequent burning.

The overall evidence from field studies and from fire control experiments indicates that fire is a component of the ecosystem that maintains the campos cerrados/savanna woodlands and the savanna grasslands in their present form. The tree and shrub species are well adapted to resist or endure its effects but likewise they are adapted to withstand and exploit the edaphic conditions. The distributions of the savannas suggest that they have not been derived from forest as a result of fire. The savanna/forest boundary as in Brazil (Cole 1960a) is abrupt. This is particularly notable in the Upper Orinoco valley where there is no evidence of irregular penetration of savanna into the forests such as would be anticipated if the latter had yielded to savanna following burning. Here the cultural practices of the very small numbers of forest dwelling Indian people are unlikely to have affected the vegetation; moreover, where they have burnt the forest to clear land for cultivation it has quickly reverted to forest after abandonment.

THE DISTRIBUTION OF THE DRY WOODLANDS, PARKLANDS AND LOW TREE AND SHRUB SAVANNAS

The dry woodlands, parklands and low tree and shrub savannas occupy the Unare basin, a broadly triangular belt of country lying between the southern foothills of the Venezuelan coastal ranges and the Llanos. This area has an average rainfall of 800–1000 mm and a dry season of five to six months. It is therefore much drier than the Llanos. For the most part it is underlain by Tertiary sediments and lacks the overlying mantle of Quaternary materials that are a feature of the area of savanna grasslands. It comprises a level to gently undulating plain drained by the Unare and Manzanares rivers that flow northwards to the Caribbean. The plain represents a Pleistocene erosion surface. In the south it is bounded by dissected country where by headward erosion the headstreams of the Unare and Manzanares rivers are cutting into the end-Tertiary planation surface. The dissected country represents the step between the two planation surfaces.

Geological evidence indicates that the Orinoco river formerly flowed northwards between the gap in the coastal range to the Gulf of Venezuela. Subsequently crustal warping tilted the land southwards and diverted the Orinoco to its present course entrenching the granite of the pre-Cambrian Shield in places. This tilting, however, initiated the new cycle of erosion that has fashioned the Pleistocene surface of the Unare plain and is actively eroding the end-Tertiary surface.

The soils of the Unare plain and of the dissected terrain at its periphery contrast with those of the Llanos. They are mostly grey and brown soils of heavy texture with a higher nutrient status than those of the areas covered by campos cerrados/savanna woodlands or savanna grasslands. On the level terrain their alternations between moisture retention after rains and deep cracking and desiccation during the dry period inhibit root development, making them less favourable for trees than the freely draining soils of the dissected terrain which favour deep rooting species.

The distribution of the dry woodlands, parklands and low tree and shrub vegetation appears overall to be related to the low rainfall and long dry season of the area they occupy. Their extension along valleys into the foothills of the coastal ranges substantiates this view. Equally, however, their distribution is related to soils and drainage conditions that are more favourable to trees and shrubs than those of the Llanos and other areas occupied by grassy savannas. In turn these more favourable conditions are related to the geomorphology for the combinations coincide with the Pleistocene planation surface and the peripheral belt of dissected country that separates it from the end-Tertiary planation surface. The significance of this is emphasized by the fact that this surface is not extensively developed in other parts of northern tropical America nor are dry woodlands, parklands and low tree and shrub savanna vegetation.

Despite the dry nature of the vegetation in the dry season, fire is not a factor in the ecosystem largely because there is not an accumulation of dry grass to act as fuel. The dry types of savanna vegetation in Venezuela are clearly related to physical environmental factors and the question arises as to the possibility of their having been derived from more mesic tropical forest.

CONCLUSION—VEGETATION, ENVIRONMENT AND DYNAMIC CHANGE

Throughout northern tropical America the distributions of the various forms of savanna reflect the interplay of many environmental factors in space and time. Everywhere the distributions of the campos cerrados/savanna wood-lands and the savanna grasslands are directly related to adverse soils and soil moisture conditions that are associated with planation surfaces, in part covered by recent colluvium and alluvium. The distributions of the dry woodlands, parklands and low tree and shrub vegetation are related partly to the low rainfall and prolonged dry season in the Unare basin of Venezuela but also to the more favourable soils and drainage conditions that characterize the area.

In northern tropical America dry types of savannas are confined to the Unare basin, where only on the Pleistocene surface and the dissected country at its periphery does the favourable combination of climatic and edaphic conditions exist, these in turn being related to the geomorphology. Here the consistent change from campos cerrados/savanna woodlands to dry woodlands along the dissected slopes separating the end-Tertiary and Pleistocene surfaces is particularly significant.

Fire is acknowledged as a factor in the ecosystem of the campos cerrados/savanna woodlands and the savanna grasslands to the extent that it modifies their composition and keeps them open. It does not derive savanna from forest and does not influence the dry types of savanna vegetation.

The sharply defined savanna grasslands within the tropical forests of the upper Orinoco valley may be a legacy from periods in the Pleistocene when the climate was drier than today. Palynological evidence indicates that such climatic changes have occurred in northern tropical America (van der Hammen 1972, 1974, Wijmstra and van der Hammen 1966).

Present distributions of the various forms of savanna vegetation in northern tropical America reflect a stage in a changing pattern. The present distribution of each form of vegetation is directly related to climatic and edaphic conditions. These are dependent on and change with geological events and the geomorphological evolution of the landscape. Today the savanna grasslands and the campos cerrados/savanna woodlands occupy the relicts of the end-Tertiary planation surface, but they are yielding on the one hand to the dry types of woodland, parkland and low tree and shrub vegetation as the Pleistocene erosion cycle progresses in the Unare basin, and on the other to tropical forests where dissection leads to improved soil and drainage conditions. The complexity of the relationships and the fineness of the balance is emphasized by the occurrence of the dry scrub vegetation over the iron orebodies at Cerro Bilivar where a combination of geology and weathering processes create extremely arid edaphic conditions in an area of humid climate.

7   The savannas of Africa

The savannas of Africa differ from those of South America in several ways, notably in the form and varied composition of the savanna woodlands, the restricted development of savanna grasslands, the great extents of low tree and shrub savannas and savanna parklands, and the complex distributional patterns of each category of savanna and of the vegetation associations and plant communities within them.

Savanna woodlands composed of relatively tall trees — between 15 and 20 m high — with a clearly defined stratum of tall perennial grasses occupy the plateaux that, bordering the Congo basin on three sides, are virtually coincident with the Tertiary planation surfaces and are characterized by lateritic soils (Figures 7.1 to 7.3). Over large areas these woodlands are dominated by *Brachystegia*, *Isoberlinia* and *Julbernardia* trees that have medium size pinnate leaves (about 2 cm in length), relatively straight trunks and large ligno tubers. Contorted trees with tough sclerophyllous leaves occur only in the less common *Uapaca*, *Monotes* and *Protea* genera found on extreme sites on the older planation surfaces. Individual species of the *Brachystegia*, *Isoberlinia* and *Julbernardia* genera, all belonging to the Leguminosae family, like the *Eucalyptus* spp. in the savanna woodlands of Australia, are sensitive to edaphic conditions and consequently the savanna woodlands exhibit marked changes of composition that are related to differences of soil and drainage that in turn are related to geomorphology and geology, notably the extent to which post-Tertiary dissection has removed the lateritic cover, exposed bedrock, led to improved drainage and provided conditions favourable for soil renewal at the periphery of the plateaux. Discrete vegetation associations whose distributions are closely related to soils, relief and drainage and geology are readily recognized.

The savanna vegetation exhibits the greatest variations in form and composition along the Congo–Zambezi watershed where repeated warpings and differential uplift have interrupted the planation cycles, and along the Luangwa and Zambezi valleys where trough faulting associated with the large scale rifting in East Africa occurred in mid-Cretaceous times. In the former area the variations in the vegetation are associated with advanced dissection that in places has uncovered rocks of Palaeozoic to Archaean age: in the latter

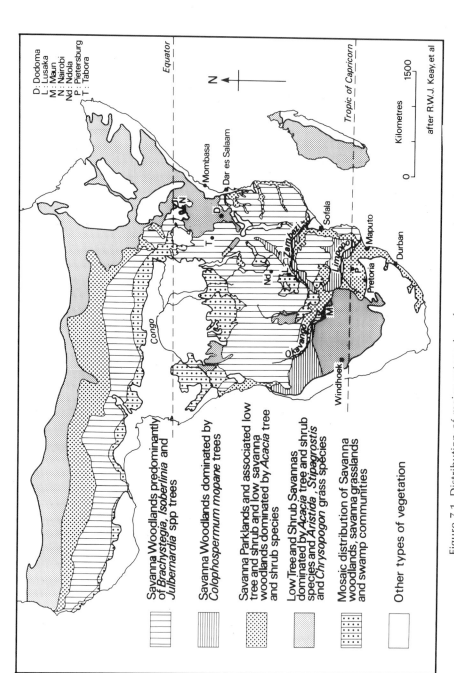

Figure 7.1. Distribution of major categories of savanna vegetation of Africa.

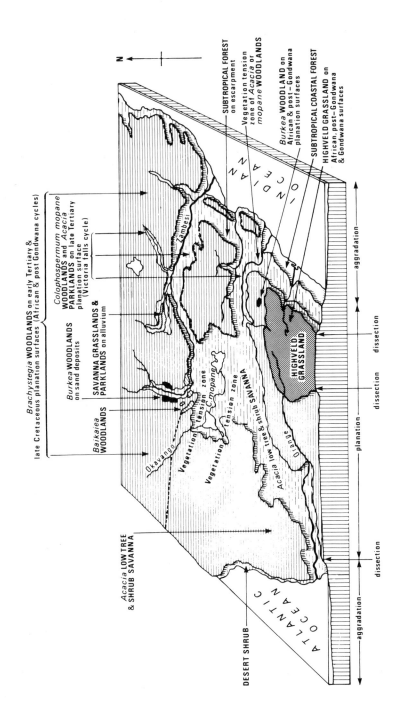

Figure 7.2. Relationships between vegetation and geomorphology in south central Africa.

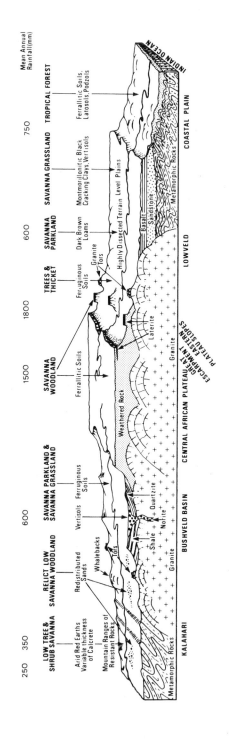

Figure 7.3. Relationships between vegetation, climate, soils, geomorphology and geology in southern Africa.

they are related to the preservation of the Karoo rocks that once covered much of the plateau, to the steep escarpments bounding the valleys and to stages in drainage superimposition progressively on to older rocks since Cretaceous times.

On relics of the older planation surfaces, notably those of Jurassic/early Cretaceous and mid-Tertiary age along the Congo–Zambezi watershed and on the Choma–Zimba plateau in Zambia, which have very poor soils that are subject to alternating waterlogging and drought, *Protea* and *Faurea* spp. of the floristically old Proteaceae family accompany and, in places, replace the *Brachystegia, Isoberlinia* and *Julbernardia* trees in open forms of savanna woodland. The *Protea* and *Faurea* spp. represent elements of the vegetation that flourished in Cretaceous and Tertiary times and their distribution, like that of the Proteaceae genera, *Banksia, Grevillea* and *Hakea*, in the savanna woodlands of Australia, is of particular significance with regard to the origin of the savanna woodland vegetation. Indeed those forms of savanna woodland containing members of the Proteaceae more closely resemble the savanna woodlands of South America, where the planation surfaces are less dissected, than do the more widespread *Brachystegia–Isoberlinia–Julbernardia* woodlands of Africa and *Eucalyptus* woodlands of Australia.

The core area of distribution of the *Brachystegia–Isoberlinia* and *Julbernardia* savanna woodlands in Africa, like that of the cerrados types of vegetation in South America, is the central plateau. There are no outliers that are strictly comparable with those in South America but the *Burkea africana* and *Terminalia sericea* woodlands near Nylsvlei in the Transvaal plateau basin and stands of *Terminalia* and *Combretum* species in the eastern Transvaal Lowveld, in western Botswana and South West Africa may represent, respectively depauperate savanna woodlands and the last vestiges of this form of vegetation in areas now too dry to support it.

In southern Africa woodlands and low tree and shrub communities dominated by *Colphospermum mopane* trees of greatly varying stature, occupy those hotter and drier parts of the savanna woodland belt that characteristically have alkaline black clay soils derived from Karoo (Triassic) basalt and shales. The distribution of these communities between the *Brachystegia–Isoberlinia–Julbernardia* savanna woodlands and the *Acacia* dominated low tree and shrub savannas provides important evidence of the interacting influences of the factors and processes influencing the distribution of all categories of savanna and of the plant communities within them (Figure 7.2).

Tall *Colophospermum mopane* woodlands occupy the alkaline black clay soils derived from Karoo basalts and shales in the low-lying hot arid section of the Zambezi valley. Their distribution, however, is interrupted by thickets of *Commiphora* and *Combretum* spp. with an occasional *Pterocarpus angolenis* tree on brown sandy soils derived from Karoo sandstone and, below Kariba dam, by *Brachystegia–Isoberlinia* woodlands where erosion has uncovered Archaean basement rocks that produce skeletal sandy soils. Here the vegetation is in a state of flux with individual categories of savanna advancing or retreating as erosion slowly strips one geological formation and exposes another and at the same time modifies the local relief and soil conditions (see Chapter 8).

Colophospermum mopane woodlands of lower or even dwarf stature occupy large areas where calcrete masks bedrock in eastern, northern and western Botswana and in the Transvaal Lowveld. In the Lowveld it also occupies red sandy soils derived from the Old Granite (see Chapter 9). In western Botswana the species forms open woodlands over riverine silts in the Okavango delta area (see Chapter 11) and in Zimbabwe it forms a low scrub in the Gwelo area. The coincidence of the extensive shallow root system of *Colophospermum mopane* and zones of maximum moisture retention in the soils in several localities in Zimbabwe has prompted the suggestion that the species occupies areas where moisture accumulates at shallow depth as where thin soils overlie either impervious bedrock (i.e. over granite) or an impervious layer of transported clay (i.e. over riverine silt) or where exchangeable sodium disperses the clay as where there is a combination of low rainfall and great heat. There is some evidence that *Colophospermum mopane* does not favour alkaline soils *per se* and that it will grow better on fertile, slightly acid permeable soils from which, however, it is usually excluded by more competitive deep rooting *Acacia* species (Cole 1967).

Colophospermum mopane is sensitive to low temperatures and appears to be unable to survive where the mean temperature for the mid-winter month of July is below 17.5°C or where light frosts occur in winter. In northern Botswana its stature is markedly lower along drainage lines where cold air accumulates on winter nights. While there and in the Transvaal Lowveld its dwarf stature may be related to seasonally low temperatures, throughout its range the distribution of *Colophospermum mopane* appears to be controlled by edaphic factors, occurring particularly on alkaline base rich soils with impeded drainage. Like *Acacia harpophylla* (the brigalow) in Australia, which shows comparable variations in form and occupies similar soils derived from rocks of comparable age, *Colophospermum mopane* appears to be ecologically aggressive and to be extending its range into areas characterized by other forms of savanna vegetation (see Chapter 8).

Savanna grasslands of comparable extent to those of the Llanos in Venezuela or of the Barkly Tableland and Great Artesian Basin in Australia are not represented in Africa. Due to altitude, relatively high latitude and consequent low winter temperatures the grasslands of the South African Highveld have the character of temperate steppes rather than tropical savannas. There is no lowland basin subject to periodic inundation comparable with that of the Orinoco or extensive plain floored with Mesozoic and later rocks or underlain by limestone bedrock producing dark brown loams and black cracking clay soils like those of central Queensland and the Barkly Tableland. The most extensive savanna grasslands in Africa are those on the Kafue Flats and Busango plains along the Kafue river valley in Zambia and on the Springbok Flats in the Bushveld Basin in South Africa. The former occupy black cracking montmorillonitic clays that have formed over alluvium laid down when the flow of the Kafue river was arrested as it became superimposed from a cover of Karoo rocks onto the more resistant rocks of the Basement Complex at the sites of the present Kafue and Meshi Teshi gorges. The savanna grasslands on the Springbok Flats also occupy black cracking clay soils derived either from alluvium or Karoo basalt. Watershed savanna grasslands of limited extent occur within the savanna woodlands, notably in Zambia where they occupy the poorest soils on the level central areas of the Tertiary planation surfaces.

Savanna parklands and low tree and shrub savannas, on the other hand, occupy very large areas in Africa occurring in the drier areas associated with the younger erosion surface where the landscape has been subjected to varying degrees of dissection, planation and deposition of wind blown material.

Savanna parklands occupy the high base status brown loam soils that have developed over Precambrian limestones near Broken Hill and south of Lusaka in Zambia, over norite in the Transvaal Bushveld Basin, over Karoo basalt in the eastern part of the Transvaal Lowveld (Figure 7.3) and in the Orapa and Magobe–Mawane areas of Botswana and over alluvium at the periphery of the Busango plains and Kafue Flats in Zambia. Everywhere the savanna parklands are characterized by *Acacia* trees and by short sweet grasses but the characteristic species vary in different areas.

Various forms of low tree and shrub savannas, sometimes with associated grasslands and parklands, cover most of South West Africa and Botswana and adjacent parts of the Transvaal and northern Cape Province in South Africa where the rainfall averages 300–500 mm concentrated in the summer period November–March and where the characteristic soils are arid red earths. In the north the low tree and shrub savannas take over from savanna woodlands, notably those dominated by *Colophospermum mopane* trees where low temperatures and light frosts occur in winter; in the west they give way to desert shrub and desert grass communities below the Great Escarpment where the annual rainfall averages less than 100 mm and is highly erratic in occurrence; and in the south they yield to Karoo shrub where the annual rainfall is less than 300 mm, the July mean temperature is below 11 °C and the mean minima 2 °C, and the frost period exceeds 90 days.

Low tree and shrub savannas, with associated parklands and grasslands, occur under climatic regimes similar to those in South West Africa and Botswana on the lower surfaces extending northwards of Mbeya through Dodoma in Tanzania into Kenya and thence through the southern Sudan into West Africa. In East Africa where sharp changes of relief and climate associated with the Great Escarpment and the rift valley system influence vegetation distributions, the low tree and shrub savannas adjoin the *Brachystegia–Isoberlinia–Julbernardia* savanna woodlands without the intervention of a belt of drier savanna woodland like that dominated by *Colophospermum mopane* trees in southern Africa. In West Africa, however, where climatic conditions are more dependent on latitude, an intervening belt of dry savanna woodland is recognized as a gradational stage between the savanna woodlands and the low tree and shrub savannas.

Bush clump savannas which may be regarded as variants of savanna parkland occur in several plains areas where groups of trees and shrubs take advantage of better drained conditions afforded by termitaria. In places thickets occupy small areas while complex vegetational mosaics embracing forest and savanna types are found along the Zambezi in Barotseland and in the Okavango inland delta area. The latter exhibits features of an ecological tension zone where the elements of different floras and different types of vegetation compete in an environment subject to long-term climatic change and periodic climatic fluctuations.

Compared with South America the more complex distribution patterns of the major categories of savanna vegetation in Africa are related to the greater diversity of relief and soils caused by the interplay of a more complex geomorphological history with major geological events and climatic changes. The presence of discrete vegetation associations within each savanna category reflects the more advanced dissection of old planation surfaces, removal of laterite, and exposure of underlying bedrock which has produced a variety of distinctive soils and micro-climatic niches to which the plants have responded. The following chapters attempt to elucidate the vegetation characterized by each of the major categories of savanna in southern Africa.

8 The savanna woodlands and associated grasslands and parklands of central and southern Africa

Savanna woodlands form the characteristic vegetation of vast areas over the level terrain of the plateau of central and southern Africa. They are interrupted by smaller areas of savanna grasslands along river valleys where impeded drainage precludes tree growth. A catenary sequence of plant communities associated with changes of soil and drainage marks the slope from plateau to valley. Over lightly dissected gently undulating country and over areas where porous bedrock promotes better drainage both types of vegetation give way to savanna parkland. The overall distribution of savanna vegetation is virtually coincident with the plateau country that has been subject to prolonged periods of planation. Evergreen tropical forests occupy the Congo basin and narrow coastal belt bordering the Indian Ocean and extend up the valleys cut into the savanna-covered plateau country. In places where the plateau is being dissected in current erosion cycles, particularly at its periphery, some forest trees are present, notably in the *Marquesia macroura* woodlands along the Congo–Zambezi watershed.

The savanna woodlands of Africa are floristically richer and more varied than those of South America. They form part of the Zambezian phytogeographical domain recognized by taxonomic botanists who have suggested that the uniformity of the vegetation, and the fact that over large areas the flora only gradually changes, are the results of the lack of strong relief and other contrasting physiographic factors (Werger 1978). Within the domain several authors have distinguished phytogeographical sectors and/or centres of endemism in Angola (Monteiro 1970), Shaba (Duvigneaud 1958), Zambia (White 1965) and Zimbabwe (Wild 1968). In each case the sectors have been distinguished by physiognomically distinct forms of vegetation associated with overall environmental conditions and the centres of endemism have been related to distinctive habitats related to geological bedrock. Thus, for example, in Angola one sector occupying the coastal zone from north of Luanda to south of Benguela is characterized by plants adapted to local arid conditions, growing in savannas interrupted by thickets. Inland, successive sectors in Angola and Shaba (Katanga) comprise savannas and thickets interrupted by gallery forests, and savanna woodlands interrupted by plateau grasslands and by gallery forests along the rivers. In Katanga and Zambia the three centres of endemism that have been identified occur respectively on the high plateau characterized by planation surfaces and lateritic soils, in the area mantled by Kalahari sand in Barotseland, and in the hot arid Zambezi valley floored by Karoo sediments.

The savanna woodlands comprise three distinctive types whose distributions are broadly related to the centres of endemism recognized by White (1965). Associations dominated by species of *Brachystegia*, *Isoberlinia* and *Julbernardia* trees cover the greater part of the plateau. Woodlands characterized by *Baikiaea plurijuga* (the Rhodesian teak) and *Cryptosepalum pseudotaxis* occupy areas of Kalahari Sand in Barotseland and smaller patches of it further east. *Colosphospermum mopane* woodlands occur mainly in the wide flat valley bottoms of the larger rivers, notably the Zambezi, Luangwa, Shire, Limpopo, Okavango and Cunene; low tree and shrub forms of this species occur along the old floors of dismembered drainage systems in Botswana as well as in the Transvaal Lowveld and Bushveld (see Chapter 9). *Colophospermum mopane* has not been cited as a species in a centre of endemism but one of its main areas of distribution, that of the Kariba section of the Zambezi valley, has. A fourth type of woodland, characterized by *Marquesia macroura*, a tall tree with buttress roots occurring around the southern periphery of the Congo basin, in dissected terrain along the Copperbelt and around the Lake Bengweula depression, has certain affinities with the tropical rain forest to which it may be regarded as transitional.

In addition to the savanna woodlands cited above, stands of *Terminalia sericea* trees occupy areas of sandy soils and often form narrow fringes of woodland at the periphery of the broad flat drainage lines called *dambos* in Zambia and *mbugas* in Tanzania. Elsewhere a low woodland of *Combretum* tree species occupies sandy soils over granite bedrock. Neither forms of vegetation comprise typical savanna woodland and in many ways they are physiognomically more akin to a low tree and shrub savanna vegetation.

The savanna grasslands that are associated with the savanna woodlands are of variable type and composition depending upon whether they occupy sites on the plateau surface or follow drainage lines where vegetation/soil/moisture catenas are found. Reflecting the variety of habitats and the range of soils from light sands to heavy clays that they occupy, the savanna grasslands of Africa are also floristically richer and more varied than those of South America.

The associated savanna parklands comprise grasslands studded with trees mainly of the *Acacia*, *Piliostigma* and *Terminalia* genera. In Zambia, they occupy the lightly dissected terrain bordering the grasslands of the Kafue Flats, Lukanga swamps, and Busanga plain and the undulating country over porous limestone bedrock south of Lusaka. Vegetation approaching that of thicket with *Acacia eriocarpa*, *Commiphora karibensis*, *Guibourtia conjugata* and occasional *Pterocarpus brenanii* trees occur in the Kariba sector of the Zambezi valley regarded by White as a centre of endemism.

Most of the accounts of the *Brachystegia–Isoberlinia–Julbernardia* woodlands, commonly referred to as miombo in Africa, and of the vegetation types associated with them, cover an individual country or region; most survey the characteristic features of the vegetation and produce classifications based on physiognomy and on dominant or prominent species. Those for Shaba (Katanga) however, are based on phytosociological data which have been used to produce a classification of the miombo communities into four alliances named the Berlinia–Marquesion, the Mesobrachystegion, the Xerobrachystegion and the Guibourtia–Copaiferon, which together make up the order Julbernardio–Brachystegietalia. All are associated with relatively high rainfall. The first named is distinguished by the occurrence of *Marquesia macroura* and the communities within it often have the character of semi-evergreen forest. The Mesobrachystegion, covering large areas in Shaba and Zambia, comprises miombo associations on relatively mesic and fertile loamy soils, whereas the Xerobrachystegion occurs on drier and poorer often shallow soils. The Guibourtia–Copaiferon is described as typical of areas of Kalahari Sand. These phytosociological surveys provide detailed information on the floristic composition of the vegetation and on the distinctive species that discriminate individual associations but they give little attention to the factors influencing either the overall distribution of the *Brachystegia–Isoberlinia–Julbernardia* woodlands or of the vegetation associations, plant communities and individual species within them.

The *Brachystegia–Isoberlinia–Julbernardia* woodlands cover plateau country spanning some 20° of latitude. This vast area experiences a relatively uniform climate characterized by hot rainy summers and warm dry winters that are frost free. The total rainfall varies from 1800 mm near the border with the rain forest of the Congo basin to only 600 mm where the vegetation changes to microphyllous thorny low tree and shrub savanna. The length of the dry season increases with latitudinal distance from the Equator while its intensity varies with both altitude and physiography. A dry season with less than 100 mm in each of three or four months precludes tropical rain forest except where subsurface water or mist makes good the deficit. The savanna woodlands or miombo woodlands are characteristic of areas with from four to seven months with less than 25 mm of rainfall. The deciduous or semi-deciduous *Brachystegia, Isoberlinia* and *Julbernardia* trees flourish under these conditions. Most species, however, shed their leaves only late in the dry season and are leafless for only a short period, usually less than three months. They produce new foliage a few weeks to a month before the summer rains begin. According to species the new foliage varies from yellow orange to deep red colour and is limp and delicate. After a few days it stiffens and the leaves become their normal green or grey-green colour. Most of the trees and shrubs in the miombo woodland also flower before the beginning of the rainy season. While the overall distribution of the *Brachystegia–Isoberlinia–Julbernardia* woodlands is broadly coincident with terrain with a marked winter drought, the behaviour of the characteristic species suggests that factors other than rainfall are also important. Most tree species possess large lignotubers which may be capable of storing moisture while, dependent on the rooting characteristics, under favourable soil conditions mature trees may be able to tap subsurface water. Some species of *Brachystegia spiciformis* and *B. boehmii* have a considerable latitudinal range whereas others, e.g. *B. taxifolia*, are restricted to the higher rainfall areas peripheral to the Congo basin. The distribution of some species has been related to rainfall, that of others to soil type or to a combination of climatic and edaphic influences.

From the author's studies in Africa it is clear that, as in other continents, the distributions of the savanna woodlands, grasslands and parklands and of the vegetation associations and plant communities within them are related not only to the prevailing climatic and edaphic conditions but also to the geomorphological evolution of the landscape, to bedrock geology and to geological events and changes of climate that on the one hand have influenced geomorphological and soil-forming processes and on the other have influenced the opportunities for individual plant species to extend their range. The influences of the geomorphological evolution of the landscape and of geological events have been studied only in Zambia and to a lesser extent in Zimbabwe. The former, however, comprises part of the core area of savanna woodlands distribution comparable with that of the campos cerrados on the Brazilian plateau in South America; hence an understanding of the influences of both the geological events and the geomorphological processes on its vegetation are of critical importance for the understanding of the overall distribution of the savanna woodlands in Africa.

THE SAVANNA WOODLANDS AND ASSOCIATED GRASSLANDS AND PARKLANDS OF ZAMBIA

Introduction

The main categories of savanna vegetation in Zambia are shown on Figures 8.1 (a) and (b). *Brachystegia–Isoberlinia–Julbernardia* woodlands with a grass layer composed mainly of *Hyparrhenia* and *Andropogon* spp. cover most of the plateau which is over 1350 m high and rises to 1500 m on the Copperbelt. These woodlands vary in both form and composition. In the south they are of relatively low stature, comprise few tree species, mainly *Brachystegia* spp. associated with *Isoberlinia globiflora*, and there are few shrubs, mainly *Uapaca*, *Pseudolachnostylis* and *Diplorhynchus* spp. Northwards the number of species increases, *I. globiflora* gives way in turn to *Julbernardia paniculata* in central Zambia and to *I. tomentosa* in the north, the trees become taller, the grass cover more luxuriant and shrubs and small trees, notably *Anisophylla*, *Baphia* and *Randia* spp., form a more definite understorey.

Forests dominated by evergreen trees, *Cryptosepalum pseudotaxis* in the north and *Baikiaea plurijuga* (the Rhodesian teak) in the south, occupy the western part of the plateau which is mantled with Kalahari Sand. They are believed to have been much destroyed by fire so that the *Cryptosepalum* forest has given way to *Brachystegia* woodland and the *Baikiaea* forest has been replaced by a woodland of *Burkea*, *Terminalia* and *Acacia* spp. (Trapnell and Clothier 1957). *Pterocarpus angolensis* is common to both the *Baikiaea* forest and *Burkea* woodland. Its distribution along with that of *P. brenaii* in the Zambezi valley and *P. rotundifolius* in the eastern Transvaal Lowveld is significant in relation to the impact of the geomorphological evolution of the landscape on vegetation communities.

Flood plain grasslands exhibiting striking species zonations parallel the major rivers on the plateau and grasslands with scattered deciduous trees, notably *Acacia*, *Combretum*, *Piliostigma* and *Bauhinia* spp. cover the adjacent more elevated and slightly dissected terrain.

Along the Copperbelt and around the Lake Bangweulu depression, where the level plateau is replaced by country of more varied relief, *Brachystegia* woodlands give way to *Marquesia* woodlands and high grass–woodlands known as *chipyas*. The former is characterized by the buttress tree. *Marquesia macroura*, which together with *Parinari mobola* is semi-evergreen and has features characteristic of forest trees. *Brachystegia spiciformis*, which is widely distributed on the more fertile soils on well-drained sites, is also common. *Pteridium aquilinum*, *Afromomum biauriculatum* and *Smilax kraussiana* are features of the undergrowth. The chipya types are closely associated. The

Figure 8.1. (a) Vegetation of northwestern Zambia. 1. *Cryptosepalum* low forest and woodlands. 2. *Marquesia* and *Marquesia-Brachystegia* woodlands and high grass-woodland or chipya types (1 and 2 are evergreen and semi-deciduous types). 3. *Brachystegi-Julbernardia-Isoberlinia* woodlands. 4. *Baikiaea plurijuga* forests. 5. Mixed *Brachystegia* and *Burkea-Colophospermum-Baikiaea* woodlands. 6. *Burkea* woodland. 7. *Acacia-Combretum, Combretum-Afrormosia* and *Pterocarpus-Combretum* grassland and thicket. 8. *Bussea-Combretum* thicket. 9. Kalahari Sand plain and watershed grasslands. 10. Valley and flood plain grasslands. 11. *Papyrus* Sudd. 12. *Colophospermum mopane* woodlands. (Figures 8.1a,b, 8.2, 8.5, 8.12a,b, 8.11, 8.13, 8.14, 8.15, 8.16, 8.17 are reproduced from Cole 1963a, with permission of the Royal Geographical Society.)

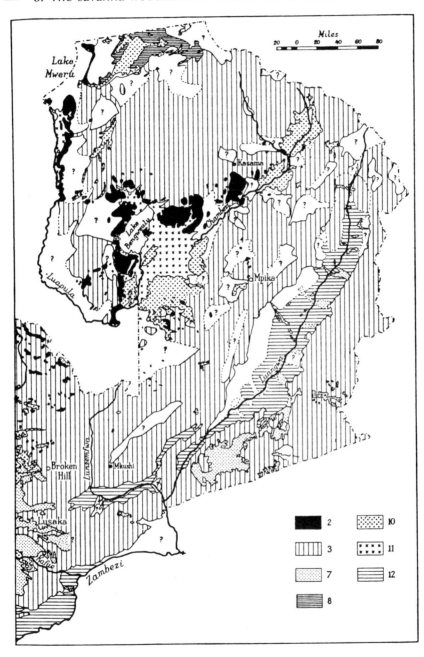

Figure 8.1(b). Vegetation of northeastern Zambia. For explanation of keys see Figure 8.1(a).

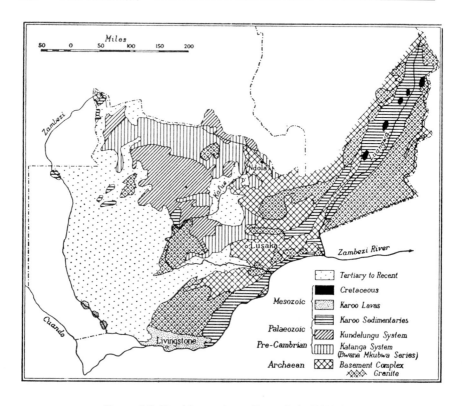

Figure 8.2. Zambia, geology. From Cole (1963a).

undergrowth is similar, but the characteristic trees are *Erythrophloeum*, *Pterocarpus* and *Afrormosia* spp., all of which are deciduous. These vegetation types occur in the areas of highest rainfall and on soils designated as lake basin type. They are considered to result from fire in areas formerly carrying rain forest. The presence of thickets containing young trees of *Entandrophragma delevoyi* and other forest species support this view.

Along the hot dry Zambezi valley, which is some 700 m below the plateau, the characteristic vegetation is the *mopani* woodland, which comprises almost pure stands of *Colophospermum mopane* on the heavy black clay soils with an excessively high pH value. Sandy soils, however, support deciduous thorny thickets of *Commiphora* and *Combretum* spp. interspersed with *Kirkia* and *Sterculia* spp. and the occasional baobab (*Adansonia digitata*), *Pterocarpus angolensis* or *P. brenanii* tree.

The physical environment

Climate   Over the Zambian plateau the total rainfall varies from about 760 mm in the relatively dry area around Lusaka to over 1400 mm on the Copperbelt and the rainy season lengthens from six months (October–March) to eight months. The rainfall decreases westwards to only 500 mm in Barotseland and is similarly low in the Zambezi and Luangwa trough valleys. Here the amount of rainfall is influenced by relief features. On the northern side of these valleys more rain falls on the escarpment hills which in turn create a local rain shadow that is responsible for the low falls around Lusaka.

Low latitude, high elevation and sharp physiographic contrasts between plateau and trough valley result in temperature extremes. Over the plateau mean maximum temperatures of around 30°C and mean minimum temperatures of about 15.5°C are experienced. In the Zambezi valley both are about 3°C higher but in Barotseland high mean maxima of around 33°C and relatively low mean minima of 15°C are usual. In all areas extremely high temperatures of 40–45°C or in Barotseland even 50°C may occur in the hot season and, dependent on the physiography, local frosts may occur in winter.

Although the climate over the plateau is comparatively equable, the vegetation has to tolerate the extremes. The deciduous habit manifest by the *Brachystegia*, *Isoberlinia* and *Julbernardia* trees may be a response to seasonally low temperatures as well as to drought. Their characteristic initiation of new leaves before the rains may be related to rising temperatures as well as increased atmospheric humidity in species whose rooting habits enable them both to store water and to tap ground water supplies.

Geology and geomorphology   It is generally believed that the fashioning of the present landscape began at the close of the Karoo period (in the Triassic) (Dixey 1938, 1942, 1943, 1944, 1955, King 1947, 1951, 1967, Cahen and Lepersonne 1952, Cahen 1954, Wellington 1955) when, following a very long period of deposition, warping occurred which brought into being the Congo–Zambezi watershed along an upfold, between the downwarped basins of the Congo and Zambezi on either side. The Zambezi drainage is believed by Wellington to have flowed towards the Kalahari where deposition continued. However, the disruption of Gondwanaland and the opening of the Mozambique Channel, which occurred at about the same time, initiated drainage towards the Indian Ocean. This proceeded by headward erosion to work its way inland. In mid-Cretaceous times trough-faulting, associated with the large-scale rifting in East Africa, occurred along the middle Zambezi (Gwembe) and Luangwa valleys where the Karoo rocks were let down many hundreds of metres. The lowering of this section of the Zambezi valley, together with headward erosion from the coast, led eventually to the diversion of all the

Zambezi drainage from the direction of the Kalahari to that of the Indian Ocean. Deposition continued in the Kalahari through Cretaceous and Tertiary and into Recent times, and in the Zambezi–Luangwa trough during the Cretaceous period.

The geomorphology of Zambia has been dominated by planation processes since the close of the Karoo deposition, with those attending drainage superimposition playing an increasingly important role since the Cretaceous. Throughout the period the erosion cycles have been interrupted by continental uplift, by regional uplift around the periphery of the subcontinent and by local warping.

On the Copperbelt, the scene of major upwarping, erosion has stripped the Karoo cover and exposed the Katanga rocks below. On the northern side of the Zambezi–Luangwa trough it has proceeded further and revealed the Archaean basement. The Karoo rocks are preserved in the Zambezi–Luangwa trough and beneath a cover of post-Karoo deposits, especially Kalahari Sand, in the western part of the country and adjacent Kalahari (Figure 8.2).

During the processes of drainage superimposition the stream flow has been arrested where resistant rocks have been uncovered. This has occurred particularly along the lines of Tertiary upwarping associated with epeirogenic uplift, its effects being particularly marked along the Kafue river and its major tributaries. Here resistant rocks have been uncovered and local base levels have been created, and following periodic continental uplift, increased erosion in the headwater region during the rainy season has produced a heavy sediment load which the rivers have been unable to carry during the subsequent dry season when their volumes are reduced. This has led to deposition above the local base levels until the rivers have regraded their valleys by cutting gorges through the resistant rocks. Reduction of stream flow during the dry season when the streams are still heavily laden with the products of erosion during the rainy season has aided the process of aggradation. In this way the Kafue Flats and the Busango Plains which lie upstream of gorges cut through the Archaean basement by the Kafue river at Kafue and Meshi Teshi, respectively, were formed.

The planation processes have produced a number of remarkably level erosion surfaces forming a stepped sequence in which each surface is separated from the one below by a scarp or belt of dissected country marking a stage of uplift. Most important is the mid-Tertiary or Miocene pediplain at an altitude of 1300 m. This was fashioned during L. C. King's Africa cycle of pediplanation. It is surmounted by the remnants of the older late Cretaceous (post-Gondwana) and Jurassic/early Cretaceous (Gondwana) surface and is cut into by the end-Tertiary (Victoria Falls) pediplain and by later surfaces ascribed to the Congo and later cycles by King. The older surfaces form the plateau country and the younger surfaces the valleys cutting into it. These surfaces have undergone relatively little deformation but warping of the end-Tertiary pediplain has produced the Bangweulu and Lukanga depressions and has accentuated the Congo–Zambezi watershed.

The slight accentuation of relief introduced by the warpings has had a marked influence on soils and vegetation (see below).

Throughout the vicissitudes of land sculpture the vegetation has changed as the drainage, soil and climatic conditions have been modified by the interplay of pediplanation and dissection and by the stripping of one geological formation and the exposure of another. As one would expect, the valleys and the escarpments have provided the avenues along which vegetation changes have progressed.

The distribution of the main types of savanna vegetation

Consideration of the broad relationship between the distribution of the main vegetation types shown on Figures 8.1 (a) and (b) and the geomorphology reveals several features of outstanding significance. Firstly the savanna woodlands (of *Brachystegia*, *Isoberlinia* and *Julbernardia* species) (Figure 8.3) and small included areas of savanna grassland occupy the extensive plateaux representing the older planation surfaces that have highly leached, infertile, and generally sandy soils with a laterite layer at a variable depth below the surface. Secondly, the *Baikiaea* forests coincide with areas of Kalahari Sand, the main area of distribution being in Barotseland with small outliers near the Kafue Flats. Thirdly, the main belt of *mopani* woodland (Figure 8.4, see also Figure 2.8), occurs on the black clay soils of the Zambezi valley, where scattered patches of thicket on sandy soils may be related to the former distribution of *Baikiaea* forest. Fourthly, the zonal distributional patterns distinguish the grasslands and *Acacia* grassland (see Figure 2.12) paralleling the Kafue river above the Kafue and Meshi Teshi gorges, this being linked with stages in the superimposition of the Kafue river from Karoo rocks on to ancient rocks below. The fifth feature is the association of *Marquesia* woodlands (Figure 8.5) and chipya with lake basin soils in the vicinity of Lake Bangweulu where basining of the end-Tertiary pediplain has introduced some relief and initiated some dissection. Finally, the juxtaposition of the post-Karoo upwarp forming the Congo–Zambezi–Kafue watershed and the depression containing Lake Bangweulu, the former suffering several periods of pediplanation punctuated by uplift, the latter experiencing recent downwarping, is associated with the mosaic of open grassland, savanna woodland (of *Brachystegia*, *Isoberlinia*, Julbernardia and *Uapaca* spp.), evergreen forests (of *Marquesia* spp.) and chipyas which characterize the Copperbelt.

From this broad outline it is clear that the savanna woodlands and associated grasslands and parklands of Africa as a whole and of Zambia in

Figure 8.3. Open savanna woodland of *Brachystegia boehmii* (left) and *Isoberlinia globiflora* (right) on the level lateritic plateau south of Choma.

Figure 8.4. *Colophospermum mopane* woodland flooding under the rising waters of Lake Kariba which are covered by *Salvinia auriculata*.

Figure 8.5. Marquesia macroura woodland near Kitwe, Zambia. From Cole (1963a).

particular are more varied than those of South America. This is due largely to the more complex geomorphological evolution of the landscape following large-scale faulting during the Cretaceous and major warpings during the Tertiary. In some areas increased dissection following these geological events has removed the relict lateritic soils and exposed bedrock. Here the varied soils, each dependent on bedrock type, support distinctive vegetation associations and plant communities displaying more complex distribution patterns than those over the lateristic plateau surface.

Against the backdrop of the broad relationships between vegetation and geomorphology, the distribution of savanna types in a few selected areas of Zambia may be examined.

The savanna woodlands and grasslands of the plateau

The savanna woodlands and grasslands are virtually coincident with the old planation surfaces recognized by Dixey, Cahen and Lepersonne, and other leading geomorphologists. Everywhere these old surfaces carry sandy to sandy clay soils, characterized by a bed of nodular laterite at a variable distance below the surface. These soils are acid (pH 5.0–5.5) and are very low in exchangeable bases and organic matter. Like the soils on the Brazilian plateau they owe their characteristic features to seasonal leaching over a long period of time on a level surface. This has left an upper horizon of old and exhausted material. Because of the absence of slope this material is not removed by the agents of normal healthy erosion and soil renewal through replacement by material weathered from the parent rock proceeds slowly, if at all. The lateritic layer formed originally at the level of a fluctuating water table which has dropped following continental uplift. Consequently, while continued leaching has progressively impoverished the surface soils, with repeated uplift the lateritic layer has become progressively thicker and more fully developed. Where it is exposed, as at the periphery of the older planation surfaces and around the margins of dambos, it has become indurated to form sheet laterite. During the rainy season the indurated laterite acts as an impervious layer causing waterlogging that few tree species can tolerate. Near Lusaka, where thicknesses of more than two metres of indurated laterite over crystalline limestone bedrock are exposed in sections in quarry faces, it is largely responsible for the stunted nature of the savanna woodlands.

The ability of *Brachystegia*, *Isoberlinia* and *Julbernardia* trees to thrive on these lateritic soils is probably associated with their large ligno tubers and with the depth of their root systems which are able to penetrate the laterite layer. Where indurated laterite outcrops or is very near surface, however, even the more tolerant species of these genera give way to species of *Uapaca*, and *Monotes* or *Protea* and *Faurea*. The absence of forest tree species is due

Figure 8.6. Eroding dambo near Choma, Zambia.

Figure 8.7. Grass-covered dambo with numerous small termite mounds and clumps of *Brachystegia* and *Julbernardia* spp. trees on large termite mounds.

Figure 8.8. *Brachystegia floribunda* woodland on yellowish red clays derived from gabbro, Chati reserve, Zambia.

partly to their inability to tolerate the soil and drainage conditions and only partly to seasonal drought. Even where the climatic conditions are favourable, as on the Copperbelt, the surface-rooting *Marquesia* trees occur only on the better soils of the dissected terrain.

Differences in the composition of the savanna woodlands are related to differences of soil and drainage that are related to geomorphology and, in areas of outcropping and near surface bedrock, to geology. The floristically older genera of *Protea* and *Faurea* occur only on the older surfaces, notably those of the mid-Tertiary pediplain along the Congo–Zambezi–Kafue watershed and on the Choma–Zimba plateau where extremely poor soils characterize the level, ill-drained terrain, and on similarly poor soils at the periphery of dambos. This mid-Tertiary pediplain, in both the cited areas, is currently being dissected in later erosional cycles. Near Choma and Kaloma, where some of the dambos are actively eroding (Figure 8.6), the relief is slight but, nevertheless, transects show zonations from open grassland studded with scattered *Protea* spp. on the highest and most level plateaux (see Figure 2.6) through woodlands dominated in turn by *Brachystegia boehmii* and *Julbernardia paniculata* to those with *B. spiciformis* and *Parinari* spp., both considered to have some affinity with tropical forest species, on the gently sloping lower ground. Grassland with clumps of trees on termite mounds characterizes the dambos (Figure 8.7), the slopes of the valleys heading into the plateaux carrying *Piliostigma* and *Acacia* spp. and an occasional *Afzelia cuanensis*. These vegetational changes are associated with improved drainage and better soils as dissection breaks up the lateritic layer and effects a balance between soil erosion and soil formation, promoting the development of dark brown clay loams.

The vegetation on the Congo–Zambezi–Kafue watershed displays an intricate mosaic. Three pediplains — the mid-Tertiary, end-Tertiary and lower Pleistocene — are represented. The younger and lower ones are growing at the expense of the older and higher ones, with each separated from the other by belts of dissected country. The mid-Tertiary pediplain carries *Uapaca–Monotes–Protea* grassland whereas the end-Tertiary surface carries poor *Brachystegia–Julbernardia* woodland. The dissected country between them, which near Chafakuma where the Bwana Mkubwa limestones are exposed is characterized by deep chocolate coloured loams, supports a *chipya* vegetation merging into *Marquesia* woodland (Figure 8.5), as also do small areas of lake basin soils similar to those of the Lake Bangweulu depression. Here and else-where along the watershed, the headstreams of the Congo and the Kafue are paralleled by *mushitus*, galleries of *Syzygium* spp., *Garcinia* spp., *Parinari excelsa* and other evergreen forest trees linked together with lianas and creepers. These mushitus extend up the valley heads cut into the plateau surface.

Some of the chipyas may represent areas of former forest destroyed by clearing and burning by shifting cultivators, but an examination of the relationship between vegetation, soils and geomorphology and an investigation of current geomorphological processes suggests that the present trend is for an extension of chipya and forest as dissection proceeds in the current cycle. Thus some of the chipyas may represent forerunners of future forest rather than relics of pre-existing forest.

Southeast of Solwezi and Chifubwa gorge and the extensive dambo above it (see Cole 1963a) provide evidence of current vegetational trends. The gorge and the dambo are the result of the superimposition of the Chifubwa river from a cover of Karoo rocks on to the Katanga rocks below. When, following epeirogenic uplift, here associated with upwarping, the river first exposed the resistant rocks, its flow was slowed down by the imposition of this local base level. At the same time the alternation of heavy sediment load from increased erosion promoted by the uplift in the upstream headwater regions during the rainy season, followed by diminished flow during the dry season, caused alluviation on the site of the present dambo. Subsequently, as the river regraded its valley by downcutting to form the gorge, the area of the dambo was drained and dissection began. This is proceeding today. It is evidenced by the outcrop of sheet laterite on the sides of the drainage channels cutting through the dambo. The dissection has given the dambo a slightly undulating surface which is reflected in its vegetation. Unlike most dambos this is not pure grassland. Grasses occupy the wet, low-lying areas and the areas underlain by laterite, but the gentle slopes below the laterite outcrops and the slopes bordering the dambo have been invaded by bracken and by *Combretum* trees, while the Chifubwa and Solwezi rivers are paralleled by *mushitus* comprising typical forest species which are also found in the gorge section. Here it is clear that the drainage and dissection of the dambo is being accompanied by the invasion and replacement of grasses by bracken and trees, the forerunners of chipya and forest.

Within this framework wherein the overall distributions of savanna woodlands and grasslands are related to soils and drainage conditions that, in turn, are related to geomorphology, there are regional and local variations of species distribution that produce distinctive vegetation associations. In some cases these are related to regional or local climatic variations; elsewhere they are related to soils whose characteristics are directly attributable to the bedrock providing their parent material. In most areas the vegetation has been disturbed by cultural practices, notably seasonal burning and shifting cultivation on the very long-term land rotation characteristic of the Chitamene system (see Trapnell 1953, Trapnell and Clothier 1957) whereby the trees are lopped to breast height, the foliage burnt and garden agriculture practised for three to seven years, after which the land is abandoned and regenerates to woodland for varying periods of thirty to sixty years before the process is repeated. Trees are also cut for house construction, for firewood and, especially on the Copperbelt, for making charcoal. These cultural practices, however, while disturbing the vegetation, appear not to have altered its fundamental character and composition which is related to physical environmental factors.

The influence of regional climatic variations is manifest in the gradual change from the lower growing open savanna woodlands with relatively few tree species in the drier cooler southern plateau to the tall woodlands with many more tree species, including some with forest affinities, in the wetter north.

Individual tree species tolerate or favour particular soil types. *Uapaca*, *Monotes*, *Protea* and *Faurea* spp. tolerate the poorest soils where indurated laterite is at or near surface or nodular laterite is abundant, and hence occupy the oldest planation surfaces. *Brachystegia boehmii* is found mainly on shallow, light textured, sandy or stony soils derived from granite, gneiss or quartzite parent material. *B. spiciformis* occupies deep loams derived from limestone and occurs particularly where dissection at the periphery of the plateaux has removed the lateritic layer, exposed bedrock and promoted good drainage and active soil formation. *Julbernardia paniculata* ranges over intermediate soil types while *B. floribunda* is characteristic of heavy, poorly drained clays around dambos and over gabbro bedrock (Figure 8.8). One of these species sometimes dominates the vegetation over large areas; elsewhere, as between Ngoma and Kalomo, zones related to the soil catena and dominated in turn by *B. boehmii*, *J. paniculata* and *B. spiciformis* are repeated from plateau summit to valley bottom in regular succession (see also Webster 1965). On the Copperbelt, where dissection has removed most of the lateritic material and soils have formed from weathered bedrock, the individual species combine in vegetation associations whose form and composition reflects the underlying geology (see Horscroft 1961).

On the Copperbelt the grey to pale brown sandy clays developed from granite and granite gneiss of the Basement Complex support a woodland of *Julbernardia paniculata*, *Brachystegia boehmii*, *B. utilis* and *Marquesia macroura* which are stunted and sparsely distributed where the soils are shallow and laterite or quartz rubble rovers the surface, but are taller and denser where the soils are deeper. Characteristically, the trees occur in clusters along joints in the bedrock. In places almost pure stands of *Marquesia macroura* are found. Similarly stunted woodlands in which *B. longifolia* is also present occupy the thinner, sandy loam and clay loams developed on Basement schists but taller woodlands with bamboo thickets occur over deeper soils. Treeless ridges mark outcrops of Muva quartzite but the deep white sands weathered from this bedrock on the slopes below support moderately tall *J. paniculata–B. longifolia* woodland.

Marked differences of vegetation distinguish the individual units of the Precambrian Katanga System. Tall, open woodland with canopy trees of *Julbernardia paniculata, Brachystegia longifolia, B. spiciformis, Isoberlinia tomentosa, Afzelia quanzensis* and *Afrormosia angolensis* attaining a height of 13.5–17 m and an understorey of *Uapaca nitida, Monotes* and *Syzygium* spp. occupy the sandy loams derived from the arkose, felspathic quartzite and quartzite of the Lower Roan Series. A *Llandorphia* creeper delineates the horizon in the Lower Roan sequence that hosts the important copper ores while treeless 'copper clearings' or 'blind dambos' occupied by *Becium homblei* and a *Cryptosepalum* sp. distinguish areas of copper-toxic ground over suboutcropping cupriferous bedrock and over seepage zones receiving drainage that has circulated over mineralized bedrock.

Similar tall woodlands occupy the deep red brown loams developed over the dolomites of the Upper Roan Series and the younger Kakontwe limestone and dolomite of the Kundelunga series of rocks. These have an upper canopy of *Brachystegia spiciformis, Julbernardia paniculata* and *B. longifolia* trees attaining heights of 17–27 m and an undercanopy of smaller *Pterocarpus angolensis, Afzelia quanzensis, Afrormosia angolensis* and *Albizia antunesiana* trees. In places the undergrowth is dense and thicket-like, with bamboos, vines, *Pteridium aquilinum*, an *Afromomum* sp. and the thorny creeper *Smilax kraussiana*. More open tall woodlands of *Brachystegia floribunda*, accompanied by *Julbernardia paniculata, B. spiciformis* and *B. longifolia*, distinguish red clay soils developed over gabbro. By contrast a stunted scrub-like growth of *J. paniculata* and *Uapaca kirkiana* with scattered *Marquesia macroura* trees scarcely attaining 5–10 m occupies the shallow yellowish clays over the Mwashia and Kundelunga shales (Figure 8.9). The stunted nature of this vegetation is partly due to the presence of indurated laterite; this outcrops in places and provides evidence that, over the less resistant rocks where the deeper profiles developed, current dissection has not yet removed all the relict lateritic soil material.

The grasslands of the Kafue Flats and Busango plains

Grasslands cover the margalitic black clay soils formed from alluvium on the Busango plains and Kafue Flats, respectively lying upstream of the Meshi Teshi and Kafue gorges along the Kafue river. The soils are base rich (pH 6.2–9.0) and have a layer of calcareous nodules below the dark grey subsoil. Their propensity alternately to swell and become highly plastic when wet, and contract, become extremely hard and develop deep cracks through the profile in dry weather, makes them inimical to tree growth. The alluvial plains were formed when the Kafue river exposed the resistant granites of the Basement Complex north of Meshi Teshi and east of Kafue during the

Figure 8.9. *Julbernardia paniculata* and *Uapaca kirkiana* scrub on yellowish clays derived from Kundulungu shale, between Kalalushi and Kitwe, Zambia. (From Cole 1965, with permission of Bedford College.)

Figure 8.10. Successional sequence of grass communities being grazed by buffalo on the Busango plains along the Kafue river. (From Cole 1965, with permission of Bedford College.)

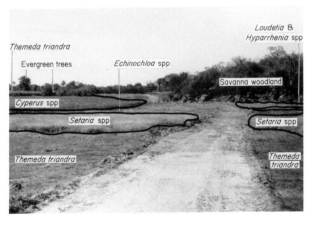

Figure 8.11. Hydrosere around an old loop of Lufupa river above outcropping granite (Kopje, right) south of Moshi camp, Kafue National Park. From Cole (1963a).

superimposition from a Karoo cover onto the older rocks below. Local base levels were created and the river flow arrested. No longer able to carry its sediment load with its flow diminished, deposition occurred upstream thereby creating the flats. Deposition occurred also along the tributary valleys and possibly extended over into the valley of the Machili which is tributary to the Zambezi. Subsequently increased dissection following continental uplift and the regrading of the river, achieved by cutting the gorges, brought about the staged lowering of the water table on the Kafue Flats and the Busango plains. The effects of this are seen in soil and vegetation zonations in both areas.

On the Busango plains the difference in elevation between the centre and edge of the plain is slight – less than one metre per mile – but clearly defined steps mark the junctions between the zone of lagoons and perennially wet grassland (of *Vossia cuspidata*, Oryza barthii and *Echinochloa* spp.) and that of seasonally dry grassland (of *Setaria, Themeda, Loudetia* and *Hyparrhenia* spp.) and between the latter and the woodland zone (Figures 8.10 and 8.12). The steps mark the stages in the uplift of the land and subsequent draining of the flood plain. At an earlier stage the seasonally wet grassland zone was occupied by the grasses of the perennially wet grassland zone. The grassland zonation is comparable with the hydroseral zonation on an old arm of the Lufuba river south of Moshi camp (Figure 8.11). On the Busango plain the grassland on the higher side of the anthill zone is studded with *Acacia, Combretum* and *Terminalia* trees which represent

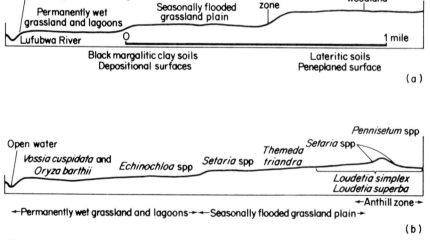

Figure 8.12 (a) and (b). Diagrammatic profile across the Busanga plain. From Cole (1963a).

invaders in the next stage in the seral succession. This stage is represented on a large-scale between Chunga and Kafwala where *Diospyros acida*, *Piliostigma* and *Bauhinia* spp. are also present in the grassland dominated by *Hyparrhenia* spp., notably *H. filipendula*. Both here and near Moshi and again at the edge of the Busango plain the change from these grassland associations to *Brachystegia–Isoberlinia–Julbernardia* woodland is abrupt, being coincident with the change from black clay soils to lateritic plateau soils. The vegetation of the termite mounds has a special significance. Due to the termite activity the soils of the mounds are better drained and more fertile, notably containing more calcium, than those surrounding them. Hence they became occupied by the vegetation of a higher successional stage. Near the Lufuba and Kafue rivers north of Chunga they carry *Diospyros mesmiliformis*, *Syzygium* spp., *Garcinia* spp. and other trees with forest affinities. In some cases the trees occur only on the southwestern side of the anthills, their establishment on the northeast side being discouraged by fires, fanned by northeasterly winds, that sweep over the plains in the dry season (Figure 8.13). It is clear, however, that the anthills function as the forerunners of vegetation change carrying evergreen tropical forest into the grassland, and not as the last bastions of forest vegetation. Further evidence of forest extension occurs along the valleys cutting back from the Kafue and the Lufubu for they likewise carry forest into the grassland zone.

The vegetation zonations on the Kafue Flats and adjacent areas follow a similar pattern. The grasses, however, are different, *Setaria*, *Chloris* and *Panicum* spp. being more important in the seasonally flooded area. As on the Busango plains two distinct steps are present. These, moreover, can be traced up the valleys of tributaries draining the Mazabuka–Monze area and indeed as far south as the Choma district, where two alluvial terraces are invariably present.

The *Acacia–Combretum* and *Combretum–Afrormosia* grasslands which parallel the Kafue Flats (see Figure 8.1(a)) and extend southwards to Pemba and northwards towards Lusaka occur on brown and red-brown loams, designated Upper Valley soils by Trapnell and derived largely from limestones of the Katanga system (Figure 8.14). Around Lusaka, however, the same limestone, where planed as the mid-Tertiary or Miocene surface, is covered by infertile soils with a near surface laterite horizon and carries either poor grassland studded with *Diplorhynchus* shrubs or a scrubby *Brachystegia boehmii* woodland. The Upper Valley soils characterizing the area between this pediplain and the Kafue valley have, in fact, developed under the current cycle of dissection which, initiated by uplift and responsible for the drainage of the Kafue Flats, is destroying the old surface and producing undulating terrain. The superior drainage and the better texture and higher fertility of the soils produced where there is a healthy balance between soil erosion and

Figure 8.13. Anthill vegetation near Moshi camp, Kafue National Park. The sides with a northeasterly exposure carry only grassland; those on the southwest, evergreen trees. From Cole (1963a).

Figure 8.14. *Acacia–Combretum-Terminalia* grassland on red-brown loams of dissected limestone country, Mount Makulu, south of Lusaka, Zambia. Left, *Terminalia sericea*, centre *T. mollis*: grassland dominated by *Hyparrhenia* spp. with lighter tone patch of *Heteropogon contortus* over a low termite mound in foreground. From Cole (1963a).

Figure 8.15. Clumps of *Colophospermum mopane* over termite mounds within *Acacia–Combretum-Piliostigma* spp.-studded *Hyparrhenia* spp. grassland in Machili-Nanzila area between Ngomo and Kaloma, Zambia. From Cole (1963a).

soil formation, permit the establishment of the *Acacia, Combretum* and *Afrormosia* trees. These naturally spread upslope from the valleys which provide the avenues for vegetational change. In this light the so-called bush encroachment, i.e. invasion of grassland by tree species, mainly thorny *Acacias*, which creates problems for cattle ranching, is seen to be a perfectly natural phenomenon which is most easily controlled by throwing back the succession by the judicious use of fire.

Both the Busango plains and Kafue Flats are grazed by wild game. Buffalo favour the wettest areas of the former; puku and lechwee graze alongside cattle in the latter. They appear not to influence the vegetation other than to maintain its stability.

The *Baikaea* forests and mopani woodland of the Livingstone–Mulobezi–Machili river area

Although the *Baikiaea* forests have been much reduced by timber cutting, it seems clear that their distribution is virtually coincident with the distribution of Kalahari Sand, whose moisture retaining capacity enables soils to remain moist to within a few feet of the surface even in late September or October. Mopani woodlands occupy the alkaline black clay soils derived from Karoo basalts and shale but black margalitic clays formed from alluvium carry either pure grassland or grassland studded with *Acacia* trees.

In the Livingstone–Muobezi–Machili river area a mosaic of all these vegetation types faithfully reflects the geomorphological picture. Most of the Kalahari Sand cover has been stripped from the area, and along the Machili and Nanzhila rivers there is evidence of the removal of the alluvium laid down at the same time as that of the Kafue Flats. This was probably never thick as the 'alluviation' feathered out in this area. In places the underlying Karoo rocks have been exposed. Where a thin cover of Kalahari Sand remains there are patches of thicket similar to that associated with the *Baikiaea* forests and possibly representing their last vestiges. Near the Nanzhila river there are stretches of grassland (of *Loudetia, Panicum* and *Hyparrhenia* spp.) with scattered *Acacia* trees (mainly *A. sieberiana*), *Combretum imberbe* and *Piliostigma thongii* trees. In some areas this is studded with clumps of *Colophospermum mopane* trees and in places this species, together with baobab trees, *Adansonia digitata, Capparis* and *Euphorbia* spp. occupy huge termite mounds (Figure 8.15). Here the *Colophospermum mopane* appears to be extending its range, coming in to occupy the alkaline black clays derived from Karoo rocks as the alluvial cover with its associated dark brown loams is removed. Where a thin alluvial cover remains the termite mounds, composed of material that includes that derived from weathered Karoo rocks brought up from depth by the termites,

Figure 8.16. Elements of three vegetation types on the lower slope of an Archaean ridge in the Gwembe valley near Chipepo, Zambia: *Brachystegia boehmii* of the *Brachystegia-Julbernardia* woodlands, *Colophospermum mopane* of the mopani woodland and *Pterocarpus angolensis* of the *Baikiaea* forest and *Combretum-Commiphora-Pterocarpus* thicket. From Cole (1963a).

constitute drier and more alkaline sites within the alluvial plain. This accounts for their distinctive vegetation which heralds the course of vegetational change. Indeed, the termite mounds act as the instigators of vegetation change by carrying mopani woodland into the *Acacia–Combretum–Piliostigma* grassland zone.

The vegetation of the Gwembe valley and the escarpment hill country

Perhaps the most interesting relationships between vegetational distributions and geomorphology are to be found in the Gwembe valley and on the bordering escarpment hill country. Here the bevelled surfaces of the escarpment hills with their thin stony soils derived from Archaean rocks carry a poor woodland of *Brachystegia allenii* or of *B. boehmii* and *Isoberlinia globiflora* with some *Uapaca* spp. This vegetation extends down the upper slopes but is replaced at lower levels by an open growth of *Kirkia* and *Sterculia* spp., with thorny shrubs and an occasional baobab (*Adansonia digitata*). The low-lying, hot, arid Gwembe valley is, for the most part, covered with mopani woodland (Figure 8.4) which alone thrives on the alkaline black and grey clays derived from Karoo basalts and shales. Here and there, however, on brown sandy soils derived from Karoo sandstone, there are thickets of *Commiphora* and *Combretum* spp., with an occasional *Pterocarus angolensis*, while the alluvium bordering the river carries thicket with tall *Acacia* trees. Ribbons of evergreen forest with *Trichelia emetica* and *Khaya nyasica* follow the rivers, extending up the tributaries into the mopani veld. Within the valley, ridges of Archaean rock protruding through the Karoo cover, as near Chipepo and Kariba, carry a poor growth of *Brachystegia boehmii* and *Isoberlinia globiflora*.

The patches of thickets are relicts of a former more widespread vegetation which may have included *Baikiaea plurijuga* and certainly included the species usually associated with it — *Pterocarpus angolensis*. Being found on soils derived from Kalahari Sand or Karoo sandstone, the latter occurring between the shales and basalt in the Karoo succession, this vegetation has retreated in some areas but extended elsewhere as the stripping of the post-Karoo and Karoo rocks has progressed. Near the Kariba dam, where the shales are exposed, it has retreated before the extension of mopani woodland. Upstream, however, where active stripping of the basalt is exposing the underlying sandstone, the thicket is gaining at the expense of the mopani woodland. Near Chipepo and Kariba, where erosion has completely removed the Karoo cover and exposed the rocks of the Archaean basement, both types of vegetation are receding in face of advancing *Brachystegia–Isoberlinia* woodland. Figure 8.16 shows the elements of all three types in close proximity on the slope of an exhumed ridge near Chipepo. The vegetation of the Gwembe valley is thus in a state of flux and the soils in a stage of instability, as remarked upon by Trapnell. Throughout the valley forest is extending as headward erosion proceeds up the tributary streams rising on the escarpment. By introducing a new base level of erosion and by creating a lake promoting increased precipitation on the escarpment hills, the construction of the Kariba dam has created conditions favourable for the initiation of further vegetational changes which as yet cannot be measured.

The forest relicts, *Marquesia* woodlands and chipyas on the southern side of the Lake Bangweulu depression

The area extending southwards from the Lake Bangweulu depression towards Mkushi and Mpika and eastwards towards Kasama is one of considerable vegetational interest. The very slightly undulating country above flood level

Figure 8.17. View westwards between Mpika and Shiwa Ngandu, Zambia, showing evergreen tropical forest along the valley, a pure stand of *Brachystegia tamarindoides* on the hilltop and *Brachystegia-Julbernardia* woodland on the end-Tertiary peneplain which forms the horizon. From Cole (1963a).

Figure 8.18. *Brachystegia-Isoberlinia* savanna woodland on the level plateau surface near Ilonga, Tanzania, with forest covering the top of the granite hill in the background.

extending around the lake is characterized by humic loams and chipya vegetation, which contrast sharply with the pallid sandy ironstone soils and scrubby *Brachystegia-Julbernardia* woodlands of the plateau to the south. The humic loams are derived from lake–basin deposits which accumulated on that part of the end-Tertiary peneplain which was downwarped in Pleistocene times. Evidence for this is provided by the occurrence of concretionary ironstone overlying bedrock below the lake–basin deposits. The humic loams, produced in a current dissection cycle which ensures a healthy balance between soil formation and soil removal, is capable of supporting forest trees. Today, however, they are characterized by high grass, mostly *Hyparrhenia* spp., and bracken with scattered *Pterocarpus angolensis*, *Erythrophloeum africanum*, *Parinari mobola*, *Burkea africanum* etc., constituting chipya. *Marquesia* woodlands occupy the low-lying belts adjacent to the valleys. The flood plains of the larger rivers carry grassland similar to that along the Kafue river, but ribbons of evergreen forest — mushitus — adjoin the rivers. These features, along with the tendency towards the formation of evergreen thickets with *Brachystegia taxifolia*, *Syzygium guineense*, *Entandrophragma delevoyi* and other forest trees together with creepers and lianas, south of Kasama, and the presence of so-called relict patches of evergreen forest in the valley heads along the ridges northeast of Mpika (Figure 8.17), have led to the belief that much of the area now covered with chipya formerly carried evergreen forest which has been destroyed by clearing and burning. In places this may well be so, but certain features of the distribution of soils and vegetation suggests a close relationship with geomorphology. Here the correlation of small outlying patches of evergreen forest and chipya with small patches of lake–basin type soils in the area between Mkushi and Mpika, is significant. Likewise the fact that *Marquesia* woodlands are confined to the lower ground adjacent to valleys whereas chipyas extend over the gentle rises. There is much evidence to suggest that the Pleistocene warping was followed by deposition over a wider area than that now characterized by lake–basin type soils. In particular, it probably occurred up the valleys as far as the areas where patches of humic loams, chipyas and evergreen forests occur in the Mkushi and Mpika areas today. Subsequent dissection has removed all but these vestiges which may therefore be regarded as relicts, but relicts due primarily to physical influences rather than man's interference. Within the main area of lake–basin soils, however, the sequence from the moisture-loving communities of *Syzygium* spp., on the ill-drained areas adjacent to the flood plains of the rivers, through the *Marquesia* woodlands and evergreen thickets of the lower slopes of the chipyas of the higher slopes, suggest a natural advance of the forests. In places, by burning and clearing, man has retarded or reversed this trend and thrown forest back to chipya, but the natural trend remains.

The Chambezi valley exhibits certain features which are comparable with those seen along the Kafue river. There is evidence of the stripping of the younger geological formations and the superimposition of the Chambezi river on to the older rocks below; where resistant rocks have been encountered, local base levels have been created and alluviation has occurred on their upstream side. The Bweli plains above the falls on the Chambezi south of

Kasama are believed to have originated in this way. They exhibit a vegetation zonation comparable with that on the Busanga plains.

Throughout this section of northeastern Zambia the current geomorphological cycle appears to be one of dissection as distinct from pediplanation. Here it is significant that the soils at the edge of the plateau and at the junction of the Bangweulu depression lack the lateritic horizon characteristic of the plateau soils and, according to analyses made in connection with the Central African Rail Link Development Survey, have a better texture and higher fertility level. As dissection proceeds into the pediplaned plateau surface the area with these soils should increase and evergreen forests may advance at the expense of the *Brachystegia* woodlands.

Conclusions

Studies of the vegetation mosaics in the above areas, selected to embrace the main categories of savanna vegetation, demonstrate close broad-scale relationships between the vegetation, soils and geomorphology of Zambia. In turn the evolution of the landscape has been influenced by geological events and climatic changes. Where dissection has exposed bedrock, both the form and composition of the vegetation and the characteristics of the soils are closely related to geology.

Since Jurassic times processes of drainage superimposition from a Karoo cover on to ancient rocks below and of pediplanation have dominated the geomorphological evolution of Zambia. In turn, these processes have been conditioned by periodic continental uplift and warping. As the landscape has slowly evolved, the various vegetation communities have gradually developed until the present picture, representing but one stage in a sequence subject to perpetual change, has been achieved. Clearly the form and composition of the vegetation is related to individual physiographic units where particular habitats prevail. The composition of the vegetation is also related to the opportunities for colonization accorded by physiographic history. Here the distribution of species of *Pterocarpus* and *Combretum*, of *Terminalia sericea*, *Burkea africana* and *Colophospermum mopane* are of particular interest and significance. Whereas the *Brachystegia*, Isoberlinia and *Julbernardia* species form the core components of the savanna woodlands to which their distribution is restricted, the other genera cited above have peripheral distributions and occur also, in some cases more characteristically, in the low tree and shrub savannas outside Zambia.

The spread of *Pterocarpus* species appears to have been limited by opportunities for colonization where suitable soils exist along valley levees so that today each species displays discontinuous distributions associated with the lighter, more fertile, loamy soils in the Zambezi valley and, beyond Zambia, along the Limpopo valley and in the Transvaal Lowveld. *Combretum* species are more widely spread but are limited to the drier sites like the margins of the Busanga plains. The genus is more characteristic of the low tree and shrub savannas where the distribution of individual species is related to soil type and bedrock geology as revealed by detailed studies in Botswana and the Transvaal Lowveld (Chapters 9–11). *Terminalia sericea* and *Burkea africana* both exhibit discontinuous distributions. Both favour sandy soils, notably in Barotseland and the latter also around the periphery of dambos elsewhere in Zambia. Stands of small *Terminalia sericea* trees are common on deep sands within the low tree and shrub savanna in Botswana and in the western part of the Transvaal Bushveld. In Zambia *Burkea africana* occurs mainly in Barotseland where it either dominates the vegetation or with *Terminalia sericea* forms mixed woodlands that have replaced the *Baikiaea* forests destroyed by fire and/or cultivation. Both *T. sericea* and *B. africana*, which in Zambia form tall trees, may be regarded as elements of the savanna woodlands and their discontinuous distributions, with numerous outliers in Zimbabwe, Botswana, South West Africa/Namibia and South Africa, indicate contractions of distribution caused by changing environmental conditions, notably those imposed by the creation of the trough-faulted valleys of the Zambezi and Limpopo and by drier climatic conditions.

By contrast, *Colophospermum mopane* is an aggressive species for which the creation of the down-faulted, semi-arid valleys with highly alkaline soils developed over Karoo sediments and lavas provided opportunities for colonization and extension, so that today the species dominates the vegetation in the Zambezi, Kafue and Luangwa valleys in Zambia, parts of the Transvaal Lowveld and the Limpopo valley in South Africa and is actively extending its range in Botswana.

Several important conclusions may be drawn from studies of the relationships between the distributions of the present vegetation types and the geomorphology in Zambia. The first is the coincidence of the *Brachystegia–Isoberlinia–Julbernardia* woodlands with the old pediplains characterized by poor drainage and 'dead' soils with a lateritic ironpan. These pediplains appear to have carried savanna woodland throughout historic times. Secondly, the evergreen forests, *Marquesia* woodlands and chipyas are restricted to dissected areas where the drainage is good and the soils constantly renewed; even before disturbance by man they were probably not much more widespread than at present. Thirdly, the *Baikiaea* forests are associated with moisture-holding Kalahari Sands and have shrunk as this cover has been stripped. Fourthly, the grasslands of the Kafue Flats, Busango plains and Bweli plains are related to soil and drainage conditions that are associated with areas of former deposition upstream of local base levels created during drainage superimposition. Fifthly, the *Colophospermum mopane* woodlands occupy the black alkaline clays derived from Karoo basalts and shales in the hot, arid Zambezi and Luangwa valleys.

Current trends vary between one region and another. At present there is an overall tendency for the extension of the tropical evergreen forests from the Congo and from Mozambique, proceeding up the valleys and along the escarpment. In the Zambezi valley, and most probably in that of the Luangwa too, the mopani woodlands are extending in some places but elsewhere are receding. On the plateau the *Brachystegia* woodlands are retreating where dissection is proceeding, but in the Zambezi valley they are coming in where the Archaean rocks are being exposed. On the open grassland areas tree invasion or bush encroachment appears as a natural accompaniment to current dissection. On dambos and other extensive valley grasslands, zonations corresponding to seral changes provide information on current trends. Within the grasslands, termite mounds may function as the vehicles of vegetational changes, as for example in carrying evergreen tropical forest trees into the Busango grassland plain and mopani clumps into the grasslands along the Machili–Nanzhila valley, or as the last bastions of a formerly more widespread vegetation.

Finally, the dynamic nature of vegetation, soils and geomorphology must be stressed. The picture is one of perpetual change with in some areas erosion, in others deposition, in some plant associations retreating, others advancing. Man cannot alter these natural phenomena although he may retard or accelerate them. Fire and shifting cultivation have been cited as agents whereby former forests have been destroyed and replaced by savanna woodlands. Experiments on fire protection in *Brachystegia* woodland near Ndola, however, have indicated that fire protection has brought little change in the canopy vegetation, notwithstanding the fact that the chosen site was a sloping one at the periphery of the plateau where dissection is currently active. The *Brachystegia–Isoberlinia–Julbernardia* woodlands that in Zambia constitute the typical savanna woodlands appear to represent the optimum vegetation on the poor soils of the pediplaned plateau surface. The associated grasslands and parklands are likewise related to specific environmental conditions that are subject to perpetual change.

THE SAVANNA WOODLANDS, SAVANNA GRASSLANDS, AND LOW TREE AND SHRUB SAVANNAS OF EAST AFRICA

Over Tanzania and the adjacent parts of Uganda and Kenya the distribution of the various categories of savanna vegetation display similar relationships with environmental factors to those in Zambia. The geologically recent tectonic events that have produced the great rift valleys and the associated volcanic activity that has created high mountains like Kilimanjaro, Kenya and Meru, however, have introduced a greater variety of landforms that is reflected in a more chequered pattern of vegetation distribution. The remnants of the peneplaned plateaux, horst blocks and trough valleys, affected to varying degrees by the present erosion cycle, are characterized by differing forms of savanna, whereas the cloud-covered escarpments and volcanic mountains, mantled by fertile soils, favour forest.

Savanna woodlands of _Brachystegia, Isoberlinia_ and _Julbernardia_ spp. cover or formerly covered the greater part of northwestern and southeastern Tanzania where the annual rainfall exceeds 760 mm distributed over the six to eight warmer months of the year (Figure 8.18).

The savanna woodlands are interrupted by a broad zone of savanna grasslands, parklands, low tree and shrub savannas and thickets variously described as grassland, wooded grasslands, bushlands and thickets (Gillman 1949) that stretch from the Kenya border across northern and central Tanzania, tapering towards Lake Malawi in the south. They occupy the central rift valley zone where the rainfall is less than 760 mm and falls below 500 mm in places.

To the west of the central rift valley zone the savanna woodlands occupy the level central plateau planed across Archaean Basement rocks, mainly granite gneiss and characterized by grey to yellow-brown soils with a layer of ferruginous concretions locally called murrum, near the surface. To the east of the central rift valley zone the savanna woodlands cover a series of high blocks that trend southsoutheastwards from Mounts Meru and Kilimanjaro towards Tanga and thence southwestwards towards the north end of Lake Malawi. Eastwards the savanna woodlands give way to evergreen forests where the high ground is bounded by steep scarp slopes that precipitate moisture brought by the onshore trade winds. From the foot of the escarpment slopes, however, almost to the coast in southeastern Tanzania, _Brachystegia_ savanna woodlands cover the plateau cut across rocks of Archaean, Palaeozoic and Mesozoic age.

Depending on rainfall, relief and edaphic conditions the vegetation of the central rift valley zone varies from grasslands and _Acacia_ parkland to low tree and shrub savanna and thicket. Around Dodoma the change from _Brachystegia_ woodland on the higher plateau surface to drier types of vegetation on the lower surface is abrupt. Grasslands studded with small _Acacia_ trees alternate with thickets of _Combretum_ and _Euphorbia_ spp. or of _Commiphora_ spp. Baobab trees (_Adansonia digitata_) are common on the lighter loam soils (Figures 8.19 and 8.20) and _Sterculia_ sp. trees occupy hillslopes including those of the hills encircling the Kongwa basin. In the northeast the _Acacia_ grasslands of Masai land verge on steppe while around Lakes Natron and Eyas the savannas give way to semi-desert.

Figure 8.19. Low tree and shrub savanna with *Acacia* spp. and the occasional baobab, *Adansonia digitata*, between Dodoma and Tabora, Tanzania.

Figure 8.20. Low tree and shrub savanna dominated by *Acacia* species west of Kongwa, Tanzania.

Figure 8.21. Savanna parkland on the better drained sites at the margin of the black soil plain between Morogoro and Ilonga, Tanzania.

Savanna grasslands occupy the heavy black clay soils formed from alluvium along all the major river valleys. They give way to *Acacia* parklands on better drained sites (Figure 8.21).

Between the escarpment slopes that bound the high blocks of the eastern part of the plateau and the outliers of the Mahenge and Uluguru mountains, savanna grasslands and *Acacia* parklands occupy the alluvial soils of the tectonic depressions of the Kilombero and Wami valleys. Here vegetation distributions are influenced mainly by drainage with countless small swamps surrounded in turn by grasslands and parklands on the higher, better drained sites.

The Rukwa valley, which lies at an altitude of about 800 m in the rift valley in southwestern Tanzania, is banded by steep scarps rising to 1600 m and is characterized by internal drainage into Lake Rukwa, the savanna grasslands display zonal patterns that are related to edaphic conditions. The zones vary seasonally with periods of above or below average rainfall and with associated fluctuations in the level of the lake (Dean 1967). On the more elevated ground where the poorly drained, sandy colluvial/illuvial soils are often flooded or waterlogged during rains but dry out rapidly in the dry season, the grasslands are dominated by *Hyparrhenia rufa* and *Chloris gayana*. By contrast the flood plain grasslands that occupy the illuvial soils of drainage lines and depressions and are flooded initially by rains and later by overflow from rivers, are dominated by *Echinochloa pyramidalis* associated with *Cyperus longus*, but they may display mosaics with *Cynodon dactylon* and *Vossia cuspidata* grasses, *Typha* sp. and *Sesbania* sp. bushes. Along the lakeshore where the grasslands are affected by the rise and fall of the lake, the grasslands show four parallel zones that are respectively dominated by *Cynodon dactylon*, *Sporobolus robustus*, *Diplachne fusca* and *S. spicatus*. In dry years the *Hyparrhenia rufa–Chloris gayana* grasslands contract, those of *Cynodon dactylon* occupy larger areas within the flood plain grassland zone, and those of *Sporobolus spicatus* extend onto the dry margins of the lake bed. By contrast, in wet years, part of the lakeshore grassland zone is submerged, and the *Echinochloa pyramidalis–Cyperus longus–Cynodon dactylon* mosaics extend into the zone of the *Hyparrhenia rufa–Chloris gayana* grasslands which are constricted. These fluctuations in the distribution of the grassland communities may be compared with those occurring in the Okavango inland delta in northwestern Botswana (Chaper 11). There drainage diversions associated with movement along rift valley faults as well as variations of rainfall may be responsible for long-term vegetational change and the possibility of such influences on changes in the grassland communities of this tectonically active area of Tanzania merit investigation.

Northwards into Uganda and Kenya the distribution of savanna vegetation is governed by influences similar to those in Tanzania. Higher and more evenly distributed rainfall, consequent on lower latitudes, favours forest rather than savanna in Uganda, while in both territories the great contrasts of relief and altitude and the greater complexity of landform associated with the maximum development of the rift valley system are responsible for more complex distributions of both vegetation types and plant communities (see Lind and Morrison 1974).

In East Africa the impact of man's cultural practices on the vegetation has been greatest in areas of former forest and savanna parkland where, respectively, the rainfall is most reliable and the soils most fertile. Cultivation is widespread in the former and sporadic in the latter. The main concentrations of population are along the railway lines and major roads and much of the intervening country is thinly peopled. Domestic stock graze the savanna grasslands, parklands and low tree and shrub savannas while large herds of wild game occupy the national parks, notably the Serengeti. Because of the prevalence of tse-tse fly the *Brachystegia* woodlands of Tanzania have been unattractive for settlement and large areas on the central and southeastern plateaux contain few people and the vegetation has been little disturbed.

Overall, within given climatic limits, the distributions of the various categories of savanna in East Africa are influenced by edaphic conditions that in turn are related to geomorphology and geology. In contrast to the savannas of other parts of Africa and of South America and Australia, tectonic influences and volcanic activity associated with the great rift valley system have played an important role and have resulted in more chequered vegetational patterns in its vicinity. Over large areas the impact of man's cultural practices on the savannas has been slight for population has concentrated in the more favourable forested areas. Within the savannas sporadic cultivation and the grazing of domestic stock and wild game appear not to have fundamentally changed the vegetation.

THE SAVANNA WOODLANDS AND ASSOCIATED SAVANNA PARKLANDS AND GRASSLANDS OF ZIMBABWE

South of the Zambezi trough the savanna woodlands and associated savanna types display marked contrasts with those of the core area in Zambia. Only four species of *Brachystegia* and one of *Julbernardia* occur in Zimbabwe. Both genera are absent south of the Limpopo trough where *Burkea africana–Terminalia sericea* woodlands on plateau sites in the Transvaal Plateau Basin of South Africa represent outliers of depauperate savanna woodland.

The floral impoverishment in the peripheral areas of savanna woodland distributions in southern Africa (and again in West Africa, Chapter 12) is comparable with that in northern South America but the distributional patterns and the nature of the barriers between core areas and outliers is different.

In central southern Africa the formation of the trough valleys of the Zambezi and Limpopo during and following the break-up of Gondwanaland created hot arid zones separating the better watered plateaux on either side. These arid zones isolated the vegetation communities of the plateaux and imposed barriers to later plant migrations between them.

The contrasts between the savanna woodlands and associated savanna types south of the Zambezi and those of Zambia stem from the isolation caused by the formation of the Zambezi trough. Over the higher parts of the plateaux in Zimbabwe and South Africa they result partly from the lower temperatures associated with higher latitude, while elsewhere they are related to the more advanced dissection of the African planation surface and consequent closer relationships between vegetation, soils and bedrock geology. These relationships were recognized by Henkel (1931) and acknowledged by Boughey (1961) in their accounts of the vegetation of Zimbabwe and are evident in detailed studies of smaller areas (Crook 1956, Wild 1953, 1955, Cole 1971b).

The physical environment

Zimbabwe comprises a central eastnortheast–westsouthwest trending spine of plateau country regarded as Highveld, flanked on either side by lower dissected terrain with ranges of hills and clusters of inselberge forming the Middleveld that descends to the trough valleys of the Zambezi, Limpopo and Sabi, regarded as Lowveld. The plateau, at an elevation of 1350 m with an offshoot rising to over 2700 m in the Inyanga mountains in the Great Escarpment, forms part of the African planation surface (Figure 8.22) on which lateritic soils are preserved whereas the dissected terrain of between 1350 and 700 m elevation is the expression of erosion in post-African cycles that have exposed bedrock. The trough valleys, lying below 700 m and descending to 200 m where the Limpopo leaves Zimbabwe, represent lower planation surfaces fashioned in the Victoria Falls and later cycles.

Most of Zimbabwe is underlain by granite gneiss and older metamorphic rocks of the Archaean Basement Complex, but younger Precambrian rocks underlie the area around Karoi and later sediments and lavas of Karoo age cover large areas in the west and in the Zambezi, Limpopo and Sabi valleys. An outlier of Karoo rocks south of Harare (Salisbury) bears witness to their former more extensive cover. In the far west Tertiary and Recent sediments,

Figure 8.22. Savanna grassland over the level plateau planed across Archaean granite gneiss which outcrops in inselberge in the background. East of Rusape, Zimbabwe.

Figure 8.23. Open savanna parkland giving way to savanna grassland on soils with toxic levels of chromium and nickel (note chrome mines) over the Great Dyke which forms the prominent range in the background, between Gwelo and Banket, Zimbabwe.

Figure 8.24. Laterite outcropping in the bed of the Hunyani river, Zimbabwe

largely Kalahari Sand, mantle large areas. An outstanding feature of the geology is the Great Dyke that, composed of norite, pyroxenite and serpentinite of the same age as the Bushveld Igneous Complex in South Africa, intrudes the older rocks and for most of its outcrop forms a prominent ridge extending for some 530 km from southsouthwest to northnortheast across the centre of this country (Figure 8.23).

Over the older planation surfaces of Tertiary age, the soils in places show evidence of lateritization; indurated laterite outcrops to the east of Harare, conglomeratic laterite occurs at the foot of the Great Dyke between Gwelo and Banket and ground water laterite outcrops in stream beds, notably that of the Hunyani river below the Ironstone range west of Salisbury (Figure 8.24). Elsewhere soil type is closely related to bedrock geology, with red clays over greenstone schists and dolerite, buff coloured gritty sands over granite, red or white sands over Karoo sandstone and Kalahari Sand, and dark brown loams and black clays over basalt and alluvium. Over the dissected terrain soil catenas follow the relief profiles.

Climate varies with altitude and latitude. The mean annual temperature averages 20°C over the Highveld plateau, decreases to 18°C at Inyanga and increases to 24°C in the Zambezi trough and to 22°C in the Limpopo and Sabi valleys. Ground forests occur on the High and Middleveld from May to September and in the former may be severe, particularly in vleis and frost hollows. The annual rainfall is generally lower than in Zimbabwe, averaging 750–1000 mm over the plateau, decreasing westwards and dropping to less than 750 mm in the trough valleys of the Zambezi, Limpopo and Sabi.

The relationships between the distributions of savanna vegetation types and the physical environment

In broad outline *Brachystegia–Julbernardia* savanna woodlands occupy the plateaux above 1350 m that represent relicts of the African planation surface but give way below this altitude to *Burkea–Terminalia* woodlands over sandy soils and to *Acacia* parklands on heavier soils. *Baikiaea* forests occupy the areas of Kalahari Sand in the west and *Colophospermum mopane* woodlands and *Acacia* dominated thickets occupy the low-lying valleys.

Regional and local distributions are more complex. Repetitive sequences of vegetation associations led Boughey (1961) to recognize a series of regional vegetation/soil/relief catenas which are characteristic of large areas and to acknowledge variants within them caused by climatic and/or edaphic conditions. Overall however, as in Australia, the variations of relief and soils are related to the advanced dissection of the old planation surfaces which in some areas have exposed bedrock and resulted in direct relationships

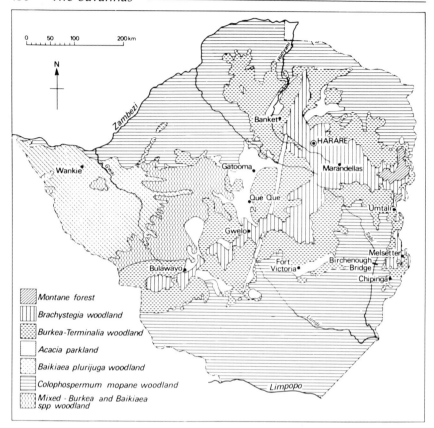

Figure 8.25. Distribution of vegetation types, Zimbabwe (a) after Henkel (1931); (b) after Boughey (1961).

between soils and geology to which plant species have responded to produce distinctive vegetation associations.

Savanna woodlands of *Brachystegia spiciformis*, associated with *Julbernardia globiflora* and, on poorer soils with *Faurea speciosa*, *Parinari curatellifolia*, *Terminalia* and *Combretum* spp., are characteristic of the Highveld plateau surface between 1580 and 2170 m extending from Harare and Mazoe in the west, to Melsetter and Inyanga in the east (Figure 8.25a and b). The woodlands reach an optimum development in the Marandellas area which, at an elevation of about 1800 m, receive an annual rainfall of about 1143 cm. At lower elevations they give way to *Brachystegia boehmii* woodlands while at higher elevations, in response to lower temperatures, *B. spiciformis* and *J. globiflora* trees become dwarfed, attaining heights of only 2–3.5 m (Figure 8.26). At high levels near the contact of the savanna

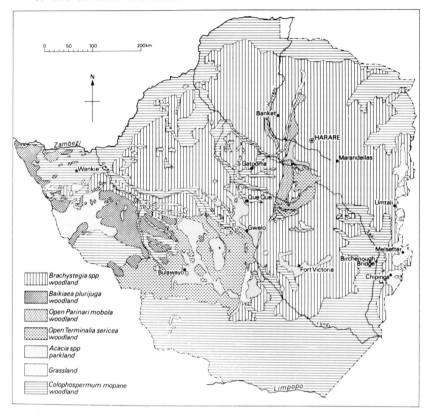

Figure 8.25b.

woodlands and the montane forest zone in the Inyanga area the dwarf
Brachystegia spiciformis woodland is intermixed with communities of tree
heathers, *Phillipia* spp. (Figure 8.27). Variants of the *Brachystegia spiciformis*
catena type occur in the warmer, drier western parts of the plateau where,
below 1700 m in the Mazoe valley, *B. tamarindoides* occurs in the upper part
of the catena and gives way to *B. boehmii* below. Further variants of the
catena occur as a result of variations of soil type related to exposed bedrock.

In the warmer, drier areas northwest and southwest of Harare the
Brachystegia spiciformis catena type gives way to one of *B. boehmii* at
elevations between 1500 and 1580 m. Upwards this extends along valleys into
the *B. spiciformis* catena sequence, while downwards it yields to woodlands
of *Burkea africana* and *Terminalia sericea* on sandy soils and to parkland
of *Acacia* spp. trees on heavy soils (Figures 8.28 and 8.29). In the upper part

Figure 8.26. Dwarf *Brachystegia spiciformis* woodland at high elevations near Inyanga, Zimbabwe.

Figure 8.27. Dwarf *Brachystegia spiciformis* (msasa) yielding to Cape heath vegetation (right foreground), Inyanga area, Zimbabwe.

Figure 8.28. *Acacia* parkland on heavy soils on the plain between the Ironstone ranges west of Harare, Zimbabwe.

Figure 8.29. Open savanna woodland of *Terminalia sericea, Faurea saligna* and *Protea* spp. trees on sandy soils near Bulawayo, Zimbabwe. Matopo hills in background.

Figure 8.30. Open savanna woodland of *Brachystegia boehmii* (left centre) *Combretum* spp. (right centre), *Uapaca kirkiana* (left) and *Protea* spp. over outcropping norite on the Great Dyke, Zimbabwe.

Figure 8.31. Woodland of *Brachystegia tamarindoides* (top right) and *Diplorhynchus condylocarpum* (centre and left) with *Cussonia* spp. (below) over outcropping norite and pyroxenite on the Great Dyke between Gwelo and Banket, Zimbabwe.

of the *Brachystegia boehmii* catena a woodland of *B. tamarindoides* may be present, as in the *B. spiciformis* catena, but more typically a woodland of *Julbernardia globiflora* is found. Where the latter extends onto the steep escarpment slopes of the Zambezi valley, as in Zambia, it is mixed with or gives way to woodland of *B. allenii* and *Sterculia* spp.

The areas of sandy soils between 1000 and 1350 m in Matabeleland, notably around and to the southwest of Bulawayo, are characterized by a *Burkea africana–Terminalia sericea* open savanna woodland catena type. In the central sections of the catena most trees are of these species but *Monotes glaber, Peltophorum africanum, Ochna pulchra, Diplorhynchus condylocarpum* subsp. *mossambicensis* and *Zizyphus mucronata* also occur. This vegetation covers large areas but is interrupted by *Acacia* parkland on heavy soils. On the lower sections of the catena where the terrain is flat and the valleys are subject to seasonal waterlogging *Colophospermum mopane* woodland prevails. Here the mopane trees colonize termitaria which form drier sites; they exhibit a regular cycle of colonization, establishment and degradation that is related to termite activity. The higher, better drained margins of the valleys carry *Acacia* parkland. As in the *Brachystegia boehmii* catena, *Julbernardia* woodland occupies the upper part of the *Burkea–Terminalia* catena.

An *Acacia* catena type has been recognized as occupying the heavier soils over virtually the same geographical and topographical area as the *Burkea africana–Terminalia sericea* catena in the Bulawayo region. *A. sieberiana, A. karoo* and *A. gerrardii* form a savanna parkland on the better drained soils in the lower parts of the catena. This yields to *Colophospermum mopane* woodland in low-lying seasonally waterlogged areas and to *Isoberlinia globiflora* woodland in the highest sections of the catena.

A *Baikiaea plurijuga* catena type occurs over Kalahari Sand in the west and southwest of Zimbabwe where, at an altitude of 1000–1300 m, it forms a continuation of the *Baikaiaea* forests found on Kalahari Sand in Botswana and in Barotseland, Zambia. In Harare the emergent *Baikiaea plurijuga* trees have an understorey of *Pterocarpus antunesii* and *Dalbergia melanoxylon* while *Burkea africana, Guibourtia coleosperma, Terminalia sericea, Erythrophloeum africanum, P. angolensis, Ochna pulchra, Acacia giraffae* and *Combretum* and *Commiphora* spp. may also be present. The lower part of the catena on Kalahari Sand is occupied by *Acacia* communities, notably *A. giraffae* and *A. galpinii*, which likewise favour areas of deep sand in South West Africa/Namibia, but low-lying areas of impeded drainage carry *Colophospermum mopane* woodland. On the upper sections of the *Baikaiaea* catena communities with *Combretum* spp., *Diplorhynchus condylocarpon* subsp. *mossambicensis* and on hillslopes, *Guibourtia coleosperma* and *Pterocarpus antunesii* are found.

A *Colophospermum mopane* catena type occupies areas not mantled by Kalahari Sand below 1000–1370 m, and is characteristic of the flatter areas of the dry Sabi, Limpopo and Zambezi valleys that receive between 250 and 650 mm rainfall annually (see Figure 2.8). The form of the vegetation varies from woodland with a continuous canopy of *Colophospermum mopane* trees in the Zambezi valley to open woodland in which the *mopane* is intermixed with *Terminalia prunioides* and *Acacia nigrescens* trees, species of *Combretum* (especially *C. apiculatum*), *Boscia* (especially *B. albitrunca*) and *Grewia* spp. shrubs in the drier areas. The upper part of the catena, stretching over broken country from the Zambezi valley to the central plateau, is occupied by *Piliostigma–Combretum* communities with, over sloping ground in the wettest catena variant, *Afzelia cuanensis*, *Kirkia* and *Sterculia* spp. trees. On the alluvial terraces in the lower part of the catena, as in the Zambezi valley, dry deciduous woodland or forest is characteristic (see p. 143). *Piliostigma* spp. are absent from the drier Sabi and Limpopo valleys where *Commiphora* spp., *Combretum* spp., *Mundulea sericea*, *Croton gratissimus*, with colonies of *Kirkia acuminata* on hilltops, occupy the upper part of the catena. Variants of the *Colophospermum mopane* catena that are related to bedrock geology exposed during the geomorphological evolution of the landscape, occur in the Zambezi and Sabi valleys where *Brachystegia tamarindoides* woodland occupies rocky ridges at altitudes of 500–830 m and *Julbernardia globiflora* woodlands cover granite ridges and kopjes above 800 m (compare with Zambezi valley of Zambia, pp. 142–143).

The vegetation catena types recognized by Boughey are comparable with the vegetation types recognized by Trapnell in Zambia. Their distributions are related to both climatic and edaphic conditions. The complex distributions of both discrete vegetation types and of vegetation associations that promoted the recognition of catenary types in Zimbabwe result primarily from the more advanced stages of dissection of planation surfaces, the removal of relict lateritic materials and exposure of bedrock in that country.

Where lateritic soils remain on the relicts of the Miocene African surface, as around Marandellas, typical savanna woodlands characterized by *Brachystegia spiciformis* and *Julbernardia globiflora* trees prevail. Partly as a result of distance from the core area of savanna woodland distribution, and partly as a result of lower temperatures consequent on higher latitude, the savanna woodlands of Zimbabwe contain fewer tree species than those of Zambia. The effect of lower temperature is particularly evident in the dwarfing of the *B. spiciformis* and *J. globiflora* in the Inyanga area where active dissection is promoting the advance of forest up the kloofs leaving relict patches of savanna woodland on the plateau spurs.

Savanna grasslands have not been recognized as a distinctive vegetation catena type in Zimbabwe but rather as a degraded form of vegetation created by man's cultural practices. However, over the central plateau some grasslands, notably those of the Gwebi, Norton and Nyabira Flats, appear to be related to edaphic conditions inimical to trees. Here the grasslands occupy the level surfaces with impeded drainage over granite bedrock. Along drainage lines where the water table is near surface *Parinari* spp. trees are common. The prevalence of these trees in such areas led Henkel to recognize a *Parinari* veld type, whereas Boughey considered their presence to be related to survival from clearing for cultivation. Relationships between their distribution and the water table level, however, is evident from sections in old quarries near Harare.

Features of the catenary sequences recognized by Boughey are the interdigitation of the communities between the catena types and the variants within them occasioned by soil variations due to bedrock geology. As in Zambia the *Baikiae plurijuga* woodlands are restricted to areas of Kalahari Sand, *Burkea africana–Terminalia sericea* woodlands and *Brachystegia boehmii* woodlands favour sandy soils. These two latter types occur at elevations below the *B. spiciformis–J. globiflora* woodlands of the highveld plateau surface in areas where dissection has exposed the Old Granite bedrock (Figure 8.29). By contrast *Acacia* parklands occupy heavier soils including those derived from basalt in the Mazoe valley. The role of geomorphology, however, is most evident in the hot, dry Zambezi and Sabi valleys where, as in Zambia, the removal of Karoo sediments and exposure of the Archaean Basement rocks has created rocky ridges and kopjes on which stands of *B. tamarindoides* and *J. globiflora*, elements typical of the savanna woodlands of the plateaux, form islands within the *Colophospermum mopane* woodlands characteristic of the valleys.

Striking across Zimbabwe in a northnortheasterly direction, the multiple ridge feature of the Great Dyke is characterized by soils that are bedrock dependent and support distinctive forms of vegetation (Figures 8.23, 8.30 and 8.31). About 70% of the outcrops is serpentinite whose high magnesium:calcium ratio and large amounts of nickel and chromium result in soils that are unfavourable or even toxic for many species. Trees are generally absent and the grassland vegetation is poor, comprising mainly *Loudetia simplex* and *Andropogon gayanus*, with, on stony sites and highly toxic sites, endemic species of *Aloe*, *Euphorbia*, *Rhus*, *Barleria* and other genera and the nickel indicator plant *Dicoma niccolifera*. On less toxic sites the grassland changes to a small tree and shrub savanna of *Diplorhynchus condylocarpum*, *Faurea speciosa* and *Protea* spp. that are tolerant of poor soils. In contrast to the areas of outcropping serpentinite, those of outcropping norite and pyroxenite which have high levels of calcium support *Brachystegia–Julbernardia* woodland in which *B. tamarindoides* is locally prominent. Indeed the distributions of savanna woodlands and grasslands faithfully reflect the changes of bedrock within the Great Dyke.

9 The savanna parklands and associated savanna types of southern Africa

Savanna parklands occupy much smaller areas than savanna woodlands in Africa, largely because they occupy the lower and warmer areas of the less extensively developed younger planation surfaces. They occur mainly in the Transvaal Plateau Basin of South Africa and in the Lowveld which, lying to the east of the Great Escarpment, extends through Swaziland and the eastern Transvaal into eastern Zimbabwe. In these areas they are associated with other forms of savanna, whose distributions are related to edaphic conditions and landscape evolution.

THE SAVANNA PARKLANDS AND ASSOCIATED SAVANNA WOODLANDS, SAVANNA GRASSLANDS AND LOW TREE AND SHRUB SAVANNAS OF THE TRANSVAAL PLATEAU BASIN OF SOUTH AFRICA

Savanna parklands, savanna grasslands and depauperate savanna woodlands separately characterize the distinctive subregions within the major physiographic region of the Transvaal Plateau Basin in South Africa. Their distribution and those of the vegetation associations and plant communities within them are related to climatic and edaphic conditions that in turn are related to the interplay of geological events and geomorphological processes over a long period of time during which the region has been subject also to major climatic changes.

The physical background

The Transvaal Plateau Basin comprises the Bushveld Basin, a surrounding girdle of ridges and valleys termed the Bankenveld, and, to the north, the

Palala (or Waterberg), Soutpansberg and Pietersburg plateaux (Figure 9.1). The first is a remarkably level basin, underlain by norite and granite of the Bushveld Igneous Complex, a great lopolith emplaced between the sedimentaries of the Pretoria Series of the Proterozoic Transvaal System as base and the Rooiberg felsites at the top of the system as roof (Figure 9.2; see also Figure 7.3). The Bankenveld comprises a series of ridges and valleys respectively developed over resistant quartzites and more readily weathered shales and diabases of the Pretoria Series which together with the underlying Dolomite and Black Reef Series of the Transvaal System were dragged down and tilted inwards at steep angles towards the centre of the Bushveld Basin as the great intrusion subsided. The Palala and Soutpansberg plateaux are level uplands developed over nearly horizontal Palaeozoic Waterberg sandstones and the Pietersburg plateau is a peneplain cut across the Archaean Old Granite.

Savanna vegetation covers the whole of the Transvaal Plateau Basin. Savanna parkland is the characteristic form over most of the Bushveld Basin. There microphyllous thorny *Acacia* trees stud a sweet grassland where dark brown loams characterize the drier lower terrain underlain by norite or basalt or alluvium (Figure 9.3). The parkland vegetation, however, gives way to low depauperate forms of savanna woodland with broad leaved semi-deciduous or deciduous trees on higher ground with acid soils and to savanna grassland where impeded soil drainage is unfavourable for tree growth. Savanna parkland alternates with open low savanna woodland in the Bankenveld. Savanna woodlands occupy the Palala (Waterberg) and Soutpansberg plateaux but grasslands similar to those of the Highveld characterize the Pietersburg plateau.

Within each category of savanna, the vegetation varies both in form and composition in response to the interplay of current micro-climatic and edaphic factors that are directly related to relief and to superficial and bedrock geology whose deposition or exposure respectively are the results of geological events and geomorphological processes operating over a very long period. The composition and the present distribution of the savanna categories and of the distinctive associations within them are related to climatic changes and geomorphological processes since the Tertiary. Changes in species composition and distribution have occurred as the climate has fluctuated between cool humid and warm dry periods, particularly during the Pleistocene and post-Pleistocene, and as the landscape has been fashioned by the processes associated with drainage superimposition from the surface developed over horizontally disposed Karoo rocks (of Permian to Liassic age) onto the steeply inclined and lithologically varied rocks of the Proterozoic Transvaal System and the intrusive rocks of the Bushveld Igneous Complex.

The drainage pattern provides a key to the geomorphological evolution

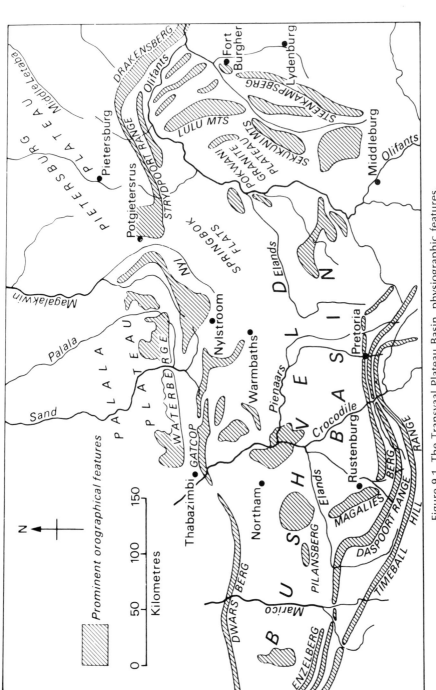

Figure 9.1. The Transvaal Plateau Basin, physiographic features.

of the landscape. The whole of the Transvaal Plateau Basin is drained by streams flowing to the Limpopo. The trunk rivers rise on the Highveld, enter the Bushveld Basin via narrow gorges cut through the southern Bankenveld, maintain with difficulty their flow across the central basin which they leave in further gorges through the northern Bankenveld rim, and finally trench the northern plateau to reach the Limpopo. Clearly this drainage pattern bears little relationship to the present surface features or to the underlying geology.

Geological evidence suggests that early Palaeozoic Loskop and Waterberg Sandstones once covered the central Bushveld Basin linking the present outcrops in the northern plateaux with those south of Loskop dam, but that they were removed in Middle Palaeozoic times and the norite and granite thereby exposed (Cole 1961). These were scraped and polished by ice movement during the Carboniferous Dwyka glacial period and then from Permian to Liassic times much of the area was buried beneath Karoo sediments and lavas which produced a fairly uniform surface sloping gently to the north and east. Geomorphological evidence suggests that the present drainage was initiated on this surface with rivers in the west and centre of the present Bushveld draining northwards and those in the east flowing northeastwards and eastwards to the Limpopo.

Palaeobotanical evidence indicates that by the late Cretaceous a fairly uniform rain forest grading from subtropical in the north to temperate in the south and containing members of the Proteaceae family—possibly the first angiosperms (Plumstead 1962, 1966)—covered the Karoo surface. The present Bushveld area occupied a central position within this area so that its vegetation was related to that further north over Zimbabwe and Zambia and that further south in South Africa.

The widespread faulting from late Jurassic to Cretaceous times, which heralded the break-up of the supercontinent of Gondwanaland, brought into being the Limpopo trough and opened the Mozambique channel, initiated geomorphological processes of fundamental significance for the vegetation. Accelerated erosion stripped the Karoo cover from much of the area and the rivers became superimposed onto the ancient rocks below. This process

---

Figure 9.2. *(opposite)*. The Transvaal Plateau Basin, geology and drainage. 1. Superficial deposits of Tertiary to Recent age. 2. Rocks of the Karoo System; mainly lavas and sandstones of Stormberg age on the Springbok Flats; shales and coal measures in the Waterberg coalfield. 3. Alkaline eruptive rocks of the Pilansberg. 4. Sandstones etc. of the Waterberg System. 5. Red Granite of the Bushveld Igneous Complex. 6. Norite of the Bushveld Igneous Complex. 7. Felsites and granophyres of the Rooiberg Series forming the 'roof' to the Bushveld Igneous Complex. 8. Rocks of the Transvaal System forming the 'floor' to the Bushveld Igneous Complex. 9. The Old Granite and rocks of the Primitive Systems. 10. Iron ore horizons. 11. Chrome ore horizons. 12 Merensky reef. (Geology after the Union Geological Survey.) (From Cole 1961.)

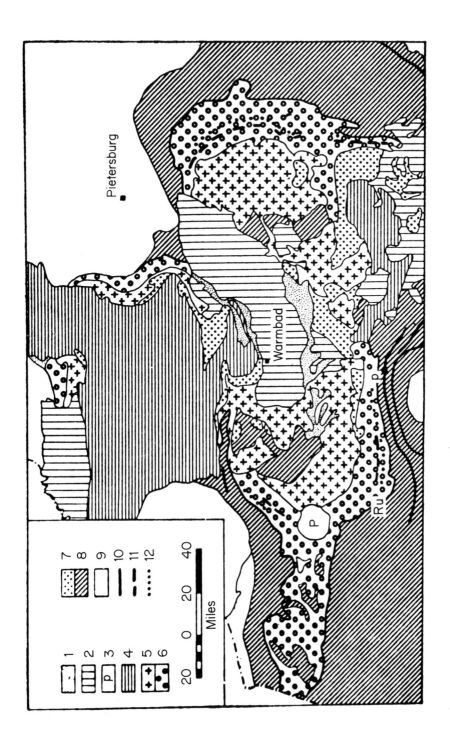

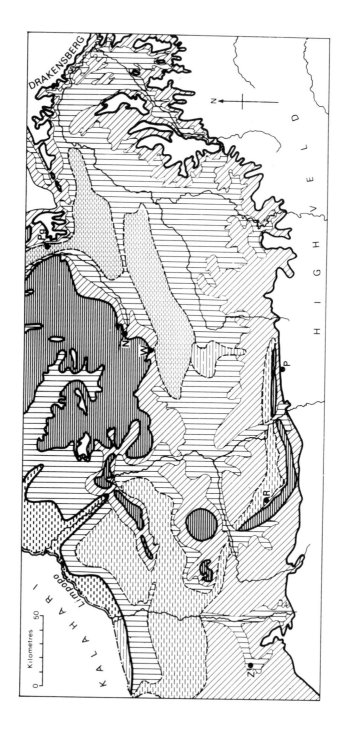

Figure 9.3. The vegetation of the Bushveld Basin and adjacent regions (after Acocks 1975). (See opposite for key.)

Savanna vegetation of the Bushveld Basin and adjacent regions

Savanna category		Diagnostic species			Veld type (Acocks 1975)
		Trees	Shrubs	Grasses	
Savanna woodland	(black vertical stripes)	Faurea saligna, Protea caffra, Combretum spp., Diplorhynchus mossambicencis, Pseudolachnostylis maprouneifolia, Burkea africana	Ochna pulchra	Schizachyrium semiberbe, Loudetia simplex, Hyparrhenia dissoluta, Trachypogon capensis; Heteropogon contortus	Sour bushveld (20)
Savanna woodland/savanna parkland mosaic	(horizontal lines)	Combretum apiculatum, Terminalia sericea, Burkea africana, Sclerocarya caffra, Acacia nigrescens, A. caffra	Woodland } Parkland	Heteropogon contortus, Aristida spp., Eragrostis spp.; Themeda triandra, Cymbopogon plurinodis	Mixed bushveld (18)
Savanna parkland	(diagonal hatch)	Acacia caffra, Acacia spp.		Cymbopogon plurinodis, Themeda triandra	Sourish mixed bushveld (19)
Savanna parkland	(dense vertical hatch)	Acacia spp.		Themeda triandra, Cymbopogon plurinodis	Springbok Flats turf thornveld (12)
Savanna parkland	(dotted)	Acacia spp.	Acacia spp.	Themeda triandra, Cymbopogon plurinodis	Other turf thornveld (13)
Low tree and shrub savanna	(dotted)	Acacia giraffae, Acacia spp., Boscia albitrunca, Terminalia sericeae (dwarf), Combretum apiculatum (dwarf)	Grewia flava, Rhigozum spp.	Eragrostis pallens, Schmidtia bulbosa, Stipagrostis uniplumis, Aristida spp.	Arid sweet bushveld (14)
Low tree and shrub savanna	(cross-hatch)	Acacia giraffae, Acacia spp.	Tarchonanthus camphoratus, Grewia flava	Eragrostis superba, Cymbopogon plurinodis, Themeda triandra	Kalahari thornveld (16)
Other types of vegetation	(blank)				

was affected by the Tertiary Miocene warpings which arched the Witwatersrand and Soutpansberg and by the persistent sagging of the Bushveld Basin. The Olifants and Crocodile rivers were able to maintain their courses through the axes of uplift but across the central subsiding area the flow of some of the smaller streams was reversed and that of the Nyl barely maintained. Along the latter alluviation led to the development of Nylsvlei. As drainage superimposition proceeded, the agents of weathering and erosion exhumed ancient landscapes in some areas and cut extensive planation surfaces across others, thereby producing the distinct subregions of the present Transvaal Plateau Basin.

As new landscapes evolved the form and composition of the vegetation changed as conditions became less suitable for formerly widespread species but more favourable for others which either advanced from adjacent areas or evolved to occupy new niches. The formation of the Limpopo trough and its rapid lowering by planation processes following the opening of the Mozambique channel, effectively disrupted vegetational links with areas farther north by interposing a belt of hot arid country. The formation of the parallel ridges and valleys of the Bankenveld by differential erosion following the stripping of the Karoo cover gave protection from cold southerly and moist easterly influences to the Bushveld Basin where planation in King's post-African cycle opened vegetational contact with the Kalahari. Within the Basin, however, relicts of post-Gondwana and African surfaces coinciding with areas of resistant rocks and acid soils remain and carry depauperate savanna woodlands related to an earlier vegetation.

Against this background of landscape evolution an understanding of the broad-scale distributions of the savanna types within the Transvaal Plateau Basin may be attempted.

Comparison of Figures 9.1, 9.2 and 9.3 shows that, notwithstanding the influence of increasing aridity towards the northwest, the distribution of the vegetation types is closely related to soils, relief and geology.

The vegetation described as thornveld by Acocks (1975) coincides with the microphyllous thorny woodland of van der Meulen (1979) and the arid savanna of Huntley (1982). It belongs to the mungu ecological element within the Zambezian phytogeographical Domain of White (1965). Its characteristic physiognomy is that of savanna parkland (Cole 1961, 1963b) which grades into savanna grassland where conditions are unfavourable for tree growth. The vegetation described as mixed bushveld by Acocks coincides with the mesophyllous woodland of van der Meulen, and moist and mesic broad leaf savannas of Huntley (1982). It is related to the miombo ecological element of White and both physiognomically and floristically constitutes depauperate savanna woodland. Within each of these savanna categories a number of discrete vegetation associations and plant communities occur.

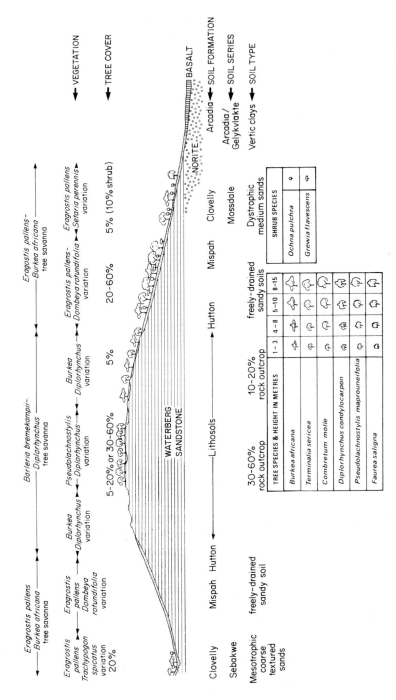

Figure 9.4. Section showing the relationships between vegetation, relief, soils and geology in the Nylsvlei area. (Original section based on information in Coetzee *et al.* 1976, with permission of the Republic of South Africa Dept of Agriculture and Water Supply.)

Apart from alluvial soils and skeletal lithosols on outcropping bedrock the soils comprise either ferruginous lateritic or fersiallitic soils and vertic black clays. The former are usually freely drained, low in organic matter content, free of $CaCO_3$ accumulation and have a medium-acid to neutral pH. Kaolinite is the main clay mineral. Although these soils may occur over most rock types they have formed particularly over sandstones, quartzites and granite: they vary considerably with relief and bedrock type, tending to red or yellow sands and loams on the more siliceous bedrock and to red loams to clays on Pretoria Shales, diabase intrusions and Karoo shales. The vertic black clays typically occur over ultra mafic rocks, particularly norite. They have strong swelling and shrinking properties with wetting and drying of the main clay mineral montmorillonite, and develop deep vertic cracks when they dry out. They are self mulching and, where the land is flat, may develop linear, gilgai features. Their pH is neutral to moderately alkaline; $CaCo_3$ concretions are usually present and the organic matter content is sometimes high. Within these two major soil groups a number of soil forms and soil series have been recognized. Their relationship to geology and relief in the Nylsvlei area are shown in Figure 9.4.

The relief features, with which are associated micro-climatic variations of importance for the plant cover, are the result of differential weathering and erosion by geomorphological processes acting over the different rock types. The characteristic features differ in the distinctive physiographic subregions.

In broad outline the savanna parklands are characteristic of the dark brown loam soils developed over norite or basalt in the warm low-lying sections of the Bushveld Basin. Depauperate savanna woodlands occupy the acid lateritic or fersiallitic soils derived from quartzites, sandstones or granite of the Bankenveld, northern plateaux and the higer ground within the Bushveld Basin; and savanna grasslands occur where impeded drainage is inimical to tree growth. The detailed picture is more complicated and an understanding of the precise relationships between vegetation, soils, relief and geomorphology and geology requires closer study of each physiographic subregion.

The Bushveld Basin

The Bushveld Basin extends over 400 km from west to east and 130 km from north to south. It has an average elevation of 1000–1350 m and is floored mainly be norite or granite of the Bushveld Igneous Complex. The surface is monotonously flat having been planed in King's post-African cycle, but here and there residual hills of inselberg type occur. In the east the country is broken where rifting in the norite parallel to the dip of its floor has produced a series of homoclinal ridges, the most striking of which builds the Lulu mountains; these attain an average height of 1700 m and rise some 700 m above the surrounding country. Elsewhere, relics of the former cover of Waterberg sandstone, remnants of the Rooiberg roof of the lopolith, unconsumed rocks of the Transvaal system within the igneous mass, and the volcanic plug of the Pilansberg give rise to minor but nevertheless well marked relief features. In contrast, remains of the horizontally disposed Karoo rocks produce the exceptionally level area of the Springbok Flats.

Savanna parkland is the typical vegetation over most of the Bushveld Basin but it gives way to deciduous broad leaf savanna woodland over relict hills and plateaux, and over very sandy soils.

The savanna parklands characterized by microphyllous Acacia *trees*
The savanna parkland that characterizes the Bushveld Basin, composed of a continuous grass stratum studded with scattered *Acacia* trees, occupies the calcareous vertic black clay soils developed over norite and basalt rocks that sub-outcrop beneath the level surface of King's post-African planation cycle (Figure 9.5). On these soils *Acacia tortilis*, *A. nilotica* and *Zizyphus mucronata* trees and *Panicum maximum*, *Setaria woodii*, *Sehima galpinii*, *Ischaemum afrum* and *Aristida bipartita* grasses are characteristic. Over diabase dykes where the soils are slightly acid to neutral, trees are more frequent, with sometimes interlocking canopies, and in addition to those named above *Sclerocarya caffra* and *Spirostachys africana* are locally dominant differential species. Over ferro gabbro outcrops like those bordering the outcrop of the Bushveld granite northeast of the Pilansberg and between Rustenburg and Pretoria, *Acacia erubescens* is the characteristic tree and *Panicum maximum*, *Urochoa brachyura*, *Aristida congesta* and *Eragrostis lehmanniana* the most common grasses. On deeper soils the vegetation is less densee, *Acacia erubescens* is less abundant and *A. tortilis*, *A. nilotica* and *A. mellifera* are prominent. In the lowest and driest parts of the basin where red sandy soils, developed from Karoo rocks and Tertiary to Recent aeolian sands, are common, *Acacia leuderitzii* occurs with *A. tortilis*, *A. mellifera* and *Boscia albitrunca* trees and the shrub *Tarchonanthus camphoratus*, the vegetation thus displaying affinities with the low tree and shrub savannas of South West Africa/Namibia and western Botswana. Similar affinities are exhibited by the *Acacia erioloba–A. fleckii* parkland which occupies deep red sandy soils around Niedverdiend and Silikaatskop west of the Great Marico river. In places over deep sand there are stands of *Terminalia sericea* and *Combretum molle* trees.

On the Springbok Flats southeast of Nylstroom sharply contrasting vegetation associations occupy the contrasting soils developed over the individual formations of the Karoo System. Typical savanna parkland characterized by scattered *Acacia karoo*, *A. arabica* var. *Kraussiana* and

Figure 9.5. Low *Acacia* spp. savanna parkland occupying vertic black clay soils over norite bedrock in the Bushveld Basin.

Figure 9.6. Open *Acacia* spp. savanna parkland over vertic black clay soils near Rustenburg in the Bushveld Basin. Dumps of platinum mines in the background.

Figure 9.7. *Acacia nilotica* and *A. heteracantha* trees and *Cenchrus ciliaris* and *Eragrostis stipitata* grasses forming savanna parkland over dark brown loams over alluvium, Nylsvlei.

Zizyphus mucronata trees in a grassland dominated by *Sehima galpinii* and usually associated with *Ischaemum afrum*, and *Setaria woodii*, occupies the vertic black clay soils derived from Karoo basalt. In the lower lying places where the soils are particularly heavy and poorly drained the trees become infrequent and the vegetation grades to grassland (see Figures 9.6 and 9.7). On the red sandy soils derived from the Karoo sandstones which outcrop around the periphery of that of the Karoo basalt, the vegetation changes abruptly to an open mesophyllous woodland of *Terminalia sericea* and *Burkea africana* trees with a sparse grass cover.

Variants of the typical microphyllous/tree savanna occur on the bottom lands and dry river beds in the gently undulating terrain underlain by the Bushveld granite. Here the physiognomy and distribution of plant communities are related to a combination of drainage and soil characteristics. The red or greyish gravelly sands usually have a neutral to slightly alkaline reaction. Some soils, however, are very poorly drained and may be under water for periods during the rainy season; in places the A horizon may be completely eroded as a result of run-off. Usually these soils are both saline and alkaline with notably high levels of sodium and potassium. They support a closed parkland or open woodland of *Spirostachys africana*, *Acacia tortilis* and *A. nilotica* trees, *Carissa bispinosa* and *Euclea undulata* shrubs and *Sporobolus iocladus* var. *usitatus*, *Eragrostis pseudo-obtusa* and *Dactyloctenium aegypticum* grasses. Similar vegetation dominated by *Spirostachys africa* trees occupies the marshy borders of the Nyl river.

The depauperate savanna woodlands characterized by mesophyllous trees Within Bushveld Basin the savanna parkland characterized by microphyllous *Acacia* trees gives way to mesophyllous woodlands on upland areas that constitute relics of King's African surface that have not succumbed to planation in his later post-African cycle. Here outcropping or near surface bedrock generally gives rise to acid sandy soils. The physiognomy and composition of the woodlands vary with relief and with bedrock type.

Where outcropping rocks of the Transvaal System that were not consumed during the intrusion of the Bushveld Igneous Complex form prominent hills with thin, poorly developed soils, open woodlands of *Combretum apiculatum* trees characterize the quartzites, whereas stands of *Spirostachys africana* trees occur over dolomite. On norite kopjes where there is hardly any soil between the outcropping rocks and boulders *Dombeya rotundifolia*, *Zizyphus mucronata*, *Peltophorum africanum*, *Croton gratissimus*, *Sclerocarpa caffra* and *Ficus* spp. trees whose roots are able to penetrate the rocks occur. Grasses, notably *Setaria lindenbergiana* and *Chrysopogon serrrulatus* occupy pockets of soil and organic matter. On comparable granite kopjes *Croton gratissimus*,

Combretum apiculatum, Clerodendrum myricoides and *Mimusops zeyheri* trees occur in a similar way. In every case the woodland is open and low, nowhere attaining the stature or floristic diversity of the savanna woodlands of Central Africa. It occupies only relatively small areas.

The largest areas of deciduous, mesophyllous or broad leaf savanna woodlands within the Bushveld Basin occur in the Nylsvley Nature Reserve between and southeast of Nylstroom and Naboomspruit on the northwestern margin of the Springbok Flats. Beyond the basin larger areas occur over the Palala (or Waterberg) plateau.

At Nylsvlei the typical deciduous broad leaf savanna woodland is characterized by *Burkea africana* trees up to 15 m high, *Ochna pulchra* shrubs and *Eragrostis pallens* and *Digitaria* of *eriantha* grasses (Coetzee *et al.* 1976) (Figure 9.8). It occupies the uplands with yellow to red sandy soils of low nutrient status derived from the Waterberg sandstone. In physiognomy and floristic composition the vegetation shows affinities with the savanna woodlands of Zambia but it contains fewer species, the trees are of lower stature, and *Brachystegia*, *Isoberlinia* and *Julbernardia* species that are characteristic of the savanna woodlands throughout Central Africa are absent. The vegetation represents a form of depauperate savanna woodland.

The structure and composition of this depauperate savanna woodland varies with differences of soil and micro-climate from the upper to the lower slopes of the uplands (see Figure 9.4). Within the characteristic *Eragrostis pallens–Burkea africana* association, three variations, one with several subvariations, occur (Coetzee *et al.* 1976). The most extensive is the *Eragrostis pallens–Dombeya rotundifolia* variation which has *Burkea africana*, *Terminalia sericea* and *Combretum molle* as the dominant trees and *Ochna pulchra* and *Grewia flavescens* as the dominant shrubs. The trees account for 20–60% of the cover and the grass and forb layer for 15–65%. The community occupies the well-drained highly leached soils of the upper and middle slopes and is differentiated from other variations on less well-drained soils below by the relatively close spacing of trees and by the presence of several species notably *Combretum molle* and *Dombeya rotundifolia* not found on the lower sites. On the lower sandstone slopes the trees become more widely spaced, the total cover usually being less than 5% and *Faurea saligna* is scattered among the *Burkea africana* and *Terminalia sericea* trees. The grass layer covers 30–75% of the ground with *Eragrostis pallens* and *Setaria perennis* as the dominant species. The third variation occurs on better drained coarse textured soils in a valley west of Maroelakop. Here the tree cover may be up to 20%, with *Terminalia sericea* trees giving a greater cover than *Burkea africana* at heights above 3.5 m and *Eragrostis pallens* and *Trachypogon spicatus* dominating the grass layer.

Where bedrock outcrops on the gentle to moderately steep slopes of the

Figure 9.8. Depauperate savanna woodland of *Burkea africana* trees and *Ochna pulchra* shrubs over sandy ferrallitic soils derived from Waterberg sandstone, Nylsvlei area, Bushveld Basin.

Figure 9.9. *Croton gratissimus, Euphorbia ingens* and *Aloe marlothi* on outcropping granite and *Acacia* spp. parkland on lightly dissected terrain below, Pietersburg plateau.

Figure 9.10. Cut out of *Acacia caffra* savanna parkland over and around a nickel-copper pipe, Rooderand, Marico district of the Bushveld Basin.

summit areas of the sandstone uplands the broad leaved savanna woodlands, described as the *Barleria bremekampii–Diplorhynchus* tree savanna
association by Coetzee *et al.* (1976), is characterized by small *Diplorhynchus
condylocarpon* trees, 4–8 m high, and *Barleria bremekampii* shrubs. In one
variation, typical of Maroelakop where rock outcrops constitute 30–60% of
the surface, *Pseudolachnostylis maprounefolia* is a differential species. Here
trees make up 5–20% and shrubs up to 15% of the cover. In another variation
which occupies the transitional zone of gentler slopes with 10–20% rock
outcrop, between the rocky sandstone summits and the soil-covered upper
slopes, widely spaced *Burkea africana* and *Diplorhynchus* trees stud a
grassland dominated by *Loudetia flavida* and *Schizachrium jeffreysii*. Here
small trees, 4–6 m high, account for 5% or less of the cover whereas grasses
and forbs account for 50–60%. The relationships between these forms of
savanna woodland and environmental factors are shown in Figure 9.4.

Comparable forms of depauperate broad leaved savanna woodlands occur
on upland areas underlain by Rooiberg felsites forming the roof of the
Bushveld lopolith. These areas are of lower elevation than the Waterberg
sandstone uplands. Their relief is gently sloping to almost level and during
winter nights frosts occur, varying in intensity from mild on the upper slopes
to moderately severe on the lower ones. In response to variations in soil and
micro-climatic conditions the *Eragrostis racemosa–Schizachyrium jeffreysii*
tree savanna and grassland associations recognized by Coetzee *et al.* (1976)
grade from open savanna woodlands on the upper slopes where shallow well-
drained soils overlie weathering felsite, to savanna grasslands on deeper poorly
drained soils with mottled perched gley horizons and soft plinthic B horizons
on the lower ground where frost is a further factor inimical to tree growth.
In each case the species composition of the vegetation differs from that over
the Waterberg sandstone uplands but shows affinities with it whereas none
exist with the microphyllous thorn savanna of the adjacent flats.

On the upper slopes of the felsite uplands an open savanna woodland
association of *Eragrostis racemosa–Combretum apiculatum*, in which small
Combretum apiculatum trees 2–8 m high form about 20% of the cover, is
characteristic over the shallow well-drained soils. In places this species forms
dense tree stands with 60% cover. Its distribution has been associated with
soils of high iron content (Theron 1973), in this case derived from felsite.
In the extensive typical *Rhus leptodictya–Combretum apiculatum* variation
of this association the dominant trees are *Combretum apiculatum, Vitex
rehmannii, Combretum molle, Peltophorum africanum, Terminalia sericea*
and *Burkea africana*. One or more of a number of grass species—*Setaria
perennis, Loudetia flavida, Themeda triandra, Trachypogon spicatus,
Rhynchelytrum repens, Schizachyrium sanguineum, Elionurus argenteus*—
may dominate the field layer. In the *Cymbopogon plurinodis–Combretum*

apiculatum variation which is transitional to the *Eragrostis racemosa–Digitaria monodactyla* grassland on the frosty lower slopes with poorly drained soils, the widely scattered trees which make up less than 5% of the cover include *Acacia caffra*, a member of the microphyllous thorn savanna, as well as *Combretum apiculatum* and *Vitex rehmanii*. On the relatively frosty poorly drained areas which form a narrow fringe on the lower slopes of both the sandstone and felsite uplands, the *Eragrostis racemosa–Digitaria monodactyla* grassland association shows two variations, one a xeric short grassland dominated by *Elionurus argenteus* on the convex slopes where shallow gravelly soils are underlain by hard plinthite which impedes drainage in wet periods, and a mesic tall grassland dominated by *Tristachya rehmanii* and *Setaria perennis* on the deep non gravelly soils on the flat to gently concave slopes.

The Bankenveld

Within the Bankenveld the form and composition of the savanna vegetation varies with relief, altitude and aspect, with soils and bedrock geology.

Around the periphery of the Bushveld Basin the Bankenveld comprises a series of ridges and valleys that owe their present form to recent resurrection of an ancient landscape and to differential erosion in rocks of the Pretoria Series of the Transvaal System following the removal of a cover of Karoo rocks during the course of drainage superimposition. Except in the southeast where the Karoo cover is preserved and in the north where, to the west of Potgietersrust, a tongue of igneous rock extends northwards, the ridges and valleys form a virtually continuous girdle around the Bushveld Basin. They are most clearly defined and show the greatest altitudinal contrast in the southwest.

On the Karoo cover the terrain is level, the main drainage lines are northward and concordant with surface and structure. East of Delmas small rocky exposures of quartzite protruding through the Karoo cover mark the first stage of resurrection of an ancient landscape. Westwards the outcrops widen; then gradually east–west trending ridges and valleys become discernible; with increasing distance from the Karoo cover these become more clearly defined and more acute, with the resistant quartzite horizons forming the Magaliesberg, Daspoort and Timeball Hill ranges and the less resistant shales and diabases forming intervening vales. The Magaliesberg forms the most marked feature: it has an average elevation of 1700 m and reaches 2000 m near Rustenburg, nearly 1000 m above the general level of the Bushveld Basin. After a gap between the Elands and Marico river valleys, the line of the Magaliesberg is continued in the Enzelberg until the outcrop swings round the western end of the Bushveld Basin and assumes a northeasterly trend in the Dwarsberg and Gatkop ridge on the northern side of the basin. A wider girdle of ridges and valleys extends around the eastern side of the Bushveld Basin but apart from the Steenkampsberge (of Magaliesberg quartzite) and the Tokane mountains (of Daspoort quartzite) the quartzites of the Pretoria Series do not produce sharply defined ridges. More prominent are the norite ridges of the Lulu mountains and, to the east, the Great Escarpment built of Black Reef quartzite whose outcrop swings westwards to form the Strydpoort range which marks the northeastern limit of the Bushveld Basin.

Because the rocks of the Pretoria Series of the Transvaal System dip inwards towards the centre of the Bushveld Basin, the quartzite ridges present steep outward-facing escarpments at the periphery of the basin and gentle dip slopes towards its centre. The combinations of slope and aspect consequently change in the different sections of the Bankenveld. The quartzites form the dip slopes and the cliffs or free faces of the escarpments below which steep slopes that are variously concave or convex are cut in diabase and shales. The soils are generally dark reddish brown sands to sandy loams over quartzite. Over diabase and shale they are of similar colour but heavier texture, tending to sandy clay loams, depending on whether the slope is convex or concave.

The characteristic vegetation on the ranges of the Bankenveld is an open savanna in which *Acacia caffra* trees stud a grassland which is dominated by *Cymbopogon plurinodis* and *Themeda triandra* in the drier western areas, by the more wiry *Trachypogon capensis* and *Tristachya hispida* in the centre, and by very sour wiry grasses, notably *Tristachya hispida*, *Eragrostis chalcantha* and *Heteropogon contortus*, on loose sandy soils in the east.

Studies on the Magaliesberg (Coetzee 1975), however, have shown that the *Acacia caffra* woodlands favour the heavier soils characteristic of the concave slopes below the cliff faces of the escarpments and of the central sections of the dipslope and give way to *Protea caffra* woodlands on the drier convex slopes of the escarpment and to seasonal grasslands with stands of *Burkea africana*, *Combretum zeyheri*, *Protea caffra* and *Faurea saligna* trees and *Ochna pulchra* shrubs on the gravelly or stony brown to dark brown soils on the flatter northern dipslopes.

Floristically the vegetation of the Bankenveld displays three distinctive affinities. The *Acacia caffra* woodlands are related to the savanna parklands of the Bushveld Basin; the stands of *Burkea africana* trees and *Ochna pulchra* shrubs are related to the deciduous broad leaf savanna woodlands of the Nylsvlei area, and the Palala Plateau and the *Protea caffra* stands are related to *Protea*-studded grasslands of the Highveld and Middleveld and the sclerophyllous vegetation of the Cape. The vegetation appears to be in a state of tension and adjustment to the varied micro-climatic and edaphic conditions of a landscape in process of active geomorphological evolution.

The northern plateaux

Open forms of depauperate savanna woodlands characterized by deciduous broad leaf trees and tall wiry grasses occupy the acid sandy and often rubbly soils derived from quartzites, sandstones and shales of the Waterberg system that form the level Palala and Soutpansberg plateaux. By contrast grasslands cover the Pietersburg plateau which is an inselberg-studded peneplain cut across the Old Granite of the Archaean Basement.

On these northern plateaux contrasting vegetation reflects differing microclimatic and edaphic conditions related to differing landscape evolution and bedrock geology.

The Pietersburg plateau which has an average elevation of 1300 m, is believed to have been the source region for the material deposited in the Bushveld Basin and also the depression north of the Soutpansberg in Karoo times. For a very long period it experienced erosion which eventually exposed the Old Granite. The planation process, however, was not completed before uplift along the Soutpansberg axis and sagging in the Bushveld Basin initiated a new erosion cycle so that the unreduced hills of the older landscape remain as inselberge. The grassland vegetation of the plateau is related to its high elevation and exposed nature. These are comparable with those of the Highveld with which the Pietersburg plateau is geomorphologically related and which likewise has a grassland vegetation. Indeed the grassland vegetation of the Pietersburg plateau has affinities with the more temperate grassland of the Highveld, a legacy of the period when, prior to the differentiation of the Bankenveld, the Miocene African surface was continuous from the Highveld across to and over the Pietersburg plateau. Today some diversity of vegetation occurs around the inselberge and along the valleys cutting into the Pietersburg plateau in the current erosion cycle. Along the warmer and drier valleys (Figure 9.9) microphyllous *Acacia* trees, notably *A. hebeclada*, *A. tortilis* and *A. nilotica*, form a savanna parkland in which the candelabra *Euphorbia ingens* is also present. With current dissection of the landscape this vegetation is extending at the expense of the grassland. Around the foot of the granite inselberge small trees, notably *Maytenus senegalensis*, *Acacia karoo*, *A. gerrardii*, *Croton gratissimus*, *Schotia brachypetala* and *Carissa* spp. and the *Aloe marlothii* take advantage of the shelter and available moisture.

The vegetation of the Palala and Soutpansberg plateaux is similar to that over the Waterberg sandstone in the Nylsvlei reserve. On the deep red sand derived from quartzite, sandstone and granite on the lower slopes of the Waterberg plateau between the Matlabas and Mogol rivers the deciduous broad leaf savanna is dominated by *Burkea africana* and *Sclerocarya caffra*, associated usually with *Peltophorum africanum* and *Grewia flava* and less frequently with *Terminalia sericea, Ochna pulchra* and *Combretum apiculatum*; the most common grasses are *Eragrostis pallens, Loudetia simplex* and *Schmidtia bulbosa*. Further north where the soils are deep grey-brown sands derived from shales, sandstones and quartzites *Burkea africana* and *Combretum apiculatum* are the dominant trees, usually associated with *Sclerocarya caffra, Protea caffra* and *Ochna pulchra*; and a grass layer composed mainly of *Digitaria eriantha* var. *stolonifera, Aristida graciliflora,* and *Schmidtia bulbosa*. A similar vegetation occupies the higher ground of the Soutpansberg but *Acacia* parkland is found in the broad east–west vales between the ridges and a variety of trees follow the deep narrow gorges cut by the streams flowing to the Limpopo.

Factors influencing the vegetation distributions

The factors influencing vegetation distribution often interplay or are interdependent. This is clearly the case in the Transvaal Plateau Basin where the micro-climatic conditions are dependent on the stage of landscape evolution and the soils are related to superficial and bedrock geology whose deposition or exposure are in turn related to the stage in the geomorphological process. The vegetation is influenced by the interplay of all these factors, with the most important factor differing from area to area.

Vegetation distributions and climatic conditions   In the Transvaal Plateau Basin the current climatic conditions are closely related to physiography which in turn is the product of landscape evolution. Throughout the year temperatures are slightly higher in the Bushveld Basin than elsewhere but the differences are not appreciable and are negligible compared with the contrasts between the region as a whole and the Highveld to the south. The ridges of the Bankenveld effectively exclude cold from the south and below 1100 m severe frosts are rare. Mild frosts, however, are frequent in flat areas and frost, possibly combined with recurrent fire, is thought to be responsible for the very low savanna parkland which in exposed parts of the Bushveld Basin has the appearance of a grassland because the scattered *Acacia tortilis* (which elsewhere may grow to 10 m) reach only 1.5 m and do not rise above the grass stratum whose protection they appear to require. The distribution of the *Protea caffra* woodlands on those slopes of the Bankenveld with a southerly aspect is also considered to be influenced by lower temperatures than occur elsewhere.

Within the Transvaal Plateau Basin the rainfall decreases westwards and varies with altitude and aspect. Differences are not great and rainfall is not a determinant on the distribution of savanna parkland and depauperate savanna woodland. In the arid western part of the Bushveld Basin aridity may favour an extension of low tree and shrub savanna but edaphic factors related to landscape evolution are also important here.

The roles of fire and overgrazing Periodic burning and overgrazing of the vegetation have been common in the Transvaal Plateau Basin for well over a hundred years. In some areas they have clearly influenced the structure of the vegetation; periodic burning by encouraging grass growth, overgrazing by causing a deterioration in the grass cover favouring encroachment of shrubs and trees. Evidence of the latter is seen in dense thicket-like communities of *Acacia nilotica*, *A. mellifera* and *A. tortilis* attaining heights of only 1–3 m within the open savanna parkland of the Bushveld Basin. The influence of fire in combination with that of frost has been cited as a possible influence where open parkland takes on the appearance of grassland in flat exposed areas of the Bushveld Basin, notably on the Springbok Flats. Overall, however, the evidence indicates that fire and grazing activities have not fundamentally changed either the structure or the composition of the vegetation which basically is related to climatic and edaphic conditions which are in turn related to superficial and bedrock geology and to landscape evolution over a very long period.

Vegetation, soils and geomorphology The fact that the depauperate mesophyllous savanna woodlands occupy the Palala plateau, the ridges of the Bankenveld and the higher sites within the Bushveld Basin, notably outliers of Waterberg sandstone rocks, all characterized by acid sandy soils, whereas savanna parklands occupy the lower terrain of the Bushveld Basin, notably that with vertic black clay soils derived from norite or basalt, suggests links between vegetation distribution and geomorphology.

Geomorphological evidence indicates that present surface features are the result of the superimposition of the present drainage system from a Karoo cover onto older underlying rocks. It would appear that these features have been associated with the resurrection of an ancient landscape and with the differential erosion of rocks of contrasting lithologies. The evidence also indicates that pediplanation processes have been operating and have produced in turn the African and post-African surfaces, the former now represented by the summits of the higher ground and the latter by the level surfaces of the Bushveld Basin.

Pedological evidence indicates that the soils, which directly influence the vegetation distributions, are the product of pedological processes that, acting on weathered bedrock material over a long period of time, have been influenced by both climatic conditions and geomorphological processes. Those of the Palala plateau, of the plateau outliers of Waterberg sandstone at Maroola Kop and of the granite and norite hills within the Bushveld Basin, are all highly leached, have an acid reaction, and exhibit indurated ferruginous material called 'ouklip' in the profile. All these features suggest legacies of laterization occurring under a formerly hotter and wetter climate on a level surface being fashioned by pediplanation.

The presence of *Burkea africana*, and locally of *Diplorhynchus condylocarpa* and *Pseudolachnostylis maprouneifolia* trees in the mesophyllous woodlands, suggests links with the savanna woodlands of Zambia where the same species occur, the first mentioned notably on sandy soils in the extreme west. The occurrence of *Protea* and *Faurea* spp. indicates links both with the savanna woodlands of Central Africa and with the sclerophyllous woodlands of the Southwestern Cape. The distribution of *Terminalia sericea* and *Combretum molle* on deep sands and of *C. apiculatum* on stony siliceous soils resembles that of these species in South West Africa/Namibia, Botswana and Zambia; the overall distribution of these species in a discontinuous girdle around the western part of the plateau is particularly significant for an understanding of current vegetation distributions.

The evidence suggests that prior to the break-up of Gondwanaland mesophyllous savanna woodland covered the level surface underlain by Karoo rocks that extended across much if not all of the present Bankenveld and Bushveld Basins. Subsequently, as the processes of drainage superimposition uncovered the pre-Karoo landscape and differential erosion produced the ridges and valleys of the Bankenveld, the savanna woodlands survived on the acid soils of the cooler ridges but savanna parkland extended into the warmer and drier valleys. At the same time planation in a new erosion cycle — that of King's post-African cycle — extended into the Bushveld Basin, uncovered the norite and granite bedrock on which respectively vertic black clays and acid sandy soils developed, and opened up vegetational links with the Kalahari to the west. Within the Bushveld Basin savanna parkland characterized by sweet grasses and *Acacia* trees extended onto the heavy soils and stands of *Terminalia sericea* and *Combretum apiculatum* trees occupied the sandy soils. Gradually the vegetation adjusted to the new habitats created by changing climate, geomorphological processes and the development of new soils from the different bedrock types as they became exposed, until the discrete associations that are recognized today were established. Thus today the mesophyllous woodlands represent outliers of savanna woodlands surviving on old land surfaces with poor acid soils. Partly because of their isolation from the savanna woodlands of Central Africa caused by the formation of the Zambezi and Limpopo troughs in Cretaceous times, and partly because of the cooler drier climate, they lack the characteristic *Brachystegia*, *Isoberlinia* and *Julbernardia* trees of those to the north and may be regarded as depauperate. The savanna parkland of the Bushveld Basin is of more recent development and has extended its range with the fashioning of the post-African surface and the creation of warmer drier habitats protected by the ridges of the southern and eastern Bankenveld. With its characteristic *Acacia* trees this parkland has affinities with the low tree and shrub savannas of the Kalahari. The stands of *Terminalia sericea* and *Combretum apiculatum* trees provide links between the mesophyllous savanna woodlands and the microphyllous savanna parkland. Characteristic of sandy sites, the former occupies in some areas soils derived from the old A horizon material removed from the lateritic profiles on which the savanna woodland originally developed.

Within both the savanna woodlands and the savanna parklands the composition of the vegetation varies with changes in the edaphic conditions that are related to bedrock geology. This sometimes results in the development of discrete vegetation associations and is particularly marked where bedrock mineralization imposes extreme conditions.

Vegetation and geology   In the foregoing sections reference has been made to broad-scale relationships between the vegetation and soils whose characteristics are attributable to the bedrock providing their parent material. Within the savanna parklands of the Bushveld Basin there are distinctive vegetation associations and plant communities whose distributions are related to the finer details of the geology of the Bushveld Igneous Complex.

The magma of the basal norite portion of the Bushveld Igneous Complex was emplaced in a series of separate intrusions or surges during each of which crystallization differentiation took place. Each successive intrusion transgressed the previous one. As a result of these processes eight distinctive rock units exist within the norite zone today. In ascending order, these comprise basal norite, harzburgite, pyroxenite, anorthosite, norite, porphyritic pyroxenite, gabbro and ferro-gabbro. Important mineralization occurs in some of these units, notably chromitite within the pyroxenite, platinum in the Merensky reef in the porphyritic pyroxenite and magnetite in the ferro-gabbro. West of the Pilansberg, several carbonatites and a series of nickel–copper pipes intrude the norite sequence. Where any of the various bedrock units cited above either outcrop or sub-outcrop at shallow depth, the vegetation differs from that typical of areas of black turf soil. The differences are particularly marked over mineralized bedrock, notably in the Marico district.

In the Marico district, lying towards the western extremity of the Bushveld Igneous Complex, where planation in King's post-African cycle has reached an advanced stage, erosion has removed the upper, middle and much of the lower divisions of the Complex. East and northeast of the Goudini carbonatite, the pyroxenites and harzburgites form a basin abutting rocks of the Pretoria Series flooring the Complex. Chromitite seams outcrop subconcentrically around the centre of the basin, while to the east birbirite (silicified and opaline harzburgite) and harzburgite from a series of concentric arcuate ridges alternating with shallow valleys developed over pyroxenite. The volcanic breccias and sovites of the Goudini carbonatite form a prominent hill rising abruptly some 100 m above the plain, which is underlain by the norite units.

Over the harzburgite and birbirite ridges thin stony sandy clay loams, only 15–60 cm deep, overlie weathering parent material, and contrast sharply with the black clays over the pyroxenite.

In this area, the typical vegetation over the black soils developed over pyroxenite is an open parkland in which the close grass cover is dominated by *Ischaemum brachyantherum* and *Cymbopogon plurinodis* with *Brachiaria cruciformis* a commonly occurring associate, and *Eragrostis curvula* abundant in hollows and in peripheral areas. Most of the scattered small trees and shrubs are *Acacia tortilis*. On the sandy clay soils overlying harzburgite, the grass cover is sparser but is characterized by a variety of forb and herb species. The principal grasses are *Cymbopogon plurinodis*, *Digitaria eriantha* and *Panicum coloratum* with *Aristida congesta*, *Brachiaria negropedata*, *Enneapogon scoparius* and a variety of other grasses and herbaceous species occurring less frequently. A variety of low trees, mainly *Acacia tortilis*, *A karoo*, *A. mellifera* and *Rhus pyroides* are scattered through the grassland. On the thin sandy loams developed over the low ridges of birbirite, trees and shrubs are more frequent: *Peltophorum africanum* and *Vitex zeyheri* are the characteristic tree species, *Acacia caffra* and *A. tortilis* are abundant, *A. karoo* and *Combretum hereroense* are common and *Rhus lancea*, *Pavetia zeyheri*, *Mundulea sericea* and *Dombeya rotundifolia* occur sporadically. *A. tortilis*, *Grewia flava* and *Zizyphus zeyheriana* form the characteristic shrubs. *Ozoroa reticulata* is common, and *O. paniculosa*, *Euclea undulata*, *Maytenus tenuispina* and a *Lycium* species occur sporadically. The thin grass cover is composed mainly of *Aristida canescens*, with *Cymbopogon plurinodis* occurring on the lower slopes where the soil is deeper. *Eragrostis curvula* and *E. rigida* occur occasionally, but the sedges *Fimbristylis exilis* and *Cyperus margaritaceus*, which are characteristic of extreme sites, are fairly common. The small herbs *Blepharis innocua*, *Chascanum heredaceum*, *Commelina erecta* and *Justicia betonica* are widespread.

Where chromitite seams sub-outcrop at shallow depth, trees are generally absent while *Themeda triandra* replaces *Ischaemum brachyantherum* and *Cymbopogon plurinodis* as the dominant grass species, the change providing an interesting example of the superior competitive ability of a species more typical of a cooler environment in occupying sites where concentrations of a toxic element in the soil adversely affect the characteristic species. The same change of grass species occurs also where the nickel–copper bearing pipes in the same area sub-outcrop beneath about one metre of black turf soil. Where the gossans related to this mineralization are exposed at surface, however, most of the surrounding area is largely bare of vegetation (Figure 9.10). In a number of instances *Dicerocaryum zanguebarium* is present, in some cases occurring with *Commelina erecta, Polygala amatymbica, Cyperus margaritaceum, Fimbristylis exilis* and *Kylinga alba*. In this area, there are no obvious anomalous plant communities over mineralized bedrock, partly because the near surface expression of the mineralization is of limited extent, and partly because the high calcium levels in the black turf soil counter the effects of heavy metal toxicity. Such changes as occur relate to the presence of out of context species with stronger competitive ability than the characteristic species, with *Dicerocaryum zanguebarium* possibly acting as an indicator plant.

The Merensky Reef has been traced for some 230 km along the western rim and for some 160 km along the northeastern and eastern sections of the Bushveld Igneous Complex. It generally underlies level terrain with black cracking clay soils and has little vegetational expression within the typical savanna parkland. Southeast of the Atok mine in Lebowa however, it outcrops or sub-outcrops at shallow depth and is only partialy covered by skeletal soils. Here changes of vegetation occur, with small *Holmskioldia tellensis* trees, *Triapsis glaucophylla* shrubs and *Aristida contorta* grass marking its position.

Conclusions

Distinctive categories of savanna vegetation characterize the individual physiographic subregions within the Transvaal Plateau Basin. In each subregion the respective distributions of the savanna parklands, savanna grasslands and depauperate savanna woodlands, and of the vegetation associations and plant communities within them, are closely related to micro-climatic and edaphic conditions which, in turn, are related to relief and aspect, geomorphology and geology. In some areas fire and overgrazing may have modified the structure of the vegetation but fundamentally the distribution, physiognomy and floristic composition of the vegetational units is the result of species adjustment to habitats created by the interplay of changing climatic conditions and geomorphological processes acting over different bedrock units for a very long period of time. Everywhere the present vegetation is in a state of dynamic equilibrium with the environment and, especially in the west where the region abuts a vegetational tension zone (see Figure 7.2), the balance is fragile so that vegetational changes may be expected in response to climatic and edaphic changes associated with the progression of current geomorphological cycles.

THE SAVANNA PARKLANDS AND ASSOCIATED SAVANNA WOODLANDS AND GRASSLANDS OF THE SOUTH AFRICAN LOWVELD

Like the Bushveld Basin the South African Lowveld is characterized by savanna parklands and associated savanna woodlands and grasslands whose distributions are related to micro-climatic and edaphic conditions, which in turn are related to landscape evolution brought about by the interplay of processes of pediplanation and drainage superimposition from a Karoo surface onto older underlying rocks. The vegetation, however, is more varied. This is partly because the major geological and relief units of the Lowveld, which extends from the Great Escarpment eastwards to the Lebombo range, have a north–south orientation whereas the drainage lines run from west to east. There have thus been natural avenues for plant species migration in both north–south and east–west directions. In the north the arid Limpopo valley provides a corridor for species links with the Kalahari while the Great Escarpment and the valleys cutting into it have offered niches for evolving species and refuges for threatened ones.

Within the Lowveld the climate varies both regionally and locally. With lower latitude and lower elevation temperatures generally increase northwards and eastwards, whereas rainfall increases with proximity to the Great Escarpment and to other areas of higher ground. In most cases relief is related to geomorphology and geology and together they introduce edaphic variations alongside the climatic variations that increase the range of habitats and favour vegetational diversity (see Cole 1956, 1961).

The physical background

Geology, relief and geomorphology   The greater part of the Lowveld is underlain by the Archaean Old Granite. More ancient metamorphic rocks of the Primitive System however, form the Barberton Mountain Land and the Murchison range. In the east these old rocks are covered by sediments and lavas of Karoo age, the upper horizons of which form the Lebombo range. Westwards the old rocks are covered in turn by igneous and sedimentary rocks of the Witwatersrand and Dominion Reef systems and by the dolomite, quartzites and shales of the Transvaal System which form the Great Escarpment. At Phalaborwa the Archaean Basement rocks are penetratred by the intrusive rocks of the Phalaborwa Igneous Complex which includes a carbonatite of Proterozoic age containing a large low grade copper orebody (Figure 9.11).

Below the sheer face of the Great Escarpment formed of Black Reef Quartzite of the Transvaal System the foothills underlain by the Old Granite

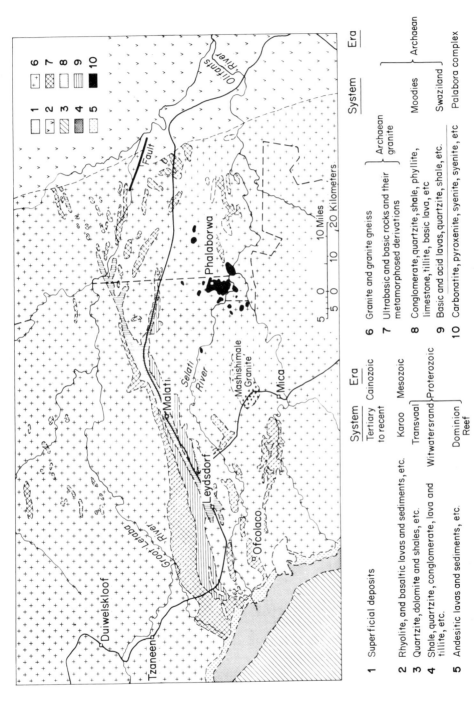

Figure 9.11. The Transvaal Lowveld. Geology of the Tzaneen–Phalaborwa area.

	System	Era
1 Superficial deposits	Tertiary to recent	Cainozoic
2 Rhyolite, and basaltic lavas and sediments, etc.	Karoo	Mesozoic
3 Quartzite, dolomite and shales, etc.	Transvaal	
4 Shale, quartzite, conglomerate, lava and tillite, etc.	Witwatersrand	Proterozoic
5 Andesitic lavas and sediments, etc.	Dominion Reef	

	System	Era
6 Granite and granite gneiss	Archaean granite	
7 Ultrabasic and basic rocks and their metamorphosed derivations		
8 Conglomerate, quartzite, shale, phyllite, limestone, tillite, basic lava, etc	Moodies	Archaean
9 Basic and acid lavas, quartzite, shale, etc.	Swaziland	
10 Carbonatite, pyroxenite, syenite, syenite, etc	Palabora complex	

are highly dissected; where percolating water causes the Old Granite to be kaolinized at depth, gulley erosion is common. This narrow belt of foothills constituting the Middleveld with an altitude of 700–1300 m passes eastwards into the Lowveld which has an elevation of between 150 and 700 m. Here the granite country is characterized by prominent inselberge surmounted by tors and by whaleback outcrops of bare rock rising above the gently sloping to hilly terrain. Eastwards the surface is less dissected and inselberge of diminishing size stud a relatively level plain. In the extreme east the cover of Karoo basalts gives rise to a featureless lowland which ends abruptly against the Lebombo range built of Karoo rhyolites. The general west to east sequence of relief features is broken where rocks of the Primitive System produce the Murchison range near Gravelotte and the Barberton Mountain Land south of Nelspruit.

The Lowveld is crossed by a number of trunk rivers whose courses are unrelated to the present relief or the the underlying geology. The Crocodile and Kaap rivers meander through gorges in the Krokodilpoort ranges of the Barberton Mountain Land and together with all the other major rivers have cut gorges through the Lebombo range.

The evolution of the Lowveld landscape dates from the break-up of Gondwanaland and the opening of the Mozambique Channel, which initiated drainage to the Indian Ocean. At that time Karoo sediments and lavas covered the whole area. Subsequent epeirogenic uplift, associated with major warping that produced the Lebombo monocline in the Miocene period, accelerated erosion which proceeded by processes of planation and scarp recession and by drainage superimposition. The former two processes have produced the Great Escarpment; the last has been responsible for alluviation upstream of gorges where resistant rocks created local base levels along the major rivers.

Climate   The climate of the Lowveld is hot and arid. Temperatures are generally higher than those in the Bushveld Basin and in winter are nowhere as low as those on the Pietersburg Plateau. They vary however from near freezing point in winter to over 38°C in the shade in summer. Marked regional differences occur with latitude and altitude and in the south light frosts may be expected in the winter months. Rainfall varies with altitude and aspect from less than 400 mm in the east to over 800 mm near Pretorius Kop and Letaba and to over 1500 mm near the Great Escarpment. It is concentrated in the summer months—November to March—and the winter months of June, July and August are practically rainless. Thus with high daily temperatures and clear skies the atmosphere may be so dry that by 3.00 p.m. the relative humidity is less than 30% and may even drop to less than 15%.

Soils   The soils closely reflect the interplay of variations of rainfall and relief on weathering processes and pedogenesis over different types of bedrock.

Over the higher terrain where at an altitude of up to 650 m the annual rainfall exceeds 750 mm the Old Granite has weathered to highly leached grey sandy soils. Under more arid conditions it has weathered to reddish sandy or sandy clay soils. These soils are often ferruginous and over eminences exhibit lateritic features suggesting formation under former wetter conditions. By contrast dark brown loams characterize the low-lying areas underlain by Karoo basalts. Skeletal soils prevail in the Murchison range and Barberton Mountain Land and over outcropping bedrock elsewhere. Calcrete development is widespread in the lower terrain and catenary sequences are evident in many areas, in places including sodic soils where drainage is poor.

Vegetation

The characteristic vegetation of the Lowveld is an *Acacia nigrescens–Sclerocarya caffra* parkland associated with dry types of low savanna woodlands variously dominated by *Combretum* spp. or *Colophospermum mopane* trees or with savanna grassland composed mainly of *Themeda triandra*, *Digitaria capense*, *Panicum maximum* and *Bothriochloa radicans* (Figure 9.12).

Two types of savanna parkland, both characterized by *Acacia nigrescens* (Knobthorn) and *Sclerocarya caffra* (maroola) trees, occur over heavy soils derived from basalt at altitudes of between 150 and 600 m where the rainfall averages 500–750 mm (Acocks 1975). In one type, termed Lowveld, *Themeda triandra* is the dominant grass (Figure 9.13); this type merges northwards into the second, the Arid Lowveld in which *Digitaria eriantha* and *D. capense* are the dominant grasses (Figure 9.14). Numerous other tree species are present in both with *Acacia tortilis* var. *heteracantha*, *A. nilotica* subsp. *kraussiana*, *A. albida* and *A. gerrardii* being the more common *Acacia* species in the south and *A. erubescens* and *A. exuvialis* in the Arid Lowveld. *Zizyphus mucronata* and *Spirostachys africana* (tambooti) occur throughout but *Peltophorum africanum*, *Dombeya rotundifolia* and *Ormocarpum trichocarpum* are found only in the south and *Terminalia prunioides* and *Combretum imberbe* (leadwood) in the Arid Lowveld where *Colophospermum mopane* appears in the north and increases in frequency until the vegetation changes to Acocks' mopani veld.

The vegetation dominated by *Colophospermum mopane* varies in physiognomy from a tall dry type of savanna woodland to a low tree or shrub savanna. The former type occurs in a broad belt of country between the Soutpansberg and the Olifants rivers; the latter type occupies parts of the Lebombo Flats and is prevalent also along shallow drainage lines in the Phalaborwa area (Figures 9.15 and 9.16).

In studies of the vegetation of the Kruger National Park the types of

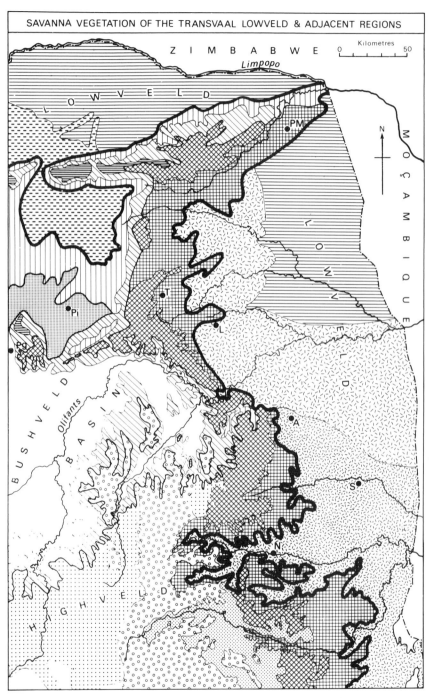

Figure 9.12. The vegetation of the Lowveld and adjacent regions (after Acocks 1975). (See opposite for key).

	Vegetation category	Diagnostic species — Trees	Diagnostic species — Shrubs	Diagnostic species — Grasses	Veld type (Acocks 1975)
	Depauperate tropical forest				N.E. Mountain Sourveld (8)
	Depauperate tropical forest				Lowveld Sour Bushveld (9)
	Depauperate tropical forest				Sour Bushveld (20)
	Depauperate savanna woodland	Faurea saligna, Protea caffra, Combretum spp., Burkea africana, Diplorhynchus mossambicensis, Pseudolachnostylis maprouneifolia		Schizachyrium semiberbe, Heteropogon contortus	
	Depauperate savanna woodland/parkland mosaic	Dombeya rotundifolia, Acacia rehmanniana, Burkea africana, Sclerocarya caffra		Themeda triandra, Eragrostis superba, Heteropogon contortus	Mixed Bushveld (18)
	Savanna woodland	Colophospermum mopane, Acacia spp.		Eragrostis spp., Cymbopogon plurinodis	Mopani Veld (15), Sourish Mixed Bushveld (19)
	Savanna parkland	Acacia caffra, Combretum spp., Dombeya rotundifolia		Themeda triandra	Lowveld (10)
	Savanna parkland	Acacia nigrescens, Sclerocarya caffra, Acacia spp.		Digitaria spp.	Arid Lowveld (11)
	Savanna parkland	Acacia nigrescens, Sclerocarya caffra, Acacia spp., Combretum spp.			
	Low tree and shrub savanna	Combretum apiculatum (dwarf), Terminalia prunioides, Commiphora spp., Boscia albitrunca	Grewia flava, Rhigozum spp., Catophractes alexandrii	Eragrostis spp., Schmidtia bulbosa	Arid Sweet Busveld (14)
	Temperate grassland			Tristachya hispida, Themeda triandra, Tristachya hispida, Eragrostis chalcantha, Eulalia villosa	N.E. Sandy Highveld (57), Bankenveld (61)
	Temperate grassland				Piet Retief Sourveld (63)
	Temperate grassland				
	Savanna grassland/temperate grassland	Acacia rehmanniana		Themeda triandra, Hyparrhenia hirta, Heteropogon contortus	Pietersburg Plateau False Grassveld (67)

Figure 9.13. Savanna parkland of tall *Acacia nigrescens* trees and *Themeda triandra* grass over dark brown loams derived from dolerite, near Gravelotte.

Figure 9.14. Savanna parkland of *Acacia nigrescens* and *Sclerocarya caffra* trees on dark brown loams derived from basalt, north of Satara, Kruger National Park (with giraffe).

Figure 9.15. *Colophospermum mopane* woodland with some *Terminalia prunioides* trees (left) and *Sanseveria* sp. (lower centre) on alkaline soils near Letsitele.

Figure 9.16. Low *Colophospermum mopane* parkland over alkaline clay soils near Olifants river camp, Kruger National Park.

Figure 9.17. Savanna woodland of *Combretum zeyheri* and *Terminalia sericea* on sandy soils derived from granite over low hills near Pretorius Kop, Kruger National Park.

Figure 9.18. Low savanna woodland of *Pterocarpus angolensis* and *P. rotundifolius* on sandy soils derived from granite, Pretorius Kop, Kruger National Park.

savanna parkland termed Lowveld and Arid Lowveld have not been distinguished (Codd 1951). However, changes from east to west have been recognized in the *Acacia nigrescens–Sclerocarya caffra* parkland south of the Olifants river as *Combretum apiculatum*, *Peltophorum africanum* and *Terminalia prunioides* become more frequent on the reddish granitic soils. This vegetation is distinguished further from that characterized by *Combretum suluense*, *C. zeyheri*, *C. gueinzii*, *Terminalia sericea*, *Pterocarpus rotundifolius* and *P. angolensis* over the more highly leached grey granitic sands where the rainfall is higher near Pretorius Kop (Figures 9.17 and 9.18). This last vegetation type is transitional between that of the Lowveld and the Northeastern Mountain Sourveld; it is related to Waterberg Sourveld, and has been termed Lowveld Sour Bushveld (Acocks 1975).

Within the Lowveld the vegetation in fact is more varied and the distribution of the savanna categories and of the plant communities within them is more complex that that outlined above.

Near the Olifants river which marks the southern limit of the mopani the vegetation varies between an open savanna parkland with *Acacia nigrescens* and *Sclerocarya caffra* trees on the lower ground and a dry type of woodland with *Combretum imberbe*, *Terminalia prunioides* and *C. apiculatum* on the eminences with more sandy soils. On poorly drained sites where sodic soils have developed from basalt a stunted form of savanna parkland prevails. South of the Olifants river this is characterized by small *Acacia exuvialis* trees together with small *Terminalia prunioides* trees, *Bothriochloa radicans* grass and *Sansevieria ethiopica* (Figure 9.19). The last named also occupies ill-drained sites elsewhere, e.g. in the mopani woodland near Tzaneen.

Between the Olifants river and Satara thence eastwards to the Lebombo range where montmorillonitic black clay soils cover the exceptionally level plain underlain by Karoo basalt, the *Acacia nigrescens* and *A. tortilis* trees, typical of the savanna parkland, become dwarfed and infrequent until the vegetation changes to a grassland (Figures 9.20 and 9.21). Within this grassland zonal distributions of species, comparable with those on the Cloncurry Plains in Australia, appear to be related to the length of time that water lies on the surface after rains. At the periphery of the planation surface where the terrain is more dissected the grasslands gives way to parkland with stands of *Sclerocarya caffra*, *Acacia nigrescens* and *Lonchocarpus capassa* trees on the dark brown loams derived from basalt. However where the surface is underlain by Karoo sediments, the tree species of the parkland changes to *Albizzia petersiana* on compacted soils formed from sandy parent material and to *Acacia welwitschi* on heavier soils. In places vegetation changes follow a soil/relief catena. Thus between Tshokwane and Skukuza depauperate savanna woodlands composed of *Combretum zeyheri*, *C. apiculatum* and *Terminalia sericea* occupy the sandy soils on the top of small

Figure 9.19. *Acacia exuvialis* and *Terminalia prunioides* low tree and shrub savanna over sodic soils derived from basalt, south of Olifants river, Kruger National Park.

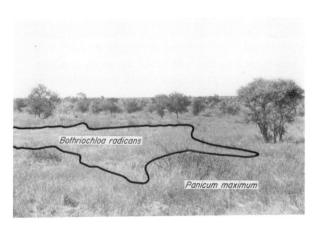

Figure 9.20. Savanna parkland of low *Acacia nigrescens* (left) and *Acacia tortilis* trees, *Panicum maximum* (foreground) and *Bothriochloa radicans* grass over black cracking montmorillonitic clay soils derived from basalt between Olifants River and Satara, Kruger National Park.

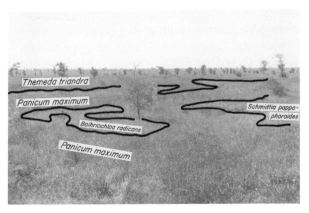

Figure 9.21. Savanna grassland with mosaic distributions of species over black cracking montmorillonitic clay soils derived from basalt between Olifants river and Satara, Kruger National Park.

relict plateau surfaces and are succeeded downslope by grassland with scattered *Albizzia harveyi*, *Acacia gerrardii* and *Combretum imberbe* trees where sandy material veneers sodic soils. The grass species also change from *Digitaria capense*, *Tricolaena monachne* and *Pogonarthria squarrosa* on top to *Themeda triandra*, *Digitaria capense* and *Hyparrhenia dissoluta* downslope. On the higher plateau surfaces in the dissected granite country between Skukuza and Pretorius Kop stands of *Pterocarpus angolensis* and *P. rotundifolius* occur within the *Combretum* spp. dominated woodlands. The presence of these species which are common in parts of the main savanna woodland belt of Zambia and Angola indicate the relationships between the broad leaved savanna woodlands of the Lowveld and those of central Africa.

Factors influencing the distribution of the vegetation

Low rainfall, 400–1000 mm annually, high temperatures and relatively alkaline soils are generally regarded as the main influences over the distribution of the savanna parkland and dry types of savanna woodlands variously dominated by *Acacia nigrescens*, *Sclerocarya caffra*, *Colophospermum mopane* and *Combretum* spp. of trees with a ground layer of perennial and annual grasses in the Lowveld.

These characteristics of the physical environment contrast with the higher rainfall (1000–1600 mm) and generally acid soils of the plateaux of Zimbabwe, Zambia, Tanzania and Angola that carry the *Brachystegia–Isoberlinia–Julbernardia* woodlands.

This relatively simple relationship, however, has been questioned by the occurrence of *Brachystegia–Julbernardia* woodland in the Gwembe section of the Zambezi valley, by that of *Burkea africana* woodlands in the Bushveld Basin, and now by that of stands of *Pterocarpus angolensis* and *P. rotundifolius* within the *Combretum* spp. woodlands as well as by the latter themselves in the Lowveld.

Within the Lowveld differing types of savanna and differing plant communities within them occupy distinctive habitats that result from the interplay of numerous environmental factors, whose relative importance varies both regionally and locally. Overall an explanation of the pattern of the vegetational distributions must be sought in the evolution of the landscape.

The role of climate   The broad-scale distributions of the *Combretum* spp. woodlands, the *Acacia nigrescens–Sclerocarya caffra* parklands and the *Colophospermum mopane* woodland appear to be related to decreasing rainfall from west to east and increasing temperatures from south to north and west to east. As indicated earlier (see p. 116) *Colophospermum mopane* is particularly sensitive to low temperatures on winter nights and its southern limit approximately coincides with the mean July isotherm of 15°C. Its stunted form along shallow valleys east of Phalaborwa where it attains a height of only 1–2 m, as in Botswana, may be related to cold on winter nights, for since the species is tolerant of poor drainage and sodic soils these factors may be discounted.

Detailed consideration of the distributions of the different vegetation types, howevers, shows that they exist side by side under the same climatic conditions, their distributions influenced by soils, relief and bedrock geology and only marginally by small differences of temperature or rainfall.

The influence of soils, relief and geomorphology   The association of the discrete types of savanna with soil type has been established. The discontinuous distribution of the woodlands dominated by *Combretum* spp. and *Terminalia sericea* and the presence of stands of *Pterocarpus angolensis* and *P. rotundifolia* between Skukuza and Pretorius Kop and of isolated trees along the Elands and Crocodile valleys merit further consideration. They occur on the higher ground, usually in soils exhibiting some lateritic features and frequently on granite. In many cases, they appear to be occupying the last vestiges of an old erosion surface, possibly one planed in King's African cycle. Their distribution appears to be related to geomorphology and in some cases the north–south alignment of the foothills of the Great Escarpment and the west–east orientation of the river valleys may have assisted their preservation. The typical savanna parklands, as in the Bushveld Basin, occupy the relatively level terrain of King's post-African planation surface and give way to savanna grasslands on the flat plain adjoining the Lebombo range.

Vegetation and geology   Broad-scale relationships between savanna parklands characterized by microphyllous *Acacia* trees on dark brown loams derived from basalt, and deciduous broad leaf woodlands on sandy soils derived from granite, are evident throughout the Lowveld.

Direct small-scale relationships between vegetation and geology are apparent over and around the Phalaborwa Complex and over areas of serpentinite bedrock in the same area.

The Phalaborwa Complex is a multiple intrusion into the Old Granite, which began with the emplacement of syenite and pyroxenite. These rocks now outcrop in broadly concentric rings parallel to the periphery of the Complex. Later a carbonatite was intruded into the centre of the Complex. Commercial concentrations of apatite and vermiculite occur in some localities within the pyroxenite while the carbonatite contains a large low grade copper orebody containing 0.5% Cu. The area underlain by the Complex forms generally level terrain but the syenite forms a series of castle kopjes or tors around the periphery of the Complex and prior to copper mining operations the carbonatite formed the hill of Loolekop.

A low open woodland of *Combretum apiculatum*, *C. hereroense*, and *Sclerocarya birrea* occupies the acid sandy soils of both the hills and the low ground underlain by syenite, whereas *Colophospermum mopane* woodland is characteristic of the heavier basic soils over pyroxenite. More tree species, notably *Acacia nigrescens*, *Ormocarpum trichocarpum*, *A. exuvialis*, and *Lonchocarpus capassa* occur over the vermiculite-bearing pyroxenite, doubtless responding to the higher phosphorus levels in the soil. Prior to mining operations a contrasting denser vegetation composed of *Acacia nigrescens*, *Dichrostachys cinerea*, *Ormocarpum trichocarpum*, *Zizyphus zeyheriana* and *Lannea stuhlmannia* trees and *Grewia hexamita* and *G. bicolor* shrubs occupied the carbonatite at Loolekop where the small shrubs *Barleria affinis*, *B. galpinii*, *B. senensis*, *Ecbolium revolutum*, *E. lugardae*, *Peristrophe cernua* and *Acalypha indica* were conspicuous over the copper orebody. Over the carbonatite high levels of calcium favoured plant growth and countered the effects of copper toxicity in the soil so that strongly anomalous plant communities did not occur. Marked changes of vegetation, however, occur over serpentinite at Laaste, north of Phalaborwa township, again south of the Selati river and in the Mashishimale Bantu Trust area. Here the vegetation is composed only of small shrubs, mainly *Grewia bicolor* and *Euclea undulata* with *Glossochilous parviflorus* in the last mentioned (Figure 9.22). Very stunted *Colophospermum mopane* trees occur at the periphery of the slight eminences formed by the serpentinite where the low calcium/high magnesium

Figure 9.22. Shrub vegetation of *Grewia bicolor* and *Euclea undulata* over serpentinite, Laaste, north of Phalaborwa. Stunted *Colophospermum mopane* trees at the periphery. Syenite hills in background.

and somewhat high nickel levels (at around 500 ppm) in the soil are unfavourable for the trees of the savanna parkland and woodlands.

The role of fire and grazing animals A large part of the Lowveld is within the Kruger National Park where the vegetation is grazed and browsed by a variety of animals and where burning is controlled. Near Satara experiments have shown that according to the time and severity of the burn *Panicum maximum* grass succumbs first, *Digitaria capense* holds on better, but both may give way in turn to *Bothriochloa radicans*, particularly on the deeper soils. Burning in successive years kills the shrubs to ground level and is followed by coppicing with *Dichostachys cinerea* becoming particularly aggressive. Today fire is infrequent and the evidence suggests that, except on the composition of the grass cover, it has little influence on the vegetation which is influenced fundamentally by the factors of the physical environment. Outside the Park, large areas along the valleys and in the foothills of the Drakensberg have been cleared for agriculture in recent decades and the savanna parklands and woodlands are now largely restricted to the interfluves and hilly terrain.

Conclusions

As in the Transvaal Plateau Basin the distributions of savanna parklands and associated savanna woodlands and grasslands in the Lowveld reflect the interplay of micro-climatic and edaphic factors that in turn are the legacy of landscape evolution.

Less is known of the geomorphology of the Lowveld than of the Transvaal Plateau Basin, but following the break-up of Gondwanaland, the opening of the Mozambique Channel and the formation of the Lebombo monocline as a result of warping in Miocene times, the Lowveld is believed to have evolved by the interplay of the processes of scarp recession and pediplanation and of drainage superimposition from a Karoo surface onto older underlying rocks. Relicts of the oldest surface occur on the summits of the Barberton Mountain Land which have the same altitude as the Highveld; those of the African surface occur over the summit plateaux and hills in the Old Granite country which have survived the post-African planation that is responsible for the level terrain of the eastern Lowveld.

The vegetation has responded to the changes in climate and edaphic conditions occasioned by the processes of landscape evolution until today in broad outline the *Acacia nigrescens–Sclerocarya caffra* parklands and associated grasslands and the *Colophospermum mopane* woodlands characterize the younger surface and the *Combretum* spp.-dominated woodlands occupy relicts of the older surfaces from the summit of the

Lebombo range to the foothills of the Great Escarpment. Within this broad outline the distribution of the individual savanna types and of the vegetation associations and plant communities within them represents an adjustment to micro-climate and edaphic conditions that in turn are influenced by relief and bedrock geology and are in a state of dynamic equilibrium.

10 The low tree and shrub savannas and associated savanna types of South West Africa/Namibia and western Botswana

Low tree and shrub savannas characterize those areas of South West Africa/Namibia and Botswana and adjacent parts of the Transvaal and northern Cape Province of South Africa where the climate is hot and semi-arid, is characterized by regular but erratic summer rains, and by great seasonal and diurnal ranges of temperature. The limits of the low tree and shrub savanna vegetation appear to be clearly defined by climatic criteria but variations in the form, composition and distribution of its component plant communities are influenced mainly by edaphic conditions related to geomorphology and geology (Cole and Brown 1976, Cole and le Roex 1978).

In the north, low tree and shrub savannas take over from savanna woodlands, notably those dominated by *Colophospermum mopane* trees where the mean annual rainfall averages less than 500 mm, the mean temperature for the mid winter month of July falls below 15°C and light frosts occur throughout the short winter season. While *Colophospermum mopane* thrives in areas of low rainfall it is sensitive to frost (see pp. 115–117), whose incidence appears to be the overriding determinant of the boundary between its distribution and that of the low tree and shrub savanna. In the west the latter yields to desert shrub and desert grass below the Great Escarpment where the annual rainfall totals less than 100 mm and is highly erratic in occurrence. In the south it gives way to Karoo shrub where the July mean temperature is less than 10°C, the mean minimum is below 2°C, and the frost period exceeds 90 days.

Throughout the great tract of country characterized by low tree and shrub savannas there are considerable variations in the physical environment and in the composition of the vegetation. Large areas are completely inaccessible but detailed studies have been made in two regions of contrasting physiography; the first embraces the western fringes of the Kalahari from Windhoek through Ghanzi and Maun to the Caprivi Strip; the second includes the Otavi Mountainland and the Etosha pan (see Chapter 11). The first comprises level terrain mantled with Kalahari Sand and calcrete that conceals bedrock; the second is characterized by mountain ranges produced by outcropping dolomites and quartzites and intervening broad valleys and plains underlain by shales, schists and unsilicified dolomites covered locally by calcrete, by transported overburden and residual soil. The inaccessible country between the two regions is characterized by long parallel west–east trending sand dunes.

The vegetation not only varies in form and composition both regionally and locally but, in some areas, it appears to have changed over historical time. The descriptions of the nineteenth century writers indicate that savanna woodlands with large *Combretum imberbe* trees occurred north of Ghanzi which was then teeming with big game. Lake Ngami was apparently much larger than it is today. The literary records that suggest that the Kalahari was then wetter are supported by evidence from Landsat satellite imagery, which shows several former shorelines for Lake Ngami indicating a once larger and shrinking lake fed by channels that are now dry (Cole 1982b; Chapter 11 and Figures 11.1 and 11.2). Sequential imagery shows that over the period 1972–79 the size of the lake has varied both annually and seasonally but has never reached its former shorelines. The Landsat imagery also reveals former shorelines of a once larger Etosha pan fed by additional channels (Cole 1982c). The evidence from both areas of an aridity trend, is, as will become apparent later, very important for explaining the present distributions of some tree species and some vegetation types.

THE WITVLETI-GHANZI-MAUN AREA

The physiognomy and the species composition of the savanna vegetation vary both regionally and over short distances within the tract of country extending from Windhoek to Maun. In the southwest it comprises a typical low tree and shrub savanna of variable composition that in places alternates with savanna parkland. The latter becomes more common towards and beyond the Botswana border. In the warmer and slightly wetter areas near Lake Ngami both types of savanna give way to low forms of savanna woodland that in places are interrupted by savanna grasslands. Within each of these savanna categories there are many discrete vegetation associations the elucidation of whose distribution patterns require prior consideration of the physical environment.

The physical environment

Climate   Within this hot semi-arid area there are some regional variations in rainfall and temperature. The rainfall averages between 300 and 500 mm but varies from 360 mm at Windhoek to 380 mm at Gobabis to 430 mm at Ghanzi and 460 mm at Maun. It occurs between October and April with about 60% falling between January and March. Characteristically it falls in local short-lived heavy convectional downpours but gentler continuous widespread rains may occur between January and March. The rainfall is unreliable in both incidence and distribution. Within a ten year period the annual total is less that 85% of the average in at least two and more usually four years.

During the summer months temperatures are high; daily maxima may exceed 38°C or even 43°C and nightly minima seldom fall below 21°C. Atmospheric humidity is usually between 50% and 60% but it may drop to 30% in clear sunny weather and of course reaches 100% during thunderstorms. The winter months are dry and characterized by temperature extremes that increase towards the centre of the Kalahari. Warm sunny days with temperatures rising well above 21°C are followed by cold nights with temperatures sometimes falling below 0°C. Frost may occur in June, July and August, particularly in valleys and depressions where cold air settles. Temperatures begin to rise in September and reach the highest maxima in November which is the hottest month of the year, the cloud and rains in the subsequent summer months being responsible for somewhat lower means. Throughout the year the high temperatures cause evaporation to exceed precipitation. Strong winds are a feature of August and September when they carry much sand and have a desiccating effect on soils and vegetation. They persist into October when their coincidence with high maximum temperatures causes peak evaporation.

Geology   Beneath an extensive cover of Kalahari Sand and calcrete the area is underlain by a diversity of Precambrian rocks (see Cole and le Roex 1978). The oldest rocks comprising metamorphosed ultrabasics, metavolcanics and metasediments outcrop only in a small area near Rehoboth. They are overlain by a suite of intermediate to acid lavas interbedded with sediments, tuffs and pyroclasts belonging to formations known as the Opdam and Skumok. Within the suite a strongly developed quartz–feldspar porphyry, resistant to weathering forms the well defined Mabeleapudi, Ngwenalekau, Kgwebe and Makabane hills in Botswana. These rocks are unconformably overlain by a sedimentary sequence of conglomerates, quartzites, arenites and argillites with, in Botswana, some limestones and dolomites as well, that form the formations known as the Tsumis in South West Africa and the Ghanzi in

Botswana. These rocks that are of equivalent age to the Proterozoic Katanga system in Zambia underlie a large tract of country extending from the Zimbabwe border through Ghanzi and Witvlei to the southwest of Windhoek. They are generally steeply inclined while near Ghanzi they are folded into a series of major anticlines and syclines. They underlie level terrain planed by erosion and hence, where not covered by Kalahari Sand and calcrete, rocks of different lithology sub-outcrop in sequence to give rise to contrasting soils supporting different vegetation communities. Between Witvlei and Dordabis and south of Gobabis predominantly dolomitic rocks of probable Cambrian age belonging to the Buschmannklippe formation and unconformably overlying the Proterozoic rocks, outcrop; north of Ghanzi much younger Karoo sandstones and basalts of Carboniferous to Triassic age floor the Mawane area.

While Precambrian to Liassic rocks underlie the area between Windhoek and Maun they rarely outcrop as most of the area is mantled by Recent deposits of Kalahari Sand and calcrete. The former varies from a thin veneer to depths of 30 m, the latter form a nodular layer overlying bedrock to thickness of tens of metres. While their origin is uncertain their deposition was probably related to changing geomorphological processes associated with increasing desiccation in post-Tertiary times. Most likely the calcium removed by leaching during lateritization under high rainfall conditions on adjacent higher plateaux in the Tertiary geological period was precipitated along drainage lines in the area under consideration. Then as the climate became drier and the ground vegetation cover deteriorated the exposed topsoil of the lateritic profiles became vulnerable to erosion and provided the material ultimately deposited as Kalahari Sand. Such events would have profoundly influenced the distribution of plant species.

Physiography and geomorphology Forming part of the great African plateau which, from an altitude of 1300–2000 m in the west slopes gradually eastwards towards the Kalahari basin, the relief is generally remarkably level. Near Windhoek there is evidence of several cyclic erosion surfaces cutting across the steeply inclined Proterozoic rocks, the more resistant of which form ranges of hills or isolated inselberge rising some 500–700 m above the general surface (Figure 10.1). Eastwards these become fewer and progressively lower until they finally disappear as a landscape feature as the sand cover increases towards the Kalahari. Around Ghanzi the featureless largely sand-covered plain exhibits some micro-relief where sub-outcrops of bedrock of differing lithologies with differing resistances to erosion cause sinuous low rises and intervening vales delimiting fold structures. Northeast of Ghanzi the Mabeleapudi, Ngwenalekau, Makabana and Kgwebe hills, produced by

Figure 10.1. Low tree and shrub savanna dominated by *Acacia* spp. trees and *Stipagrostis uniplumis* grass over surface planed across steeply inclined Proterozoic rocks between Windhoek and Rehoboth. Range of resistant quartzites and ironstones of Damara system (background) with accordant summit levels cut into by Naaus poort.

Figure 10.2. Savanna parkland dominated by *Acacia giraffae* trees over sandy terrain between Witvlei and Windhoek, South West Africa.

Figure 10.3. Savanna parkland of *Terminalia sericea* (left foreground) and *Acacia giraffae* trees and *Stipagrostis uniplumis* and *Aristida* spp. grasses between Windhoek and Gobabis, South West Africa.

outcropping resistant quartz prophyry rocks, provide the only relief in the otherwise featureless sand plain.

There are no perennial rivers in the southern part of the area. South of Windhoek the generally dry water courses of the White and Black Nossob eventually unite with that of the Molopo, an intermittent tributary of the Orange river. South of Dordabis the Usib and Schaf river courses which are also dry for most of the year are characterized by spectacular gorges—the Nauas and Klein Nauas poorts—through the hills of resistant Tsumis quartzites. Here the present drainage pattern being transverse to the alignment of the hills and the geological strike is quite unrelated to relief and geology. Apparently it originated on a surface above the summit level of the ranges during a wetter climatic epoch. Eastwards towards the Kalahari, notably southeast of Dordabis and Ghanzi, sand dunes, now fossilized, have dismembered former stream courses. In the Ghanzi area individual pans and chains of pans are the only relics of former drainage systems. On the Ghanzi ridge the smaller pans normally fill with water after rains but others, including those on the sand plain south of the Tsau hills, rarely do so. Large pans, that may be up to 2 km across, occur infrequently and usually in groups both on the Ghanzi ridge and on the Kalahari Sand plain. Some like the Ghanzi pan are floored by calcrete and crystalline limestone and yield water at shallow depth. Others, including those on the sand plain south of the Tasu hills, are floored by heavy calcareous clay or silty clay that swells and becomes sticky after rains but cracks deeply on drying. These pans rarely fill with water but small pools accumulate in them after rains. The relatively large Ngwaku and Tale pans southeast of Lake Ngami are of intermediate type.

Except in the Okavango delta and Lake Ngami there is no permanent surface water in the area. Borehole records however suggest that the alternating sequence of quartzites, arenites and argillites in the Tsumis–Ghanzi system is favourable for the accumulation of ground water and that, where this sequence is exposed or covered by thin calcrete, ground water is available at shallow depth and within reach of the roots of most trees and many shrubs characteristic of the area. Ground water appears to be available also around the quartz porphyry hills where the cover of Kalahari Sand and/or calcrete is thick; however, the water table may be very deep.

In the extreme north, the Okavango river brings water from the higher rainfall plateau of southern Angola and distributes it in a labyrinth of channels in the Okavango swamps from which some filters through to Lake Ngami and some spills over into the Botete river and thence the Makarikari depression. The exceptional conditions in the Okavango swamp–Lake Ngami area produce mosaic distributions of differing types of savanna and forest and are considered separately (Chapter 11).

The physiographic features of the western fringe of the Kalahari are thus the result óf geomorphological processes involving planation and drainage superimposition followed by climatic changes causing increasing desiccation, the deposition of wind blown sand and the dismemberment of drainage systems. The effect on the vegetation has been profound, leading to complex patterns of plant communities whose distribution is related to varied edaphic conditions associated with the interplay between geomorphology and geology.

Soils and overburden The characteristic soils are either immature or skeletal arid red earths with virtually no horizon development. Their precise nature varies with relief, geomorphology and geology. Over hills of outcropping bedrock and over level terrain where bedrock is relatively near surface soils are related to lithological type. Elsewhere they are related to the thickness of the mantle of Kalahari Sand and calcrete. Only skeletal sandy soils are present over Kalahari Sand and outcropping quartz porphyries, arenites and quartzites. Skeletal dark brown soils occur over surface calcrete. Somewhat deeper immature soils of variable texture have formed over level terrain where near surface bedrock has weathered to soil parent material with which some wind blown sand may be incorporated. These soils are generally sandy arid red earths but over argillite bedrock they tend to be heavier brown sandy loams. In some areas near Witvlei and on the Ghanzi ridge a gravel layer that is a legacy of the planation processes that fashioned the landscape during Tertiary times occurs in the soil profile below the surface sandy material and above the bedrock. On and around pans skeletal grey and brown soils of heavy texture are found while dark brown to black clays surround Lake Ngami, occupying areas formerly covered by water.

The soils generally lack humus and are low in mineral nutrients, other than calcium. There are variations related to bedrock type, depth of Kalahari Sand and extent of calcrete development (see Tables 10.2a,b) with the dark brown loams derived from Karoo basalt having the highest nutrient status and the 'soils' over deep Kalahari Sand the lowest. The soil pH varies from between 6.0 and 7.0 over near surface bedrock and calcrete to only 5.0 over deep sand.

The characteristic vegetation—savanna categories, vegetation associations and dominant species

Between Windhoek and Witvlei the low tree and shrub savanna is dominated by *Acacia mellifera* (wait-a-bit thorn) associated with *A. hereroense* trees, *A. hebeclada*, *Tarchonanthus camphoratus*, *Grewia flava*, G. flavescens and *Phaeoptilum spinosum* shrubs and *Stipagrostis uniplumis* tussock grass over level terrain where skeletal sandy soils cover relatively near surface bedrock.

Figure 10.4. Low woodland of *Terminalia sericea*, *Combretun collinum* and other *Combretum* spp. with bare sand between the trees north of Mamona, Botswana.

Figure 10.5. Savanna grassland dominated by *Aristida* spp. in the Okwa valley in Botswana changing to low tree and shrub savanna on the valley sides where bedrock outcrops.

Figure 10.6. Low savanna woodland of *Terminalia prunioides* trees (left and right) with *Acacia erubescens* and *A. leuderetzii* trees and *Combretum* spp. shrubs near Ngwaku pan, Botswana.

It gives way to a more open parkland characterized by taller *Acacia giraffae* trees, where deep sand mantles bedrock (Figure 10.2).

Northeast of Witvlei the above named associations alternate with an open parkland co-dominated by *Terminalia sericea* and *Acacia giraffae* trees where the cover of Kalahari Sand is deeper and more extensive (Figure 10.3). North of Mamona, where the deep sand cover is ubiquitous over large areas, a low woodland of *Terminalia sericea*, *Combretum collinum* and other *Combretum* spp. prevails (Figure 10.4). Around Ghanzi, however, low tree and shrub savanna again characterizes areas with skeletal soils over near surface bedrock. Its composition differs from that at Witvlei, notably in the additional presence of *Boscia albitrunca*, *Acacia reficiens* and *Combretum hereroense* trees and shrubs, and sporadic occurrence of large *Combretum imberbe* trees and the widespread occurrence of the suffruticose *Petalidium englerianum*. Northeastwards a low shrub savanna of *Combretum apiculatum*, *Bauhinia macrantha* and *Croton gratissimus* alternates with savanna grassland dominated by *Aristida meridionalis* over the level sand-covered terrain of the Kalahari (Figure 10.5).

North of Ghanzi a parkland of *Acacia erubescens* and *Commiphora pyracanthoides* trees and the perennial grasses *Stipagrostis uniplumis*, *Aristida scabrivalvis*, *A. hordeacea* and *Eragrostis porosa* occupies the dark brown loam and black clay soils developed over basalt bedrock and stands of *Terminalia sericea*, sometimes accompanied by *Acacia giraffae* trees occur over deep sands. Towards Lake Ngami the vegetation becomes a low type of savanna woodland composed of *Terminalia prunioides*, *Acacia erubescens* and *A. leuderetzii* with numerous shrubs, notably *Combretum* spp. (Figure 10.6). This alternates with areas of *Combretum apiculatum* trees, with *Acacia erubescens* parkland and, along drainage lines, with *Schmidtia pappophoroides* grassland. Between Lake Ngami and Maun these vegetation types are interrupted by belts of *Terminalia sericea* trees over west–east trending sand dunes. North and northwest of Maun vegetation distributions are influenced by the great inland drainage system of the Okavango and are considered separately (see Chapter 11). Throughout the area from Windhoek to Maun shrub communities characterized by *Catophractes alexandrii* occupy areas of calcrete development.

The distributions of vegetation associations and plant communities throughout the area between Windhoek and Maun are more complex than is suggested by the above summary description. As revealed both by studies of satellite and airborne imagery and by field investigations, they are influenced fundamentally by the extent and depth of Kalahari Sand and calcrete cover and by differing lithologies in areas of near surface bedrock.

Figure 10.7. *(opposite)* Distribution of vegetation associations in the Witvlei area based on aerial photograph interpretation and field investigations by M. M. Cole and M. M. Mason (1968–1970). From Cole and le Roex (1979).

Low tree and shrub savanna	Habitat
1. Characterized by *Combretum apiculatum* and *Albizia anthelmintica* trees, *Grewia bicolor, G. flavescens, Commiphora pyracanthoides, Croton gratissimus* and *Mundulea sericea* shrubs.	Conglomerate ridge of Witvlei berg and quartzite hills on Eskadron, Okajirute and Grunental.
2. Characterized by variable association of *Acacia hereroensis, A. mellifera* and *A. hebeclada* trees, *Grewia flava, Phaeoptilum spinosum* and *Tarchonanthus camphoratus* shrubs and *Stipagrostis uniplumis* grass.	Level terrain with near surface bedrock.
3. Characterized by *Terminalia sericea* and *Acacia giraffae* trees, *Tarchonanthus camphoratus, Grewia flava, Oroza paniculosa* and *Rhus ciliata* shrubs and *Stipagrostis uniplumis* and *Schmidtia pappophoroides* grasses.	Thick sand cover.
4. Characterized by *Acacia mellifera* trees, *Tarchonanthus camphoratus* shrubs and *Stipagrostis uniplumis* and *Aristida congesta* grasses.	Sand and gravel accumulation on the northern side of Witvlei berg and around the quartzite hills on Eskadron.
5. Characterized by *Acacia giraffae* and *A. mellifera* trees, *Catophractes alexandrii* and *Grewia flava* shrubs, the suffrutices *Leucasphaera bainesii* and *Aptosimum leucorrhizum* and the grass *Fingerhuthia africana*.	Calcrete capped ridges.
6. Characterized by tall *Acacia mellifera* and *Boscia albitrunca* trees, *Catophractes alexandrii* shrubs, the suffrutices *Leucas pechelli, Hermannia damarana* and *Pseudogaltonia clavata* and the grass *Enneapogon cenchroides*.	Thick calcrete sheets masking bedrock.
7. Characterized by *Acacia giraffae, A. karoo, A. hebeclada* and *Zizyphus mucronata* trees.	Fossil drainage lines and pans floored by calcrete.
8. Characterized by *Acacia giraffae* and *A. karoo. A. hebeclada* and *Zizyphus mucronata* trees.	Alluvium along current drainge lines.

Shrub savanna

9. Characterized by *Catophractes alexandrii* and *Grewia flava* śhrubs with the suffrutices *Leucasphaera bainesii, Hermannia damarana, Pseudogaltonia clavata* and *Pegolettia pinnatiloba* and the grass *Fingerhuthia africana*.	Shallow calcrete over shales and limestones of the Buschmannsklippe.

Savanna grassland

10. Characterized by *Aristida stipitata* and *Eragrostis pallens* grasses.	Thick sand cover.

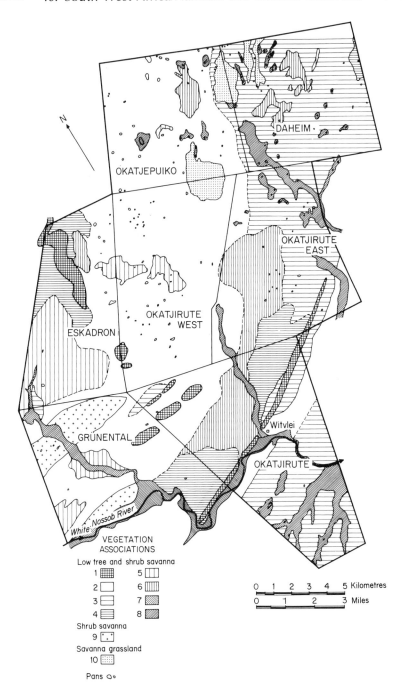

DAHEIM

OKATJEPUIKO

OKATJIRUTE
EAST

OKATJIRUTE
WEST

ESKADRON

Witvlei

GRÜNENTAL

OKATJIRUTE

White Nossob River

VEGETATION
ASSOCIATIONS

Low tree and shrub savanna
1   5
2   6
3   7
4   8

Shrub savanna
9

Savanna grassland
10

Pans

0 1 2 3 4 5 Kilometres
0 1 2 3 Miles

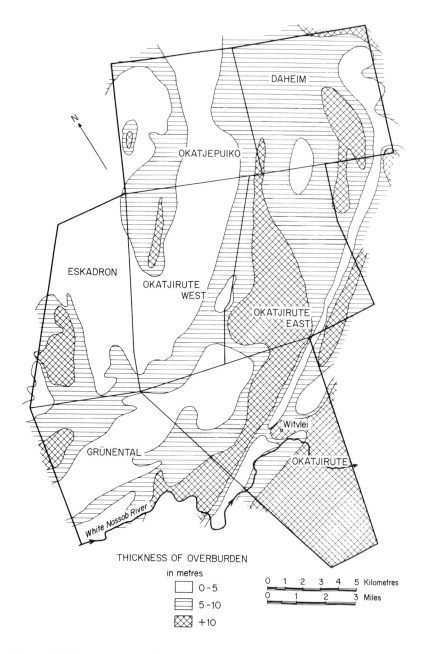

DAHEIM

OKATJEPUIKO

N

ESKADRON

OKATJIRUTE
WEST

OKATJIRUTE
EAST

Witvlei

GRÜNENTAL

OKATJIRUTE

White Nossob River

THICKNESS OF OVERBURDEN

in metres

☐ 0-5

▤ 5-10

▨ +10

0 1 2 3 4 5 Kilometres
0 1 2 3 Miles

Figure 10.8. Thickness of soil and overburden in the Witvlei area based on seismic investigations by Anglovaal geologists. From Cole and le Roex (1979).

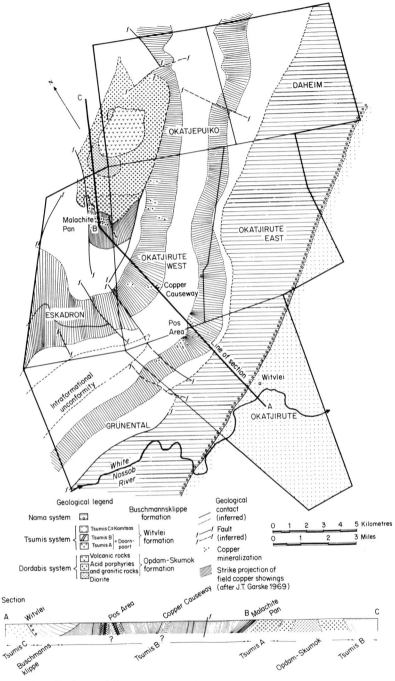

Figure 10.9. Geology of the Witvlei area based on aerial photograph interpretation by J. Garske and field investigations by Anglovaal geologists. From Cole and le Roex (1979).

The Witvlei–Dordabis area

Studies made over seven farms in the Witvlei area show that the distributions of the savanna types and of the plant associations within them are related in the first instance to the depth of Kalahari Sand and calcrete cover and to bedrock geology (Figures 10.7–10.9; Mason 1975, Cole and le Roex 1978).

A low tree and shrub savanna association characterized by *Terminalia sericea* and *Acacia giraffae* trees with the shrubs *Tarchonanthus camphoratus*, *Grewia flava*, *Ozorea paniculosa* and *Rhus ciliata* and the grasses *Stipagrostis uniplumis* and *Schmidtia pappophoroides* (numbered 3 on Figure 10.7) is virtually coincident with areas of deep sand exceeding 5 m and reaching over 30 m over quartzites at the top of the Tsumis formation and over dolomites of the Buschmannklippe.

Figure 10.10. Shrub vegetation of *Pentzia calcarea*, *Leucasphaera bainesii*, *Ocimum americanum*, *Barleria lanceolata*, *Optoptera burchellii*, etc. (foreground) over calcrete near Witvlei, South West Africa. Characteristic low tree and shrub savanna of *Acacia* spp. trees and *Stipagrostis uniplumis* grass behind.

Four distinct types of low tree and/or shrub savanna distinguish areas of disparate calcrete development (Figure 10.10). One composed of *Acacia giraffae* and *A. mellifera* trees with *Catophractes alexandrii* and *Grewia flava* shrubs, *Leucasphaera bainesii* and *Aptosimum leucorrhizum* suffrutices and *Fingerhuthia africana* grass characterizes ridges where the calcrete cover may be from 5 to 23 metres thick. A second association of *Acacia mellifera* and *Boscia albitrunca* trees with *Catophractes alexandrii* shrubs, the suffrutices *Leucas pechelli*, *Hermannia damarana* and *Pseudogaltonia clavata* and the grass *Enneapogon cenchroides* (numbered 4 on Figure 10.7) occupies areas covered by extensive sheets of calcrete from 10 to 36 m thick that probably overlie limestones and shales of the Buschmannsklippe formation. Where the latter outcrop or are covered by thin calcrete a shrub savanna association of *Catophractes alexandrii* and *Grewia flava* with the suffrutices *Leucasphaera bainesii, Hermannia damarana, Pseudogaltonia clavata* and *Pegoletta pinnatiloba* and *Fingerhuthia africana* grass occurs. A fourth type of low tree and shrub savanna comprising *Acacia giraffae, A. karroo, A. hebeclada* and *Zizyphus mucronata* trees occupies fossil drainage lines and pans that are floored by calcrete. The differences in the composition of the vegetation over the different thicknesses of calcrete are believed to be related to variations in the availability of water below the calcrete cover.

Two contrasting and distinctive low tree and shrub savanna associations delineate respectively areas of outcropping bedrock and of near surface bedrock covered by less than 5 m of overburden. One association of *Combretum apiculatum* and *Albizia anthelmintica* trees and *Grewia flavescens, Commiphora pyracanthoides, Croton gratissimus* and *Mundulea sericea* shrubs (numbered 1 on Figure 10.7) occupies the conglomerate ridge of the Witvleiberg and quartzite hills north of Witvlei. The other association comprising *Acacia hereroensis, A. mellifera* and *A. hebeclada* trees with *Grewia flava, Phaeoptilum spinosum* and *Tarchonanthus camphoratus* shrubs and *Stipagrostis uniplumis* grass (numbered 2 on Figure 10.7) covers a broad belt of shallow overburden within which plant distributions over different lithologies such as arenites and argillites reflect geological contacts, regional geological strike and faults and fold structures so faithfully that they are readily distinguished on conventional aerial photographs.

Figure 10.11. Anomalous plant community of *Helichrysum leptolepis* (centre) occupying copper toxic soils over mineralized bedrock within the low tree and shrub savanna, Witvlei area, South West Africa.

In places the last mentioned vegetation association suddenly gives way to anomalous plant communities of small *Helichrysum leptolepis* plants, sometimes associated with *Fimbristylis exilis* and sometimes with *Aristida congesta* at the peripheral contact with the typical low tree and shrub savanna vegetation (Figure 10.11). Numerous *Helichrysum leptolepis* communities occur in the Witvlei area. In every case they delineate areas of copper toxic soils associated with cupriferous horizons in argillite bedrock (Mason 1975, Cole and le Roex 1978). Here the *Helichrysum leptolepis* is a copper indicator plant occupying sites that, with copper levels of between 25 and 800 ppm in the surface soil and up to 4% in mineralized bedrock at a depth of 1–4 m, are too toxic for other plants.

The Ghanzi area of Botswana

The Ghanzi area of Botswana is remarkable for the way in which the distribution patterns of plant communities within the low tree and shrub savannas outline fold structures with intricate drag folds and faults that, apparent from aerial reconnaissance, are displayed on aerial photographs (Figure 10.12). The vegetation over some of these fold structures has been mapped from species frequency data recorded along transect lines orientated across the inferred geological strike, supplemented by aerial photograph interpretation and field checking of boundaries (Cole and Brown 1976). Investigations of plant rooting systems and major and trace element analyses of both plant and soil samples have provided further detailed information on the vegetation which must be considered in the context of the broad-scale vegetation distributions in Botswana.

Maps depicting physiographic and floristic classifications of the vegetation of Botswana (Figures 10.13 and 10.14) show a three-fold division of the low tree and shrub savanna within the Ghanzi area. This division closely follows the patterns of geology and relief. Thus the Kalahari Sand plains north and east of the Ghanzi ridge carry an open low tree savanna characterized by *Terminalia sericea* and *Lonchocarpus nelsii*, whereas those to the south carry one of *Acacia leuderetzii*, *A. giraffae* and *L. nelsii*. The Ghanzi ridge has a variable vegetation in which *Boscia albitrunca* and *Acacia* species are usually present. This has been subdivided primarily by de Beer (1962) into two categories, namely (i) shrub savanna of *Catophractes alexandrii* and *Rhigozum brevispinosum* in the southwest; and (ii) low tree and shrub savannas that have been secondarily subdivided by Blair Rains and Yalala (1970) into those characterized by (a) *Combretum imberbe*, *Acacia giraffae* and *A. mellifera* northeast of Ghanzi, (b) by *Combretum spiculatum*, *C. imberbe* and *Lonchocarpus nelsii* near Kuke, and (c) by *Acacia mellifera*, *C. hereroense*, *Zizyphus mucronata* and *Mundulea sericea* in depressions

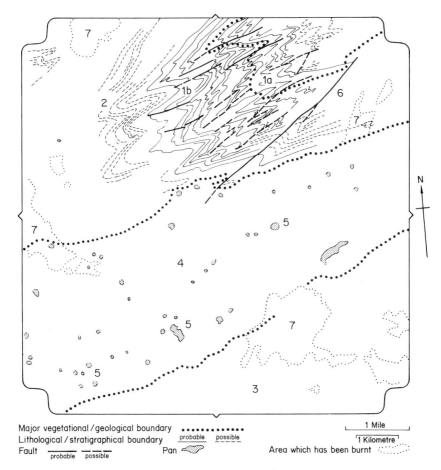

Figure 10.12. Interpretation of vegetation/physiography/geology relationships shown on 28BC/21 No. 064 covering the area southeast of Ghanzi. (Interpretation by Cole and Brown, 1976.)

Key. (1) Apparent fold structure outlined by belts of grassland dominated by *Stipagrostis uniplumis* in silt-filled vales alternating with low tree and shrub savanna characterized by *Boscia albitrunca* on ridges. (a) Ridges with denser tree growth, possibly promoted by increased water supply at the contact of argillite and arenite bedrock at depth. (b) Ridges with more open tree growth, possibly over near surface arenites. (2) Discernible but less well defined apparent fold structure weakly outlined beneath sand cover of up to 4 m depth by narrow bands of low *Acacia giraffae* trees and *Grewia flava* shrubs which probably delineate water-bearing horizons at the contact of quartzites and shales. (3) Uniformly speckled textured areas where a low tree and shrub savanna characterized by *Combretum imberbe*, *C. hereroensis* and *Terminalia sericea* trees and *Grewia* spp. and *Combretum* spp. shrubs occupies thick sand cover of over 4 m depth. (4) Area of darker tone with evenly distributed large *Combretum imberbe* trees on calcrete cover obscuring bedrock geology. (5) Approximately circular pans, often calcareous, carrying a dense grass cover with a ring of trees of various species at their periphery. (6) Belt of dense *Combretum imberbe* and associated trees species defining a linear feature, possibly a fault, which may be associated with increased ground water. (7) Irregular areas of darker tone produced by the effects of fire.

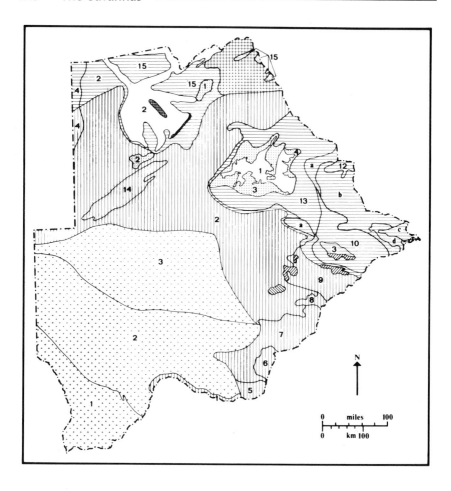

throughout the area. De Beer regards the presence of large *Combretum imberbe* trees as indicative of a former cover of savanna woodland that has been progressively destroyed by timber cutting, fire and grazing. Repetitive sequences in the distribution patterns of the individual plant associations notably over the apparent fold structures show, however, that the vegetation is very closely related to environmental parameters. This suggests that biotic factors may have modified but not fundamentally changed the character and composition of the vegetation.

Vegetation units over the Ghanzi ridge   The low tree and shrub savanna of the Ghanzi ridge is characterized by *Boscia albitrunca* trees some 3–4 m

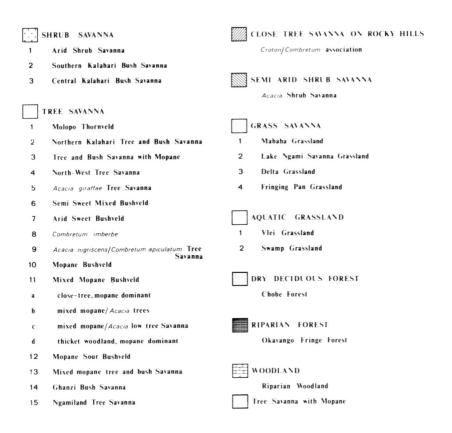

SHRUB SAVANNA
1   Arid Shrub Savanna
2   Southern Kalahari Bush Savanna
3   Central Kalahari Bush Savanna

TREE SAVANNA
1   Molopo Thornveld
2   Northern Kalahari Tree and Bush Savanna
3   Tree and Bush Savanna with Mopane
4   North-West Tree Savanna
5   *Acacia giraffae* Tree Savanna
6   Semi Sweet Mixed Bushveld
7   Arid Sweet Bushveld
8   *Combretum imberbe*
9   *Acacia nigriscens/Combretum apiculatum* Tree Savanna
10 Mopane Bushveld
11 Mixed Mopane Bushveld
a   close-tree, mopane dominant
b   mixed mopane/*Acacia* trees
c   mixed mopane/*Acacia* low tree Savanna
d   thicket woodland, mopane dominant
12 Mopane Sour Bushveld
13 Mixed mopane tree and bush Savanna
14 Ghanzi Bush Savanna
15 Ngamiland Tree Savanna

CLOSE TREE SAVANNA ON ROCKY HILLS
Croton/Combretum association

SEMI ARID SHRUB SAVANNA
Acacia Shrub Savanna

GRASS SAVANNA
1   Mababa Grassland
2   Lake Ngami Savanna Grassland
3   Delta Grassland
4   Fringing Pan Grassland

AQUATIC GRASSLAND
1   Vlei Grassland
2   Swamp Grassland

DRY DECIDUOUS FOREST
Chobe Forest

RIPARIAN FOREST
Okavango Fringe Forest

WOODLAND
Riparian Woodland
Tree Savanna with Mopane

Figure 10.13. Vegetation of Botswana. Physiognomic classification (after Weare and Yalala 1971).

high and by *Acacia mellifera* subsp. *detinens* shrubs up to 1.5 m high. Neither dominates the vegetation which is composed also of scattered *Combretum hereroense* and *Zizyphus mucronata* subsp. *mucronata* trees and numerous shrubs, notably *Grewia flava*, *Tarchonanthus camphoratus* and *Rhus tenuinervis* with a grass layer usually dominated by *Stipagrostis uniplumis*. The distribution of the major associations within this low tree and shrub savanna are shown in Figure 10.15.

Over the Ghanzi ridge repetitive sequences of vegetation associations produce remarkable banded patterns of apparent stratigraphic horizons, drag folds and faults within the major fold structures seen on the aerial photographs (Figures 10.12 and 10.16). The distribution of the individual

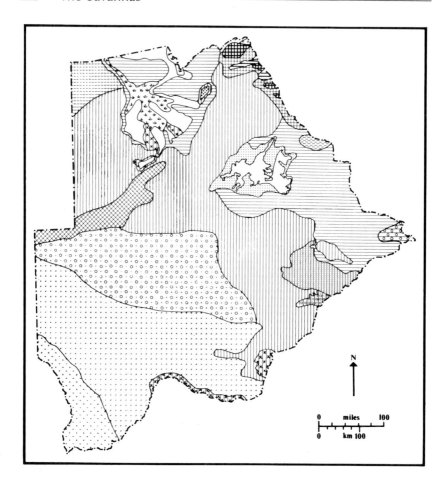

associations forming these bands is influenced mainly by minor variations of physiography occasioned by the contrasting weathering characteristics of the arenites, argillites and limestones comprising the underlying Ghanzi beds, and by local differences in the thickness of the calcrete and Kalahari Sand which mantles them.

While the terrain is remarkably level over extensive areas, within the apparent major fold structures there is a succession of low ridges and broad valleys that are believed to follow individual lithological units. The rises are only some 5 m higher than the valleys. Calcrete occurs as a weathering/soil formation product over most rock types but is believed to be more strongly developed over arenites and limestones. It outcrops over the ridges, but in the valleys is partially or completely obscured by deposits washed down from

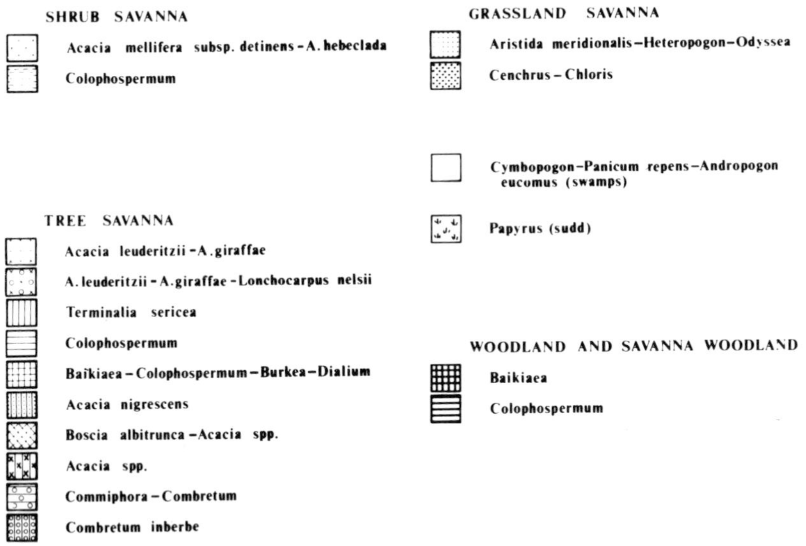

SHRUB SAVANNA

Acacia mellifera subsp. detinens – A. hebeclada

Colophospermum

TREE SAVANNA

Acacia leuderitzii – A. giraffae

A. leuderitzii – A. giraffae – Lonchocarpus nelsii

Terminalia sericea

Colophospermum

Baikiaea – Colophospermum – Burkea – Dialium

Acacia nigrescens

Boscia albitrunca – Acacia spp.

Acacia spp.

Commiphora – Combretum

Combretum inberbe

GRASSLAND SAVANNA

Aristida meridionalis – Heteropogon – Odyssea

Cenchrus – Chloris

Cymbopogon – Panicum repens – Andropogon eucomus (swamps)

Papyrus (sudd)

WOODLAND AND SAVANNA WOODLAND

Baikiaea

Colophospermum

Figure 10.14. Vegetation of Botswana. Floristic classification after Wild and Barbosa (1967) (Wild and Fernandes 1967–68).

the adjacent ridges. Thus a series of grey calcrete-capped ridges usually with a quartzite or arenite core alternates with red silt- and gravel-filled valleys which are probably underlain by limestone or shale. Each unit carries a characteristic vegetation association, which produces the well defined banding into apparent fold structures visible on the air photos (Figure 10.16).

A low tree and shrub savanna (Figure 10.16, communities 1–3) characterized by *Boscia albitrunca* and a variety of shrubs occurs typically over the crests of the calcrete-capped rises where ground water is usually encountered just below the calcrete. Within this association, *Rhigozum brevispinosum*, *Catophractes alexandrii* and *Ximenia americana* occur in patches locally while *Acacia nebrownii* and *Maytenus senegalensis* occupy overgrazed areas. The very dark green leaves of *Boscia albitrunca* contribute

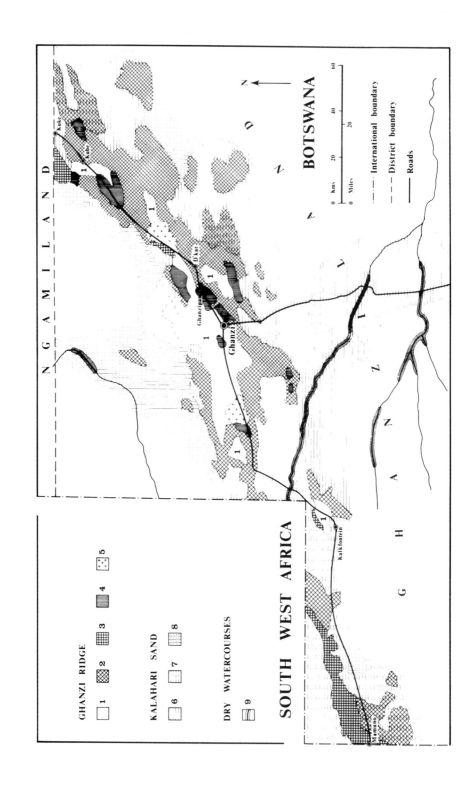

to the dark tones that this association produces on the aerial photographs. On some rises, however, the small grey-leaved shrubs *Petalidium englerianum* and *Leucasphaera bainesii* form very distinctive bands that produce a lighter tone on the aerial photographs.

Shrub communities of *Catophractes alexandrii* flank the *Boscia albitrunca* associations occurring where fine sand and silt mantles the calcrete to a depth of a metre or more on the slopes below the crests of the calcrete rises (Figure 10.17). Throughout South West Africa and western Botswana this species occurs wherever massive calcrete features the soil profile. It spreads readily by rhizomes and forms virtually monospecific communities. Its grey leaves produce distinctive tones on aerial photographs that outline its banded distribution on either side of the crests of the calcrete ridges.

Savanna grassland (Figure 10.16, communities 6 and 7) dominated by *Stipagrostis uniplumis* var. *pearsonii* occupies the silt- and sand-covered linear depressions between the calcrete ridges. Here, where over half the surface is bare, *S. uniplumis* var. *pearsonii* covers one third of the remainder. Scattered *Combretum hereroense*, *Acacia giraffae* and *A. tortilis* subsp. *heteracantha* trees may occur; the last named occurs in the moister localities whereas *A. giraffae* forms stands of 10 to 20 small trees over deep sand. Shrubs are more common than trees; *Grewia flava* and *Petalidum englerianum* occur most frequently and *Acacia nebrownii*, *Rhus tenuinervis*, *Commiphora pyracanthoides* subsp. *pyrancanthoides* occasionally. In areas that receive flash floods, *Aristida congesta* and *Eragrostis* spp. locally

---

Figure 10.15 *(opposite)*. Vegetation associations of the Ghanzi area (mapping by R. C. Brown according to categories of M. M. Cole).

Key to vegetation associations: Ghanzi ridge: (1) Complex vegetation patterns reflecting concealed fold structures and showing a repetitive banded sequence of low tree and shrub savanna characterized by *Boscia albitrunca* over low rises of outcropping calcrete, shrub savanna dominated by *Catophractes alexandri* on the slopes below locations where calcrete is present in the soil profile, and savanna grassland over linear sand-filled vales. (2) Low tree and shrub savanna characterized by *Combretum hereroense* and *Acacia fleckii* trees, *Grewia flava* shrubs, *Tylosema esculentum* and a variety of herbs over apparent fold structures concealed by sand cover. (3) Low tree savanna dominated by *Combretum apiculatum* over outcropping quartzites and over areas mantled by ferruginous sands. (4) Tree savanna characterized by *Combretum imberbe* trees associated with *Acacia mellifera*, *A. tortilis* and *A. giraffae* trees which locally may be dominant, occurring over hard crystalline pan limestone. (5) Shrub savanna dominated by *Catophractes alexandrii* where calcrete occurs in the soil profile.

Kalahari Sand plain: (6) Low tree and shrub savanna dominated by *Terminalia sericea* on deep red Kalahari Sands. (7) Low tree and shrub savanna characterized by *Acacia leuderetzii*, *A. giraffae* and *Terminalia sericea* on shallower Kalahari Sands. (8) Open savanna parkland characterized by *Acacia giraffae*, *A. leuderetzii*, *A. fleckii* and *A. mellifera* trees associated with *Stipagrostis uniplumis*, *Schmidtia pappophoroides*, *Anthephora pubescens* and other grasses.

Dry watercourses: (9) Tree savanna dominated by *Acacia tortilis* and *A. giraffae*.

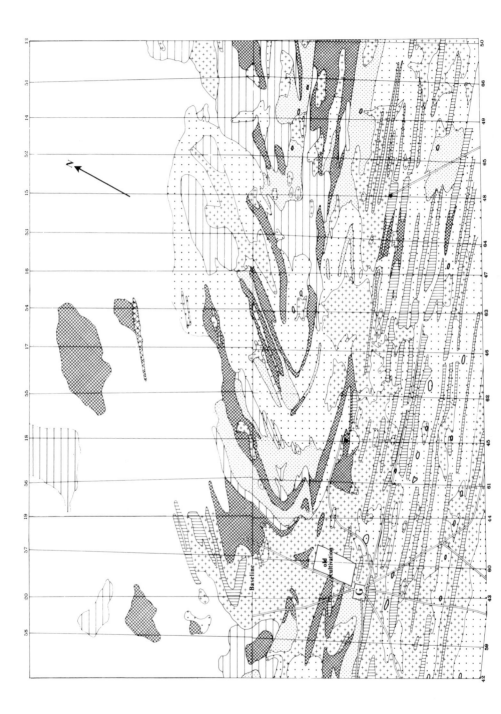

dominate the grass layer. In overgrazed areas *Maytenus senegalensis*, *Acacia mellifera* and *A. hebeclada* replace the grasses and other shrub species.

Along the limbs of the apparent folds, large ill-defined vleis or pans that receive intermittent flood waters and are filled with a red silty sand similar to that in the valley depressions, carry a savanna grassland characterized by the perennial grasses *Cynodon dactylon*, *Aristida congesta* subsp. *congesta*, *Schmidtia pappophoroides* and *Stipagrostis uniplumis*, associated with a variety of annual grasses, notably *Pogonarthria squarrosa* and *Eragrostis porosa*. Trees, mostly *Zizyphus mucronata* subsp. *mucronata*, although infrequent, are more common than in the linear silt-/sand-filled depressions. *Grewia flava* and *Acacia hebeclada* are the most common shrubs.

The distribution patterns of the above vegetation associations are complex. Individual associations usually occupy narrow zones that are often only a few metres wide, but extend for hundreds of metres, sometimes curving at acute angles and sometimes being offset, reflecting the minor features of drag folds and faults in the underlying geology. The patterns produced by the sequences of individual vegetation associations are repeated in each of the major fold features that are apparent from the air in the Ghanzi area.

Where the depth of sand is sufficient to obscure the micro-relief but not to eliminate vegetational response to underlying geology, a low tree and shrub savanna of heterogeneous composition, showing weak zonal banding occurs

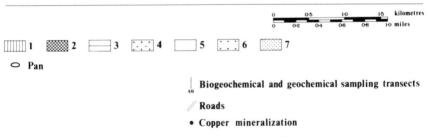

Figure 10.16. The plant communities over the fold structure on the farms Hartebeestfontein and Wellington north and east of Ghanzi.
Key to plant communities. Low tree and shrub savanna: (1) characterized by *Boscia albitrunca*, *Acacia nebrownii*, and *Commiphora* spp. trees, *Leucasphaera bainesii* and *Barleria lancifolia* shrubs and *Enneapogon brachystachyus* grass on calcrete ridges; (2) characterized by *Combretum hereroense*, *Dichrostachys cinerea Commiphora* spp. and *Ximenia americana* trees and *Rhigozum brevispinosum*, *Rhus tenuinervis* and *Bauhenia macrantha* shrubs on sandy ridges; (3) characterized by *Terminalia sericea* trees, high sandy ground. Shrub savanna (4) characterized by *Catophractes alexandrii*, calcrete present in the soil profile. (5) Undifferentiated low tree and shrub savanna, on sand cover. Savanna grassland: (6) characterized by *Stipagrostis uniplumis* grass, on low areas and vales between low ridges, (7) characterized by *Stipagrostic uniplumis* grass with some scattered *Combretum hereroense*, and *Grewia flava* shrubs and some scattered *Acacia giraffae* trees, on low areas. Data collected by R. de Hoogh, R. C. Brown and M. M. Cole.

Figure 10.17. Belts of Catophractes alexandrii (left foreground) occupying the flanks of successive calcrete ridges north of Ghanzi. From Cole and Brown (1976) with permission.

as around Ghanzi, between Ghanzi and D'kar and near Mamuno and Kalkfontein (Figure 10.15, association 2). In this mixed association, the trees follow the subsurface contact of the arenaceous and argillaceous rocks and thereby identify structural lineations. *Combretum hereroense* is the most common species. It occurs with *C. imberbe* and *Acacia fleckii* north and east of Ghanzi and with *A. mellifera* subsp. *detinens* around D'kar, where *Dichostachys cinerea* is the most common shrub, particularly on land disturbed by overgrazing and by rodent burrows. *Grewia flava* and *Petalidium englerianum* are widespread, *Rhigozum brevispinosum*, *Ximenia americana* and *Rhus tenuinervis* occur less frequently and *Bauhinia macrantha* appears where the sand cover thickens. *Tylosema esculentum* is typical of the association. Its vines spread over the surface below which it develops a large water storing root (sometimes exceeding 1.5 m in diameter). This creates a 'crater' some 500 mm or more across, and brings to the surface large fragments of the sub-outcropping bedrock, thereby providing geological information. *Stipagrostic uniplumis* var. *pearsonii*, *Schmidtia pappophoroides* and *Eragrostic rigidior* form a grass layer except in overgrazed areas where the small shrub *Hermannia angolensis* is usually common.

As the sand cover thickens away from the margins of Ghanzi ridge, these vegetation associations merge into those characteristic of the Kalahari Sand plain.

Significant changes in the form and composition of the vegetation of the Ghanzi ridge occur between Ghanzi and the Ngamiland border (Figure 10.15).

These are associated with increasing rainfall and decreasing frost incidence and with the greater depth of sand cover which obscures the bedrock geology. Trees become larger and more numerous, and the low tree and shrub savanna characterized by *Boscia albitrunca* passes into a form of low savanna woodland with *B. foetida*, *Combretum albopunctatum*, *Acacia erubescens*, *Terminalia prunioides* and even an occasional frost-sensitive *Adansonsia digitata* tree. The distribution of individual species, and the form and composition of discrete vegetation association reflects differences in the soils and drainage caused by variations in the depth of sand and in the concealed bedrock. *Combretum apiculatum* trees are characteristic where sandy soils overlie arenaceous bedrock, whereas *Terminalia prunioides* and *Acacia erubescens* trees occupy the heavier dark brown loams where argillite sub-outcrops. In the shrub layer, *Grewia flava* is accompanied or replaced by *G. bicolor* and *G. retinervis* and by *Combretum* spp., particularly *C. engleri*.

Commiphora pyracanthoides subsp. *glandulosa* and *Croton menyhartii* are particularly common in sand cover, including that overlying calcrete, where they are associated with *Catophractes alexandrii*. The composition of the grass cover is similar to that further south, but *Enneapogon cenchroides* takes over from *E. brachystachys* over calcrete. The herb layer is richer and the variety of annual species is greater.

On the borders of Ngamiland, areas of savanna grassland are more sharply differentiated from the low savanna woodland than they are from the low tree and shrub savanna farther south. This is due partly to the greater contrast between the vegetation units themselves, and partly to abrupt changes in drainage conditions which are a feature of the north.

Near the South West African border at Mamuno, where the Ghanzi ridge forms an elevated series of outcropping or sub-outcropping quartzite platforms some 30–40 m above the surrounding plain, a low savanna woodland dominated by *Combretum apiculatum* subsp. *apiculatum* occupies the rocky slopes and hilltops. The trees, which reach a height of about 5 m, often occur in nearly pure stands. Locally an aloe, *Aloe littoralis*, characterizes the rocky slopes. Where the soil cover is deeper, scattered trees of *Acacia mellifera* subsp. *detinens*, *Albizia anthelmintica*, *Combretum hereroense*, *Boscia albitrunca* and *Rhus lancea* and a sparse shrub layer of *Grewia* spp., *Phaeoptilum spinosum*, *Montinia caryophyllacea*, *Catophractes alexandrii* and *Commiphora pyracanthoides* form a low tree and shrub savanna. This has a sparse grass cover of *Eragrostis porosa*, *Stipagrostis uniplumis* var. *pearsonii*, *Rhynchelytrum villosum* and *Oropetium capense*. Locally treeless areas characterized by the small shrub *Petalidium parvifolium* occur over areas which may have been disturbed by cultivation or overgrazing.

An atypical form of savanna woodland occupies the extensive level areas of hard crystalline limestone or calcrete flooring the large pans which occur sporadically throughout the Ghanzi district. Here the trees may attain a height of up to 15 m. Shrubs are less common than in adjoining associations and a ground layer occurs only where the pan limestone is covered with sand or soil. *Combretum imberbe* is the most characteristic tree species and, northeast of Ghanzi and D'kar, occurs in belts which are several kilometres long and about 1 km wide. It is associated with *Acacia mellifera* subsp. *detinens*, *A. giraffae*, *A. tortilis* subsp. *heteracantha* and *Zizyphus mucronata* subsp. *mucronata*. Towards the Ngamiland border, *Acacia erubescens*, *Terminalia prunioides* and *Boscia foetida* become progressively more common in this form of woodland. The understorey of scattered shrubs is composed of *Grewia flava*, *Ximenia americana*, *Dichrostachys cinerea* subsp. *africana*, *Rhus tenuinervis*, *Diospyros lycioides* subsp. *sericea* and *Acacia hebeclada*. More species are present where ground water is relatively near the surface, e.g. in Ghanzi pan where *Maytenus senegalensis* and *Ximenia americana* occur as tall shrubs or small trees alongside *Maerua angolensis*. Small shrubs of the *Hermannia* genus frequently occur with the grasses *Stipagrostis uniplumis* var. *pearsonii*, *S. uniplumis* var. *neesii* and *Cymbogon excavatus*. In places, *Acacia mellifera* subsp. *detinens* and *A. fleckii* form thickets in this woodland.

Belts of *Acacia tortilis* subsp. *heteracantha* and *A. giraffae* trees follow the abandoned watercourses that are often associated with the large pans, and they also follow the dismembered river systems of the Hanahai, Okwa and Groot Laagte. In each case, the shrubs characteristic of the calcrete-floored pans constitute the understorey. Along the old river systems, however, variations in the composition of vegetation occur in consequence of differences in slope and soil moisture conditions occasioned by the presence of sand, calcrete or bedrock outcrop.

Contrasting with the limestone- or calcrete-floored pans, the large relict pans characterized by surface accumulations of fine powdery clay carry a savanna grassland dominated by *Cynodon dactylon*, which is associated with various bulbous species including *Dipeadi gracillimum*, *Lapeirousia caerulea*, *Crinum charnsii* and *Nerine laticoma*. The grassland is ringed by *Petalidium englerianum* and *Acacia nebrownii* and by occasional *A. tortilis* subsp. *heteracantha* trees on the periphery of the pan.

The small pans which are a feature of the Ghanzi ridge also carry a distinctive vegetation, which breaks the continuity of the associations delineating the stratigraphical horizons within the apparent fold features. The centres of the pans may be occupied by annual grasses such as *Urochloa brachyura*, but for most of the year are usually bare. The periphery is marked by rings of *Petalidium englerianum*, *Grewia flava*, *Rhigozum brevispinosum* and *Acacia nebrownii* shrubs, and of *Zizyphus mucronata*, *Acacia tortilis* subsp. *heteracantha*, *A. mellifera* subsp. *detinens* and *Combretum hereroense* trees, with a grass layer of *Cenchrus ciliaris, Eragrostis barbinodis, E. rigidior* and *Aristida congesta* subsp. *congesta*.

The sand dune, sand-covered ridges and sandy plains that occupy parts of the Ghanzi ridge carry a similar vegetation to the Kalahari Sand plains, and will be considered in the context of the latter.

Vegetation units of the Kalahari Sand plain The areas deeply mantled by Kalahari Sand to the north and south of the Ghanzi ridge carry a relatively uniform low tree and shrub savanna vegetation that reflects similarity of habitat conditions over great distances. The contrast with the Ghanzi ridge is sharp.

There is no surface water over the Kalahari Sand plain where boreholes often have to penetrate at least 100 m before reaching water. The water table is beyond the reach of most plant species which must therefore depend on the moisture held in the sand after rains for their water requirements.

South of the Ghanzi ridge, the characteristic low tree and shrub savanna is usually dominated by *Terminalia sericea* trees (see Figures 10.3, 10.4, and 10.15, associations 6–8). These sometimes form pure stands but more often are associated with, and in some places may give way to *Acacia giraffae*, *A. leuderetzii* var. *leuderitzii*, *A. fleckii* and *A. mellifera* subsp. *detinens*, or *Combretum collinum* subsp. *gazense* and *Zizyphus mucronata* subsp. *rhodesica*. The shrub layer is composed largely of *Grewia flava, G. flavescens* var. *olukondae, G. avellana, Dichrostachys cinerea* subsp. *africana, Bauhinia macrantha, Rhus tenuinervis, Commiphora africana, C. angolensis* and *Ximenia caffra* var. *caffra* and the grass layer, which may occupy only up to 20% of the ground, leaving the rest bare, is a mixture of *Stipagrostis uniplumis* var. *pearsonii, Aristida meridionalis, Eragrostis rigidior, E. pallens* and *Schmidtia pappophoroides*; where the trees and shrubs are closely spaced, however, *E. pallens* alone forms a sparse ground cover. Other species occur less commonly; the small trees *Combretum engleri, C. mossambicense* and *Maerua angolensis* and the shrub *Croton gratissimus*, which are common in Ngamiland, occur northeast of Ghanzi, and *Combretum zeyheri* and *Acacia hereroensis* trees and the shrub *Ozoroa paniculosa* occur near the border with South West Africa.

Outlying patches of *Terminalia sericea* trees occur where deep sand mantles the Ghanzi ridge. This species is most common, however, east and south of Ghanzi, where it occurs alone or with *Acacia giraffae* and *A. leuderetzii*.

Over the sand plain north of the Ghanzi ridge, the Kalahari Sands tend to be greyer in colour and more compacted than further south and the vegetation tends to be more open, in places assuming the character of a savanna grassland with occasional large trees. The grass cover, which may occupy up to 60% of the surface, is composed largely of *Eragrostis rigidior*, with *Schmidtia pappophoroides, Anthephora pubescens* and *Stipagrostis uniplumis* var. pearsonii; an annual grass, *Eragrostis biflora*, occurs where trees cast shade. *Acacia giraffae*, either singly or in clumps of young trees, *A. leuderetzii, A. fleckii* and *A. mellifera* subsp. *detinens*, sometimes as thickets, occur occasionally as do groups of *Albizia anthelmintica* trees. Shrubs are rare, *Grewia flava, G. avellana, Bauhinia macrantha* and *Dichrostachys cinerea* subsp. *africana* occurring infrequently.

In places north of D'kar and west of Kuke this open savanna grassland or parkland gives way to a denser growth, comprised of the same tree species with a prominent shrub layer of *Grewia flava, Rhus tenuinervis, Croton gratissimus* and *Rhigozum brevispinosum*, while the vast plains adjoining the Groot Laagte watercourse carry an open parkland savanna in which small shrubs and trees of *Ochna pulchra* occur along with the species characteristic of the sand plains near Ghanzi.

Relationships between the distribution of vegetation associations, plant communities and environmental conditions   In order to elucidate the relationships between the distribution of the vegetation associations, plant communities and the environmental conditions in the Ghanzi area, the life form spectrum of the vegetation, the seasonal growth rhythm and the rooting systems of the characteristic species, and the content of major mineral elements in both plant tissues and soils were ascertained.

The life-form spectrum of the vegetation: The life-form spectra of the vegetation in the Ghanzi area and in the southern Kalahari were compared using the Raunkiaer classification (Raunkiaer 1934), as modified by Leistner (1967) and simplified by the omission of categories defined by morphological and physiological features not directly influenced by environmental parameters (Table 10.1 and Figure 10.18). This showed that in both areas the majority of species are hemicryptophytes, geophytes and therophytes and that most of those bearing their perennating buds above ground level are chaemaephytes and nanophanerophytes. These distributions reflect the importance of morphological characteristics assisting survival under arid conditions, a fact emphasized by the lower percentages of microphanerophytes, nanophanerophytes and chaemaephytes in the drier southern Kalahari than in the Ghanzi area.

In the Ghanzi area, of the eight evergreen phanerophytes present in the spectum seven are restricted to areas where ground water is available at rooting depth; i.e., to the Ghanzi ridge, where *Boscia albitrunca* trees occupy the calcrete rises, and to old watercourses where *Acacia tortilis* trees dominate. Microphanerophytes and nanophanerophytes, although contributing a relatively small percentage of species to the spectrum, are the characteristic

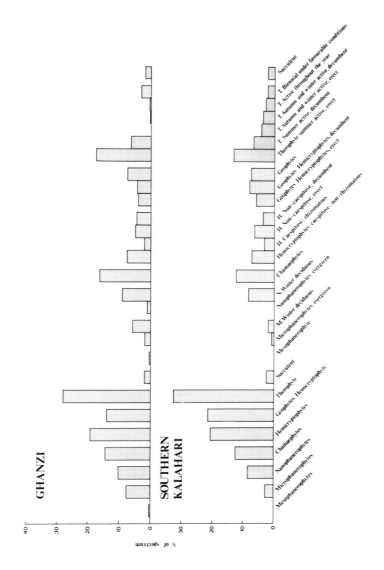

Figure 10.18. The life-form spectra of the vegetation of the Ghanzi area of Botswana and of the southern Kalahari (Cole and Brown 1976 after Raunkiaer 1934, as modified by Leistner 1967).

Table 10.1. Comparison of life-form spectra of the vegetation of the Ghanzi area and the southern Kalahari

Life-form	Ghanzi area		Southern Kalahari (after Leistner 1967)	
	No. of species	Spectrum (%)	No. of species	Spectrum (%)
Mesophanerophyte				
Winter deciduous	2	0.4	0	0.0
Microphanerophyte				
Evergreen	6	1.3	3	0.7
Winter deciduous	29	6.3	9	2.0
Nanophanerophyte				
Evergreen	2	0.4	—	—
Winter deciduous	44	9.6	37	8.3
Chaemaephyte	75	16.4	54	12.2
Hemicryptophyte				
Caespitose				
Rhizomatous	33	7.2	32	7.2
Non-rhizomatous	10	2.2	14	3.2
Non-caespitose	44	9.6	45	10.1
Hemicryptophyte/Geophyte	42	9.2	62	14.0
Geophyte	35	7.6	33	7.4
Therophyte				
Summer active	111	24.2	88	19.8
Autumn and winter active	1	0.2	35	7.9
All season active	2	0.4	12	2.7
Biennials	14	3.1	10	2.3
Succulent	8	1.7	10	2.3
Total	458	100.0	444	100.0

Note: The position of the perennating beds is as under:
Mesophanerophyte — more than 8 m above soil level
Microphanerophyte — 2–8 m above soil level
Nanophanerophyte — 250 cm to 2 m above soil level
Chaemaephyte   — 0–25 cm above soil level
Hemicrytophyte   — at soil level
Geophyte   — below soil surface
Therophyte   — annuals
From Cole and Brown (1976) with permission.

life-forms of the area. The former category embraces most of the typical *Acacia*, *Combretum* and *Terminalia* trees and the latter includes the widespread shrubs *Grewia flava*, *G. bicolor*, *G. flavescens*, *Catophractes alexandrii*, *Rhigozum brevispinosium* and *Croton gratissimus*. The microphanerophytes and nanophanerophytes, together with the hemicryptophytes which include the widespread perennial grasses, produce the typical low tree and shrub savanna. Of the numerous species in the chaemaephyte category, only *Petalidium englerianum* is both widespread and common, being characteristic of the plant communities over calcareous bedrock and compacted pan deposits, where *Leucosphaera bainesii* may be locally co-dominant or dominant.

Most of the species classified as geophytes in the Ghanzi area are bulb-producing members of the Amaryllidaceae and Liliaceae families, and corm-producing members of the Iridaceae. There are fewer species characterized by tubers or rhizomes, but these include *Tylosema esculentum*, and *Vellozia humilis*. The latter frequently occupies the relatively heavy soils developed over pan sediments where bulb- and corm-producing species are also common. Some species favour sites where 1–2 m of sand overlie calcrete or bedrock. Geophytes are not common in the Ghanzi area, largely because the rainfall occurs in summer, the most favourable period for plant growth, and water and food storage are not essential for survival.

The high percentage of therophytes reflects the equilibrium with environmental conditions of those species able to complete their life cycle from seed to seed again during the short period after favourable summer rains, and to remain dormant in the seed state for long unfavourable periods. These species are particularly characteristic of pans and shallow depressions with heavy clay soils, and of areas of outcropping calcrete where perennial plants are absent or infrequent and where competition in favourable periods is minimal. Elsewhere they are widely but sparsely distributed except in areas of deep sand cover, where they cannot compete with the trees and shrubs whose well developed lateral root systems draw on the available vadose water.

The rooting systems of selected plant species: In order to establish the relationships between the distribution of plant species and soil and ground moisture conditions, the root systems of characteristic species occupying sites representative of particular habitats were exposed and examined (see Cole and Brown 1976). The sites included those with near surface bedrock, with calcrete cover, those on the Kalahari Sand plains and those in depressions with cracking clay soils.

The investigations revealed significant differences in the rooting habits between different tree and shrub species, and confirmed fidelity of habit in individual species occupying contrasting habitats.

Except for *Acacia mellifera*, the characteristic *Acacia* tree species have both large tap roots and well developed lateral root systems, which enable them both to draw on ground water and to utilize the moisture held in the surface soils after rains. *Combretum imberbe*, *Commiphora pyracanthoides* subsp. *pyracanthoides*, and *Terminalia prunioides* exhibit similar rooting characteristics, the first two developing exceptionally large tap roots and relatively small laterals in heavy soils, and the third a smaller tap root and more laterals in sandy areas. *Acacia tortilis* has contorted roots which enable the tree to draw water from a larger area. *Boscia albitrunca* and *Commiphora africana* have large tap roots, but lack lateral root systems. Of the characteristic shrub species the nanophanerophytes *Combretum hereroense* and *Catophractes alexandrii* and the chaemaephyte *Petalidium englerianum* have several major descending roots as well as laterals.

Combretum apiculatum trees and *Grewia bicolor* and *Lycium* sp. shrubs develop extensive lateral root systems which can draw on vadose water held in the soil and sand overburden after rains; the first mentioned may develop a tap root in heavy soils.

Terminalia sericea trees and *Rhizozum brevispinosum*, *Grewia flava* and *Lonchocarpus nelsii* shrubs and *Stipagrostis uniplumis* and other perennial grasses have adventitious roots extending outwards in all directions from a central rootstock and in some cases penetrating as deeply as the tap roots of the species cited earlier.

The depth of root penetration of most species is not known, only the top two metres of taproots of the species cited having been exposed. Fragments of *Acacia* roots, which have a characteristic smell, have been brought up from 30 m during drilling operations, and the roots of *Acacia nigrescens* have been encountered at 50 m in an exploration shaft in eastern Botswana. There appears to be little doubt that many of the characteristic tree species root deeply and thereby can tap ground water.

Plant response to environmental conditions: While the climate is semi-arid, the meagre rainfall occurs in summer when temperatures are favourable for plant growth. Most species show a precise response to the climatic conditions. The deep rooting tree and shrub species, able to draw on ground water, respond to rising temperatures and increasing atmospheric humidity from September onwards, and flower and leaf before the rains. They include most of the *Acacia* species, *Albizia anthelmentica* and *Rhigozum brevispinosum*. These carry their leaves into the dry season and shed them only after the first frosts, which exert a greater influence than drought on the seasonal rhythm. A few species, notably *Boscia albitrunca*, retain their leaves throughout the year. Of the deep rooting shrubs, *Catophractes alexandrii* flowers throughout the year and *Petalidium englerianum* in the dry winter period. The plants with underground storage organs, notably *Tylosema esculentum* and most of the Liliaceae and Amaryllidaceae, which are more typical of winter rainfall areas, flower and leaf before the rains, die down and produce their bulbs, corms and tubers before the heat of summer.

The trees and shrubs with lateral rooting systems are leafless until the ground has been well moistened by several good rainstorms. *Terminalia sericea*, which occupies deep sand, is particularly slow to respond. The annuals germinate only after rains.

All species produce large quantities of seed which germinate only when the ground is moist. In the early-flowering species of *Acacia*, this may be in the same year.

Most species possess features and mechanisms for reducing transpiration; some have specific ones for withstanding the semi-arid conditions. Thus some species develop deciduous roots which use soil moisture when it is available and are shed when the ground dries out; perennial grasses form protective sand sheaths around their roots, possibly as a result of mucilaginous secretions of pectic substances (Oppenheimer 1960, Leistner 1967).

Throughout western Botswana, response to available moisture and sensitivity to frost both influence the distribution of plant species. North of Ghanzi, the greater frequency of the deep-rooting *Boscia foetida, Terminalia prunioides, Acacia erubescens, Combretum engleri* and *Commiphora pyracanthoides* subsp. *glandulosa* is due partly to lesser incidence of frost and slightly higher rainfall, but more particularly to available ground water associated with calcrete cover and nearer surface bedrock. By contrast, southwest of Ghanzi the prevalence of species with lateral rooting systems, particularly *Combretum collinium* and *Terminalia sericea*, reflects increasing sand cover.

Around Ghanzi, the distribution of individual species, and their time of flowering and leafing, reflect the relationship between rooting habit and available moisture. Trees and shrubs with well developed tap roots, notably *Boscia albitrunca, Combretum imberbe, Acacia fleckii, A. giraffae, A. mellifera* subsp. *detinens, Commiphora pyracanthoides* subsp. *pyra-canthoides, C. africana, Catophractes alexandrii* and *Petalidium englerianum*, are a feature of the Ghanzi ridge, where ground water is available at depth throughout the year. By contrast, *Combretum apiculatum* and *Terminalia sericea*, which respectively have lateral and adventitious root systems, favour sand-covered areas where they can draw on vadose water after rains. *T. sericea*, together with *C. collinum, Lonchocarpus nelsii* and *Croton gratissimus*, characterize the vegetation of the Kalahari Sand plain. Thus, the contrasts in the form and composition of the vegetation between the Ghanzi ridge and the Kalahari Sand plain are due to differences of species distribution occasioned by relationships between rooting habit and available moisture. Over the Ghanzi ridge, similar relationships influence the distribution of the contrasting associations that are related to micro-habitat conditions over individual lithological units within the concealed sequence of Proterozoic sedimentary rocks forming the apparent fold features.

The mineral status of the soils and vegetation: Major mineral nutrients, other than calcium, are low in most soils, but vary with the nature of the

Table 10.2a. Analyses of soil samples for major elements, ppm (−270 mesh fraction: digested in 1N HNO₃ for 1.25 h: analysis for calcium and iron by atomic absorption spectrophotometry, for potassium and sodium by flame photometry, for phosphorus by colorimetry)

Site	Calcium			Phosphorus			Iron			Potassium			Sodium		
	Number of analyses	Mean value	S.D.	Number of analyses	Mean value	S.D.	Number of analyses	Mean value	S.D.	Number of analyses	Mean value	S.D.	Number of analyses	Mean value	S.D.
Ghanzi ridge															
(1) Calcrete ridges	182	4830	5814	79	97	40	302	4972	2415	80	1070	828	80	47	21
(2) Sand- and silt-filled vales	186	4223	6527	71	87	45	350	5477	1910	112	1303	1020	112	46	32
Kalahari Sand cover															
(1) Red sand	83	3110	1841	83	60	25	219	2289	1153	137	812	380	136	46	36
(2) Grey sand							151	1265	244	151	514	178	151	16	8
Areas of plateau calcrete and shallow water limestone	262	2913	3633	66	86	40	378	5409	2366	79	2003	780	79	308	446

From Cole and Brown (1976) with permission.

Table 10.2b. Analyses of soil samples for major elements, ppm (−80 mesh fraction: digested in 1N HNO₃ for 1.25 h: analyses for calcium and iron by atomic absorption spectrophotometry, for potassium and sodium by flame photometry, for phosphorus by colorimetry)

Site	Transect no.	Calcium			Phosphorus			Iron			Potassium			Sodium		
		No. of samples	Mean	S.D.	No. of samples	Mean	S.D.	No. of samples	Mean	S.D.	No. of samples	Mean	S.D.	No. of samples	Mean	S.D.
Ghanzi ridge																
(1) Calcrete ridges	70	12	2100.0	790.5	12	104.2	41.2	12	2091.7	202.1	12	897.5	140.0	12	93.3	26.1
	72	8	1662.5	1414.2	8	29.3	20.3	8	3537.5	796.3	8	870.0	198.3	8	46.3	9.2
(2) Sand- and	70	8	1680.0	577.5	8	66.7	27.3	8	2112.5	164.2	8	1058.8	217.0	8	75.0	8.7
silt-filled vales	72*	12	1623.2	869.8	12	30.1	5.5	12	5200.0	1381.1	12	1486.7	451.9	8	58.3	22.1
		22	1294.5	774.7	22	27.7	5.2	22	5360.0	1128.2	22	1301.4	450.0	22	57.1	18.7
	78	16	1010.0	570.5	16	75.6	19.4	16	3512.5	685.9	16	1433.3	617.2	16	61.8	17.2
	80	12	850.0	335.5	12	38.8	26.0	16	5218.2	1960.0	16	1045.5	564.7	16	52.5	12.9
Kalahari Sand cover																
(1) Red sand cover	79	10	3188.0	56.5	11	112.0	40.2	11	1750.0	786.3	11	843.0	486.6	11	83.0	9.1
(2) Grey sand cover	92	28	490.4	173.9	28	23.2	4.8	28	1222.6	185.8	28	595.0	141.2	28	14.4	4.9
Areas of plateau calcrete and shallow water limestone	70	16	1643.8	435.1	16	85.3	29.7	16	1650.0	196.6	16	728.3	130.0	16	68.1	21.7
	72	14	2142.9	646.5	14	37.9	29.9	14	3046.4	445.7	14	781.4	163.7	14	75.7	28.5

*For transect 72 analyses are given for the sites at which both Grewia flava and Stipagrostis uniplumis were collected and also for these plus the additional sites at which the latter species only was collected. For transects 78 and 80 analyses are given for the sites at which both Grewia flava and Stipagrostis uniplumis plus those at which the latter species only was collected. No −80 mesh fraction samples were available for transect 91.

From Cole and Brown (1976) with permission.

Table 10.3. Analysis of Stipagrostis uniplumis for major elements, ppm per dry weight of sample (analysis on unmilled, dry ashed material digested in 1N HNO$_3$ for 1.25 h: analyses for calcium and iron by atomic absorption spectrophotometry, for potassium and sodium by flame photometry, for phosphorus by colorimetry)

Site	Transect no.	Calcium			Phosphorus			Iron			Potassium			Sodium		
		No. of samples	Mean	S.D.	No. of samples	Mean	S.D.	No. of samples	Mean	S.D.	No. of samples	Mean	S.D.	No. of samples	Mean	S.D.
Ghanzi ridge																
(1) Calcrete ridges	70	11	6000.0	1897.4	12	335.5	75.3	11	52.3	16.0	12	3558.3	1042.3	12	53.7	13.2
(2) Sand- and silt-filled vales	72	7	3842.9	1238.1	7	527.1	93.9	7	174.3	43.9	7	5700.0	583.1	7	60.0	17.8
	70	9	3244.4	1756.5	9	335.6	110.5	9	65.5	22.0	9	7725.0	2166.7	9	84.8	26.7
	72*	12	2978.5	1413.7	13	462.5	128.6	13	171.4	65.9	13	7939.4	3125.6	13	87.0	
		22	3102.4	1169.7	21	450.7	134.7	23	162.8	63.1	22	7209.6	2950.1	23	81.1	
	78*	16	3268.8	826.8	14	387.4	109.3	16	106.0	40.4	16	2566.5	2787.7	16	60.6	
	80*	12	4208.3	912.0	12	398.3	53.6	12	125.4	70.3	12	3500.0	514.0	12	94.6	14.4
Areas of plateau calcrete and shallow water limestone	70	11	5820.0	133.0	6	203.8	60.6	11	50.6	14.7	11	7858.4	1816.7	11	77.1	20.9
	72	12	3831.5	1083.1	11	382.5	91.4	12	102.4	30.7	13	8914.6	1481.4	12	105.6	22.3

*Note: Stipagrostis uniplumis is sparsely represented in areas of Kalahari Sand cover. It is well represented in the sand- and silt-filled vales where samples were collected at additional sites to those at which Grewia flava samples were collected. For transect 72 analyses are given for the same sites as those for Grewia flava and also for the same plus additional sites. For transects 78 and 80 they are given for the same plus additional sites. From Cole and Brown (1976) with permission.

Table 10.4. Analyses of leaves of Grewia flava for major elements, ppm per dry weight of sample (analyses on unmilled, dry ashed material digested in 1N HNO$_3$ for 1.25 h; analyses for calcium and iron by atomic absorption spectrophotometry, for potassium and sodium by flame photometry, for phosphorus by colorimetry)

Site	Transect no.	Calcium			Phosphorus			Iron			Potassium			Sodium		
		No. of samples	Mean	S.D.	No. of samples	Mean	S.D.	No. of samples	Mean	S.D.	No. of samples	Mean	S.D.	No. of samples	Mean	S.D.
Ghanzi ridge																
(1) Calcrete ridges	70	12	21600.0	4845.8	12	1512.4	365.2	12	52.9	10.6	12	13408.3	1058.7	12	135.4	23.5
	72	8	17188.8	4398.1	6	1166.7	86.2	8	93.5	22.4	8	12032.5	2189.2	8	170.1	22.0
(2) Sand- and silt-filled vales	70	8	11253.5	4925.4	9	1418.8	340.4	9	42.0	12.3	9	10437.8	2958.7	9	173.1	34.7
	72	13	14890.0	4925.2	13	1055.4	234.7	13	74.5	37.7	13	11326.3	3629.2	13	199.3	40.7
	78	6	17533.3	4512.0	6	1091.5	192.4	6	57.3	10.3	6	10483.3	1079.7	6	168.3	31.3
	80	6	13250.0	1839.3	6	1846.7	439.6	6	146.7	25.8	6	13833.3	1254.9	6	170.8	61.4
Kalahari Sand cover																
(1) Red sand cover	79	10	29888.9	4196.6	10	1467.7	243.0	11	45.4	9.5	11	12800.0	2932.6	10	147.4	19.8
	91	11	10435.4	2417.7	11	1244.5	85.4	10	36.7	8.2	11	13472.7	2662.7	10	102.8	33.8
(2) Grey sand cover	92	26	14003.9	1691.0	27	915.4	155.3	28	56.6	10.6	28	12080.0	3410.0	28	180.9	65.1
Areas of plateau calcrete and shallow water limestone	70	16	40000.0	7081.2	15	1558.2	187.6	16	58.1	7.6	16	11516.3	2572.2	16	204.5	24.0
	72	14	17627.9	3709.8	14	1083.7	222.5	14	67.1	27.2	14	12377.1	1928.1	14	251.5	57.2

From Cole and Brown (1976) with permission.

Table 10.5. Analyses of the leaves of selected species for major elements

Species	Calcium			Phosphorus			Iron			Potassium			Sodium		
	Number of analyses	Mean value (%)	S.D. (%)	Number of analyses	Mean value (ppm)	S.D. (ppm)	Number of analyses	Mean value (ppm)	S.D. (ppm)	Number of analyses	Mean value (%)	S.D. (%)	Number of analyses	Mean value (ppm)	S.D. (ppm)
*Stipagrostis uniplumis**	126	0.5	0.2	113	299	134	173	63	27	57	0.45	0.16	58	62	20
Grewia flava	51	2.8	1.0	65	1427	442	241	71	39	117	1.24	0.28	117	137	58
Petalidium englerianum	38	8.1	2.7	44	1199	459	136	136	48	31	1.82	0.35	31	226	63
Dichrostachys cinerea	16	3.3	0.8	19	1536	290	108	61	26	44	1.08	0.22	44	142	81
Acacia mellifera	20	3.8	1.2	24	1393	583	99	47	18	53	0.88	0.27	53	133	53
Acacia tortilis	6	3.4	1.1	6	1189	122	40	73	29	37	0.66	0.24	37	239	110
Combretum hereroense	25	2.3	0.7	29	988	359	106	75	30	40	0.96	0.22	40	142	39
Combretum imberbe	1	2.3	0	1	174	0	15	35	16	8	1.29	0.29	8	142	50
Boscia albitrunca	43	2.0	0.8	43	1321	424	43	57	19	19	1.05	0.46	19	102	66
Terminalia sericea	10	2.1	0.5	10	1216	389	51	29	10	25	0.66	0.15	25	107	44

*Analysis of whole plant of *Stipagrostis uniplumis*.
From Cole and Brown (1976) with permission.

overburden. The soils over the Ghanzi ridge and over areas floored by plateau calcrete and shallow water limestone contain more calcium, phosphorus, iron and potassium than those over areas mantled by Kalahari Sand (Tables 10.2a,b). Over the Ghanzi ridge, the soils on the calcrete ridges contain more calcium but less iron and potassium than those of the intervening sand- and silt-filled vales. The soils from those sand covered areas where calcrete occurs at shallow depth, however, have very high calcium levels which are reflected in the presence of the *Grewia flava* shrubs.

Different in mineral status as well as in soil texture and moisture availability help to explain the contrasts between the vegetation associations of the Ghanzi ridge and the Kalahari Sand plains and between the communities respectively dominated by shrubs on the calcrete ridges and by grasses in the sand- and silt-filled vales.

Compared with the dominant grass, *Stipagrostis uniplumis*, which affords the main grazing for cattle, the leaves of some of the trees and shrubs contain much larger quantities of calcium, phosphorus, potassium and sodium (Tables 10.3–10.5) and those of *Grewia flava*, *Acacia mellifera* and *Boscia albitrunca* in particular provide valuable browse for wild game and domestic cattle.

The influence of fire and biotic factors on the composition and stability of the vegetation: Some authors believe that timber cutting, cattle ranching and fire have had a considerable influence on the composition and stability of the vegetation (de Beer 1962, Blair Rains and Yalala 1970).

The cutting of *Combretum imberbe*, *Acacia giraffae*, *A. tortilis* subsp. *heteracantha* and *A. leuderitzii* for fence poles and of *Terminalia sericea* for African buildings, has reduced the number of trees in some areas, but the small number of farms and the sparse population throughout the area, makes it doubtful whether this has had a significant effect on the vegetation of the area as a whole. Today cutting is restricted to woodland areas, trees are valued as shade for cattle and only dead wood is used for fuel.

Cattle ranching on both the organized farms and on unrestricted grazing areas in the Ghanzi district depends on the natural vegetation. Stocking rates are related to the low carrying capacity and grazing and browsing by cattle has little effect on the composition or character of the vegetation; during studies in 1967–70 no detectable change could be discerned in the associations that straddle grazed areas in the Ghanzi farming blocks and the State lands where no ranching is practised.

However significant changes in the vegetation were evident around boreholes, farmsteads and townships where overgrazing by goats and cattle occurs. This was most severe on the unrestricted grazing areas around Ghanzi, Mamuno and the very important watering point at Kalkfontein. These areas were virtually devoid of all grasses and other herbs, the more palatable shrubs, notably *Grewia flava*, had been eaten back to ground level, and unpalatable thorny shrubs, particularly *Acacia nebrownii*, *A. hebeclada*, *A. mellifera* subsp. *detinens* and *Maytenus senegalensis* had taken over.

Although efforts are made to prevent fire, the vegetation is burnt intermittently by lightning strike and by Bushmen. This has little lasting effect on the vegetation. Because the cover is sparse, fire passes quickly and scarcely affects the deep rooting trees and shrubs. It destroys the dry grass thereby promoting new growth and facilitating the germination of new plants after the next rains.

Relationships between vegetation distribution and the interplay of environmental factors: Detailed studies have revealed close relationships between the distribution of vegetation associations and plant communities and many interacting environmental factors in the Ghanzi area.

The three-fold division between low tree and shrub savanna characterized by *Terminalia sericea* on the Kalahari Sand plain to the east and west of the Ghanzi ridge, by *Acacia leuderetzii*, *A. giraffae* and *Lonchocarpus nelsii* on that to the south, and by *Boscia albitrunca* and *Acacia* spp. on the Ghanzi ridge is broadly related to edaphic conditions. On the Ghanzi ridge complex sequences of plant associations characterize and delineate individual lithological horizons within a succession of Proterozoic sedimentary rocks that are disposed in a series of spectacular folds near the small town of Ghanzi.

The life-form spectra of the vegetation indicate a close adjustment between the position of the perennating buds of the component members of the plant communities and the prevailing climatic conditions. Studies of the rooting systems of characteristic species reveal that most of the plants of the Kalahari Sand plain have lateral roots which utilize the vadose water held in the sands after rains, whereas most of those occupying the Ghanzi ridge, where ground water is available at relatively shallow depth, have tap roots that can reach this source. Clearly, an ability to utilize available moisture in each type of habitat is critical for survival. The seasonal growth rhythm of characteristic species also reflects this ability, the deep-rooting species flowering and leafing as temperatures rise and atmospheric humidity increases before the rains, when they set and shed seeds. The shallow-rooted species commence vegetative growth only after good rains have soaked the soil and overburden.

Analyses indicate that in most soils the levels of major mineral nutrients other than calcium are low, and vary with the nature of the overburden. Differences in soil nutrient status, texture and moisture availability, help to explain the contrasts between the vegetation of the Ghanzi ridge and the Kalahari Sand plains. On the Ghanzi ridge, the adjustment between plant distributions and edaphic factors is so close that individual plant communities

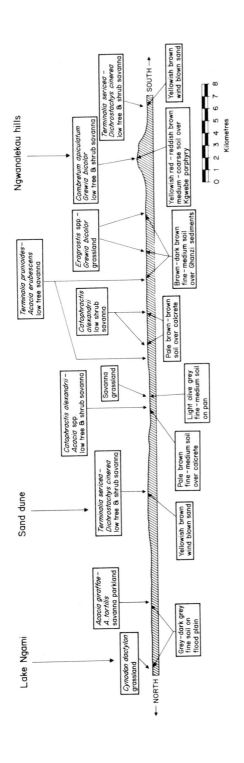

Lake Ngami

Cynodon dactylon grassland

Acacia giraffae – A. tortilis savanna parkland

Grey – dark grey fine soil on flood plain

NORTH →

Sand dune

Terminalia sericea – Dichrostachys cinerea low tree & shrub savanna

Yellowish brown wind blown sand

Catophractis alexandrii – Acacia spp. low tree & shrub savanna

Pale brown fine – medium soil over calcrete

Savanna grassland

Light olive grey fine – medium soil on pan

Terminalia prunoides – Acacia erubescens low tree savanna

Catophractis alexandrii low shrub savanna

Pale brown – brown soil over calcrete

Eragrostis spp. – Grewia bicolor grassland

Brown – dark brown fine – medium soil over Ghanzi sediments

Ngwanalekau hills

Combretum apiculatum – Grewia bicolor low tree & shrub savanna

Terminalia sericea – Dichrostachys cinerea low tree & shrub savanna

Yellowish red – reddish brown medium – coarse soil over Kgwebe porphyry

Yellowish brown wind blown sand

SOUTH →

0 1 2 3 4 5 6 7 8
Kilometres

Figure 10.19. Transect from Lake Ngami to the Ngwenalekau hills (Buerger 1976).

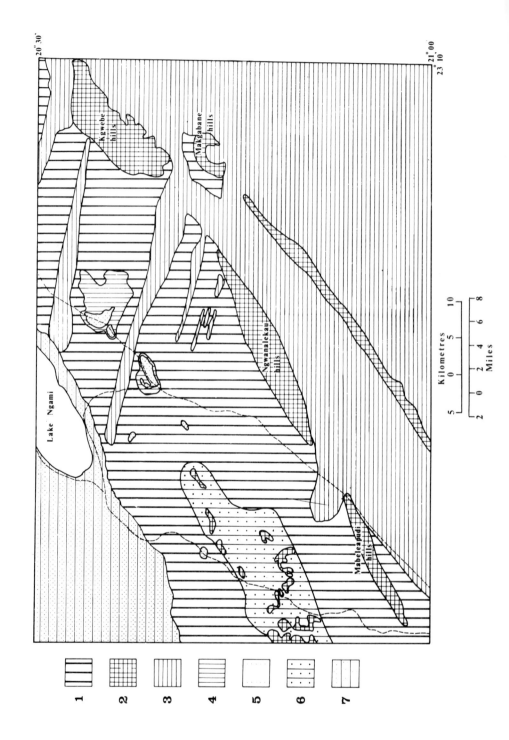

Lake Ngami

Kgwebe hills

Makgabane hills

Ngwanalekau hills

Mabeleapudi hills

20° 30'

21° 00'

23° 10'

1
2
3
4
5
6
7

Kilometres

10 8

5 6

0 4

0 2

5 0

2

Miles

delineate the sub-outcropping bedrock, and faithfully reflect concealed fold structures.

The Lake Ngami–Ngwenalekau hills area

In the area between the Mabeleapudi, Ngwenalekau and Kgwebe hills and Lake Ngami to the north of Ghanzi, strong banding in the low tree and shrub savanna vegetation is evident from aerial reconnaissance and studies of aerial photographs. The banding, broken only by areas of open grassland along drainage lines and by a uniform cover of trees and shrubs over fossil sand dunes, follows the inferred geological strike of the Precambrian rocks and suggests close relationships between vegetation and bedrock geology. On the ground the close cover of trees and shrubs over level terrain obscures visual appreciation of vegetation distributions and ubiquitous cover of soil, Kalahari Sand and calcrete conceals bedrock.

Detailed field studies, supported by laboratory analyses and drilling to ascertain bedrock geology, however, have elucidated the relationships between vegetation distributions and environmental parameters (Buerger 1976, Cole and le Roez 1978) and studies of Landsat imagery have assisted accurate mapping of vegetation, geomorphological and geological features over large areas.

Within the area of strong vegetational banding a low tree and shrub savanna of small *Combretum apiculatum* trees associated with occasional larger *Sclerocarya caffra* and *Markhamia acuminata* trees occupies the areas of outcropping quartz porphyry rocks that form the Mabeleapudi, Kgwebe and Makabana hills while an alternating sequence of low tree and shrub

---

Figure 10.20 *(opposite)*. Vegetation associations in the Lake Ngami–Ngwaku pan area (after Buerger 1976).
Key. (1) Low tree savanna woodland characterized by *Terminalia prunioides* and *Acacia erubescens* associated with *Boscia foetida*, *A. tortilis* and *Commiphora pyracanthoides* subsp. *glandulosa* trees, *Croton menyhartii*, *Grewia bicolor*, *Dichrostachys cinerea* and *Combretum erythrophyllum* shrubs and *Aristida hordeacea*, *A. scabrivalvis* and *Cenchrus ciliaris* grasses. (2) Low tree and shrub savanna dominated by *Combretum apiculatum* trees and *Grewia bicolor* shrubs and *Eragrostis superba* and *Stipagrostis uniplumis* grasses. (3) Low tree and shrub savanna dominated by *Terminalia sericea* and *Dichrostachys cinerea* trees, *Croton gratissimus*, *C. menyhartii* and *Maerua angolensis* shrubs and *Aristida meridionalis*, *Eragrostis horizontalis* and *Stipagrostis uniplumis* grasses. (4) Low tree and shrub savanna characterized by *Acacia mellifera*, *A. karoo*, *A. nebrownii* and *Dichrostachys cinerea* trees and *Catophractes alexandrii* shrubs. (5) Savanna grassland of *Enneapogon brachystachus*, *Sporobolus spicatus* and *Oropetium capense* studded with suffructicose *Leucasphaera bainesii* and *Plinthus karrooicus*. (6) Savanna parkland dominated by *Acacia erubescens* trees and *Stipagrostis uniplumis*, *Aristida scabrivalvis*, *A. hordeacea* and *Eragrostis porosa* grasses. (7) Savanna parkland characterized by *Acacia giraffae* and *A. tortilis* trees and *Enneapogon brachystachus* grass.

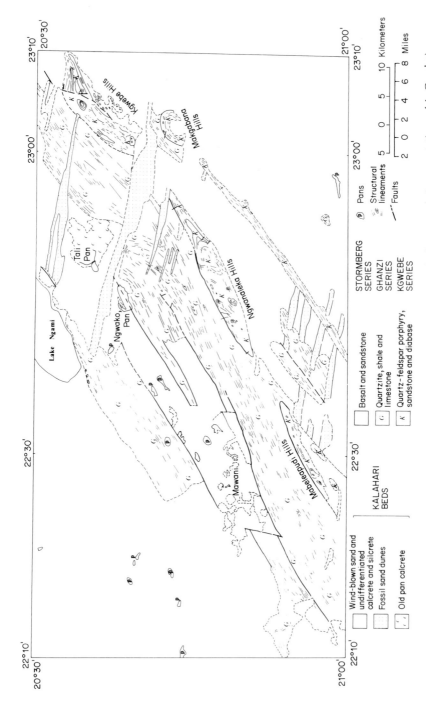

Figure 10.21. Geology of the Lake Ngami-Ngwenalekau hills area (after aerial photograph interpretation of J. Garske).

savanna, shrub savanna and low tree savanna woodland occurs over the different lithological units within the concealed sedimentary sequence of the Proterozoic Ghanzi Beds between these hills and Ngwaku pan (Figures 10.19–10.21). Here woodland characterized by *Terminalia prunioides* and *Acacia erubescens* trees associated with *Boscia foetida*, *A. leuderetzii* and *A. tortilis* trees, *Grewia bicolor*, *Croton menyhartii* and *Combretum erythrophyllum* shrubs and a wide range of perennial grasses that includes *Cenchrus ciliaris*, *Aristida stipagrostis*, *Eragrostis porosa*, *E. echinochloides*, *Aristida scabrivalvis* and *A. hordeacea* occupies heavy dark brown soils derived from argillite and limestone overlain by calcrete. By contrast a low tree and shrub savanna dominated by *Combretum apiculatum* trees associated with *Commiphora pyracanthoides* subsp. *glandulosa* and *Dichrostachys cinerea*, *Grewia bicolor* and *Combretum erythrophyllum* shrubs, *Aristida scabrivalvis* and *A. hordeacea* grasses occupies the red sandy soils where red quartzites sub-outcrop.

Within the *Terminalia prunioides–Acacia erubescens* low tree savanna woodland a major geobotanical anomaly in which the blue flowered shrub of the *Acanthaceae* family, *Ecbolium lugardae* replaces all other shrubs, herbs and grasses in the ground layer, outlines an area some 7 km long and up to 1 km wide where a copper deposit in argillite bedrock causes toxic conditions in the soils (Figure 10.22).

In areas from which vegetational banding is absent a uniform vegetation of *Terminalia sericea* trees, *Dichrostachys cinerea*, *Bauhinia macrantha* and *Croton gratissimus* shrubs, *Aristida meridionalis*, *Eragrostis horizontalis* and *Stipagrostic uniplumis* grasses occurs where deep Kalahari Sand mantles bedrock. This community gives way to one of *Aristida meridionalis*, *A. kalahariensis* and *A. hordeacea* grasses and scattered *Lonchocarpus nelsii* and *Croton gratissimus* shrubs where the sand is exceptionally deep. Major west–east trending sand dunes carrying these forms of vegetation are disclosed on Landsat imagery of the area south of Maun.

Open parkland of *Acacia* trees and *Eragrostis porosa* grass occurs around pans and along drainage lines. Communities of *Acacia mellifera*, *A. karoo*, *A. nebrownii*, *Catophractes alexandrii* and *Dichrostachys cinerea* surround Tale pan and Ngwaku pan where *Petalidium englerianum* is prominent in the ground layer. Over the centres of these pans savanna grassland of *Enneapogon brachystachus*, *Sporobolus spicatus* and *Orepetium capense* prevails. Around Lake Ngami the vegetation patterns are more complex but parkland of *Acacia giraffae* and *A. tortilis* trees with *Enneapogon brachystachus* as the dominant perennial grass is characteristic of the dark grey to black soils of the flood plain.

Figure 10.22. Anomalous ground vegetation of *Ecbolium lugardae* occurring within the *Terminalia prunioides-Acacia erubescens* low tree savanna woodland where copper toxic soils occur over mineralized bedrock concealed by calcrete, northwest of the Ngwenalekau hills.

Figure 10.23. Savanna parkland of *Acacia erubescens* trees and *Stipagrostis uniplumis, Aristida scabrivalvis, A. hordeacea* and *Eragrostic porosa* grasses over dark brown loams derived from Stormberg basalt, Mawane-Magobe area, Botswana.

Figure 10.24. Low tree savanna of *Combretum apiculatum* over a low hill where an inlier of Cave Sandstone gives rise to sandy soils within the plain floored by Stormberg basalt, Mawane-Magobe area, Botswana.

The Mawane–Magobe area

Northwest of Ghanzi the low tree and shrub savanna that characterizes the arid red earth soils derived from the Proterozoic sedimentary rocks gives way abruptly to savanna parkland over lower ground where dark brown loams and black clay soils have developed from Stormberg (Karoo) basalts (Figure 10.23). Typically this parkland is composed of widely spaced *Acacia erubescens* trees studding a grassland of perennial *Stipagrostis uniplumis*, *Aristida scabrivalvis*, *A. hordeacea* and *Eragrostis porosa*. The distribution of this parkland association is governed by the texture, moisture and nutrient characteristics of the soil, the trees and grasses developing extensive and finely ramifying lateral and vertical root systems that fully utilize the moisture retentive properties and high base mineral reserves of the soil. The parkland is interrupted by shrub communities of *Catophractes alexandri* over surface calcrete and by low tree and shrub savanna or low tree savanna where slight eminences occur and by savanna grassland where slight depressions occur, both features appearing as circular features on aerial photographs.

The vegetational changes over the apparent circular features are related to changes of soil, relief and bedrock geology that were established by field investigation and have been accorded a regional perspective by studies of Landsat imagery. Over the slight eminences the low tree and shrub savanna or low tree savanna, composed mainly of small *Combretum apiculatum* trees or shrubs, occupies red sandy soils derived from Cave Sandstone. The slight eminences represent the tops of hills in the Cave Sandstone landscape that existed before the outpourings of the Stormberg lavas. Their distribution is clearly outlined by distinctive colours on colour composites generated from Landsat imagery. Within the areas of parkland over the Karoo basalts the circular features associated with slight depressions are characterized by grassland surrounded by belts of *Terminalia prunioides* and *Acacia erubescens* trees and *Aptosimum leucorrhizum* and other shrubs over the more elevated rim.

CONCLUSIONS

Detailed studies of the low tree and shrub savannas and associated vegetation types in South West Africa and Botswana have revealed very close relationships between plant species and plant community distributions and environmental parameters.

Individual species have morphological features and physiological responses that enable them to survive the hot semi-arid conditions. Some features exhibited by most species combat atmospheric aridity and are a response to climatic conditions; others enable species to exploit particular edaphic conditions and are related to the nature and depth of superficial cover and to differences of bedrock lithology.

Some tree species, notably *Boscia albitrunca, B. foetida, Acacia giraffae, A. hereroensis, A. erubescens* and *A. nigrescens* develop deep tap roots to reach ground water. Others like *Terminalia sericea, Acacia mellifera, A. hebeclada* and *Combretum collinum* have extensive lateral root systems enabling them to draw moisture from a wide area after rains. Similarly some shrubs like *Phaeoptilum spinosum* and *Rhigozum trichotomum* root deeply whereas others like *Grewia flava, G. bicolor* and *G. flavescens* and *Tarchonanthus camphoratus* have extensive lateral systems. The distribution of individual species is influenced by their rooting habit which enables them to obtain water in some edaphic environments but not in others.

The characteristic umbrella shaped crowns of the taller *Acacia* trees, notably *A. tortilis* and *A. giraffae*, reduce the foliage surface exposed to water loss. Their leaves are small and pinnate and they turn their edges to the direct sunlight, all devices to reduce transpiration. The shrubs *Phaeoptilum spinosum* and *Rhigozum brevispinosum* have very small leaves. In these species, the *Acacia* species, *Catophractes alexandri* and many other species some leaves are reduced to thorns. The leaves of many species, including the *Acacias* are protected by resins, those of *Catophractes alexandrii* and *Terminalia sericea* by numerous fine hairs, those of *Boscia* and *Combretum* species are sclerophyllous—all characteristics that combat drought. Some species, notably *Catophractes alexandrii, Petalidium englerianum, Leucasphaera bainesii* and other grey leaved shrubs have excessive uptakes of calcium that may likewise combat drought. Many species shed their leaves during the dry season.

Most tree and shrub species produce masses of colourful flowers that form large quantities of seeds. These are usually enclosed in protective casings that in *Acacia giraffae* and *Catophractes alexandrii* are very thick.

The ground layer comprises mainly perennial and annual grasses. The former have a tussock form and narrow rolled leaves enclosed in a protective sheath. Plants with underground storage organs that enable them to complete their life cycle in a short period after rains are also present. These include bulbous plants of the Liliaceae family in South West Africa and the legume *Tylosema esculentum* in the Ghanzi area of Botswana.

The trees and shrubs that root deeply flower, fruit and come into leaf towards the end of the dry season and before the first rains. Able to draw sufficient moisture from ground water sources they respond to rising temperatures and increasing atmospheric humidity. The early seeding favours germination during the ensuing rainy season. Some shrubs, notably *Ocimum americanum*, flower in January and again in March, taking advantage of two rainy periods to produce seed, some of which germinates in the same season and some in the following one.

While most species have mechanisms for withstanding the hot arid conditions, some are suited to areas of near surface bedrock where ground water is available within rooting depth; others can survive in deep sand. The differing characteristics of individual species and the differing edaphic habitats created by bedrock geology and superficial deposit result in the remarkably close relationships between the distribution of plant communities and geology seen in this harsh environment.

11 Mosaic distributions of savanna woodlands, parklands, grasslands and low tree and shrub savannas and tension zones in Africa

In several areas of Africa, notably in Barotseland in Zambia, in the Okavango delta in Botswana, in the Otavi Mountainland–Etosha pan area of South West Africa and along the Nile in the Sudan, sharply defined and mosaic distributions of the major categories of savanna vegetation occur. This is a result of contrasting edaphic conditions caused by the juxtaposition of differing combinations of relief and drainage, bedrock and superficial geology variously related to the geomorphological evolution of the landscape and to both long-term and short-term climatic changes. In this chapter two areas of complex vegetation distributions exhibiting sharply contrasting physiographic conditions are considered — the Okavango delta and the Otavi Mountainland–Etosha pan area.

THE OKAVANGO DELTA AREA

In northwestern Botswana the Okavango drainage system, fed by streams from the high rainfall area of the Benguela plateau in southeast Angola, introduces areas of periodic, seasonal and permanent inundation into an area of semi-arid terrain. Within the area a great variety of superficial deposits, representing the products of erosion cycles and drainage histories, covers the bedrock geology. In response to the variety of habitats a complex mosaic of different categories of savanna vegetation and of the plant communities within them reflects the influences of soils, geomorphology and geology under

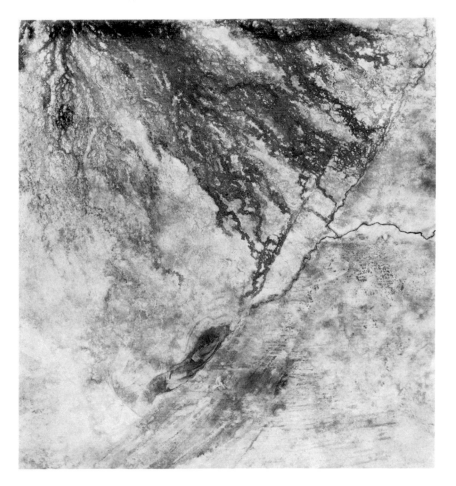

Figure 11.1. The Okavango–Lake Ngami area. Landsat 1, MSS band 5 imagery. Scene ID 1054-07571, 15 September 1972.

the impact of long-term climatic changes and short-term fluctuations in rainfall.

The Okavango delta occurs where, below Muhembo, the Okavango river divides into an anastomosis of channels most of which are eventually collected by the Thamalekane river which flows southwestwards along the base of the delta (Figures 11.1–11.3). In years of high flood, waters flow from the Thamalekane southeastwards into the Botletle river and overflow into Lake Dow and the Makarikari depression which is the focus of all the drainage in northern Botswana. Two channels, the Kwaai and the Mogolelo, flow

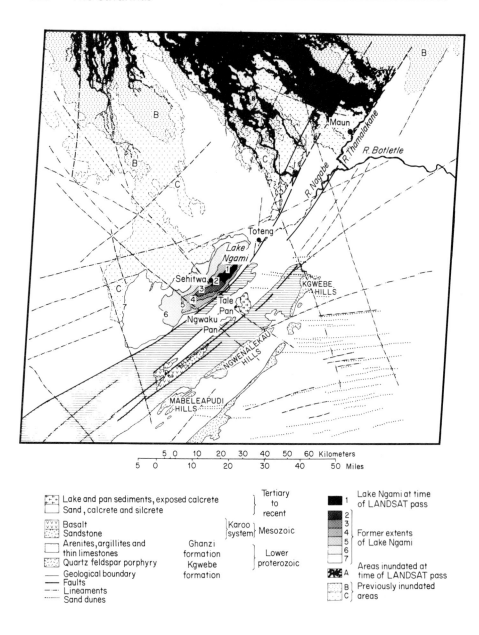

Figure 11.2. The Okavango–Lake Ngami area. Geology and hydrology interpreted from Landsat imagery, Scene ID 1054-07571, 15 September 1972.

Figure 11.3. Vegetation mosaics and flooded areas, Okavango delta. View south from near Maun along Thamalekane (top right).

Figure 11.4. *Acacia* trees and shrubs over silty sand along a stream course between the Kwaai and Savuti channels, Okavango area. In the background *Colophospermum mopane* woodland.

Figure 11.5. *Colophospermum mopane* woodland on riverine silt, between Kwaii and Poha, Okavango area.

towards the Mababe depression, which is no longer flooded. Another, the Taoghe, flows towards Lake Ngami, which is flooded periodically. It is believed that waters formerly flowed along the Savuti channel to the Mababe depression and thence to the Thamalekane, but that river captive by the Linyanti has diverted the waters to the Zambezi (Wellington 1949, 1955).

Today Lake Ngami is much smaller than formerly and until the recent series of wet years the Mababe and Makarikari depressions were believed to be drying up. Climatic and geomorphological evidence has been advanced to account for the desiccation of the area, which is of vital importance for an understanding of the present distribution of plant communities. Palynological, geomorphological and archaeological evidence indicates that during the Quaternary era major climatic oscillations occurred in Africa with pluvial and dry periods corresponding with the glacial and interglacial periods in Europe. During the Recent period the contraction of the Equatorial rain belt and a shortening of the rainy season (Veryard 1962) has been regarded as responsible for falling lake levels and river discharge and for a contraction of savanna and forest and an increase of desert and steppe. The combination of drier climatic conditions and the diversion of waters to the Zambezi has led to the progressive desiccation of the Okavango delta area.

The Okavango area straddles a major vegetational ecotone (tension zone) between the *Colophospermum mopane* woodlands north of Maun and the low tree and shrub savannas characterized by *Acacia* spp. to the south. This ecotone is associated with a climatic transition zone with periodic fluctuations of rainfall. The vegetation is sensitive to climatic oscillations which, however, affect the ground layer rather than the trees and shrubs. The vegetation is also highly vulnerable to degrading factors such as overgrazing by domestic cattle and wild game and damage by elephants which, however, only affect limited areas.

Within the Okavango area the distribution of plant communities reflects edaphic conditions. These are related to the nature of superficial deposits and the extent of inundation by flood waters which superimpose a northwest-southeast pattern over the southwest–northeast trend of the largely concealed Karoo, Proterozoic and Archaean rocks which underlie the surface. Alluvial sands, silts and clays have been laid down along the present distributaries and the former channels of the Okavango while the interfluves, including those beween the Mogolelo and the Kwaai flood plains and those between the latter and the Savuti channel are characterized by a mosaic of wind blown Kalahari Sand and waterlaid sand and clay deposits, the latter a legacy of the periods when the swamps were more extensive. In the north, quartz porphyry bedrock is exposed in the Goha hills while sand dunes border the Savuti channel and Mababe depression.

Away from the aquatic communities which occupy the permanently inundated sites the alluvial soils of areas adjoining the river channels are occupied by flood plain grasslands and riverine and marginal flood plain woodland and parkland. The old alluvium and Kalahari Sand on extensive interfluve areas are covered by various forms of savanna woodland and low tree and shrub savanna.

The flood plain grasslands occupy areas subject to inundation annually. As along the Kafue river in Zambia, *Echinochloa* spp. dominate in the wettest areas and *Setaria, Chloris, Panicum* and *Hyparrhenia* species on the drier sites. The lawn-forming *Cynodon dactylon* covers extensive areas while *Sporobolus spicatus* is confined to white saline powdery soils (Tinley 1966). Riverine and marginal flood plain woodland and parklands occupy the alluvial soils of slightly elevated flat ground which represents an earlier flood plain surface now above present day flood level. Here *Acacia nigrescens* is the characteristic tree except on sandy alluvium where *A. giraffae* dominates. *Colophospermum mopane* is present where there is a compacted layer below the surface. Palm savanna woodland characterized by *Hyphaene ventricosa* occurs in places at the margins of the flooded areas.

Over the extensive areas which normally are no longer flooded between the Kwaai and the Savuti channels and west of Taoghe, savanna woodlands occupy areas of old alluvium whereas low tree and shrub savanas characterize areas of Kalahari Sand (Figure 11.4). *Acacia tortilis* is the most common tree where the alluvium is a silty sand, and *A. giraffae* where it is sandy. *Colophospermum mopane* woodlands occur over dark grey to black clay soils and soils with a clay pan (Figure 11.5). They form a complex mosaic with *Terminalia sericea–Combretum mechowianum* low tree and shrub savannas over Kalahari Sand. North of the Savuti channel, tall *Colophospermum mopane* woodlands occupy deep grey sands overlying black clay while *Kirkia africana* trees distinguish the vegetation over the Goha hills where quartz porphyry bedrock outcrops (Figure 11.6). The major sand dune west of the Mababe depression carries low tree and shrub savanna dominated by *Terminalia sericea* (Figure 11.7).

That the complex mosaic of savanna woodlands, parklands and grasslands in the Okavango area represents a delicate adjustment to edaphic conditions related directly to geomorphology and to geology under the influence of climatic changes, is confirmed by the imagery from successive Landsat passes. This reveals the vegetation distributions, some of which outline the former extents of Lake Ngami and reveal former channels that fed the larger lake (Figure 11.2; Cole 1982b). The imagery also shows numerous fault structures which have clearly controlled the drainage and influenced the vegetation patterns.

Movements along these faults could easily have diverted waters towards the Zambezi and brought about progressively drier conditions in the Lake

Figure 11.6. Woodland of *Kirkia africana* and *Adansonia digitata* (baobab) over outcropping quartz porphyry, Goha hills, Okavango area. From Cole (1982a).

Figure 11.7. *Terminalia sericea* low tree savanna over sand dune (foreground) near Mababe depression (background).

Figure 11.8. Dead *Acacia* spp. trees on black clay soils possibly killed by alternation of dry and wet periods around Lake Ngami.

Figure 11.9. Trees killed by flood waters along the Savuti channel.

Ngami area (Figures 11.8 and 11.9). The imagery shows that in 1975 Lake Ngami was larger than in 1972 and that some of its former channels were again occupied by flood waters. The lake, however, was nowhere near as extensive as at one time, as evidenced by the maximum extent of former shorelines. It is possible that at the time when there was a considerable body of water in Lake Ngami the savanna woodlands may have extended into this area and that the presence of *Combretum imberbe* trees in the area between Ghanzi and Maun and the stands of *Terminalia sericea* trees and of *Combretum* tree and shrub species in deep Kalahari Sand throughout western Botswana represent the last vestiges of that vegetation.

THE OTAVI MOUNTAINLAND–ETOSHA PAN AREA

Sharp contrasts of relief characterize the Otavi Mountainland–Etosha pan area lying to the west of the sand dune country that separates it from the Okavango delta area.

The Otavi Mountainland is built of a suite of Proterozoic sedimentary rocks that have been folded and faulted and injected with pseudo aplite pipe-like bodies that are mineral bearing. Resistant dolomites and quartzites form a series of east–west trending ranges which extend from northwest of Otavi to Grootfontein and to Tsumeb in the north and rise some 60–240 m above the flanking valleys which have average elevations of 1200–1800 m above sea level (Richter-Zwanziger 1978). The broad level valleys and adjacent plains are underlain by less resistant grits, shales, schists and unsilicified dolomites that are locally covered by calcrete and residual and transported soils of variable thickness. Near Grootfontein the Otavi valley drains via the Omuramba to the Okavango river whereas near Otavi the drainage is southwestward to the Uchab and Atlantic Ocean. North of Tsumeb the drainage is to the Etosha pan. Karstic features characterize the areas underlain by dolomite. Surface water is absent for most of the year but springs, underground caverns and sink holes are common features in the valleys.

Over the rugged dolomite mountain ranges the soils are skeletal brownish sands. Deeper brown sands and red and brown loams occur over dolomite in the valleys while grey loam and dark grey clays occur over calcrete.

The vegetation is closely related to the relief and geology. An open savanna woodland of *Terminalia prunioides*, *Kirkia acuminata* and *Commiphora pyracanthoides* trees with a sparse cover of *Croton gratissimus* shrubs, and *Aristida*, *Eragrostis* and *Enneapogon* spp. of grasses cover the rocky upper sloper of the ranges whereas on the deeper sandy soils of the foothills and lower slopes *T. prunioides* is associated with *T. sericea* and *Combretum apiculatum* trees. By contrast the valleys have a low tree and shrub savanna or savanna parkland vegetation that is characterized by *Acacia hereroensis*, *A. mellifera*, *Dichrostachys cinerea* and *Combretum* spp. trees over sands and calcrete and by *A. reficiens*, *Peltophorum africanum* and *Lonchocarpus nelsii* trees over sandy loams (Figure 11.10). Within this broad framework, however, the form and composition of the vegetation varies with the soils and bedrock. Virtually pure stands of *Terminalia sericea* low savanna woodland occupy deep sands developed over a tillite horizon within the Proterozoic sequence. Shrub communities of *Croton gratissimus* mark zones

Figure 11.10. *Acacia* parkland on floor of Otavi valley and *Kirkia acuminata-Terminalia prunioides-Commiphora pyracanthoides* woodland on the rocky slopes of the ranges.

of outcropping schist and dense stands of small *Dichrostachys cinerea* trees occur over cupriferous epidosite and breccia. The copper indicator plant *Helichrysum leptolepis* delineates areas of toxic ground over small copper orebodies associated with pseudo aplite plugs near the Kombat copper mine as well as toxic soils over cupriferous bedrock at other localities.

The vegetation associations and plant communities in the Otavi Mountainland appear to be closely adjusted to environmental conditions and to be stable under present conditions. Studies of Landsat imagery indicate that the Etosha pan, like Lake Ngami southwest of the Okavango delta, was once larger than it is today (Cole 1982c). Discrete variations in the plant communities occur around the Etosha pan where low tree and shrub savannas and low savanna woodlands of *Terminalia prunioides* and *Acacia* spp. alternate with stands of *Colophospermun mopane* on soils with high pH values and with savanna grasslands on heavy clay soils (see Figure 3.6). There is some evidence for a vegetational tension zone north of the Etosha pan, but because the area does not receive such large inflows of drainage from outside the region and because it is less subject to climatic fluctuation, under present conditions the vegetation is more stable than in the Okavango delta area.

12   The savannas of West Africa and the southwestern Sudan

Geographical location and a long history of human occupation results in marked differences between the West African savannas and those of other areas.

The West African savannas occur within latitude 5° and 15°N between the tropical forests of the Guinea coast and Congo basin and the semi-desert steppes and deserts of the Sahara. This narrow latitudinal extent contrasts with the great latitudinal expanse of the East, Central and South African savannas which cover vast areas between 5° and 25°S and extend northwards to the equator and southwards to 35°S (Figure 12.1). Although they span 50° of longitude the West African savannas are virtually detached from those of the core area of savanna distribution in central southern Africa. Their distribution may be likened to that of the savannas of northern tropical America which are isolated from the core area of South American savanna distribution in Brazil.

As in northern tropical America, the peripheral distribution of the West African savannas is associated with fewer species than in the savanna core areas of central southern African. Because of the narrow latitudinal extent the impacts of individual physical factors on the distribution of the major savanna categories differs from those in other parts of Africa, while greater population pressures have severely affected the vegetation. Fire, cultivation and grazing have disturbed or destroyed much of the vegetation and, coupled with prolonged drought, have caused desertification in the low tree and shrub savannas of the Sahel.

In West Africa three categories of vegetation have been recognized between the tropical forests and the semi-desert steppes and deserts (Chevalier 1900, Keay 1952). These are the savanna woodlands of the Guinea zone, the drier types of savanna woodland of the Sudan zone to the north, and the low tree and shrub savannas of the Sahel described as thorn savanna or steppe by Keay (1952, 1959) (Figure 12.1).

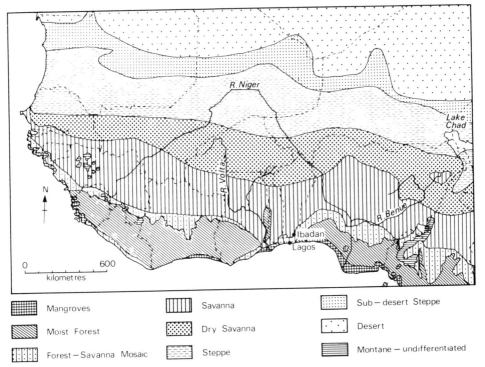

Figure 12.1. Distribution of major vegetation zones in West Africa (after Morgan and Pugh 1969).

Mangroves	Savanna	Sub–desert Steppe
Moist Forest	Dry Savanna	Desert
Forest–Savanna Mosaic	Steppe	Montane – undifferentiated

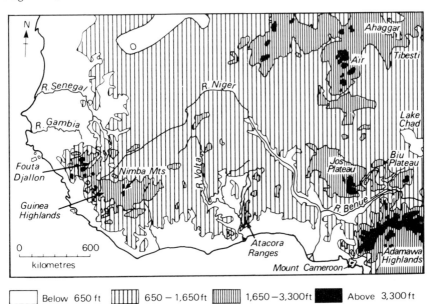

Below 650 ft   650 – 1,650 ft   1,650 – 3,300 ft   Above 3,300 ft

Figure 12.2. Relief and drainage of West Africa (after Morgan and Pugh 1969).

The savanna woodlands of West Africa, like those of central southern Africa, are composed of deciduous trees and tall grasses. Their physiognomy and seasonal growth characteristics are similar throughout the Guinea zone but floristic differences have occasioned a subdivision between south and north.

Although many species have a widespread distribution some are more typical of one subzone than of the other. Generally speaking, a variety of tree species, some with rain forest affinities, characterizes the southern Guinea subzone whereas communities dominated by one species are more typical of the northern subzone.

In the southern subzone *Anogeissus leiocarpus* and *Lophira lanceolata* are the most common trees. Along with *Daniella oliverii, Terminalia glaucescens, Hymenocardia acida, Burkea africana* and *Afzelia africana*, the last three of which are common in central southern Africa, they may attain heights of 12–15 m. In the northern Guinea subzone, which for centuries has experienced frequent burning but less extensive cultivation than the southern subzone, the dominant trees *Isoberlinia doka* and *I. tomentosa* attain heights of only 6–12 m. Only these two species of the *Isoberlinia* genus are present while species of *Brachystegia* and *Julbernardia*, which with *Isoberlinia* are so typical of the 'miombo' savanna woodlands of central southern Africa, are absent. Smaller more contorted trees of *Uapaca togoensis* and *Monotes kerstingii*, like other species of the same general in central southern Africa, respectively replace the *Isoberlinia* spp. on outcrops of concretionary ironstone or indurated laterite and on eroded areas farther downslope. On these sites each genus is represented by only one species in West Africa whereas several occur in the core areas of the savanna woodlands in central southern Africa. *Terminalia macroptera* occupies the depressions with poorly drained clays in West Africa where again the vegetation is floristically poorer than in central southern Africa. *Parinari curatellifolia* and *Cussonia barteri* occur throughout both Guinea subzones, while small *Gardenia* spp., *Piliostigma thonningii* and *Stereospermum kunthianum* trees are common in both subzones; *Bridelia ferruginea, Maytenus senegalensis* and *Psorosporum febrifugum* are more typical of the southern Guinea subzone and *Annona senegalensis, Combretum* spp., *Grewia mollis, Protea elliottii* and *Ximenia americanum* of the northern subzone. Tall grasses, mainly *Hyparrhenia, Andropogon* and *Pennisetum* spp. form the ground layer which has an average height of 1.5–3 m in the south and of 0.5–1.5 m in the north.

Within the savanna woodland zone, the Jos plateau of Nigeria—which averages 1200 m and rises to 2000 m in places—is largely treeless. Relics of savanna woodland, confined to its periphery, contain typical northern Guinea zone species and also some species with affinities with those of East and Southern Africa, e.g. *Faurea speciosa*.

In the drier forms of savanna woodland of the Sudan zone where the annual rainfall averages 500–1000 mm, some relatively tall trees, 7–15 m high, notably *Anogeissus leiocarpus*, *Sclerocarya birrea* and the baobab, *Adansonia digitata*, occur with the typical small trees, mostly *Acacia* spp., 5–7 m high. The locust bean tree, *Parkia clappertoniana*, shea butter tree, *Butyrospermum paradoxum*, kapok tree, *Bombax costatum* and *Hyphaene thebaica* palm are common in old cultivation areas. *Colophospermum mopane*, which occupies such large areas of the dry savanna woodlands of south central Africa, however, is absent. Shrubs and a layer of relatively short grasses that commence vegetative growth before the rains occupy the ground between the trees.

Northwards, the dry savanna woodland gives way to the low tree and shrub savanna of the Sahel. This is composed mainly of small, thorny *Acacia* spp. trees, thorny shrubs like *Commiphora africana* and short wiry grasses of the *Aristida* genus. *Acacia seyal* trees favour the clay soils of depressions whereas *A. raddiana* trees occur in light sandy soils. *A. nilotica* occupies flood plains like that of the Senegal river and *A. sieberiana* trees follow watercourses where they may attain a height of 12 m.

FACTORS INFLUENCING THE DISTRIBUTION OF SAVANNAS IN WEST AFRICA AND THE SOUTHWESTERN SUDAN

Climate, fire and man's cultural practices have long been cited as the main influences over the physiognomy, composition and distribution of savanna vegetation in West Africa (Aubreville 1938, Clayton 1958a, Hopkins 1962, 1965a,b, Jones 1963, Keay 1949, 1951, 1952, 1953) although the importance of soils has been acknowledged in some areas of Nigeria (Keay 1952, 1959a) and repetitive catenary sequences of associated vegetation, soils and relief conditions have been recognized in the southwestern Sudan (Morrison *et al.* 1948) and the Ivory Coast (Menaut and Cesar 1979, 1982). The influence of edaphic factors on the distribution of forest and savanna and on the stability of the forest/savanna boundary in Nigeria has been established (Morgan and Moss 1965; Moss and Morgan 1970), while the roles of climatic change and of termite activity have been cited to explain vegetational patterns in the savannas of the Sudan zone. As in other regions of Africa the vegetation of West Africa and the Sudan is the legacy of the interplay of physical and biotic environmental factors whose relative importance today, as in the past, varies from place to place. Most studies of the vegetation have been undertaken either in forest reserves or around research stations, particularly in Nigeria and the Ivory Coast, and investigations of the interplay between vegetation and environmental factors over major regions have not been made. Nevertheless examination of the roles of individual factors and of their interplay on vegetation patterns is merited and some evaluation of the evolution of these patterns is warranted.

The influence of climate, fire and cultural practices

The broad coincidence between the distribution of the main categories of savanna vegetation and the amount and seasonal incidence of rainfall, the long history of human settlement, the widespread and frequent occurrence of fires and the extent of cultivation have focused attention on the overriding influences of climate, fire and cultural practices on the form, composition and distribution of savanna vegetation in West Africa.

Evergreen tropical forests give way to semi-deciduous and deciduous savanna woodlands where the average annual rainfall is below 1500 mm and there is a marked dry season, exceeding one month when less than 2.5 mm is received, and the lowest mean monthly relative humidity is below 70%. Northwards the composition of the savanna woodlands changes to more xerophytic species where the average annual rainfall is below 1000 mm, the dry season lengthens to four or five months, temperatures are more extreme and the intensity of the harmattan, the dry northeasterly wind that brings tropical continental air from the Sahara, lowers the relative humidity to daily maxima of 75% and daily minima of 20% in the dry months. The dry savanna woodlands in turn give way to low tree and shrub savannas where the annual rainfall averages 500–700 mm, the dry season lasts from five to seven months and is characterized by very low relative humidities and great extremes of temperatures with mean daily maxima of 30–50°C and mean daily minima of 10–28°C. The low tree and shrub savannas finally yield to semi-desert steppe and to desert where the meagre and unreliable rainfall of less than 500 mm concentrated in less than four months of the year is inadequate to support tree growth.

Despite the gradual change from constantly hot, humid conditions on the coast to those of increasingly prolonged aridity and extremes of temperature inland, the boundaries between rain forest and savanna woodland and between savanna woodland and low tree and shrub savannas are usually abrupt. One author believes that before the vegetation was affected by burning and cultivation there was a continuum from complex rain forest in the wetter areas to simpler savanna woodland in the drier areas (Hopkins 1965a). Another has suggested that the areas covered by Quaternary sand in the Sudan zone of Nigeria may once have carried woodlands comparable with those characterized by *Baikiea plurijuga* in Zambia (Keay 1952).

West Africa has a long history of human occupation. The open character and healthy climate of the low tree and shrub savanna zone of the Sahel attracted early settlement. In the 11th century the Arab chronicler Bekri wrote of vast and prosperous fields in ancient Ghana; in Medieval times the Sudanic kingdoms were sited in the Sahel (Morgan and Pugh 1969). In this zone the vegetation has been severely affected by clearing for cultivation and by grazing of cattle, sheep and goats. Fire has not been important for the short grasses, which shoot only after rains, are valued for grazing and do not provide combustible dry matter. The Sahel is particularly susceptible to oscillations of climate that are governed by the global movements of pressure and wind systems; the combination of recent prolonged droughts and of animal and human population pressures exceeding the resource capacity have caused widespread loss of vegetation and the onset of desertification.

Within the savanna woodland of southern Guinea, fire has been used widely and frequently to drive out wild game, to obtain grazing for domestic stock and to prepare lands for cultivation. Here some authors (Aubreville 1949, Hopkins 1965a) contend that the present savanna woodland has been derived from forest — a suggestion that is questioned by the sharpness of the forest/savanna boundary and by the differences of tree species between the two forms of vegetation. When the tall grasses of the savanna woodlands shrivel as the dry season advances they are highly susceptible to fire, which burns off the dead matter. Thick barks protect the savanna woodland trees from the effects of fire and their well developed lignotubers favour regrowth. The fires do not readily penetrate moist forests where there is a paucity of dry grass to provide tinder. In many instances soil differences enhance the contrasts of moisture status between savanna woodland and forest. The evidence indicates that the savanna woodlands are associated with the interplay of environmental factors with fire as one of the factors they are able to tolerate. This view is supported further by the change inland from the woodlands dominated by *Anogeissus leiocarpus* or *Isoberlinia* spp. to the drier types of woodland characterized by *Acacia* spp., *Sclerocarya birrea* and *Adansonia digitata* trees where the shorter grasses provide good grazing throughout the year and fires are infrequent and unwelcome. These changes parallel those in central southern Africa and indicate basic interrelationships with physical environmental factors.

Relationships between the seasonal growth of individual savanna species and the interplay of climatic and edaphic factors that influence moisture availability are evident from studies made on a savanna site within the Okokemeji Forest Reserve of Nigeria. These showed a general correspondence between vegetation growth and the onset of rains in February but *Pterocarpus erinaceous*, which flowers when leafless in December–January, commenced extension growth before late January, and *Acacia sieberiana*, *Cussonia barteri* and *Daniella oliverii* trees, the grasses *Andropogon tectorum* and *Monocymbium ceressiforme* and the sedge *Fimbristylis exilis* flushed at that time (Hopkins 1970a).

Pre-rains flushing is a characteristic feature of savanna vegetation in Africa, and in the author's view is both dependent on the rooting systems of individual species and related to temperature conditions and moisture availability as determined by soils and geology (see Chapter 10). The pre-rains flushing of *P. erinaceous* parallels that of *P. angolensis* in Tanzania (Boaler 1963). Hopkins regards fire as the most important stimulant to the pre-rains flush but suggests that where budbreak occurs in its absence a slight increase in day length could be responsible. As elsewhere in Africa flushing in species whose roots can draw on ground water is most probably a response to a rise in temperature which may or may not be fire induced. In West Africa as elsewhere a deciduous habit and deep rooting systems enable savanna species to endure extremes of temperature and moisture availability and to respond to the onset of favourable conditions. The shallow rooted evergreen species of the rain forests cannot do this. It follows that, notwithstanding the importance of fire, vegetation distributions including those of forest and savanna and of different categories of savanna are controlled by interacting physical factors upon which fire and man's cultural practices impose a secondary influence. Attention must therefore be accorded to the edaphic influences which will vary with the geomorphology and geology.

The influence of soils, geomorphology and geology

On a broad regional scale the distribution of savanna woodlands coincides with areas of ferruginous soils and that of low tree and shrub savannas with brown loam soils. In turn within the broad climatic limits that influence major soil type, the soils of West Africa are related to relief, geomorphology and bedrock geology (Figures 12.2–12.4). Deep weathering and laterite development are characteristic features over large areas and ferruginous duricrusts, laterite or ciurasse are well developed and widespread even in the drier zones (Morgan and Pugh 1969). They are associated with a series of planation surfaces, 200–500 m high, cut across Precambrian rocks (Harrison Church 1957, King 1962). Particularly in the drier areas they represent relict features from periods of wetter climate.

Relationships between the form and composition of the vegetation and the soils have been cited by several authors (Morrison *et al.* 1948, Clayton 1958a, 1961, Hambler 1964, Jones 1963, Keay 1959a, Menaut and Cesar 1979, 1982, Morgan and Moss 1965, Ramsay 1964, Ramsay and de Leeuw 1964, 1965, White 1965). Vegetational changes related to the disposition and outcrop of concretionary ironstone (laterite or cuirasse) and of bedrock have

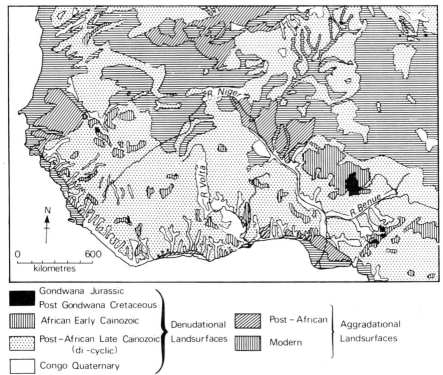

Figure 12.3. Geomorphological surfaces of West Africa (after Morgan and Pugh 1969).

- ■ Gondwana Jurassic
- Post Gondwana Cretaceous ⎫
- African Early Cainozoic ⎬ Denudational
- Post-African Late Cainozoic (di-cyclic) ⎬ Landsurfaces
- Congo Quaternary ⎭

Post – African ⎫
Modern ⎬ Aggradational Landsurfaces

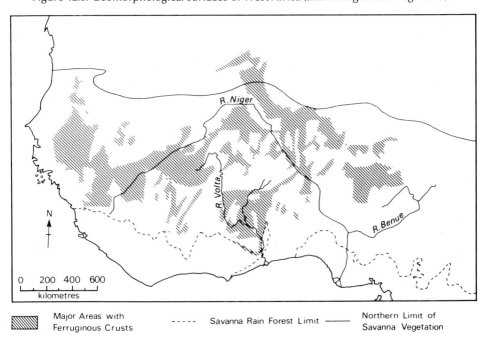

Major Areas with Ferruginous Crusts — ---- Savanna Rain Forest Limit — Northern Limit of Savanna Vegetation

Figure 12.4. Distribution of ferruginous crusts in West Africa (after Morgan and Pugh 1969).

been noted by some writers (Keay 1953, 1959a, Jones 1963). Relationships between soils and geomorphology and between vegetation, soils and geology have been described by others (Clayton 1958b, 1961, Ramsay 1964, Ramsay and de Leeuw 1964, 1965). For several areas linear vegetational patterns have been ascribed to edaphic variations related to old sand dunes and to the breakdown of old termitaria, in each case occasioned by climatic oscillations. Assessment of the interacting influences of all environmental factors, including those of soils, geomorphology, geology and climatic change, however, is essential for a full understanding of present vegetation distributions.

Edaphic influences on the savanna/forest boundary

Studies of the savanna/forest boundary and of forest outliers within the savanna woodland zone of Nigeria indicate that edaphic factors exert an important influence over the form of vegetation. Forest outliers occupy soils with more exchangeable calcium (Jones 1963) and a better moisture status (Morgan and Moss 1965) than those of the surrounding savanna woodlands. These relationships are recognized by local people who grow different crops on the forest and savanna sites. Because of the moister soils and paucity of grass, fire rarely enters the forest and, as studies of aerial photography of the area between Ibadan and the Dahomey border for 1953–54 and 1962–63 have shown, the savanna/forest boundary is remarkably stable even under the pressure of increasing population density. Only minor changes in the boundary, mainly of forest advancing into savanna on the savanna ward edges of forest reserves, have occurred. Moreover, burning is not universal and whereas some areas are fired twice in the same dry season, others are rarely burnt. Thus, although there may be strong ecological evidence for a change from forest to savanna as a result of cultivation and burning (Clayton 1958a, Hopkins 1965a) in some areas of West Africa, this may not be representative of the savannas as a whole; indeed the savanna/forest boundary may be influenced or even determined by edaphic conditions affecting soil moisture relationships.

Vegetation/soils catenas

Clear relationships between vegetation, soils, relief and geology have emerged from detailed investigations in the southwestern Sudan (Morrison *et al.* 1948), the Anara forest reserve (Keay 1959a), Kabba province (Clayton 1958b, 1961), the middle Gongola valley (Ramsay and de Leeuw 1964, 1965) and the area northwest of Ibadan in Nigeria (Hambler 1964) and the Lamto research station in the Ivory Coast (Menaut and Cesar 1979, 1982).

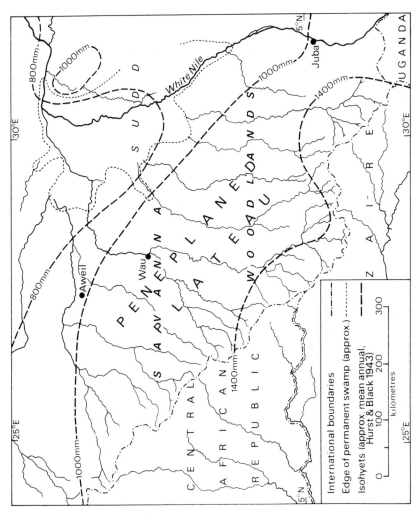

Figure 12.5. The southwestern Sudan, rainfall and drainage and vegetation distributions (after Morrison *et al.* 1948).

The southwestern Sudan   The southwestern Sudan comprises a level plateau that is planed across Precambrian Basement gneiss and slopes gently northeastwards from the Congo–Nile watershed towards the permanent swamps of the Sudd. Its altitude declines from 800 m in the southwest to 400 m in the northeast and its surface is lightly dissected by shallow valleys cut by the northeastward flowing rivers. These become sluggish in their lower reaches where they seasonally inundate the flood plain region bordering the swamps (Figure 12.5) (Morrison *et al.* 1948).

From the Congo–Nile watershed northeastwards across the plateau the vegetation shows regional changes in response to decreasing annual rainfall and lengthening dry season, and exhibits catenary variations related to soils and relief that produce repetitive patterns over large areas.

Dense savanna woodlands broken by gallery forests along the valleys occupy the dissected watershed region where the rainfall averages 1250–1400 mm distributed over nine to ten months. This changes to open deciduous savanna woodlands on the plateau where 1000–1250 mm of rainfall occurs over seven to eight months and to savanna grasslands and parklands with thorny trees and shrubs in the flood plain region which receives only 800–1000 mm in six to eight months. The savanna woodlands resemble those of the Guinea zone of West Africa and the parklands with thorny species are comparable with areas that seasonally are partially inundated within the Sudan zone.

Within each physiographic region the distribution of the characteristic vegetation is interrupted by catenary variations of vegetation, soil and relief whose repetitive patterns produce discrete complexes. On the higher plateau savanna woodlands occupy the eluvial soils over ironstone or indurated laterite but, in response to varying soil and drainage conditions, exhibit mosaic distributions of discrete associations producing the eluvial vegetation complex. The colluvial soils of the slopes below the plateau edge carry a more open woodland of smaller trees belonging to fewer and different species. This shows zonal variations related to changes of soil texture with increasing distance from the plateau edge. A treeless grassland occupies the heavy illuvial soils with impeded drainage of the periodically flooded lower ground but it comprises discrete plant communities that reflect variations of soil texture and drainage, and exhibits mosaic distributions to produce the illuvial vegetation complex.

While these vegetation/soil/relief catenas occur throughout the southwestern Sudan, the eluvial vegetation complex is best developed within the savanna woodland area of the southwestern plateau whereas the illuvial complex is more characteristic of the flood plains region. In all areas and on all sites the vegetation may be further influenced by fire and cultivation and by termite action.

The interactions between moisture conditions and fire on the higher eluvial levels and the lower illuvial levels of the catenary sequence have been shown schematically as follows:

Higher levels
↓
Ground drier

Wet season:		Dry season:
No flooding		Little moisture at grass-root depth
↓		↓
Trees encouraged	→ Shading →	*Sparser grass*
↑		↓
Saplings survive	←	Slight burning

Lower levels
↓
Ground wetter

Wet season:		Dry season:
Flooding		Fair moisture at grass-root depth
↓		↓
Trees discouraged	→ Little shading →	*Denser grass*
↑		↓
Saplings suffer	←	Severe burning

(after Morrison *et al.* 1948)

The form and composition of the savanna woodlands of the eluvial complex varies with the depth of soil. It comprises mixed stands of *Prosopis africana*, *Burkea africana*, *Isoberlinia doka*, *Daniella oliveri*, *Parinari curatellifolia*, *Sclerocarya birrea* and *Khaya senegalensis* in which most trees attain 9–15 m and some reach 15–18 m where the soils are relatively deep. Locally stands of *Khaya senegalensis* and *Anogeissus leiocarpus* reaching 12–20 m occur where soils with a higher percentage of clay have formed around termite mounds. A lower woodland of *Lannea schimperi*, *L. kerstingii* and *Terminalia mollis*, some 6–12 m high, occurs where the soil comprises only a shallow A horizon over pisolotic laterite (pea grit). On eroded sites where there is no A horizon material and pisolitic laterite occurs at surface, only small trees, notably *Hymenocardia acida*, and shrubs occur; these may form a thicket some 2–4.5 m high. Where the ironstone actually outcrops there is no vegetation at all. These distinctive communities whose distributions are related to the depth of soil over the laterite or ironstone produce vegetation mosaics over the eluvial complex.

The vegetation over the colluvial slopes is composed of small trees mostly *Combretum* spp. reaching 7.5 m in a tall grassland that is denser than that on the eluvial soils of the plateaux. Both grass and tree species exhibit simple zonal patterns of distribution between the plateaux and valley sites.

The vegetation of the illuvial complex displays more irregular mosaic distribution patterns. On the lighter, better drained soils the vegetation comprises a tall grassland composed mainly of *Hyparrhenia rufa* and other *Hyparrhenia* spp. with widely spaced *Terminalia macroptera* and *T. laxiflora* trees up to 11 m high. This has the character of savanna parkland (or orchard savanna) which is interrupted by dense clumps of deciduous and evergreen trees, including *Anogeissus schimperi*, *Acacia campylacantha*, *A. sieberiana* and *Diospyros mespiliformis* on termite mounds with better drained soils. By contrast the brownish grey and grey soils with impeded drainage support only a tall grassland of *Vetiveria nigritana* with single trees or clumps of trees on elevated ground, notably termite mounds, where *Mitragyna inermis*, *Acacia sieberiana* and *Piliostigma thonningii* may occur. The dark grey fine textured soils with impeded drainage found mainly in the flood plains region carry a vegetation of tall grassland with small thorny *Acacia seyal* trees 3–9 m high, while the 'black cotton' soils of basin sites without drainage may carry either a similar vegetation or, in extreme cases, be completely bare. These communities whose distributions are related to soil texture and soil drainage produce mosaics or zonal vegetation patterns in the illuvial complex.

The Kaduna and Kabba province areas of Nigeria   Vegetation, soils and relief catenas comparable with those of the eluvial plateau complex of southwestern Sudan have been described from the Anara forest reserve between Kaduna and Zaria in Nigeria (Keay 1959a).

The Kaduna area of Nigeria is characterized by three erosion surfaces, the upper two of which are capped by lateritic ironstone. The underlying granites and gneisses of the Precambrian Basement Complex outcrop both above and below the highest ironstone plateau. This has an altitude of about 640 m and is slightly and irregularly tilted towards the northwest. The ironstone forms hard massive sheets that are generally covered by variable depths of soil but, in places, outcrop to form barren pavements. The individual plateaux are separated from one another by low but steep escarpments that mark the steps between the erosion surfaces.

The vegetation of the lateritic plateau, like that of similar plateaux throughout the northern Guinea zone, has been relatively little disturbed by man's cultural practices. This is attributed to the poor, stony ground, the lack of permanent streams for domestic water on the watershed plateau country, the prevalence of tse-tse flies and the backwardness of the inhabitants, who were constantly harried by the Hausa and Fulani of the Sudan zone to the north and often carried off as slaves.

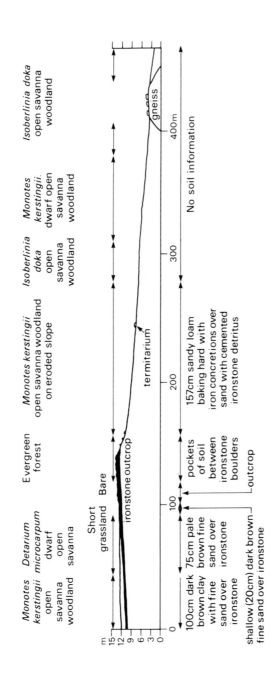

Figure 12.6. Transect showing the relationships between vegetation, soils and relief Kaduna area, Nigeria (after Keay 1959a).

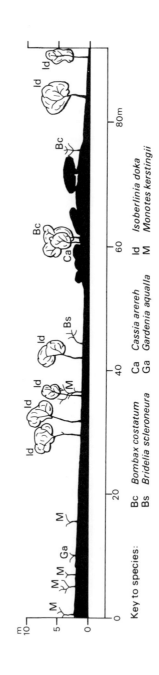

Figure 12.7. Transect showing the relationships between vegetation, soils and relief Kaduna area, Nigeria (after Keay 1959a).

Key to species:

Bc	*Bombax costatum*	Ca	*Cassia arereh*	Id	*Isoberlinia doka*
Bs	*Bridelia scleroneura*	Ga	*Gardenia aqualla*	M	*Monotes kerstingii*

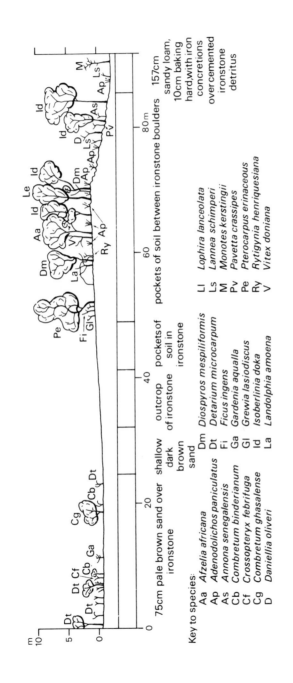

Figure 12.8. Transect showing the relationships between vegetation, soils and relief Kaduna area, Nigeria (after Keay 1959a).

Key to species:
Aa Afzelia africana
Ap Adenodolichos paniculatus
As Annona senegalensis
Cb Combretum binderianum
Cf Crossopteryx febrifuga
Cg Combretum ghasalense
D   Daniellia oliveri
Dm Diospyros mespiliformis
Dt Detarium microcarpum
Fi Ficus ingens
Ga Gardenia aqualla
Gl Grewia lasiodiscus
Id Isoberlinia doka
La Landolphia amoena
Ll Lophira lanceolata
Ls Lannea schimperi
M   Monotes kerstingii
Pv Pavetta crassipes
Pe Pterocarpus erinaceous
Ry Rytigynia henriquesiana
V   Vitex doniana

75cm pale brown sand over ironstone

shallow dark brown sand

outcrop of ironstone

pockets of soil in ironstone

pockets of soil between ironstone boulders

157cm sandy loam, 10cm baking hard, with iron concretions overcemented ironstone detritus

In the Kaduna area, as elsewhere within the northern Guinea zone, savanna woodland dominated by *Isoberlinia doka*, 10–14 m high, occupies the deeper soils of the ironstone plateaux, the gentle slopes with colluvial soils below their edge and relatively well drained sites on the upper edges of flood plains. *Isoberlinia doka* is rare and always stunted on the shallow soils of the ironstone plateaux but is frequent in rocky areas with granite outcrops. It gives way to stunted open savanna woodland of *Detarium microcarpum* and *Combretum binderianum* on shallow soils over laterite.

The ironstone escarpments carry evergreen forests that include *Afzelia africana* and *Diospyros mespiliformis*, which occur on similar sites in central southern Africa. Open woodlands of *Monotes kerstingii* occupy the eroded slopes below the escarpments, while *Bombax costatum* is characteristic of fissures in outcrops of granite gneiss exposed by erosion on the lower ground (Figures 12.6–12.8); it may be accompanied by *Erythrina senegalensis*, *Entada africana*, Boswellia dalzielii, *Diospyros mespiliformis* and other trees that seldom attain 12 m. Fringing or gallery forests composed of *Khaya senegalensis*, *Syzygium guineense* and *Anogeissus leiocarpus* linked by climbers follow the streams cutting into the plateau surface. These appear to resemble the mushitus along the headstreams cutting into the lateritic plateau in Zambia where *Syzygium guineense* is also present.

Contrasts in the catenary relationships between the Kaduna area and the Sudan arise from differences of geomorphology, notably the greater erosion that has exposed bedrock from beneath the lateritic cover in the former, whereas deposition resulting from periodic flooding is a feature of the latter.

Vegetation, soil, relief and geomorphological conditions resembling those near Kaduna occur in the 'derived savanna' zone in the western part of Kabba province, Nigeria (Clayton 1958b, 1961). There three forms of savanna woodland characterized by *Daniellia oliveri* occur. Where the species is associated with the oil palm *Elaeis guineensis* the vegetation is regarded as clearly derived from forest by fire and cultivation but where it occurs with *Prosopis africana* the vegetation forms part of the southern Guinea savanna. The third form, the *Daniellia–Uapaca* complex, which commonly includes *Afzelia africana* and *Syzygium guineense* var. *macrocarpum*, occurs within a humid climatic zone capable of supporting forest and is considered as transitional between forest and the *Daniellia–Elaeis* complex. The presence of *Uapaca togoensis*, however, suggests affinities with the northern Guinea savanna, a link strengthened by the presence of *Monotes kerstingii* on steep slopes of the escarpments. Moreover, the complex occupies excessively drained shallow soils along dissected escarpment country and effects a link with the northern Guinea savanna woodlands where they extend southwards towards the 'Dahomey Gap' where there is a break in the distribution of coastal zone forest. These relationships between vegetation, soils and relief along escarpment slopes at the periphery of planation surfaces where concretionary ironstone is near surface or actually outcrops suggest important geomorphological influences on vegetation distributions that are manifest in the interplay between climatic and edaphic factors. This is reinforced by comparable vegetation/soil relationships in eastern Kabba which is underlain mainly by Cretaceous sediments, mostly sandstones. There, however, under somewhat lower rainfall conditions, a drier type of forest characterized by *Albizia* spp. is more uniformly distributed through the 'derived savannas' which display a mosaic of *Daniellia–Elaeis*, *Daniellia–Prosopis*, secondary forests and transitional types. The *Daniellia–Prosopis* complex of the lower rainfall areas, however, penetrates into the moister vegetation types to the south as islands on shallow soils, on ironstone outcrops and on dry skeletal escarpment soils while the *Daniellia–Uapaca* complex again occurs on escarpments, in this case those flanking the Benue valley. These distributions pose wider questions of vegetational tension in zones that have been subject to climatic oscillations and processes of landscape evolution as well as interference by man.

The Lamto area, Ivory Coast   Vegetation, soils and relief catenas occur in the Lamto savannas of the Ivory Coast (Menaut and Cesar 1979, 1982) which adjoin the dense, humid forest, are maintained by fire in an area of forest climax and are characterized by an impoverished savanna flora that is likely to yield to forest species if fire is excluded. Along the catena the vegetation changes from savanna woodlands and dense shrub savannas occupying the red ferruginous soils with concretionary laterite on plateau surfaces through transitional shrub savannas and stands of small *Cochlospermum planchoni* trees at the break of slope to savanna grasslands with scattered *Borassus aethiopum* palms on hydromorphic pseudo gley soils in the lower areas. Further variations in the vegetation and soils relate to whether the underlying bedrock is granite or amphibolite; the former, which underlies most of the area, produces ferruginous soils able to support trees and shrubs as well as grasses, whereas the latter, whose outcrops are localized, gives rise to vertisols supporting treeless grassland in small restricted areas. Thus within an area of forest climax both the occurrence of savanna vegetation and its composition are expressions of edaphic conditions influenced by both relief and geology.

The middle Gongola valley, Nigeria   In the vicinity of the middle Gongola river, a tributary of the Benue in Nigeria, relationships between vegetation, soils, geomorphology and geology provide significant clues for an understanding of the ways in which present vegetation distributions over wider areas in West Africa have come about. In the north steep escarpments, formed

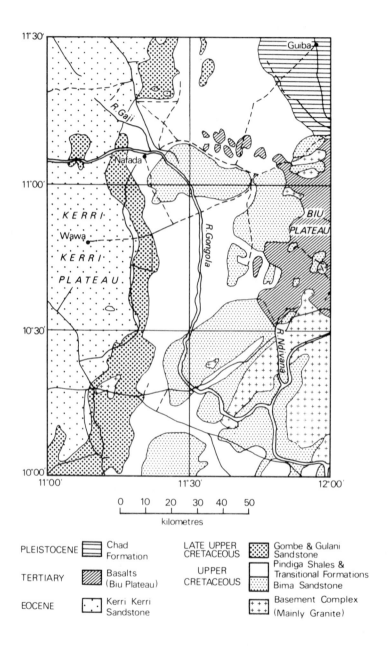

Figure 12.9. Geology of the middle Gongola valley (after Ramsay and de Leeuw 1965).

by headward erosion of the Gongola headstreams cutting back into the surface of the Lake Chad basin, separate the middle Gongola and Benue drainage from the Lake Chad basin. The scarps mark the step between two planation surfaces, on the lower and younger of which bedrock has been exposed. Here the vegetation varies greatly as it is adjusting to the edaphic conditions created by differing lithological units, whereas on the surface draining to Lake Chad it is remarkably uniform.

The floor of the middle Gongola Valley, which has an altitude of 270–300 m, is underlain by Upper Cretaceous rocks comprising the Bima sandstone, a continental deposit which outcrops over large areas in the east, the Pindiga and Fika marine shales that underlie the central valley and the Gombe sandstone that outcrops in the western section (Ramsay and de Leeuw 1964, 1965) (Figure 12.9). To the east the valley is defined by the steep scarp forming the western edge of the Biu plateau built of Tertiary basalt; to the west it is bounded by the Kerri Kerri plateau formed of Tertiary sandstones, grits and clays. In the southeast irregular terrain has formed over the coarse grained granites of the Archaean Basement Complex.

Open savanna scrub and woodland representing secondary vegetation much affected by cultivation occupies the thin sandy soils developed over Bima sandstone. It is characterized by *Combretum* spp., notably *Combretum glutinosum*, which is accompanied by *Terminalia avicennioides*, *Steganotaenia araliacea*, *Commiphora pedunculata* and *C. africana* shrubs on the deeper soils on the lower slopes, by *Detarium microcarpum*, *Crossopteryx febrifuga*, *Afrormosia laxiflora* and *Boswellia dalzielli* on skeletal soils on the upper slopes and by *Anogeissus leiocarpus* and *Balanites aegyptiaca* in depressions and along drainage lines. Comparable vegetation occupies the skeletal soils over the Gombe sandstone where, however, *Combretum nigricans* var. *elliottii* and *Gueira senegalensis* form important components of the shrub savanna. The former species, together with *Isoberlinia doka* and *Anogeissus leiocarpus*, occur on the deeper soils of colluvial sites and *C. nigricans* var. *elliottii* and *A. leiocarpus* are joined by *Prosopis africana* on colluvial/alluvial soils on flat sites. On the light gravelly sands and loams around outcropping granite of the Basement Complex the vegetation is again characterized by *Combretum glutinosum* with *Boswellia dalzielii*, *Detarium microcarpum* and *Strynos spinosa* on stony soils. On deeper soils *Anogeissus leiocarpus* is joined by *Pterocarpus erinaceous*, *Bombax costatum* and *Sterculia setigera*.

The vegetation of the heavier soils of the lower lying sections of the Gongola valley contrasts with that over the sandy soils of the Cretaceous sandstones and Basement Complex granite. An open woodland, some 10.5 m high, dominated by *Anogeissus leiocarpus* accompanied by *Bombax costatum*, *Combretum ghasalense*, *Pterocarpus erinaceous*, *Sterculia setigera* and *Terminalia laxiflora*, covers the deep, fairly heavy soils formed over transitional sandstone and mudstone, and a very open woodland in which a few *Balanites aegyptiaca* and *Combretum ghasalense* trees share the upper canopy with *Acacia seyal* occupies the poorly drained swelling and cracking clays derived from marine shales in the low-lying areas. Here there is no shrub layer and fierce fires that sweep through the dense tall grass in the dry season keep the vegetation open.

West of the Gongola valley a distinctive vegetation known as 'Wawa bush' covers the Kerri Kerri sandstone plateau. This comprises a dry woodland of *Combretum nigricans* var. *elliottii*, *Anogeissus leiocarpus*, *Burkea africana* and other *Combretum* spp. which survives in a mature state on the acid, free-draining, highly permeable and nutrient deficient sands that are too infertile for cultivation. The high shrub density precludes a vigorous grass layer and fierce fires do not occur.

East of the Gongola valley the vegetation over the Tertiary basaltic lava flows, cones and craters of the Biu plateau and its outliers varies with the relief, soil depth and cultural practices. A low savanna woodland of *Boswellia dalzielii*, *Acacia senegal* and *Combretum glutinosum* occupies the shallow, stony soils of low outlying basaltic hills; on the edge of the high basalt plateau to the east these are accompanied by *Sterculia setigera*, *Anogeissus leiocarpus*, *Sclerocarya birrea* and *Afzelia africana*. The vegetation is floristically richer than that on the Bima or Gombe sandstone and the species of *Detarium*, *Afrormosia* and *Crossopteryx*, typical of skeletal, sandy soils are absent. Savanna woodland dominated by *Isoberlinia doka* covers the stony soils on the ridges and plateaux in the centre of the basalt area; here *Boswellia dalzielii* and *Acacia senegal* are important and other Northern Guinea zone species, such as *Cussonia barteri*, occur occasionally. In this area the vegetation over the deeper soils has been largely cleared for cultivation.

Northeast of the middle Gongola valley the area draining to the Chad basin is underlain by lacustrine and fluviatile clays and sands of Pleistocene age. Deep free-draining sands to sandy loams occasionally grading into sandy clay loams showing an increasing number of iron concretions with depth, occur over the gently undulating relief, but in the lower parts of the area underlain by clays, imperfectly drained mottled loams with iron concretions occur. The remains of large termitaria occur in wide valleys and depressions that are flooded during the wet season. The characteristic vegetation over the deeper soils is a savanna woodland dominated by *Anogeissus leiocarpus* and *Bombax costatum* trees and *Combretum glutinosum* and *Gueira senegalensis* shrubs. One tree, usually *Anogeissus leiocarpus* or *Tamarindus indica*, or occasionally *Adansonia digitata*, and a tangle of scandent shrubs and climbers occur over the old termitaria.

The hills northwest of Ibadan   Further evidence of the influence of geologically controlled edaphic factors on vegetation distributions is manifest on granite inselberge within the Guinea savanna woodland zone and the zone of derived savanna northwest of Ibadan in Nigeria (Hambler 1964). Around the peripheries of Shabe hill and Addo Awaiye hill where drainage from the granite domes provides a soil water regime within the tolerance of rain forest trees, there are patches of forest that are floristically similar to the lowland rain forest of the Idanre hills eastsoutheast of Ibadan. On the boulder slopes above the forest patches, woodland comprising both rain forest and savanna woodland trees occur on Addo Awaiye hill where prehistoric grinding holes provide evidence of prolonged habitation that has doubtless influenced the vegetation. On similar sites on Okepologum hill a pioneer *Markhamia tomentosa* forest occurs. By contrast on shallower soils farther from the granite domes a woodland of savanna species, notably *Detarium macrocarpum*, *Pterocarpus erinaceous* and *Burkea africana* prevails. Over the granite domes communities of *Monocymbium ceressiforme* and *Andropogon linearis* grasses or *Trilepis bilosa* sedge form on thin soil mats while forest forms or regenerates in hollows in the hills.

The influences of climatic change and termite activity

Vegetation communities producing arc stripe and ripple patterns in the drier areas of the Sudan and Sahel zones, linear vegetation patterns possibly associated with the degradation of termitaria and the presence of montane forest species in some higher areas like the Jos plateau, are believed to represent legacies of former differing climatic and geomorphological conditions.

In the Hadeijia region of northern Nigeria broad stripes with a southeast–northwest orientation mark the crests of old sand dunes formed during a previous desert advance (Clayton 1958a,b). South of Katsina east–west bands of vegetation in shallow soils separated by deeper soils now under cultivation (Clayton 1963) are believed to be related to sand streaming from the great erg to the east through gaps in the chain of hills running south from Daura (Grove 1957, 1958). Near Gummi in Sokoto province, ripple-like patterns caused by differences in the height and composition of the vegetation may be related to differences of soil moisture status between the former dunes and swales that were formed along the borders of the great erg at right angles to the prevailing wind during a previous desert advance. Over the ripples where water penetrates downwards the vegetation comprises *Combretum nigrescens* trees, some 10 m high with occasional tall *Anogeissus leiocarpus* and *Sclerocarya birrea* trees, whereas smaller *C. nigrescens* and *Gueira senegalensis* only 3 m high occupy the inter-ripple areas where water tends to spread laterally in the first few centimetres of soil where most roots occur.

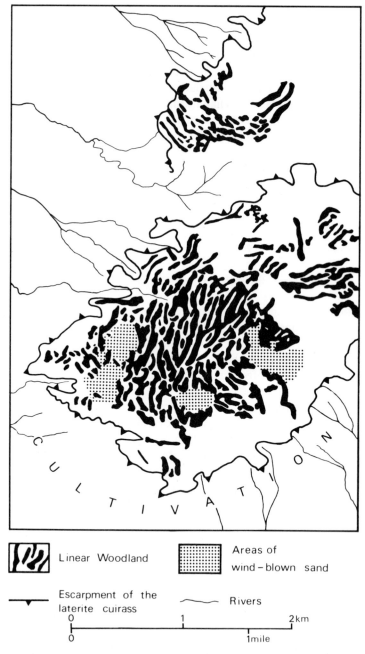

Figure 12.10. Areas with woodland stripes (after White 1965).

Other linear vegetation patterns known as 'brousse tigree' that occur in the Sahelian low tree and shrub savanna zone in the southern part of the Republic of Niger are thought to result from soil water variations related to termite activity in areas where shallow soils and limited rainfall cause intense root competition (White 1965). The patterns occur on shallow, gravelly soils of plateaux with a massive laterite cuirass of Tertiary age in areas where the rainfall is about 700 mm. They consist of alternating lines of *Combretum* spp. woodland about 4 m high and intervening stripes of bare or sparsely covered ground (Figure 12.10); they occur close to and parallel with the escarpment edge of the plateau. Elsewhere an irregular mosaic of *Combretum* woodland and bare ground characterizes most of the laterite cuirasse surface.

Where not covered by patches of wind blown sand the laterite plateau is remarkably level. It is covered by some 10 cm of sandy loam soil over ironstone gravel extending to laterite cuirasse at a depth of 10–40 cm. The combination of shallow soil over impermeable laterite cuirasse and level terrain inhibits percolation and results in the accumulation of surface water after rains. There are no significant differences between the soils of the woodlands and bare areas. It has been suggested that the linear vegetation patterns formed when, with a change of climate (Clos-Arceduc 1956) debris from degraded termitaria smothered adjacent vegetation while the unaffected trees, benefitting from extra run-off from the collapsed termitaria, extended their roots beneath the bare areas. Once established the pattern became self perpetuating for the compact soils of the degraded mounds and the root competition from the existing woodland trees discouraged seedling establishment on the bare stripes. The alignment of the woodland belts parallel to the escarpment edge and to large patches of sand are considered to be related to run-off from these areas (White 1965).

Further evidence of linked vegetational and climatic changes is provided by the occurrence of mounds that are believed to be deserted termitaria within the Okomu forest reserve in southern Nigeria (Jones 1956). These mounds must have been built under drier climatic conditions than those now prevailing and within an area of more open vegetation, probably savanna woodland. Such a more southerly extension of savanna woodlands would help to explain the nature of the present forest/savanna boundary which in most areas is stable but shows a tendency for forest advance rather than retreat.

The interacting influences of environmental factors on savanna distribution in West Africa and the Sudan

The vegetation, soils, relief catenas that occur in all vegetation zones, the vegetation patterns associated with old sand dunes and degraded termitaria, and the close links between vegetation, soils and geology on the lower erosional surfaces in the landscape support the view that the form, composition and distribution of the savannas of West Africa and the Sudan are the result of the interplay of many environmental factors that have changed over time, rather than the result of burning and cultivation on a former continuum from forest to savanna woodland governed by decreasing rainfall and increasing extremes of temperature and relative humidity from the coast towards the interior.

Although many detailed studies of the form and composition of the vegetation have been made, due perhaps to acceptance of the influences of climate, fire and cultural practices, the relationships between vegetation and other environmental factors have received little attention.

The literature cites geomorphological features. It refers to widespread planation surfaces, the prevalence of deep weathering, the extent of laterite formation and presence of indurated laterite or ironstone or cuirasse. The savanna woodlands are characteristic of the planation surfaces and of soils with lateritic or ironstone horizons. In the southern Sudan the dense savanna woodlands that cover the dissected country forming the Congo–Nile watershed resemble those along the Congo–Zambezi watershed in Zambia. Gallery forests like the mushitus on the Zambian Copperbelt follow the valleys cutting back into the peneplaned plateau. In both regions forest vegetation is replacing savanna woodland as dissection in current erosion cycles proceeds. Near Kaduna in Nigeria, as in Zambia, evergreen forests follow the escarpments separating erosion surfaces and gallery forests again follow the streams cutting into the plateau surfaces. The same genera and some species are common to all areas.

On eroded plateaux in the Kaduna area, changes in the form and composition of the savanna woodlands paralleling those on the older planation surfaces on the Zambian Copperbelt, occur as the soils become shallower, ironstone or laterite approaches the surface and eventually outcrops. *Uapaca* spp. occupy poorly drained sites with near surface laterite and *Monotes* spp. occupy eroded sites in both countries. Where granite gneiss bedrock outcrops in West Africa, as in Zimbabwe, trees including *Diospyros mespiliformis* grow in the joints.

Where erosion of the lower planation surfaces has exposed bedrock, as in the middle Gongola valley of Nigeria, the vegetation varies with the soils and geology. In this it contrasts with the uniform vegetation covering the older surface draining to Lake Chad which is separated from the lower surface by an escarpment.

Thus, within the climatic limits that govern the broad vegetation zones of West Africa and the Sudan, the form and composition of the vegetation is related to edaphic conditions that in turn are related to geomorphology and geology. Savanna woodlands are characteristic of the older planation surface with lateritic soils. They give way to *Acacia* parkland or grass-land on the heavier soils of the younger planation surfaces as in the Sudan and in the middle Gongola valley of Nigeria. They are replaced by evergreen woodlands or forests along escarpments separating planation surfaces, over dissected terrain along major watersheds and along valleys cutting back into the peneplaned plateaux. The pattern and processes are similar to those in central and southern Africa but they are less obvious because the legacies of fire and man's cultural practices are greater. The vegetation has also been influenced by climatic oscillations which are responsible for the 'brousse tigree' patterns in the Sudan and have had an impact on the savanna/forest boundary in West Africa. There is evidence that forest is currently advancing at the expense of savanna woodland but prolonged pressures in excess of resources is leading to desertification within the low tree and shrub savanna zone.

CONCLUSIONS

On a broad regional scale the distribution of savanna woodlands coincides with areas of ferruginous soils and that of low tree and shrub savannas with brown loam soils. In turn within the broad climatic limits that influence major soil type, the soils of West Africa are related to relief, geomorphology and bedrock geology (Figures 12.1–12.4). Deep weathering and laterite development are characteristic features over large areas and ferruginous duricrusts, laterite or cuirasse are well developed and widespread even in the drier zones (Morgan and Pugh 1969). They are associated with a series of planation surfaces, 200–500 m high, cut across Precambrian rocks (Harrison Church 1957, King 1962). Particularly in the drier areas they represent relict features from periods of wetter climate.

Relationships between the form and composition of the vegetation and the soils have been cited by several authors (Morrison *et al.* 1948, Clayton 1958a, 1961, Hambler 1964, Jones 1963, Keay 1953, 1959a, Menaut and Cesar 1979, 1982, Morgan and Moss 1965, Ramsay 1964, Ramsay and de Leeuw 1964, 1965, White 1965). Vegetational changes related to the disposition and outcrop of concretionary ironstone (laterite or cuirasse) and of bedrock have been noted by some writers (Keay 1953, 1959a, Jones 1963). Relationships between soils and geomorphology and between vegetation, soils and geology have been described by others (Clayton 1958b, 1961, Ramsay 1964, Ramsay and de Leeuw 1964, 1965). For several areas linear vegetational patterns have been ascribed to edaphic variations related to old sand dunes and to the breakdown of old termitaria, in each case occasioned by climatic oscillations. Assessment of the interacting influences of all environmental factors, including those of soils, geomorphology, geology and climatic change, is essential for a full understanding of the present vegetation distributions.

13   The savannas of India and Southeast Asia

In India and Southeast Asia the status and origin of the forms of vegetation that might be included within the savanna category pose controversial questions (Blasco 1983) and any assessment of the interplay of environmental factors influencing their distribution is prejudiced by the lack of detailed data on regional and local scales. Hence coverage comparable with that for the other continents is not possible in this text.

THE SAVANNAS OF INDIA

Tropical subhumid and dry deciduous forests are thought to have covered those areas of India where various forms of savanna vegetation are now recognized (Misra 1983). The country has a history of human occupation extending back to 4000 BC and during this long period man has cleared forest land for cultivation, grazing and settlement, cut trees for timber and fuel and used fire in hunting wild animals. The vegetation has been so disturbed that the distributions of the various forms of savanna cannot be equated with environmental parameters such as climate–soil complexes and geomorphological influences with any degree of confidence (Spate and Learmonth 1967).

Dry deciduous woodlands occur in the dry subhumid zone of the Deccan plateau of peninsular India where the annual rainfall brought by the southwest monsoon varies from 800 to 1250 mm and is distributed over seven months of the year with a pronounced dry season from November/December to March/April. The plateau surface, of 500–700 m elevation, is level to gently undulating; the soils derived from ancient gneisses and schists are lateritic shallow sands or clays with a pH 6.0–6.2 in the surface horizons; they are moisture deficient during the dry season. The woodlands are characterized by *Anogeissus latifolia*, usually associated with *Terminalia tomentosa* trees in a grass stratum of *Heteropogon contortus* or *Andropogon* spp. (Champion 1936) or of *Sehima* and *Dichanthium* spp. (Misra 1983). *Boswellia serrata* trees, which are absent from the moist deciduous forests, are widespread; among other species *Pterocarpus marsupium* and *Diospyros melanoxylon* may be present while thorny *Acacia catechu* and *Zizyphus jujuba* occur on heavily grazed areas where the annual rainfall exceeds 1250 mm. Woodlands of *Tectona grandis* (teak) usually associated with *Terminalia, Lagerstroemia* and *Diospyros* spp. trees occupy soils of higher base status (pH 6.5–7.5), notably those with high levels of calcium and phosphorus derived from the basalts of the Deccan trap lava flows (Puri 1960). They give way, however, to a stunted scrubby vegetation of *Acacia, Terminalia* and *Boswellia* spp. on the soils derived from the interbedded amydaloidal lavas. Teak is absent also from soils with a pH above 8.5.

Dry deciduous woodlands of *Anogeissus latifolia, Terminalia tomentosa, Sterculia* and other tree species occur also in northern India where they occupy dry sites, notably on south-facing hillsides and flat hilltops within the moist deciduous forests that extend to the foot of the Himalayas. In this area woodlands of sal, *Shorea robusta*, at the dry limit of its distribution, occur on sandy soils, notably those derived from the sandstones and conglomerates of the Siwaliks.

Comparable types of dry deciduous woodland occur in central upper Burma where the annual rainfall is again between 850 and 1250 mm with a seasonal distribution similar to that in southern India. Close relationships between species dominance and geology have been observed with teak favouring the moister, heavier, more base rich soils and sal the light sandy soils derived from sandstones (Puri 1960). *Vitex, Terminalia, Albizzia* and *Dalbergia* spp. form important components of the tree and shrub layers.

The dry deciduous woodlands of India and Burma resemble the savanna woodlands of Africa. They occur under similar environmental conditions and show some affinity of tree genera, *Anogeissus* occuring in West Africa and *Terminalia, Pterocarpus* and *Diospyros* throughout Central, East and West Africa. In India these woodlands are considered to have been derived by cutting, fire and grazing from the moist deciduous forests which contain many more species. However, they occur within given climatic limits and occupy edaphically dry sites. They may in fact represent the climax vegetation on poor soils that have discouraged agricultural usage.

Where the annual rainfall is less than 750 mm, as in the lee of the Western Ghats, in Bangalore in southern India and in Rajasthan and Sind in the northwest, the vegetation is that described as thorn forest (Champion 1936, Puri 1960). This resembles some of the thorny types of vegetation in Africa and South America that have been included in the low tree and shrub savanna category. It is characterized by the same tree genera and occurs under similar environmental conditions. Small *Acacia* trees, notably *A. catechu, A. leucophloia* or *A. arabica*, dominate the vegetation, but may be accompanied by *Zizyphus jujuba, Capparis aphylla* and *Prosopis spicigera*. The ground layer is composed of short grasses that form a continuous cover after rains but, under grazing pressure, give way to bare ground in the dry season. In the Bangalore area of southern India these thorn forests or low tree and shrub savannas cover shallow dry soils over a variety of different rock types but an open vegetation with scattered *Acacia arabica* trees is typical of the black cracking clays, locally called black cotton soils, and a *Euphorbia* scrub occupies the poorest, shallowest soils and stony sites. In the Punjab, Sind and Rajasthan, *Acacia arabica* occupies land that is flooded by the Indus but gives way to *Prosopis spicigera* as the levels are raised above floodwater. Low tree and shrub vegetation of *Acacia, Prosopis*, and *Capparis* spp. extends over areas of concretionary limestone or kankar that parallel those of calcrete in Africa. In the north vegetation described as *Acacia* scrub forest is believed to have retrogressed from sal forest and, under grazing and browsing pressures, especially by goats, the vegetation composed of *Acacia, Prosopis, Capparis* and Zizyphus shrubs and *Dichanthium, Cenchrus* and *Lasiurus* short grass spp. in Rajasthan is considered vulnerable to desertification.

The influence of man on the savanna vegetation of India

Most writers on the vegetation of India consider that the dry deciduous woodlands and thorn forests represent vegetation that has been degraded from moist deciduous forest by man's cultural practices. The change from *Heteropogon contortus* and *Andropogon* spp. of grass cited by Champion (1936) to *Dichanthium* and *Sehima* spp. cited by Misra (1983) suggests species retrogression in the grass layer that may be reversed if fire and grazing are withheld. In the Chandraprabba sanctuary at Varanasi on the Vindhyan upland in the north of the Deccan, where there is a Man and the Biosphere (MAB) site, grazing in the recent past is considered to have reduced the dry deciduous mixed forest of *Anogeissus latifolia* and *Diospyros melanoxylon* trees in some places to 'scrub and savanna'. Where the latter has been protected from grazing for two years the vegetation now comprises grassland of *Heteropogon contortus* and *Bothriochloa pertusa* with small *Zizyphus jujuba* trees and shrubs whereas where it is open to grazing the ground cover consists of *Desmostachya bipinnata*. Many years must elapse before it will be known whether, under protection, this form of vegetation will progress to *Anogeissus latifolia–Diospyros melanoxylon* woodland from which it is believed to be derived, and thence to moist deciduous woodland.

Relationships between the vegetation and interacting environmental factors

Notwithstanding the impact of man, the literature suggests that the discrete forms of dry deciduous forest or savanna woodland and of thorn forest or low tree and shrub savanna occur within given climatic limits and are influenced by specific edaphic conditions. Both forms of vegetation are characteristic of peninsular India which, until the Cretaceous formed part of Gondwanaland. The presence of trees of the same genera in India and Africa are legacies of the former continental linkage. Since the break-up of Gondwanaland the block that now forms peninsular India has been linked to the Eurasian plate by the building of the Himalayas and infilling of the Indo-Gangetic plain. Concomitant with and following this great orogeny, great changes of climate have occured since the Tertiary. These profoundly affected the distributions of species and of the vegetation units that they compose. The dry deciduous woodlands of peninsular India represent the depauperate relics of the moist deciduous forests of the Tertiary, augmented by species from the northern forests that found refuge in the south during the Pleistocene and adjusted to the drier conditions that have since prevailed. The dry deciduous woodlands occupy the older surfaces and poorer, often lateritic, soils. The thorn forests are more recent and, as in other continents, their characteristic tree species, notably of the *Acacia* genus, are able to survive on the heavy poorly drained soils of the younger surfaces. The precise relationships between the dry deciduous woodlands and the thorn forests or low tree and shrub savannas are not clear. While some authors consider that the latter have been derived from the former, the distributional relationships of each to climatic and edaphic conditions suggest that they represent responses to the interplay of changing environmental conditions over a long period of time, upon which man's activities have imposed a recent additional influence.

THE SAVANNAS OF SOUTHEAST ASIA

Mosaic distributions of open forests (or woodlands) and dense evergreen rain forests are a characteristic feature of continental Southeast Asia whereas shrub savannas and grasslands are restricted to very small areas (Blasco 1983).

The most characteristic and most commonly occurring type of vegetation below 900 m in Cambodia, Laos, Thailand and Vietnam is the deciduous or dry dipterocarp forest which Blasco (1983) has likened to the *foret claire* of the French speaking botanists. He concedes that while everyone agrees that these forests 'are strongly influenced by human interference and annual burning, their status and origin still pose controversial questions'; and acknowledges that 'careful investigations of environmental conditions and of the flora involved, as well as an understanding of the dynamics of the woody species' are required.

The physiognomy of the deciduous or dry dipterocarp forests, described as 'having only one discontinuous tree layer, often ranging between 10 and 20 metres high', composed of deciduous trees of less than 40 cm diameter, with small boles and crowns that rarely touch each other and an herbaceous ground layer of uneven height and density, resembles that of the denser forms of savanna woodlands in Zambia and the adjacent territories of Africa. The species composition of the tree layer, characterized by *Dipterocarpus tuberculatus*, *Pentacme suavis* and *Shorea obtusa*, however, is very different.

In Southeast Asia deciduous or dry dipterocarp forests are unknown where the rainfall exceeds 2000 mm and the dry season is less than four months. There degradation of rain forest leads regressively to derived shrub savanna or derived grassland, notably of *Imperata cylindrica*, which progressively reverts back to rain forest when burning is withheld and cultivation abandoned. The dry dipterocarp forests that appear to represent the Southeast Asian equivalent of savanna woodlands are restricted to warm semi-dry or semi-humid areas where the annual rainfall is between 1000 and 2000 mm, and the dry season (December–March or November–April) is from four to seven months long and is associated with a mean monthly saturation deficit of 7–12 mm. They occur only where the mean temperature for the coldest months exceeds 15°C, the absolute minimum never falls below 8°C and the mean annual thermal amplitude is less than 10°C. Such conditions occur only in plains and on low plateaux below 1000 m at latitudes between 20°N and the equator.

Within the climatic limits cited above the deciduous open forests or woodlands co-exist in mosaic distributions with dense deciduous and semi-deciduous forests and rain forests. Their distributions appear to be closely related to edaphic conditions which are considered to be responsible for maintaining their apparent stability. While dependent on parent material and local topography, there is a great variety of soils within the climatic zone favourable for the dipterocarp open forests or woodlands. These woodlands are restricted to areas with acid lithosols or skeletal soils or with red and yellow podzols or grey podzolic soils. The former predominate on hilly areas in northern Thailand, southern Cambodia and east of the Mekong. The latter cover the flat landscapes that characterize much of Southeast Asia including the Korat plateau of Thailand. The leached A horizon and zone of clay accumulation in the B horizon are usually clearly differentiated: iron compounds such as laterite and iron concretions are common while indurated laterite or 'hardenable' laterites occur at various depths. Both the acid

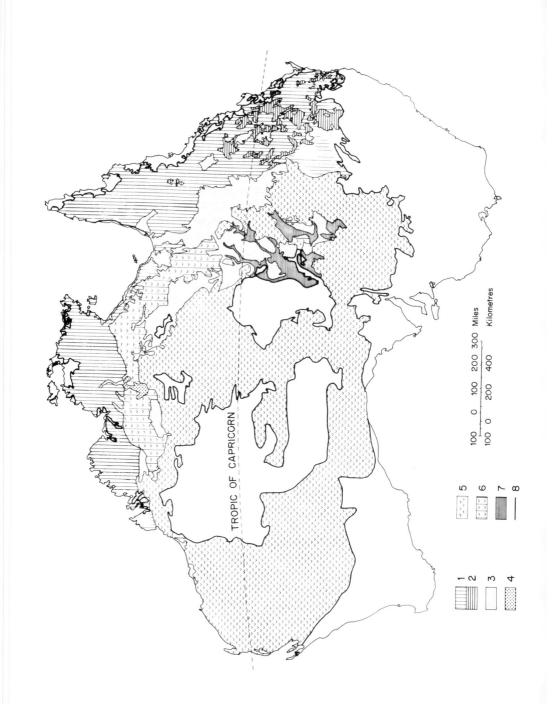

TROPIC OF CAPRICORN

1
2
3
4

5
6
7
8

100   0   100   200   300 Miles
100   0   200   400 Kilometres

and savanna grasslands along the north coast (Figure 14.1–14.3). The savanna woodlands give way to tropical forests and coastal woodlands along the east coast, but occur again to the north of the Torres Strait in southern New Guinea.

The savanna grasslands cover larger areas in Australia than in the other continents with the greatest extents occurring over the Barkly Tableland and the plains of the Great Artesian Basin, where in both cases their distribution is governed largely by edaphic conditions. Savanna parklands are of relatively limited extent, occurring mainly over basaltic soils along the tributary valleys of the rivers Burdekin and Mackenzie in eastern Queensland and those of the Victoria and Roper rivers in the Northern Territory. The typical savanna grasslands are dominated by tussock grasses of the *Astrebla* genus whereas the grass stratum in the savanna parklands is usually dominated by *Dichanthium* spp. The composition of the grass layer of both forms of vegetation thus contrasts with that in the other continents but the characteristic trees belong to genera that are the same or closely related to those in Africa, namely *Acacia*, *Bauhinia* and *Terminalia*. In contrast to the pinnate leaved *Acacias* of Africa and South America, those of Australia are leafless. They develop phyllodes or expanded stems to carry out photosynthesis, after their leaves have been lost following the early stages of growth.

As in Africa, low tree and shrub savannas occupy large areas underlain largely by Precambrian rocks at the drier interior margins of the savanna woodlands in Australia. Here, according to the relief and edaphic conditions, they interdigitate with areas of arid woodland comparable with the low savanna woodlands of Botswana. Generally speaking they are characterized by *Eucalyptus* rather than *Acacia* trees, but *Acacias* are prominent in the shrub layer. Narrow resinous rolled leaved *Triodia* species of grass form the ground layer, contrasting with the dominant flat bladed *Stipagrostis uniplumis* grass in Africa.

The actual distributions of the major savanna categories is more complex than in South America or Africa, a result of the greater dissection of the Tertiary planation surfaces which has produced a greater variety of habitat

Figure 14.1 *(opposite)*. Distributions of major categories of savanna vegetation in Australia.
Key. (1) Savanna woodlands dominated by *Eucalyptus* spp. trees. (2) Dry savanna woodlands and scrub dominated by *Acacia harpophylla*. (3) Savanna grasslands. (4) Savanna parklands. (5) Low tree and shrub savannas. (6) Mosaic distributions of savanna woodlands and low tree and shrub savannas. (7) Mosaic distributions of the five major categories of savanna vegetation in the Channel Country of southwest Queensland and the neighbouring states of New South Wales and South Australia.

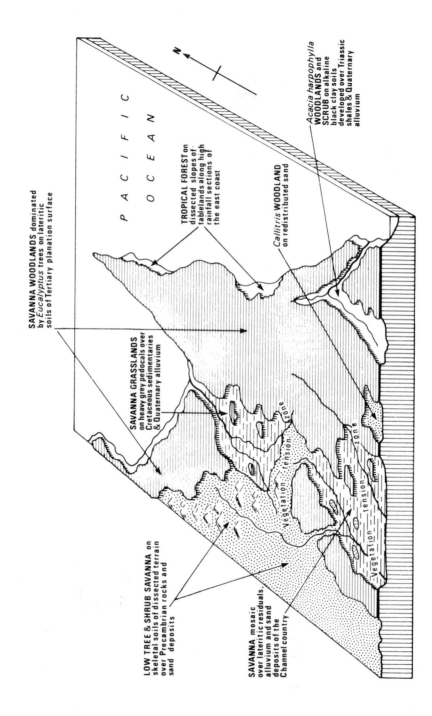

SAVANNA WOODLANDS dominated by *Eucalyptus* trees on lateritic soils of Tertiary planation surface

TROPICAL FOREST on dissected slopes of tablelands along high rainfall sections of the east coast

Callitris WOODLAND on redistributed sand

Acacia harpophylla WOODLANDS and SCRUB on alkaline black clay soils developed over Triassic shales & Quaternary alluvium

PACIFIC OCEAN

SAVANNA GRASSLANDS on heavy grey pedocals over Cretaceous sedimentaries & Quaternary alluvium

LOW TREE & SHRUB SAVANNA on skeletal soils of dissected terrain over Precambrian rocks and sand deposits

SAVANNA mosaic over lateritic residuals, alluvium and sand deposits of the Channel country

Vegetation tension zone

N

Figure 14.2. Relationships between vegetation and geomorphology, northern Australia. From Cole (1982a).

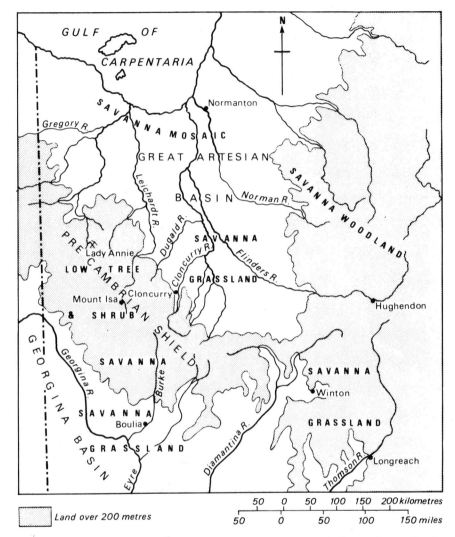

Figure 14.3. Distribution of the major savanna categories in northwest Queensland.

conditions over relatively short distances. The interdigitating mosaic distributions of the major savanna categories are indeed so complex that over large areas it is possible to map them only on a very large scale. Moreover the distributions between savanna woodlands and sclerophyllous woodlands and between low tree and shrub savannas and steppe are less clear than in Africa and South America. In Western and South Australia the woodlands, that like the savanna woodlands are dominated by *Eucalyptus* tree species, are excluded from the savanna woodland category because they have a ground layer that is characterized by shrubs and not grasses. Where they occupy lateritic soils on the relicts of Tertiary planation surfaces they resemble the savanna woodlands to which they are related by virtue of their derivation from the vegetation that occupied these surfaces in Tertiary times. The gradations from low tree and shrub savanna to steppe south of the central desert areas are related to the general absence of relief features and to the seasonal incidence of periodic rainfall in either summer or winter.

Mosaic distributions of the various forms of savanna vegetation occur in the Channel Country of southwestern Queensland and the neighbouring states. Like comparable distribution patterns in the Pantanal of Brazil and in Barotseland and the Okavango areas of Africa, they reflect varying edaphic conditions related to the geomorphological evolution of the landscape. Like the comparable areas of South America and Africa, the Channel Country also constitutes a vegetational tension zone in which plant distributions, sensitive to climatic fluctuations that accelerate or retard the geomorphological processes, are in a state of flux.

In the chapters that follow the relationships between vegetation distributions and the interplay of environmental factors in areas that are characterized by each of the major savanna categories are examined.

15   The savanna woodlands and associated savanna grasslands and parklands of Australia

The savanna woodlands of Australia occur within an arcuate belt of country parallelling the north and east coasts. This area receives between 500 and 1500 mm of rainfall annually which is concentrated in the summer months, December–March. The area is characterized by winter drought which is more pronounced in the north of Western Australia and the Northern Territory than it is in Queensland where the growing period, as defined by the formula for effective rainfall based on work at the Waite Agricultural Research Institute*, is longer (CSIRO 1960). This is due partly to the fact that whereas northern Australia depends on monsoonal rainfall, in eastern Queensland this is supplemented by rainfall emanating from moist air masses associated with the onshore southeasterly winds and with low pressure systems passing up the coast. Temperatures are high during the summer months when there is little difference between the western and eastern parts of the savanna woodland zone. Monthly maxima exceed 30°C and monthly minima are above 21°C. In winter the differences are greater with temperatures being markedly lower particularly at night in southern Queensland. Monthly maxima exceed 26°C but in eastern Queensland the monthly minima fall below 15°C near the coast and below 10°C inland where a nighttime minimum around freezing point may be experienced.

The main areas of savanna woodlands occur in Western Australia and the Northern Territory northwards of latitude 17°S and in eastern Queensland where they extend southwards to and beyond the border with New South Wales at latitude 29°S (Figure 14.1). These areas are virtually separated from one another by the belt of savanna grassland which extends across central Queensland to the Gulf of Carpentaria near Normanton. In the area bordering

*All rain in excess of $0.4E^{0.75}$ where E is the evaporation from free water, is taken as being effective.

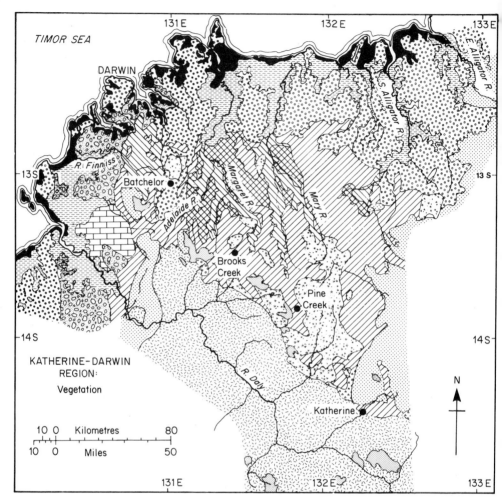

KATHERINE–DARWIN
REGION:

Vegetation

the southern shore of the Gulf of Carpentaria, savanna woodlands alternate with savanna grasslands, parklands and low tree and shrub savannas to form mosaic patterns of distribution in the area described as the Gulf Fall region. Savanna woodlands occur again in a mosaic with savanna categories in southwestern Queensland.

In contrast to the position in Africa and South America, the savanna woodlands of Australia do not adjoin extensive tropical forests, being separated from the main forest belt of Southeast Asia and Melanesia by the Timor, Arafura and Coral seas. Significantly the savanna woodlands extend into the southern part of New Guinea which is separated from the Cape Yorke Peninsula of Australia by the relatively narrow Torres Strait. On the Australian mainland the savanna woodlands are in direct contact only with

SAVANNA WOODLAND dominated by:

Tall *Eucalyptus tetrodonta*
E. miniata trees and tall
Heteropogon triticeus,
Sorghum spp. grasses.

E. tetrodonta and *E. miniata*
trees with *Livistona humilis*
palms and *Calythrix* spp.
shrubs and with marginal zone
of *Acacia shirleyii* trees.

E. tetrodonta, *E. miniata*,
E. confertiflora, *E. grandifolia*
trees with understorey of
Petalostigma banksii
Grevillea spp. trees.

E. phoenicea, *E. dichromophloia*
and *E. miniata* trees and *Triodia*
microstachys grass.

E. foelscheana, *E. confertiflora*
trees and *Themeda* and *Sehima*
spp. grasses.

E. foelscheana, *E. grandifolia*,
E. tectifica and *E. confertiflora*
trees with abundant *Livistona*
humilis palms and *Heteropogon*
triticeus and *Sorghum* spp.
grasses.

E. foelscheana *E. confertiflora*
and *E. tectifica* with *Erythrophloeum*
chlorostachys trees and *Heteropogon*
triticeus and *Sorghum* spp. grasses
with smaller areas of savanna
parkland with *Eucalyptus papuana*,
E. microtheca, *Bauhinia cunninghamii*,
Erythrophloeum chlorostachys
Terminalia volucris and *Acacia*
bidwillii trees and *Dichanthium* spp.
grasses.

SAVANNA PARKLAND of

Bauhinia cunninghamii,
Eucalyptus microtheca,
Erythrophloeum chlorostachys
and *Terminalia volucris* trees
and *Dichanthium* spp. grasses.

PALM SCRUB dominated by

Livistona humilis and *Pandanus*
spiralis.

SAVANNA GRASSLAND dominated by

Themeda australis and *Eriachne* spp.

SWAMP GRASSLAND of

Oryza and *Eleocharis* spp.

Littoral communities.

Figure 15.1. *(opposite)* Katherine–Darwin area, vegetation. For key, see above. Reproduced with permission of the Land Research and Regional Survey Division (now Water and Land Resources).

small areas of tropical forest. The change to forest occurs in places along the east coast of Queensland, on the Atherton tablelands, on the dissected seaward-facing slopes of the Great Dividing Range and on the steep slopes of the Glasshouse mountains where the rainfall exceeds 1500 mm and is either fairly evenly distributed throughout the year or is supplemented by mist, and where the terrain is dissected and characterized by well drained soils derived from deeply weathered parent material, frequently of volcanic origin. At several localities in the Northern Territory the savanna woodlands give way over soils of heavy texture and in areas with impeded drainage to savanna grasslands.

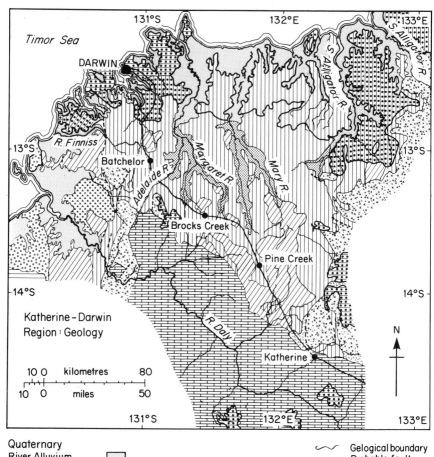

Katherine – Darwin
Region : Geology

10 0   kilometres   80
10 0   miles   50

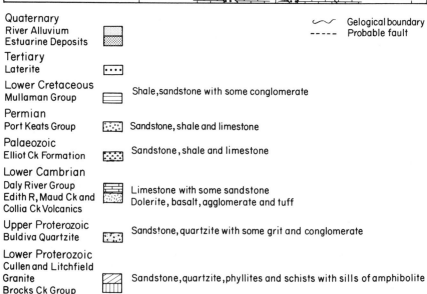

Quaternary
River Alluvium
Estuarine Deposits

Tertiary
Laterite

Lower Cretaceous
Mullaman Group   Shale, sandstone with some conglomerate

Permian
Port Keats Group   Sandstone, shale and limestone

Palaeozoic
Elliot Ck Formation   Sandstone, shale and limestone

Lower Cambrian
Daly River Group
Edith R, Maud Ck and   Limestone with some sandstone
Collia Ck Volcanics   Dolerite, basalt, agglomerate and tuff

Upper Proterozoic
Buldiva Quartzite   Sandstone, quartzite with some grit and conglomerate

Lower Proterozoic
Cullen and Litchfield
Granite   Sandstone, quartzite, phyllites and schists with sills of amphibolite
Brocks Ck Group

Gelogical boundary
Probable fault

The distribution of the savanna woodlands in Australia, as in Africa and South America, appears to be related closely to the distribution of laterite and lateritic soils, to that of the planation surfaces on which these soils developed, and to the subsequent breakdown of the lateritic soil profiles and dissection of the planation surfaces by geomorphological processes influenced by climatic changes and by crustal movements and eustatic changes of sea level. Peneplanation and lateritization appear to have occurred over vast areas of Australia in Tertiary, Pleistocene and Recent times and evidence has been advanced to suggest that the latter process is still operative on parts of the coastal lowlands between Caboolture and Battle Creek in Queensland. The great extent of savanna woodlands in Australia is due largely to the fact that planation and laterization occurred over enormous areas. The precise relationships between the present distribution of the savanna woodlands, soils and geomorphology are complicated because widespread differential crustal movements have led in some places to the dissection of the old peneplaned surfaces and in others to large-scale deposition over them (Cole 1982a). However in areas that have been subjected to detailed study these relationships have been established.

THE SAVANNA WOODLANDS AND ASSOCIATED SAVANNA GRASSLANDS AND PARKLANDS OF NORTHWESTERN AUSTRALIA AND THE NORTHERN TERRITORY

In the area extending from Broome eastwards to the mouth of the Roper river and including the Kimberley district of Western Australia, the Katherine–Darwin area and Arnhem Land in the Northern Territory, the present vegetation is derived from the flora that was widespread over northern Australia in the Tertiary period when the landscape was a monotonous peneplain characterized by lateritic soils. The subsequent destruction of this surface during the several geomorphological cycles inaugurated by tectonic movements, major changes of climate and eustatic fluctuations of sea level in the Quaternary and Recent periods, created new and varied habitats in which the present day vegetation associations and communities evolved. The present distribution of the savanna woodlands and of the vegetation associations and plant communities within them is influenced by the amount of rainfall and the length of the rainy season and by the relief, drainage and soil conditions that are related to the stage of dissection of the Tertiary

Figure 15.2. *(opposite)* Katherine–Darwin area, geology. Reproduced with permission of the Land Research and Regional Survey Division (now Water and Land Resources).

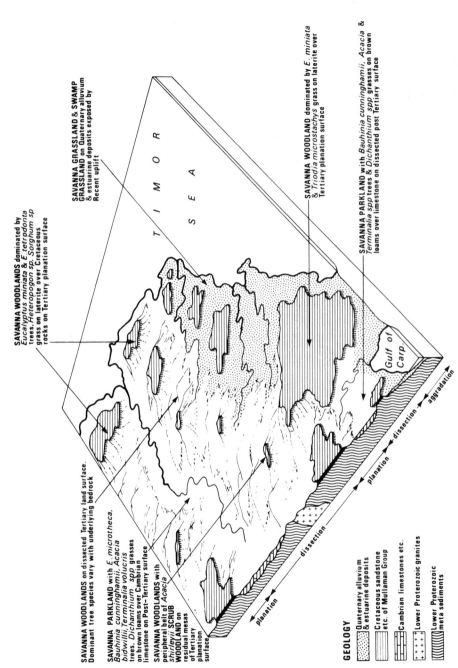

Figure 15.3. Relationships between vegetation, geomorphology and geology in the Northern Territory.

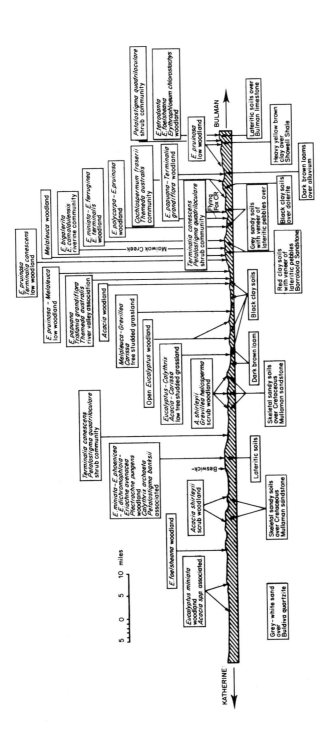

Figure 15.4. Relationships between vegetation, relief, soils and geology between Katherine and Bulman, Northern Territory. From Cole *et al.* (1968) with permission.

planation surface, removal of lateritic cover and exposure of bedrock, and to the interplay of geomorphological and pedological processes acting on remaining lateritic material and different types of bedrock (Figures 15.1–15.4).

The physical environment

The greater part of the savanna woodland belt that extends from the mouth of the Daly river eastwards to Katherine and northwards into Arnhem Land is underlain by Precambrian rocks (Figures 15.1 and 15.2). In the Katherine–Darwin area these comprise steeply folded metamorphosed Lower Proterozoic slates, sandstones, quartzites, phyllites and schists that have been intruded by granite batholiths and amphibolite sills, and subhorizontally bedded Upper Proterozoic sandstones, quartzites and conglomerates (Christian and Steward 1952). Near Bulman the Lower Proterozoic rocks comprise limestones and intrusive dolerite sills disposed in a domed structure (Sturmfels 1952, Cole *et al.* 1968). Rocks of Palaeozoic and Permian age occur over relatively small areas but the Mullaman Group of subhorizontally bedded Lower Cretaceous sediments caps numerous relict tablelands and mesas and appears formerly to have extended over most of the area. Following the exposure of the land in post-Cretaceous time the terrain was subjected to a long period of erosion which, because of the low relief, was associated with peneplanation and lateritization. By the Late Middle Tertiary the remaining sediments of the Cretaceous Mullaman Group had been laterized, as had older rocks where exposed on the peneplaned surface. The most resistant Precambrian rocks were not affected and formed prominent ridges rising above the Tertiary land surface. Subsequently uplift, which included both warping and faulting at the end of the Tertiary, initiated a new cycle of erosion while changes of sea level in Quaternary times led to the exposure of extensive post-Tertiary alluvium along the coast (Christian and Stewart 1952). The distribution of the vegetation associations within the savanna woodlands is closely related to the extent of the lateritized Tertiary planation surfaces and to the exposure of both old rocks and recent alluvium, with which in turn are associated variations in the soil, relief and drainage conditions that influence plant growth.

The Daly river–Darwin–Katherine–Alligator river area

Between Darwin and the Alligator river savanna woodlands dominated by tall *Eucalyptus miniata* and *E. tetrodonta* trees, by tall perennial grasses, notably *Heteropogon triticeus*, *Eriachne trisecta* and by the tall annual grass *Sorghum intrans* occur where the Tertiary lateritic surface is preserved and is associated with Tertiary lateritic red earths and Tertiary lateritic podzols over level to gently undulating terrain underlain by Lower Proterozoic metamorphic rocks of the Brocks Creek group or by shales of the Cretaceous Mullaman Group (Figure 15.4). An understorey of *Eugenia* subsp. *orbicularis*, *Eucalyptus porrecta*, *E. papuana*, *Gardenia* spp. trees, *Livistona humilis* palms and *Acacia* spp. shrubs may be present. Permanent or semi-permanent lagoons occupying depressions within the level surface are fringed by *Pandanus* palms and by dense communities of *Melaleuca symphyocarya* that are surrounded in turn by grassland flats characterized by *Pseudoraphis spinescens* and *Vetiveria pauciflora* and by a *Tristania–Grevillia–Banksia* community. These communities show distribution patterns that are related to drainage conditions. They may be compared with those forming lozenge-shaped patterns in the savanna grasslands occupying dark brown loams or black cracking clay soils within the semi-arid country characterized by low tree and shrub savannas of the Cloncurry area.

On the elevated mesa-like residuals where resistant lateritic horizons cap shales of the Cretaceous Mullaman Group, an open savanna woodland of *Acacia shirleyii* trees, *Grevillea heliosperma*, *Calythrix archaeta* shrubs and *Livistona humilis* palms occupies the shallow gravelly sandy loams of the plateau surface (Figure 15.4); it is succeeded on the slopes below the breakaway by mixed communities in which *Petalostigma quadriloculare* and *Terminalia canescens* are prominent. On the flats at the base of the mesas the vegetation varies with the nature of the soils and with the bedrock geology, with *Eucalyptus pruinosa* communities being common on heavy yellow brown clays derived from shale parent material (Figure 15.4). This sequence of savanna woodland communities occurs on and around the laterite-capped residuals of Cretaceous Mullaman rocks between Darwin and Katherine and again between Katherine and Bulman (Figure 15.4) (Cole *et al.* 1968).

Where the Tertiary lateritic surface has been partially or wholly eroded the composition of the savanna woodlands varies according to the relief and soils over different types of bedrock. Where Cambrian or Palaeozoic limestones give rise to red sandy loams an open savanna woodland characterized by *Eucalyptus foelscheana*, *E. tectificia*, *E. confertiflora*, *E. grandifolia* and *Erythrophloeum chlorostachys* trees, and by *Heteropogon contortus*, *Chrysopogon pallidus* and annual *Sorghum* spp. grasses, prevails over widely separated areas such as those around Katherine and near Bulman (Figure 15.5). Where heavy grey pedocals have formed in depressions subject to past alluviation and present day seasonal flooding, the vegetation changes to a savanna parkland of *Eucalyptus microtheca*, *E. papuana*, *Bauhinia cunninghamii*, *Erythrophloeum chlorostachys*, *Terminalia volucris* and other tree species scattered in a grassland of *Dichanthium* spp., *Chrysopogon* spp. *Themeda australis*, *Sehima nervosum* and other species (Figure 15.6). Where

Figure 15.5. Savanna woodland of *Eucalyptus miniata* with some *Erythrophloeum chlorostachys* trees and *Heteropogon contortus* grass over laterite over limestone bedrock, Rum Jungle area, Northern Territory.

Figure 15.6. Open savanna woodland of *Eucalyptus papuana* trees and *Heteropogon contortus* grass occupying heavy clay soils derived from shale bedrock near Rum Jungle. Smaller *Xanthostemon paradoxus* trees with grey trunks occur over the wetter sites along Rum Jungle Creek.

Figure 15.7. Savanna woodland of *Eucalyptus grandifolia* and *Grevillea* spp. over granite bedrock, Rum Jungle area.

the soils develop deep cracks in the dry season, the trees are few in number and deciduous in habit.

Where yellow podzolic soils have formed over sub-outcropping Precambrian granites a savanna woodland composed of *Eucalyptus grandifolia*, *E. clavigera*, *Eugenia bleeseria* and *Owenia vernicosa* trees associated with *Grevillea pteridofolia*, *G. parallella* and *Petalostigma quadriloculare* shrubs, *Livistona* and *Pandanus* palms and *Eriachne arenacea* grass occurs (Figure 15.7). On lateritic soils the *Livistona* palm is more frequent while on extreme rocky sites the rolled leaved *Plectrachne pungens* grass replaces the broad leaved species. Similarly on rocky outcrops of the Upper Proterozoic Buldiva quartzite the vegetation consists only of *Triodia microstachya*; on gentler slopes underlain by this formation a savanna woodland of *Eucalyptus phoenicea*, *E. miniata* and *E. dichromophloia* prevails.

In the areas which were not peneplaned or lateritized during the Tertiary and where the Precambrian metamorphic rocks of the Brocks Creek Group formed and still form hills rising above the general level, the composition of the savanna woodland varies with soils that are directly related to bedrock type. Over limestone bedrock *Eucalyptus miniata*, *E. foelscheana*, *Erythrophloeum chlorostachys* and *Eugenia bleeseri* trees occur in association with *Planchonia careya*, *Persoonia falcata* and *Acacia difficilis* shrubs, whereas over shale bedrock *Eucalyptus papuana*, *Eugenia suborbicularis* and *Terminalia pterocarpa* are the characteristic trees. The small *Xanthostemon paradoxus* tree which is present in some areas has been instanced as a uranium indicator at Rum Jungle where the Lower Proterozoic shale hosted an important orebody. The tree also occurs at the edge of a seasonally flooded area characterized by Pandanus palms near the Mount Finnis tin mine (Figure 15.6).

The Marrakai plains

Over the Marrakai plains which encompass the middle courses of the Adelaide, Margaret, McKinlay and Mary rivers where extensive alluviation occurred on the mature land surface following the Quaternary rise of sea level, the vegetation distributions are governed by the soils, by slight variations of relief and by the degree of seasonal flooding to which the area is subject. The low-lying level areas that are flooded after the summer rains and are characterized by acid alluvial soils are inimical to tree growth and carry a savanna grassland composed mainly of *Themeda* and *Eriachne* spp. The slightly higher ground of the low residuals of lateritized Precambrian rocks that have gravelly yellow podzolic soils have a low savanna woodland of *Eucalyptus bleeseri* or *E. papuana* and *Erythrophloeum chlorostachys* trees and *Jacksonia* spp. and *Melaleuca viridiflora* shrubs (Figure 15.8). Between

Figure 15.8. Savanna grassland over low-lying generally flooded areas and low savanna woodland over lateritic residual, Marrakai plains, Northern Australia.

Figure 15.9. Savanna woodland of *Eucalyptus foelscheana* (framing picture) and *Gardenia megasperma* with *Vetiveria elongata* grass over planation surface, Bulman area, Arnhem Land, Northern Territory. From Cole *et al.* (1968) with permission.

Figure 15.10. *Cochlospermum fraseri* trees over outcropping dolerite, south of Mainoru, Bulman area, Northern Territory. From Cole *et al.* (1968) with permission.

the plains and the rises, a narrow transition zone, which is above the level of the floods but has heavy soils, is characterized by savanna parkland in which *Eucalyptus latifolia*, *E. bigalerita*, *E. grandifolia*, *E. papuana* and *E. apodophylla* stud *Themeda australis* grassland. A similar parkland community in which *Tristania grandiflora* may also be present occupies the levees along the rivers.

Despite the differences of altitude the grassland and parkland communities of the Marrakai plains are comparable with the valley grasslands and parklands of the Busanga Plains and Kafue Flats in Zambia. In both countries they occupy the lower lying areas of a lateritized peneplaned surface on which alluviation occurred following changes of base level and on which today vegetation distributions are strongly influenced by soil and drainage conditions.

The Katherine–Bulman area

Detailed studies have revealed close relationships between vegetation, soils, geomorphology and bedrock geology in the Katherine–Bulman area (Cole *et al.* 1968).

The regional vegetation pattern is displayed in the broad sequence of vegetation associations along a transect from Katherine to Bulman (Figure 15.4). As in the Katherine–Darwin area *Acacia shirleyii* woodlands delineate mesas capped by the lateritized remnants of Cretaceous Mullaman sandstone. Open savanna woodlands of *Eucalyptus miniata*, *E. tetrodonta*, *E. ferruginea* and *E. terminalis*, with smaller *Erythrophloeum chlorostachys* and *Petalostigma banksii* trees and *Calythrix archaeta* shrubs, occupy level plateaux representing relicts of the Tertiary planation surface where laterite mantles the Borroloola sandstones at Beswick. The dominance of *Plectrachne pungens* and *Eriachne avenacea* in the grass layer distinguishes areas with sand-veneered indurated laterite, as on the Beswick plateau, from those characterized by more weathered material, as on the lower ground near Maiwok Creek where *Themeda arguens* and a *Sorghum* spp. prevail. Small trees of *Terminalia canescens* diagnostically occur over marginal zones where redistributed lateritic gravel veneers pallid zone material. Southeast of Bulman similar vegetational patterns are associated with comparable geomorphological conditions.

In the Bulman area the vegetation reflects the underlying geology. Southwest of Bulman an open woodland of stunted *Eucalyptus pruinosa* trees covers the heavy yellowish brown to grey soils of the flats underlain by shales of the Showell Formation; these trees become more numerous and are associated, in turn, with *Melaleuca viridiflora*, *M. acacioides* and *Petalostigma quadriloculare* near the base of mesas formed of the overlying Borroloola Sandstone (Figure 15.4). Grassland usually dominated by *Themeda australis* characterizes the black cracking clay coils of the alluvial flats, but near their better drained margins this is studded with small *Acacia* and *Bauhinia* trees. Where the soil material, derived by erosion from the pallid zone of the old laterite, is very fine, producing 'bull dust' in the dry season, *Eucalyptus polycarpa* and *Carissa* spp. occur in the grassland. These vegetational patterns resemble those in the belt of country bordering the Gulf of Carpentaria between Borraloola and Normanton (Chapter 16). Everywhere they are interrupted by well defined galleries of trees along the stream courses, where *Tristania grandiflora* and *Eucalyptus camaldulensis* occupy the stream bed and *Eucalyptus papuana*, *Terminalia* and *Bauhinia* spp. occur on the banks.

Within the Bulman area savanna woodland composed of *Erythrophloeum chlorostachys*, *Gardenia megasperma*, *Eucalyptus ferruginea*, *E. tectifica*, *E. tetrodonta* and *E. jenseni*, with a grass layer of *Chrysopogon pallidus* and various species of the *Andropogoneae* family, cover most of the country north and west of Waimuna Springs, where re-weathered laterite and silicified pallid zone material masks the lower limestone of the Bulman Formation. A similar but more open community of scattered *Eucalyptus foelscheana*, *Erythrophloeum chlorostachys* and *Gardenia megasperma*, with occasional *Grevillea dimidiata* and *Acacia pallida* trees studding a tall grassland dominated by cane grass, *Vetiveria elongata* and *Chrysopogon pallidus*, covers the low hills and rises formed by the siliceous dolomite and bedded carbonate rocks of the upper limestone at Bulman (Figure 15.9). In sharp contrast a sparse community of scattered small trees, mostly *Cochlospermum fraseri* and widely spaced *Heteropogon contortus* and *Vetiveria elongata*

Figure 15.11. *Terminalia platyphylla* trees in heavy dark brown soils, Bulman area, Northern Territory. From Cole *et al.* (1968) with permission.

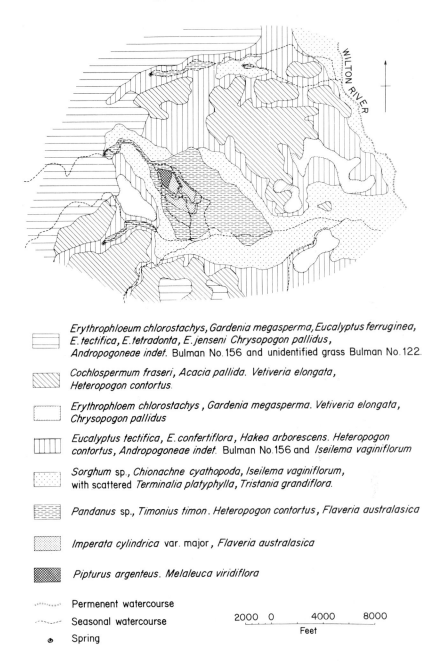

Erythrophloeum chlorostachys, Gardenia megasperma, Eucalyptus ferruginea,
E. tectifica, E. tetradonta, E. jenseni Chrysopogon pallidus,
Andropogoneae indet. Bulman No.156 and unidentified grass Bulman No.122.

Cochlospermum fraseri, Acacia pallida. Vetiveria elongata,
Heteropogon contortus.

Erythrophloem chlorostachys , Gardenia megasperma. Vetiveria elongata,
Chrysopogon pallidus

Eucalyptus tectifica, E. confertiflora, Hakea arborescens. Heteropogon
contortus, Andropogoneae indet. Bulman No.156 and *Iseilema vaginiflorum*

Sorghum sp., *Chionachne cyathopoda, Iseilema vaginiflorum,*
with scattered *Terminalia platyphylla, Tristania grandiflora.*

Pandanus sp., *Timonius timon. Heteropogon contortus, Flaveria australasica*

Imperata cylindrica var. major *, Flaveria australasica*

Pipturus argenteus. Melaleuca viridiflora

Permenent watercourse

Seasonal watercourse

Spring

2000 0   4000   8000

Feet

Figure 15.12. Bulman area, vegetation. From Cole *et al.* (1968) with permission.

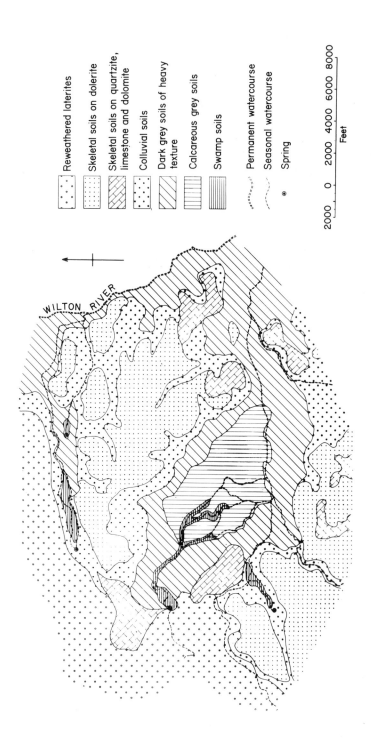

Figure 15.13. Bulman area, soils. From Cole *et al.* (1968) with permission.

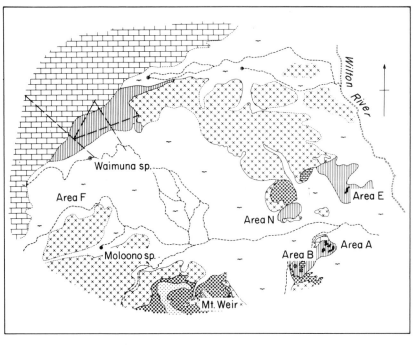

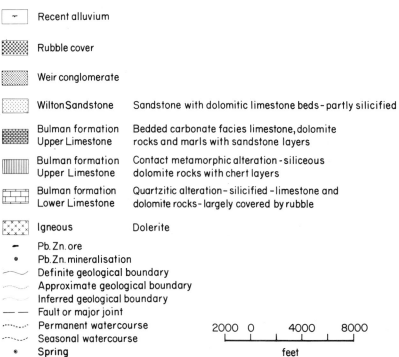

Wilton River
Waimuna sp.
Area F
Area E
Area N
Area A
Area B
Moloono sp.
Mt. Weir
Recent alluvium
Rubble cover
Weir conglomerate
Wilton Sandstone
Sandstone with dolomitic limestone beds - partly silicified
Bulman formation Upper Limestone
Bedded carbonate facies limestone, dolomite rocks and marls with sandstone layers
Bulman formation Upper Limestone
Contact metamorphic alteration - siliceous dolomite rocks with chert layers
Bulman formation Lower Limestone
Quartzitic alteration - silicified - limestone and dolomite rocks - largely covered by rubble
Igneous
Dolerite
Pb. Zn. ore
Pb. Zn. mineralisation
Definite geological boundary
Approximate geological boundary
Inferred geological boundary
Fault or major joint
Permanent watercourse
Seasonal watercourse
Spring
2000 0 4000 8000
feet

Figure 15.14. Bulman area, geology. From Cole *et al.* (1968) with permission.

grasses, distinguishes the low hills and rises formed of dolerite boulders and bedrock (Figure 15.10). A parklike savanna occupies the deeper colluvial soils which form aprons around the limestone and dolerite hills. *Eucalyptus tectifica* and *E. confertiflora* are the most common tree species, while the grasses *Heteropogon contortus* and *Iseilima vaginiflorum* characterize the ground layer. As the colluvial soils give way to dark brown or grey soils of heavy texture over the flood plain alluvia the vegetation changes to tall grassland dominated by a *Sorghum* sp., *Chionachne cyathopoda* and *Iseilima vaginiflorum*. Here *Tristania grandiflora* and *Terminalia platyphylla* may occur as scattered solitary trees (Figure 15.11), while the former also forms galleries along stream courses.

South and east of Waimuna Springs a sequence of specialized vegetation communities occurs over calcareous soils believed to be derived from Recent travertine; these soils are of lighter texture than the black cracking clays characteristic of the river flats. The community that occupies the largest area is that in which *Timonius timon* and a *Pandanus* sp. palm form a fairly open tree straum over a ground layer of *Heteropogon contortus* grass and the tall herb *Flaveria australasica*. On the interfluves between the braided stream courses this is replaced, in turn, by a tall grassland of *Imperata cylindrica* var. *major*, sometimes accompanied by *Flaveria australasica*, and by dense low thickets of *Pipturus argenteus* associated with *Melaleuca viridiflora* in wet places.

The distributions of individual vegetation associations and plant communities within the Bulman area are influenced mainly by soil and drainage factors that, in turn, are largely governed by geomorphology and geology (Figures 15.12–15.14). The strong contrasts between the northwest and southeast of the area result from the influences of these factors. Thus the uniformity of vegetation over a wide area on the northwest is attributable partly to the preservation of lateritic material over the old Tertiary peneplain and partly to the presumed extent of underlying lower limestone of the Bulman Formation. The soils are remarkably uniform, possessing certain qualities derived from features of the old lateritic profiles, which are now frequently truncated and re-weathered, and others attributable to the bedrock at depth. In the southeast, where erosion has exposed bedrock and produced a varied relief, sharply contrasting vegetation associations distinguish high ground and river flat and areas underlain by limestone, dolerite and alluvium.

Over the plains alternate waterlogging and drought, coupled with the high montmorillonitic clay content of the soils, which causes them to swell when wet and crack deeply when dry, discourage tree growth and are primarily responsible for the grassland vegetation. Improved drainage and/or more favourable soil texture, resulting in less cracking and better moisture retention, is reflected in the presence of trees. Southeast of Waimuna Springs the sequence of specialized vegetation communities is directly related to variations in the edaphic conditions over a restricted area.

Over the uplands free drainage and easy root penetration through the shallow gravelly soils favour trees whose frequency is governed mainly by available water during the dry season — hence their sparsity over the dolerite outcrops and greater frequency over dolomite, especially where the latter carries remnants of residual laterite.

Within the Bulman area there are marked vegetational changes over areas of known lead–zinc mineralization that occur on or near the summits of the low hills formed of the upper limestone of the Bulman formation at the Bulman Prospect. Here there are few trees. Those characteristics of the vegetation over carbonate rocks become infrequent, *Erythrophloeum chlorostachys* being totally absent from some areas and *Gardenia megasperma* represented by relatively few specimens. The characteristic grass species *Vetiveria elongata* and *Chrysopogon pallidus* are joined by, and in places give way to, an assemblage of *Polycarpaea synandra* var. *gracilis*, *Gomphrena canescens*, *Tephrosia* aff. *polyzyga*, *Fimbristylis schultzii* and *Aristida browniana*.

THE SAVANNA WOODLANDS AND ASSOCIATED SAVANNA GRASSLANDS AND PARKLANDS OF EASTERN QUEENSLAND

The break in the distribution of the savanna woodlands caused by the Gulf of Carpentaria and by the extensive grasslands over the Great Artesian Basin to the south is associated with some differences in the dominant tree species between the Northern Territory and eastern Queensland. These differences appear to be related fundamentally to landscape evolution, for whereas the dominant trees over the level plateaux of the mid-Tertiary planation surface tend to be the same in both areas, those over the terrain where subsequent dissection has exposed bedrock differ even where soils and lithologies are similar. In eastern Queensland further differences in the characteristic tree species are related to lower temperatures from north to south and decreasing rainfall between the coast and the interior. The relationships will be illustrated by reference to the Cape Yorke Peninsula, the Mareeba–Chillagoe area, the Townsville–Bowen area, the Charters Towers–Burdekin river valley area and the Lake Galilee–Alice Tableland area.

The Cape Yorke peninsula

In the northern part of the Cape Yorke peninsula, the savanna woodlands, like those of the Darwin–Rum Jungle area of the Northern Territory, are

Figure 15.15. *Eucalyptus tetrodonta–E. miniata* savanna woodland, Weipa, Cape Yorke Peninsula, Queensland.

Figure 15.16. Open savanna woodland of *Eucalyptus crebra* and *Heteropogon contortus* grass over basalt, Lolworth area, Burdekin valley, eastern Queensland.

Figure 15.17. Savanna woodland of *Eucalyptus melanophloia* and *Heteropogon contortus* grass on the Lake Galilee plateau, eastern Queensland.

dominated by *Eucalyptus tetrodonta* and *E. miniata* trees and *Heteropogon contortus* grass (Figure 15.15). These woodlands are coincident with the mid-Tertiary planation surface where laterite caps Cretaceous rocks. At Weipa and Pera Head where the laterite cap yields commercial bauxite deposits, the form and composition of the savanna woodland vary with slight changes of soil associated with minor dissection of the planation surface. Over the level plateau, the dark reddish grey to dark reddish brown loamy sands that change downwards to sandy clays overlying the bauxite support a close woodland in which *E. tetrodonta* and *E. miniata* trees are accompanied by *Grevillea parallela* and *G. pteridofolia*. On the gentle slopes of slightly dissected areas these species are joined by *E. confertiflora*, *E. nesophila* and *Erythrophloeum chorostachys* on dark reddish brown loamy sands passing downwards to dark sandy clays. Areas of redistributed ferruginous gravel along creek lines cut below the laterite carry a sparse tree cover of small *Petalostigma pubescens*, *Alphitonia excelsa*, *Melaleuca viridiflora* and *Grevillea glauca*. Where erosion has exposed water bearing Cretaceous sandstone patches of forest occur where springs issue at surface.

The Mareeba–Chillagoe area

The savanna woodlands over the level tablelands near Mareeba are of different composition. Those over the lateritic soils developed over granite bedrock are characterized by *Eucalyptus leptophleba* which is accompanied by *Grevillea parallela*, *G. pteridofolia* and *G. glauca*, by occasional *Erythrophloeum chorostachys* and *E. intermedia* trees and have a grass layer in which *Themeda australis*, *Heteropogon triticens* and *H. contortus* are the most common species. Over the more dissected terrain between Mount Garnet and Chillagoe the composition of the savanna woodlands is closely related to soils and in turn to bedrock geology. A typical open savanna woodland dominated by *Eucalyptus drepanophylla* (narrow leaf ironbark) or by *E. cullenii* and *Heteropogon contortus* grass occupies the sandy soils of areas underlain by sandstones and greywackes of the Siluro/Devonian Herberton Beds and by the Carboniferous Almaden granite. It gives way abruptly to a low growth of dwarf *Eucalyptus pruinosa*, *Petalostigma quadriloculare* and *Grevillea* trees accompanied by *Calythrix* spp. shrubs on the skeletal soils over Permian featherbed porphyry and porphyritic rhyolite rocks. The change of vegetation over the contact of the Herberton Beds and the Featherbed porphyries is extremely sharp. Further sharp changes of vegetation occur where mineralization is present. Thus patches of *Polycarpaea spirostylis*, *Bulbostylis barbata*, *Crotalaria trifoliastrum* and *Eriachne obtusa* displace the *Heteropogon contorta* grass where copper mineralization occurs at the contact of the Silurian Chillagoe limestone and the Carboniferous Almaden granodiorite and *Eucalyptus terminalis* takes over from *Eucalyptus drepanophylla* at the periphery of the area with toxic soils. Similar changes occur at Ruddigore where the quartz monzonite phase of the Almaden granodiorite is copper bearing, at Mungana where shales have similar mineralization, and along the continuation of the lead bearing Otho line of lode.

The Burdekin, river–Charters Towers area

South of Mount Garnet and in the upper Einasleigh and upper Burdekin valleys the composition of the savanna woodland varies according to the nature of the soils, which are either lateritic or derived directly from alluvium, Tertiary basalt or granite. A typical savanna woodland of *Eucalyptus racemosa* and *E. crebra* trees with a grass stratum of *Themeda australis* and *Chrysopogon fallax* occupies the lateritic red sandy soils derived from granite bedrock over the higher plateaux of the mid-Tertiary planation surface. *Grevillea parallela* and *G. pteridofolia* are usually present and *E. citriodora* and *E. setosa* occur in some areas. *Callitris glauca* trees occur where the soils are particularly sandy. Where the upper layers of the lateritic profiles have been removed and dark reddish brown loamy clays have weathered from mottled zone material the savanna woodlands are dominated by *E. racemosa* and *E. setosa* trees, again with a grass stratum of *Themeda australis*, whereas the grey brown soils formed over pallid zone material are favoured by *E. orgadophylla* and *E. hemiphloia* trees. Near Lyndhurst savanna woodlands of *E. racemosa*, *E. citriodora* and *E. tessellaris* occupying the dark reddish brown loams derived from basalt contrast with those of *E. siderophloia*, *Petalostigma quadriloculare*, *Grevillea glauca* and *G. pteridofolia* and *Melaleuca* spp. over sandy soils derived from granite; over flats with ill-drained sandy soils low woodlands of *Melaleuca* spp. prevail.

Over the basalt lava flows that produce a series of platforms and steps bearing repetitive sequences of soil types in the Burdekin river valley, the form and composition of the savanna woodlands vary with the changes in the soil and drainage conditions. In turn the woodlands change from those dominated by *Eucalyptus crebra* and *E. hemiphloia* trees over dark reddish brown clay loams on the most freely drained areas (Figure 15.16) to those of *E. hemiphloia* and *E. populnea* trees on dark brown loamy clays to more open parkland with *E. populnea* and *E. microtheca* trees on the heaviest black soils. *Planchonia careya* and other *Eucalyptus* species are infrequently distributed throughout the woodlands whose grass stratum varies in composition from *Heteropogon contortus* on the lightest soils to *Dichanthium* and *Astrebla* species on the progressively heavier soils. Because of the value of the latter grasses for grazing purposes the savanna woodlands on the heavier soils of the Burdekin valley have been managed to increase the grass cover, a factor that partly accounts for their more open character compared with those on the planation surfaces of the tablelands. At the other extreme, on the most recent lava flows that produce rough terrain with skeletal soils near Valley of Lagoons homestead, the vegetation is that of a vine scrub that is considered to represent depauperate tropical forest.

The Townsville–Bowen area

Contrasts in the savanna woodlands occur again over different types of terrain in the Townsville–Bowen area (Christian *et al.* 1953). There, however, the physiographic features and the soils are the result of erosion to maturity, modified to some extent by Pliocene or early Pleistocene warping near the present coast, rather than of planation processes. The area consists essentially of nearly flat alluvial plains and scattered mountainous residuals near the coast and of maturely dissected rugged hills inland. The skeletal soils of the freely draining sites over the hills carry a savanna woodland of *Eucalyptus drepanophylla* and *E. dichromophloia* with a grass layer of *Heteropogon contortus*, *Bothriochloa intermedia*, *Themeda australis* and *Sehima nervosum*. This passes through one of *E. drepanophylla* and *E. papuana* to one dominated by the latter species where strongly solonized soils with a hardpan in the subsoil occur on sites subject to waterlogging after rains. Here the grass layer is composed of *Aristida contorta*, *Heteropogon contortus*, *Bothriochloa intermedia* and *Chrysopogon fallax* with some patches of *Chloris* spp. By contrast savanna woodlands of *E. polycarpa* associated with *E. alba*, *Petalostigma quadriloculare*, *Melaleuca* spp. and *Heteropogon contortus* occupy the deeper sandier soils. Communities variously dominated by *E. tessellaris*, *E. alba* or *E. shirleyi* occupy respectively sandy, sandy solonized and stony skeletal soils over relatively small areas. The savanna woodlands give way to savanna grasslands of *Dichanthium* species with scattered *E. alba* and *E. microtheca* on the heavy clay soils of the flats and to stands of *Acacia harpophylla* on the alkaline black clay soils near Collinsville.

The Alice Tableland

South of Charters Towers the more typical savanna woodlands occur again over the Alice Tableland, a plateau of some $20\,000\,\text{m}^2$ that, with an elevation of 350–500 m, forms part of the Great Divide for some 400 km to beyond Alpha. Over the extensive plateau the mid-Tertiary planation surface has suffered little dissection and it has a more or less continuous lateritic cover. Over the centre of the plateau the full profile is preserved but dissection at the margins has removed the upper horizons. Indeterminate drainage and shallow lakes are a feature of the surface, the largest being Lake Buchanan and Lake Galilee.

On the higher parts of the plateau a savanna woodland dominated by the narrow-leaved ironbark, *Eucalyptus drepanophylla* and the silver-leaved ironbark, *E. melanophloia* and the bunch spear grass, *Heteropogon contortus* occupies the red sandy loam soils characteristic of the fully developed lateritic profile (Figure 15.17). *Grevillea* spp., notably *G. striata* and *G. parallela*, form a sparse lower tree layer. On exceptionally level terrain where the drainage is impeded *Grevillea* spp., in places accompanied by *Banksia* spp., tend to replace the dominant trees to form a more open woodland comparable with that near Kalomo in Zambia (see Figure 2.6). As in the latter area this form of savanna woodland, characterized by species of *Proteaceae*, occurs in the most central area of the old planation surface. It occurs also to the south of Charters Towers where small *Grevillea* and *Banksia* trees and *Triodia* spp. grass occupy areas with outcropping indurated laterite and again to the southwest of Lake Galilee where there is a large number of shallow circular depressions in which water accumulates. These depressions are believed to result from the weathering of the softer kaolinitic material within the mottled zone of the lateritic profile from which the upper horizon has been removed (Whitehouse 1940). In places both on the Lake Galilee plateau and around its periphery the typical savanna woodland gives way to plant communities characterized by *Triodia* sp. grass and by *Calythrix* sp. shrubs where fairly deep red sands, representing the redistributed A horizon material, have accumulated.

Around Lake Galilee and along the creek draining from it and towards the Thompson river there are significant changes in the vegetation that are related to differences of soil associated with the dissection of the plateau and the removal of the lateritic material. A narrow belt of the narrow-leaved box, *Eucalyptus brownii*, occurs around the edge of the lake. This is succeeded by a belt of *Acacia cambagei* trees with *Astrebla squarrosa* and *Dichanthium* sp. grasses which occupies the dark brown to black clay soils which have developed subsequent to the removal of the lateritic material. On the lighter brown soils the white gum, *Eucalyptus papuana*, *E.melanophloia*, *Atalaya hemiglauca* and *Grevillea* spp. occur with *Astrebla squarrosa*. *Acacia cambagei* occupies the dissected terrain paralleling the creeks where it is sometimes associated with *Myoporum platycarpum*. In places where the dark brown to black clay soils tend to gilgai, *Acacia harpophylla* occurs.

Between Lake Galilee and Jericho a repetitive sequence of plant associations confirms the relationship between vegetation, soils, relief and geomorphology. In this sequence the communities of *Eucalyptus melanophloia* trees and *Heteropogon contortus* or *Astrebla squarrosa* grass occupying the red sandy soils of the rises are succeeded by one characterized by *E. brownii* and *E. alba* on the heavier soils of the lower ground and by odd patches of *Acacia harpophylla* on black cracking clays. East of Jericho the sandy soils of the summits of a series of lateritic ridge carry stands of *Acacia aneura*, whereas the lower ground has a woodland of *E. tessellaris*, but nearer Alpha the previous sequence occurs again.

CONCLUSIONS

Thus over the savanna woodland belt of eastern Queensland the most typical forms occupy the extensive remains of the mid-Tertiary planation surfaces, notably in the Cape Yorke Peninsula in the north and over the Alice Tableland in the south, whereas variants showing close relationships between species distribution and geology occupy the dissected terrain where post-Tertiary erosion has removed the Tertiary lateritic cover and exposed bedrock. As in the Northern Territory the savanna woodlands give way to savanna grasslands over black clay soils that are subject to alternating waterlogging and drought, and to parklands on better drained brown loams of higher nutrient status.

16   The savanna grasslands and associated savanna types of Australia

In Australia savanna grasslands cover very large areas on the Barkly Tableland of the Northern Territory and over the plains of central and northwest Queensland where the edaphic conditions are remarkably similar although the bedrock that has provided the soil parent material differs in both age and type—Cambrian sediments, mainly dolomites and limestones on the Barkly Tableland, and Cretaceous and later sediments, mainly calcareous shales and alluvium, on the plains in Queensland. Smaller areas of savanna grassland occur in widely scattered areas, on heavy soils along valleys where, like those of the Victoria and Roper, they are associated with savanna parklands (Chapter 17) or on highly leached lateritic soils on the central parts of plateaux fashioned by Tertiary planation where they are associated with savanna woodlands (Chapter 15). Further areas of savanna grassland occur in the Georgina basin and along the channels draining to Lake Eyre where they form complex mosaics with other types of savanna vegetation (Chapter 19).

THE SAVANNA GRASSLANDS AND ASSOCIATED SAVANNA TYPES OF THE BARKLY TABLELAND AND ADJACENT AREAS

Savanna grasslands cover some 250 000 km² on the Barkly Tableland. In the south and east, with increasing aridity, they give way to predominantly low tree and shrub savanna and in the north and west, with increasing rainfall, to predominantly savanna woodland. Variations in the plant cover occur within the savanna grasslands of the Tableland while complex distributions of the three savanna categories are a feature of its margins. These distributional patterns are the result of the interaction between plants and environment over a long period of time and their elucidation requires attention to both the current physical conditions and to the geological and geomorphological evolution of the landscape.

Geology and geomorphology

The Barkly Tableland forms part of the northeastern corner of the Australian Precambrian Shield. This has been relatively stable since Precambrian times. It has been subject to long periods of erosion interrupted by shallow marine transgressions during which the sediments of the Upper Proterozoic, Middle Cambrian and Lower Cretaceous were laid down. For the most part these sediments remain unfolded. Since the Cretaceous the greater part of the area has been above sea level and subject to prolonged erosion. The only Tertiary deposits are of terrestrial origin. At the beginning of the Recent, gentle warping of the surface depressed the area now forming the Gulf of Carpentaria and arched the land to the south, while minor differential uplifts occurred along the eastern and western margins of the area. At the same time differential movements in South Australia rejuvenated the drainage system of southwestern Queensland, eventually affecting the upper Georgina river. Subsequently a major eustatic rise of sea level in the late Pleistocene completed the flooding of the Gulf of Carpentaria and led to the deposition of extensive estuarine alluvial deposits, some of which were uncovered by a slight fall in sea level in mid-Recent time.

Today the area where Middle Cambrian and Lower Cretaceous sediments and terrestrial deposits of Tertiary age overlie the folded Precambrian basement constitutes the Barkly Tableland. This is delimited on the east, north and west by rugged terrain where the folded and metamorphosed Precambrian rocks of the Shield outcrop along the lines of differential uplift.

The Cambrian sediments that underlie the Barkly Tableland consist mainly of dolomite and limestone, sandstone, chert and shale. They are disposed more or less horizontally with, probably, basin structures beneath the Barkly basin and Georgina valley. Remnants of the Lower Cretaceous Mullaman Group, which once covered most of the area extending to the Gulf of Carpentaria, occur in the north of the Barkly basin with isolated outliers near the Gulf. Tertiary deposits of lake limestone and both Tertiary and Recent spreads of alluvium occur in the Barkly basin and Georgina valley.

The fashioning of the present landscape began when the region was uplifted after the deposition of the Cretaceous sediments. A long period of erosion ensued in Tertiary times when the land surface was reduced to a peneplain — a level or gently undulating plain with extensive swamps and some lakes in the centre, west and south, and some residual hilly country in the east and north. Lateritization occurred over much of the region except where there were swamps and lakes, steep hills and calcareous sediments.

The present landscape has been sculptured from this Tertiary, probably Miocene, laterite covered peneplain. Over much of the area the old surface has been preserved but in places erosion and deposition have produced younger surfaces and wrought changes in the soil profiles that in turn have caused changes in the vegetation cover. The major forces motivating the erosive and depositional processes have been the warpings and differential land movements that occurred at the beginning of the Recent, a period of aridity sometime during that period and eustatic changes of sea level in the late Pleistocene and mid-Recent. The first mentioned initiated erosion particularly in the belt peripheral to the Gulf of Carpentaria where the coastal flowing streams were rejuvenated. The subsequent onset of arid conditions caused the drying up of inland lakes and swamps, upset the vegetation balance and induced erosion which led to the destruction of the old lateritic soil profiles, and the deposition of the topsoil in dunes and sand tracts and of the decomposed laterite as veneers of ironstone gravel. With a return to moister conditions new soils developed on the truncated lateritic profiles or exposed bedrock while pedogenesis commenced on the depositional material. The eustatic changes of sea level led to the creation of areas of coastal alluvium. Throughout the period of changing environmental conditions the vegetation responded with some species retreating in the face of unfavourable conditions and others evolving and spreading to occupy the newly created niches.

The interaction of geomorphological processes and geological events produced four topographically distinct zones within the Barkly region— namely, the plains of the Barkly Tableland, the belt of dissected hilly country along its eastern and northern margins, the coastal plains bordering the Gulf of Carpentaria and a belt of low hills in the west. The Barkly Tableland has an altitude of around 200 m in the south and centre, which features internal drainage, rising to 330 m at its periphery. The eastern and northern hilly country has an altitude range from 330 m near Mount Isa to 17 m at the edge of the coastal plains where altitude varies from sea level to 100 m. The western hills are 350–430 m high.

Three major geomorphological divisions have been recognized within the Barkly region—the Gulf Fall, the Georgina basin and the Barkly basin (Christian *et al.* 1954). The first is drained by streams that flow to the Gulf of Carpentaria and includes the coastal plains and most of the eastern and northern hilly belt. The Georgina and Barkly basins include the Barkly Tableland and small areas of the surrounding hill belts. Within each of the divisions stable, erosional and depositional land surfaces have been distinguished, the first being little altered relics of the Tertiary lateritized peneplain and the others young surfaces created by either erosion or deposition. The relationships between these surfaces in each of the divisions is shown in Figure 16.1.

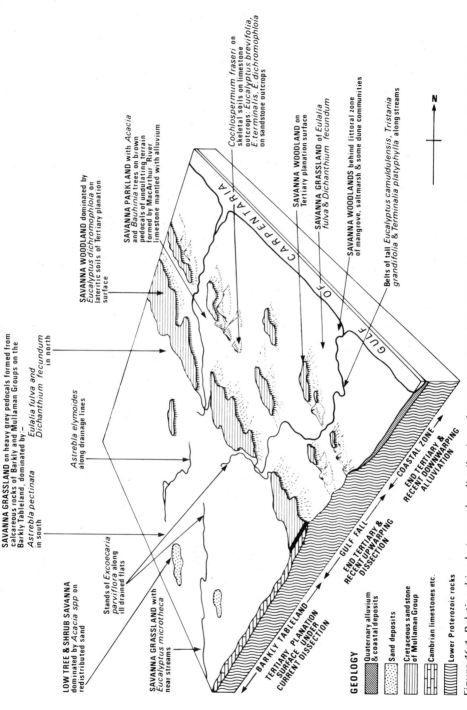

SAVANNA GRASSLAND on heavy grey pedocals formed from calcareous rocks of Barkly and Mullaman Groups on the Barkly Tableland, dominated by:—
Eulalia fulva and *Dichanthium fecundum* in north
Astrebla pectinata in south

Astrebla elymoides along drainage lines

LOW TREE & SHRUB SAVANNA dominated by *Acacia spp* on redistributed sand

Stands of *Excoecaria parviflora* along ill drained flats

SAVANNA GRASSLAND with *Eucalyptus microtheca* near streams

SAVANNA WOODLAND dominated by *Eucalyptus dichromophloia* on lateritic soils of Tertiary planation surface

SAVANNA PARKLAND with *Acacia* and *Bauhinia* trees on brown pedocals of undulating terrain formed by MacArthur River limestone mantled with alluvium

Cochlospermum fraseri on skeletal soils on limestone outcrops: *Eucalyptus brevifolia, E. terminalis & E. dichromophloia* on sandstone outcrops

SAVANNA WOODLAND on Tertiary planation surface

SAVANNA GRASSLAND of *Eulalia fulva & Dichanthium fecundum*

SAVANNA WOODLANDS behind littoral zone of mangrove, saltmarsh & some dune communities

Belts of tall *Eucalyptus camuldulensis, Tristania grandifolia & Terminalia platyphylla* along streams

GULF OF CARPENTARIA

COASTAL ZONE
— END TERTIARY & RECENT DOWNWARPING — ALLUVIATION

GULF FALL —
— END TERTIARY & RECENT UPWARPING — DISSECTION

— BARKLY TABLELAND — TERTIARY PLANATION SURFACE UNDER CURRENT DISSECTION

N

GEOLOGY

- Quaternary alluvium & coastal deposits
- Sand deposits
- Cretaceous sandstone of Mullaman Group
- Cambrian limestones etc.
- Lower Proterozoic rocks

Figure 16.1. Relationships between the distribution of savanna vegetation, geomorphology and geology on the Barkly Tableland and adjacent areas.

The grasslands of the Barkly Tableland

The characteristic grassland of the Barkly Tableland is an association dominated by the perennial tussock grass *Astrebla pectinate* (barley Mitchell grass) which attains a height of 30–75 cm and an individual tussock diameter of 22–30 cm (Christian *et al.* 1954). Other tussock grasses, notably *Astrebla squarrosa* (bull Mitchell grass), *A. elymoides* (weeping Mitchell grass), *Aristida latifolia* and *Chrysopogon fallax* (golden beard grass) may occur while patches of the tall *Sorghum*, *Panicum decompositum*, *P. whitei*, *Aristida unaequiglumis* and *Spathia nervosa* may be common in some seasons. During and after a season of good rains the spaces between the tussock grasses are occupied by shorter grasses and herbs some 7–30 cm high. Most of these are annuals with *Iseilima* spp. (Flinders grasses) and *Brachyachne convergens* (native couch) as the most important grasses.

The *Astrebla pectinata* grassland occupies the heavy grey pedocal soils that have formed from material derived from the calcareous rocks of the Barkly and Mullaman groups in places intermixed with fine textured alluvium which accumulated in swamps of the Tertiary peneplain. The level terrain, its tendency to flood for periods after rains and the self mulching characteristics of the soils are at once generally inimical to tree growth and favourable for grasses.

In the northern part of the Barkly Tableland where the rainfall is slightly higher *Eulalia fulva* (brown top) and *Dichanthium fecundum* (blue grass) replace *Astrebla pectinate* as the dominant grass. They are associated with *Astrebla squarrosa*, *A. elymoides*, *Aristida latifolia*, Chrysopogon fallax, *Sehima nervosa* (white grass) and *Bothriochloa* spp. to produce a somewhat taller grassland—between 1 and 2 m—than that dominated by *Astrebla pectinata*. *Themeda australis* (kangaroo grass), *Sorghum* and *Panicum* spp. may be present while the ground layer of *Iseilema vaginiflorum* (red Flinders grass), *Brachyachne convergens*, *Eragrostic japonica* (delicate love grass) and numerous herbs is usually denser and taller.

Throughout the area a grassland dominated by *Astrebla elymoides* (weeping Mitchell grass) occupies the slightly wetter habitats such as shallow depressions and shallow drainage lines. The species is usually accompanied by *A. squarrosa*, *Aristida latifolia*, *Eriachne nervosa*, *Panicum whitei*, *P. decompositum* and a variety of lower growing annual grasses, notably *Iseilima vaginiflorum*, and herbs to produce a denser cover than that of the *Astrebla pectinata* association. In places dense stands of *Sesbania benthamiana*, which attains 2 m, occur in some seasons, giving rise to what are known as pea bush swamps.

In all three tussock grassland associations a sparse low tree layer of *Eucalyptus microtheca*, the coolibah, may occur where the surface is more undulating and more moisture is available from run-off from nearby areas. This tree also occurs along the streams tributary to the Barkly inland drainage system. On the ill-drained flats near the streams that are flooded for short periods annually the gutta percha tree, *Excoecaria parvifolia*, forms a virtually monospecific community (Figure 16.2).

In places where calcimorphic soils of somewhat lighter texture, mostly dark brown pedocals formed from the Barkly limestones occur, pure grassland gives way to a parkland characterized by deciduous *Bauhinia cunninghamii* and *Terminalia volucris* (rosewood) trees and a grass layer of *Themeda australis* associated with *Heteropogon contortus*, *Cymbopogon* and *Chrysopogon* spp. and variable densities of annual grasses and herbs. This parkland, whose composition varies, occupies only relatively small areas, notably in the north between Brunette Creek and Mallapunyah station where erosion following the end Tertiary/Recent warping has uncovered the limestone bedrock. Further south *Bauhinia cunninghamii* trees occupy anthills that rise through the heavy grey pedocals and provide better drained sites and a rooting stratum of lighter texture. Currently parkland is extending as erosion reduces the cover of Tertiary alluvium and assists the formation of lighter textured soils derived directly from limestone bedrock. The *Bauhinia cunninghamii* trees on the anthills within the grasslands occupying the heavy grey pedocals represent the forerunners of this change.

The typical tussock grasslands of the Barkly Tableland are interrupted where relicts of lateritic material mantle the surface. The nature of the vegetation change depends on whether the plains surface is thinly veneered with the last vestiges of lateritic material or whether the Tertiary planation surface with its lateritic soil profiles has been largely preserved.

A low grassland dominated by annual species, particularly *Sporobolus australasicus* and *Enneapogon* spp. which seldom exceed 15 cm, occurs on low gravelly rises where chert fragments overlie the heavy grey pedocal soils. Grassland, however, gives way to patches of *Acacia georginae* (gidgee) scrub over ground veneered with ferruginous lateritic gravel. On some low rises, which form relatively drier habitats, scattered low straggly *Grevillea striata*, *Ventilago viminalis*, or *Atalaya hemiglauca* trees or scattered *Carissa lanceolata* bushes may occur. Frequently this form of vegetation occupies a narrow zone of variable transition soils between the grasslands of the heavy, grey pedocals and the relict savanna woodlands on lateritic remnants on the one hand and the low tree and shrub savanna on the sandy depositional soils on the other.

Where relict lateritic red earths, lateritic red sands and lateritic podzolic soils, formed over a variety of rocks during the Tertiary period, remain *in situ* over residual hills or low eminences within the plains, savanna woodlands form the characteristic vegetation. These woodlands occur mainly in the

Figure 16.2. Stands of *Excoecaria parviflora* on ill-drained flats on the Barkly Tableland.

Figure 16.3. Laterite residual with *Eucalyptus* trees above the *Astrebla–Iseilima* spp. grasslands over the dark brown soils of heavy texture of the plains of central Queensland between Morella and Muttaburra.

Figure 16.4. *Astrebla* spp. grassland near Kynuna, Queensland.

northern part of the Barkly Tableland, notably on Anthony Lagoon station. In areas with lateritic red earths they are characterized by *Eucalyptus dichromophloia*, sometimes associated with *E. ferruginea* trees, the shrubs *Grevillea wickhamii*, *G. striata*, *G. dryandri*, *Acacia lysiphloia* and other *Acacia* spp. The ground layer is composed of sclerophyllous tussock grasses, mostly *Triodia pungens* associated with other *Triodia* and *Plectyrachne* spp. which form a discontinuous cover especially where indurated laterite outcrops at or near surface. Where the A horizon is deeper *Aristida pruinosa* may replace *Triodia pungens* as the dominant grass. Where indurated laterite outcrops and where the surface soils are composed largely of ferruginous gravel *Eucalyptus brevifolia* or *Acacia shirleyii* replace *E. dichromophloia* as the dominant tree and the vegetation changes to low tree and shrub savanna or scrub, respectively. Where the soils developed over truncated lateritic profiles are deeper and display features of yellow podzolics *Eucalyptus argillaceae*, *E. terminalis* and *E. tectifica* are the dominant trees, the first occurring particularly where the soils are derived from limestone bedrock. *Sehima nervosum*, *Sorghum plumosum*, *Heteropogon contortus*, *Themeda triandra* and *Chrysopogon pallidus* form a fairly dense grass cover 1–1.3 m high. The dissected gravel-strewn slopes below the lateritic relicts typically carry a sparse low tree and shrub vegetation in which small *Terminalia canescens* and *Petalostigma quadriloculare* trees are prominent, while the level frequently poorly drained land at their foot is occupied by low woodland dominated by the silver box *Eucalyptus pruinosa*. This gives way to the typical tussock grasslands of the plains.

The continuity of the *Astrebla pectinata* tussock grasslands of the Barkly Tableland is also interrupted where sand, sometimes in the form of sand hills, covers the surface. This sand is believed to represent A horizon material from the Tertiary lateritic soil profiles that were eroded during an arid period and deposited particularly in the southern and western parts of the area as well as beyond its confines. Today these sandy areas carry a low tree and shrub savanna characterized by *Acacia* species. On Alexandria Station in the south *Acacia lysiphloia*, *A. coriaceae* and *A. xylocarpa* form the dominant shrub species, sometimes being accompanied by *Grevillea striata*, while *Triodia pungens* dominates the ground layer. In the west near Elliott *Jacksonia odontoclada* co-dominates with *Acacia* species in the shrub layer.

Thus within the Barkly Tableland the distribution of the characteristic tussock grassland dominated by *Astrebla pectinata* and allied species in closely influenced by current climatic and soil conditions. This distribution however is interrupted by savanna woodlands over Tertiary lateritic relicts and by low tree and shrub savannas where sand mantles the surface. Overall the present vegetation is the expression of the interplay of climatic and edaphic factors, geomorphological processes and geological events over a long period. Beyond the Barkly Tableland the vegetation becomes predominantly savanna woodland in the north where mosaic patterns of savanna woodland, savanna grassland and parkland feature the Gulf Fall where vegetation distributions are intimately related to soils and geomorphology. It becomes predominantly low tree and shrub savanna in the east and south where vegetation distributions are closely influenced by soils and bedrock geology.

The mosaic of savanna woodland, savanna grassland and parkland of the Gulf Fall area south of the Gulf of Carpentaria

In the Gulf Fall area dissection and deposition since the Tertiary period has produced a complex pattern of physiographic features, some of which are relict remains of the Tertiary lateritic peneplain whereas others are controlled by bedrock geology. The vegetation reflects the interrelationships between soils, geomorphology and geology.

At the edge of the Barkly Tableland on Mallapungah station laterite caps the Cambrian limestone to produce a clearly defined breakaway feature. To the northeast over the axis of the end Tertiary/Recent upwarp the terrain has been severely dissected by the tributaries of the MacArthur river. Initiated on a Mesozoic surface these have now become superimposed onto the Proterozoic rocks below. Most of the area northeast of the breakaway is underlain by the MacArthur river limestones and dolomites equivalent in age to the Bulman limestones of Arnhem Land but Borroloola sandstones, together with the Three Knobs Shale and Bauhinia sandstone, respectively equivalent to the Showell Shale and Wilton sandstone formations in Arnhem Land, have been preserved in the Abner range while nearer the coast younger Bukalara sandstone, capped by Tertiary laterite, is preserved near Borroloola. The last mentioned forms part of the low-level Tertiary lateritic plain. Between the breakaway on Mallapungah and this plain the physiography varies with the extent of Tertiary lateritic remnants and the degree of dissection of the Proterozoic rocks. The MacArthur river and its tributaries occupy open valleys over the limestone bedrock but are confined in gorges through the sandstone ranges. In places alluviation has occurred upstream of the local base levels imposed by the resistant sandstone rocks. Near the Gulf there are wide spreads of coastal alluvium.

The vegetation is closely related to the nature of the soils which in turn are influenced primarily by geomorphology and bedrock geology. Below the breakaway the brown pedocals formed from the MacArthur river limestones with some admixture of alluvium carry a parkland characterized by *Bauhinia cunninghamii* and *Acacia* spp. trees and *Eulalia fulva* and *Dichanthium fecundum* grasses. This is interrupted by savanna woodland mainly composed of *Eucalyptus terminalis*, *E. argillacea*, *Erythrophloeum chlorostachys* and *Grevillea striata* trees and *Heteropogon contortus*, *Chrysopogon pallidus*, *Sehima nervosum* and other grasses where red soils with loose lateritic boulders occur and by one dominated by *Eucalyptus brevifolia*, *Erythrophloeum chlorostachys*, *Carissa lanceolata* and *Melaleuca acacioides* on red sands probably derived from the old A horizon of the lateritic profile near Mallapungah station. Where near surface limestone bedrock weathers to red sandy soils an open savanna woodland of *Eucalyptus terminalis* and *E. papuana* with a ground layer of *Triodia* and *Plectrachne* grasses occurs while small *Cochlospermum fraseri* trees occupy the skeletal soils associated with outcropping limestone. The skeletal soils over the range of Borroloola and Abner sandstones support open woodland of *Eucalyptus brevifolia*, *E. terminalis* and *E. dichromophloia* trees associated with *Grevillea*, *Verticordia* and *Calythrix* shrubs and *Triodia* spp. grass while the poorly drained heavier soils at the base of the hills, as in the Bulman area, are thinly covered by *Eucalyptus pruinosa* trees. Near Borroloola a taller savanna woodland of *Eucalyptus tetrodonta*, *E. miniata*, *E. ferruginea* together with *Callitris intratropica* and *Terminalia canescens* trees, *Calythrix microphylla*, *Petalostigma pubescens* shrubs, *Triodia* and *Plectrachne* grasses and in places dense patches of *Gomphrena canescens* occupies a zone where massive indurated laterite occurs at surface. Elsewhere in this coastal area stands of *Eucalyptus papuana–E. tectifica* woodland occupy the river levees, those of *Melaleuca leucadendron* feature the Tertiary lateritic and yellow podzolic soils of poorly drained areas flooded for part of the year while patches of *Excoecaria parvifolia* occupy ill-drained zones along valley lines. Belts of tall trees, including *Eucalyptus camuldulensis*, *Tristania grandifolia* and *Terminalia platyphylla* follow the perennial streams to the Gulf of Carpentaria where mangrove swamps, salt marshes and sand dunes support specialized communities to add to the vegetation complexity of the area.

THE SAVANNA GRASSLANDS AND ASSOCIATED SAVANNA WOODLANDS AND PARKLANDS OF CENTRAL AND NORTHWESTERN QUEENSLAND

The savanna grasslands that occupy the level plains of central and northwestern Queensland where grey and brown soils of heavy texture have formed over calcareous shale of Cretaceous age, are more varied in form and composition and have a more broken distribution than those of the Barkly Tableland. These differences are due to more varied soil and relief conditions that in turn are related on the one hand to the more widespread legacies of Tertiary planation and lateritization and on the other hand to the greater dissection that has occurred since that period.

Compared with the Barkly Tableland the plains of central Queensland are slightly undulating and they are broken by residual mesas capped by lateritic ironstone (Figure 16.3). In places extensive spreads of lateritic gravel mantle the surface of the plains. Two distinctive categories of soils may be distinguished. Very fine grained grey to dark grey soils which are friable but tend to swell when wet and to crack deeply on drying characterize the central parts of the plains which are free of lateritic gravel. These soils have formed either from calcareous shale bedrock or from recent alluvium. Where the surface is mantled by lateritic gravel more compact yellowish brown clay silts and clay loams occur. These have formed at least in part from the kaolinitic horizon of old lateritic soil profiles. Within areas characterized by these latter soils shallow depressions free from gravel tend to swell and puff, producing the features known as 'gilgais' or 'crab-holes'.

Treeless grasslands dominated by *Astrebla lappacea* (common Mitchell grass) and *A. elymoides* or, in the badly drained areas, by *A. squarrosa*, characterize the areas with grey to dark grey soils. These grasslands resemble those of the Barkly Tableland. Grassland dominated by *A. pectinata* and usually studded by trees occupy the yellowish brown soils. Over lateritic gravel the trees are *Acacia cambagei* which, in places near residual mesas, form a scrub woodland with only a sparse ground layer of grasses. Farther from the mesas scattered *Acacia homalophylla* (the boree) trees form a parkland savanna (see Figure 2.13). In places there is an admixture of both tree species. In contrast to the grasslands and tree studded grasslands, savanna woodlands that are characterized by either *Eucalyptus* spp. trees or by *Acacia cambagei* trees with a ground layer of *Triodia* grass occupy the relict lateritic soils of the residual mesas.

Detailed studies, based on interpretations of Landsat and air survey imagery, followed by field investigations, have elucidated the relationships between vegetation and environmental parameters over the plains between Kynuna and Winton and around Cloncurry. These studies have established that in the former area the composition of the cover and the percentage of bare ground is closely related to stages in the dissection and removal of Tertiary lateritic material, whereas in the latter it is related to soil/drainage conditions and the lowering of the water table.

Over the plains in the headwaters region of the Diamantina river near Kynuna the cover of *Astrebla* and *Iseilima* spp. grasses thins out and is replaced by one of *Aristida contorta* and *Enneapogon arenaceous* over spreads of lateritic gravel where there are stands of *Eucalyptus cambagei* trees that frequently sucker vigorously where the ground is bare (Figures 16.4–16.6). Where all vestiges of a former laterite cover have been removed and Mesozoic sediments either outcrop or approach surface there are some stands of small *Atalaya hemiglauca* trees whose distribution is probably

Figure 16.5. *Astrebla* spp. grasses yielding to *Aristida contorta* and *Enneapogon arenaceus* grasses over lateritic gravel (dark areas) near Kynuna, Queensland.

Figure 16.6. *Acacia cambagei* trees over lateritic gravel within the *Astrebla* spp. grasslands, near Kynuna, Queensland.

related to phosphorus levels in the substrate. Elsewhere over the dark brown loam soils the grass cover usually exceeds 60% and is dominated by *Astrebla pectinata* or *A. lappacea* with *A. squarrosa* following moister drainage lines.

Over the plains north of Cloncurry there are remarkable vegetation patterns that are intimately related to soils, drainage and geology (Figures 16.7 and 16.8) (Cole 1982a, Cole and Owen-Jones 1977). Over the central part of the

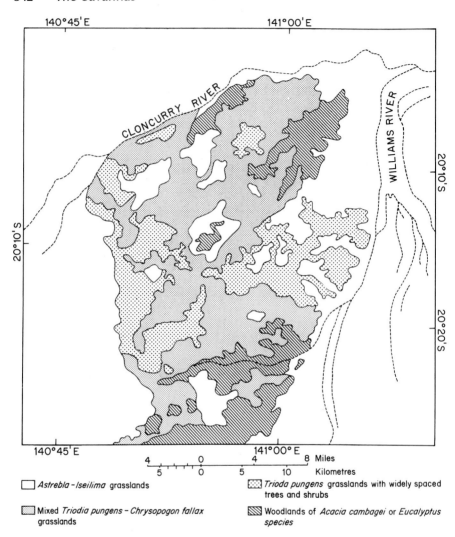

Figure 16.7. Distribution of vegetation communities between the Cloncurry and Williams rivers, Cloncurry Plains, Queensland. (Interpreted from Landsat and air survey imagery and field investigations.)

plain between the Cloncurry and Williams rivers, pure grasslands composed mainly of perennial *Astrebla* and annual *Iseilima* spp. occupy yellow brown to grey clay loams derived from Older Alluvium, whereas a low tree and shrub savanna, comprising scattered *Eucalyptus pruinosa* trees and *Carissa lanceolata* shrubs in a grassland in which the annuals *Aristida contorta* and

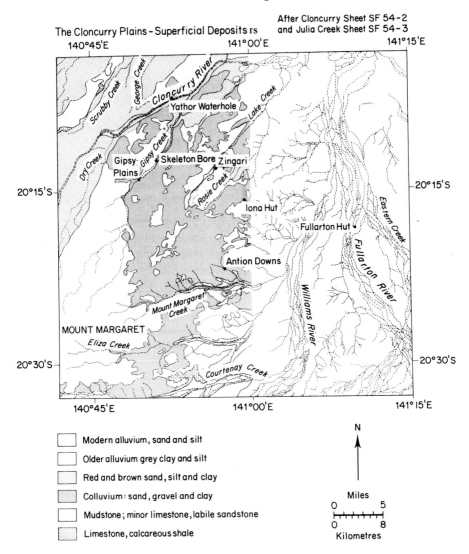

Figure 16.8. Superficial deposits, Cloncurry Plains (after Bureau of Mineral Resources maps).

Sporobolus australasicus occupy the spaces between the perennial clumps of *Triodia pungens*, characterizes the reddish brown sandy clays developed over the colluvial sand and gravel that is a legacy of the former lateritic cover. In places, stands of *Acacia cambagei* trees cover spreads of ferruginous gravel. Along the creeks open woodlands characterized either by *Eucalyptus* spp.

Figure 16.9. The Cloncurry Plains. Tall *Eucalyptus* spp. trees and *Cenchrus pennisetiformis* grassland on alluvial soils along the Williams river, east of Cloncurry.

or by *Acacia cambagei* trees occupy areas underlain by Modern Alluvium or by Lower Cretaceous Allaru mudstone (Figure 16.9).

Within the area characterized by the *Eucalyptus pruinosa–Triodia pungens* association on the plains north of Cloncurry there are pockets of treeless grassland in which patterns of lozenge or almond shaped features, produced by concentric distributions of different plant communities, are evident on aerial imagery. Due to inaccessibility the species composition of these communities is not known but that of the communities producing comparable features over much larger areas between the Dugald river and Cabbage Tree Creek northwest of Naraku and again below the confluence of these streams has been studied in detail (Figures 16.10 and 16.11) (Cole and Owen-Jones 1977). There, within a grassland dominated by *Brachyachne convergens*, *Iseilima macratherum* and *Sporobolus australasicus* with some *Ocimum sanctum*, *Sida acuta* and *Ptilotus spicatus* plants, the outer 'shell' or 'ring' of each 'almond' or 'lozenge' is characterized by *Astrebla squarrosa* and *Ocimum sanctum* with subsidiary *Brachyachne convergens* and *Iseilima macratherum*. This is succeeded inwards by a 'shell' or 'ring' of *Sporobolus australasicus* and *Cleome viscosa* with some bare areas and this in turn by an inner sparsely vegetated centre of *Enneapogon arenacous*, *Aristida contorta* and *Sporobolus australasicus* grasses and much bare ground. The vegetational sequence shows some relationship to soil changes, with the characteristic *Brachyachne convergens–Iseilima macratherum* grasslands occupying dark brown to black clay loams and clay soils and giving way successively to the other communities as the soils become heavier towards

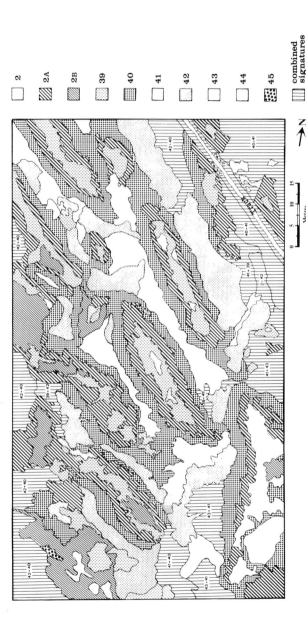

Figure 16.10. Distribution of plant communities in lozenge shaped patterns, Little Eva plains. Interpreted from infra red colour film 27 frame 155.

Key: (2) *Sporobolus australasicus* dominated grassland on red sandy soils over mixed colluvial and residual material. (2A) *Sporobolus australasicus* dominated grassland on heavy black clay soils. (2B) *Sporobolus australasicus* and *Cleome viscosa* community on heavy black clay soils. (39) Sparse cover of *Enneapogon arenaceous* and *Aristida contorta* grasses with *Sporobolus australasicus* with much bare ground on heavy black clay soils. (40) *Ocimum sanctum* and *Astrebla squarrosa* co-dominant in association with *Brachyachne convergens*, *Sida acuta* and *Iseilema macrantherum* on dark brown to heavy black clay soils. (41) *Brachyachne convergens* and *Sida acuta* co-dominant in association with *Iseilema macrantherum* and *Ptilotus spicatus* on sandy brown to black clay loams. (42) *Brachyachne convergens*, *Sporobolus australasicus* and *Iseilema macratherum* dominating association with some *Sida acuminata*, *Crotalaria trifoliastrum* and *Ocimum sanctum* on dark brown to black clay soils. (43) *Brachyachne convergens* dominant in association with *Enneapogon polyphyllus*, *Cleome viscosa* and *Boerhaavia diffusa* on black clays with impeded drainage where water lies after rains. (44) Largely bare with sparse cover of *Dichanthium tenuiculum* and *Sporobolus australasicus* and some *Portulaca* sp. nov. (45) Dense *Acacia chisholmii* shrub with scattered *Eucalyptus argillacea* and *E. terminalis* trees and *Triodia pungens* grass on brown to reddish brown sandy clay loams. (46) Mixed vegetation communities. From Cole et al. (1974).

Figure 16.11. Little Eva plains. Grass communities with concentric distributions producing lozenge shaped patterns on aerial photographs.

the centres of the lozenge features. The changes in turn are related to soil moisture conditions and in particular the length of time that water lies on the surface after rains. The overall distribution pattern of the lozenge features outlines a subsurface drainage system that appears to reflect the lowering of the water table since the Tertiary (see Cole and Owen-Jones 1977). Similar but more diffuse patterns of grass and herb communities, again related to the extent to which water lies at surface after rains, occurs on the plains south of Cloncurry where they resemble patterns observed also in southern Africa (see Chapters 8 and 9) and Tanzania. This suggests that such patterns are a common feature, associated with the particular soil/drainage relationships, on the black soils plains that in Australia and Africa constitute vast areas of inaccessible and potentially valuable grazing land. The identification and elucidation of the patterns in Australia is thus of considerable importance.

17 The savanna parklands and associated savanna grasslands and savanna woodlands of Australia

Savanna parklands cover relatively small areas in widely separated areas of Australia. They occupy the areas with reddish brown to dark brown loams that have formed over Tertiary basalt in the Peak Downs–Springsure area of eastern Queensland and over basalts, Proterozoic limestone and alluvium along the valleys of the MacArthur, Roper and Victoria rivers in the Northern Territory and along the Ord river in the northern part of Western Australia. In all these areas the savanna parklands are characterized by small widely spaced trees of the *Acacia* and *Bauhinia* genera and by *Dichantium fecundum* or *Astrebla* spp. of grass. Physiognomically and floristically they exhibit similarities with the savanna parklands of Africa which are reinforced by the presence of occasional baobabs, *Adansonia gregorii* along the Ord and Victoria river valleys (Figure 2.11). In both continents the characteristic genera are the same or closely related but the species are different, and while the *Acacias* of Africa are thorny most of those in Australia are thornless, lack leaves and develop phyllodes (expanded stems) to carry on photosynthesis.

The savanna parklands occur where there is a combination of rolling terrain with moderately good surface drainage and fairly heavy base rich soils with a good internal drainage; they give way to other forms of savanna where any of these conditions is not met. Thus southeast of Springsure, a small area of savanna parkland characterized by clumps of *Bauhinia hookeri* trees occupying a small outlier of Tertiary basalt around Bauhinia Downs station is separated from the main savanna parkland belt by *Acacia harpophylla* woodland and scrub which covers the alkaline black clay soils derived from Triassic shales. Open savanna woodlands dominated by *Eucalyptus siderophloia* and *E. melanophloia* occupy the sandy soils of the laterite residuals and taller woodlands characterized by *E. populnea* follow the heavier soils adjoining the creeks (Figure 17.1). At the margins of the savanna

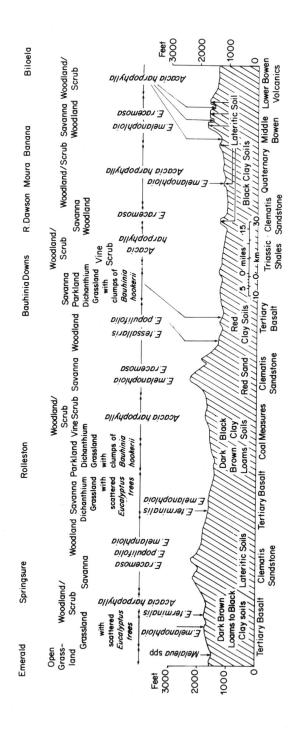

Figure 17.1. Transect showing the relationships between vegetation, soils, geomorphology and geology between Emerald and Biloela, eastern Queensland.

Figure 17.2. Savanna parkland of *Dichanthium fecundum* grass and groups of *Bauhinia hookeri* trees in dark brown loams derived from basalt between Biloela and Rolleston, eastern Queensland; behind *Acacia harpophylla* (brigalow) scrub occupying slightly lower land with alkaline black clay soils derived from Triassic shales.

Figure 17.3. *Acacia* spp. invading the savanna grasslands near Winton, Queensland.

Figure 17.4. Savanna parkland of *Bauhinia cunninghamii* trees and *Dichanthium fecundum* grass between Tennant Creek and Katherine, Northern Territory.

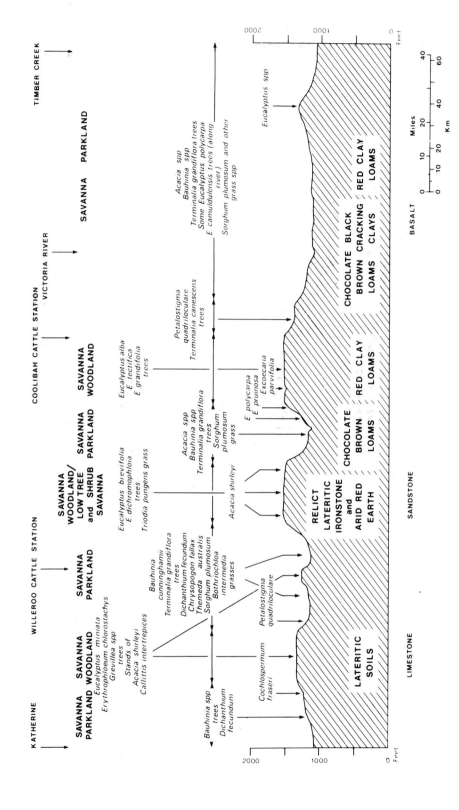

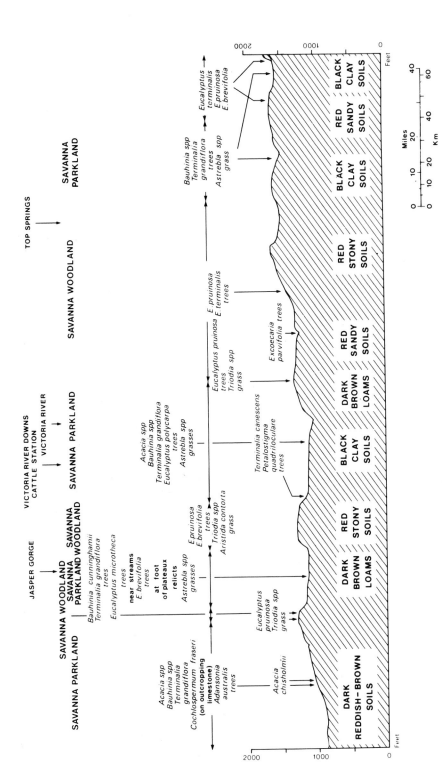

Figure 17.5. Transect showing the relationships between vegetation, soils, geomorphology and geology between Katherine and the Victoria river and Top Springs station, Northern Territory.

parkland on Bauhinia Downs, where the dark brown loam soils feather out and alternate with alkaline black clays, the brigalow *Acacia harpophylla*, whose distribution and behaviour resemble that of *Colophosphernum mopane* in Africa, appears to be extending its range, in places occurring with *Bauhinia hookeri* in the grassland (Figure 17.2). Over dissected terrain east of Bauhinia Downs, near Rolleston and between Emerald and Capella, savanna parklands gives way to the so-called vine scrub with trees of the *Brachychiton* and *Flindersia* genera and shrubs of the *Geijera* and *Myoporum* genera prominent in the dense growth which is considered to represent depauperate rain forest. North of Clermont the savanna parklands are interrupted by patches of *A. cambagei* trees where lateritic gravel mantles the surface.

In central Queensland savanna parkland appears to be extending at the expense of savanna grasslands wherever dissection in current erosion cycles is producing a more undulating surface and so improving the internal drainage that the soils tend to become dark brown loams rather than black cracking clays. Since the 1960s there has been a marked increase in the spread of *Acacia* and *Bauhinia* trees into the grassland areas south of McKinlay and Winton and in the Blackall and Barcaldine areas (Figure 17.3).

In the Northern Territory the savanna parklands characterized by *Bauhinia cunninghamii*, *Terminalia grandiflora* and *T. volucris* along the MacArthur, Roper and Victoria river valleys are also restricted to the better drained areas of brown loam soils (Figures 17.2 and 17.4). They give way to sparse stands of *Cochlospermum fraseri* trees where limestone outcrops, and are interrupted by stands of *Excoecaria parviflora* trees along seasonally inundated drainage lines and by savanna woodlands over lateritic soils associated with relicts of Tertiary planation surfaces (Figures 17.5 and 17.6).

Both in Queensland and the Northern Territory the savanna parklands occupy restricted areas where the particular combination of moderately well drained rolling terrain with base rich soils occurs over alluvium or over volcanic or limestone bedrock in the zone of dissection below the level of the old Tertiary planation surface. In eastern Queensland this zone adjoins the area where Triassic shales, comparable in age and character with the Karoo shales of Africa, have been exposed and give rise to alkaline black clay soils occupied by the agressive *Acacia harpophylla*. Here there is tension in the savanna parkland/*A. harpophylla* ecotone. Everywhere the savanna parklands occupy edaphic niches where their distribution is related to geomorphology and geology. As dissection in current erosion cycles produces improved drainage that permits the establishment of *Acacia* trees, savanna parkland replaces savanna grassland; where the dissection exposes the Triassic shales the savanna parklands in turn give way to *Acacia harpophylla* scrub. The interplay between vegetation, soils, geomorphology and geology is clearly displayed in the environs of the Arcadia valley. North of Injune the light

Figure 17.6. *Excoecaria parviflora* on yellow brown clays along seasonally inundated drainage line, Roper river valley. *Bauhinia cunninghamii* on brown loams derived from basalt frames the picture (right).

Figure 17.7. *Acacia harpophylla* woodlands, Arcadia valley. *A. leiocalyx* and *A. crassa trees* in foreground and right.

Figure 17.8. *Bauhinia cunninghamii* tree remaining from former savanna parkland on alluvial soils, now cleared and sown to pasture grasses, Arcadia valley.

Figure 17.9. Vine scrub with *Brachychiton* sp. trees (bottle trees) at the periphery of the Arcadia valley.

sandy soils carry savanna woodlands of *Eucalyptus siderophloia, E. melanophloia* and *E. populnea* with variable amounts of *Callitris glauca* (Cypress pine). Over the ridges of outcropping Triassic sandstone at the periphery of the Arcadia valley the woodlands are dominated by *Acacia* spp., notably *Acacia leiocalyx* and *A. crassa.* Where the Triassic shales are exposed, on the slopes below and in the valley, these give way abruptly to *Acacia harpophylla* woodland (Figure 17.7). Much of this has been cleared for pasture but along the valleys the remaining *Bauhinia cunninghamii* trees indicate the former presence of savanna parkland on alluvial soils while remnants of vine scrub with *Brachychiton* spp. (bottle trees) on the dissected slopes at the periphery of the valley mark the tension zone between savanna and forest (Figures 17.8 and 17.9).

18   The low tree and shrub savannas and associated savanna types of Australia

Low tree and shrub savannas occupy most of inland Australia where the annual rainfall is between 500 and 100 mm but their limits are less clearly defined than in southern Africa. They form a broad girdle around the central deserts extending to the savanna woodlands in the north and east and the sclerophyllous woodlands in the southwest and southeast. In the north, where the rainfall occurs in summer, they interdigitate with savanna grasslands and savanna woodlands. Southwards they give way to desert shrub and steppe on the borders of the Tanami, Simpson, Great Australian and Gibson deserts where sand cover rather than low rainfall limits vegetation growth. To the south of these deserts where the meagre rainfall occurs mainly in winter, but is periodically augmented by heavy falls from summer storms, the low tree and shrub savannas, here characterized by small trees of mallee habit and by tall shrubs, interdigitate with and finally give way to shrub steppe and scrub where July mean minimum temperatures fall below 2°C and frosts are common in the south and southeast.

The relationships between the distribution of the low tree and shrub savannas and climatic factors are broadly similar to those in southern Africa, but because the greater longitudinal extent causes more extreme climatic conditions, the low tree and shrub savannas of Australia occupy a relatively smaller area than shrub steppe and sclerophyllous shrub communities. As in Africa the form and composition of the vegetation vary in response to variations of physical environment. The most typical low tree and shrub savannas occur in northwest Queensland, and in the northern part of Western Australia. The low tree and shrub vegetation of the southern part of Western Australia and of South Australia is regarded as shrub savanna by Australian authors, but the general absence of grasses and the preponderance of shrubs, notably *Atriplex*, *Cratystylis* and *Kochia* species in the ground layer, accords with steppe that is modified by the presence of trees imparting a savanna-like appearance.

THE LOW TREE AND SHRUB SAVANNAS AND ASSOCIATED SAVANNA GRASSLANDS AND SCRUB WOODLANDS OF NORTHWEST QUEENSLAND

Like those covering the western fringes of the Kalahari in South West Africa and Botswana, the low tree and shrub savannas of northwest Queensland occupy areas underlain by sequences of Proterozoic sedimentary rocks of contrasting lithologies. They give way to savanna grasslands and associated parklands where, to the northwest, southwest and east, these rocks are respectively covered by Cambrian limestones on the Barkly tableland and by Mesozoic and later deposits in the Georgina basin and in the Great Artesian basin, the latter drained northwards by the Cloncurry river and its tributaries and southwestwards by the Diamantina and Coopers Creek and their tributaries. Within their main areas of distribution the low tree and shrub savannas are interrupted by scrub woodlands over relict planation surfaces with lateritic soils.

The physical environment

Climate   The climatic conditions are similar to those in South West Africa and western Botswana but droughts are more severe and prolonged and are usually broken by heavier rains and more violent floods. In summer the daily maximum temperatures average 35–38°C and nightly minima 23–25°C but on occasions temperatures exceeding 52°C may be experienced. Winter temperatures average 18–21°C with daily maxima of 25–28°C and nightly minima of 10.5–13°C. After light rains that occasionally occur in July or August however the temperatures may fall below 3.5°C. The rainfall normally occurs between November and March with the main falls in February and March. In years of heavy rains following droughts continuous rains may extend throughout April and into May, as happened in 1971 when nearly 750 mm were received. The annual fall, however, is usually between 250 and 500 mm and droughts are frequent.

   Widespread evidence of lateritization and kaolinization testifies to wetter conditions in the past when the mobilization, leaching and precipitation of the more soluble minerals must have taken place. Moreover, in some areas patterns of plant species distribution reveal features suggesting that the water table has dropped (see pp. 346). In these features northwest Queensland contrasts with South West Africa and Botswana, although there too is found evidence of wetter conditions in the past.

Geology In contrast to much of South West Africa and Botswana, in northwest Queensland the Proterozoic rocks outcrop and differential erosion of the individual lithological units has produced a belt of rugged dissected terrain extending from the Lawn Hill area southwards towards Dajarra and Boulia and from Mount Isa eastwards to Cloncurry (see Figure 14.3). Areas with calcrete and sand cover are of limited extent. The Proterozoic rocks were originally laid down in a major geosyncline which early in its history became divided into eastern and western sections by a narrow meridional axial zone of uplift along which today the Archaean Leichardt metamorphic rocks and the Kalkadoon granites are exposed between Mount Isa and Cloncurry. The sediments laid down in the western and eastern geosynclinal belts differed and they were subject to differing orogenic events in their respective areas of deposition. The result is that today in the eastern belt extending from Dobbyn through Cloncurry to Kuridala and Mount Elliot acid lavas, predominantly rhyolites, form the basal unit known as the Argylla formation. This is followed in turn by the Ballara quartzites, Marraba volcanics, basalts and metasediments of the Soldiers Cap formation, the Mitakoodi quartzite and slates, quartzites, greywacke and calc silicate rocks which in different localities are known as the Marimo, Staveley and Kuridala formations or as the Corella formation. In the western geosyncline extending from Lawn Hill through Lady Annie to Mount Isa, acid lavas of the Argylla formation are absent; the basal unit is the Leander or Mount Guide quartzite (probably equivalent to the Ballara quartzite) which is succeeded by the Eastern Creek volcanics, the Myally and Judenham sandstones and quartzites, and the dolomites, siltstones, shales and fine sandstones of the Ploughed Mountain Beds, the Surprise Creek Beds and Mount Isa Shale, the Gunpowder Creek and Paradise Creek formations. Orogenic movements during sedimentation in both geosynclines caused considerable local variations in the nature of the sediments laid down which is now manifest in the varied lithologies in the exposed bedrock. Granite intrusions occurred during orogenic deformations following the sedimentation and are exposed today in the outcrops of Wonga and Naraku granites.

Relief, drainage and geomorphology The relief and drainage features of northwest Queensland in some ways contrast with and in others resemble those of South West Africa and western Botswana. The contrasts arise from the greater extent of exposed bedrock. The area with outcropping and near surface Precambrian rocks comprises a highly dissected peneplain which, like that in southern Africa, is of Miocene or mid-Tertiary age. This forms

Figure 18.1. The Dugald river area north of Cloncurry. View southeastwards across *Eucalyptus brevifolia-Triodia pungens* low tree and shrub savanna over calc silicate rocks and savanna grassland over alluvium to the Knapdale quartzite range.

Figure 18.2. Low tree and shrub savanna of *Eucalyptus argillacea* trees and *Triodia pungens* grass, Dugald river area, north of Cloncurry. In foreground *Polycarpaea glabra* over mineralized bedrock.

Figure 18.3. Savanna woodland of *Acacia cambagei* trees and *Triodia pungens* grass over lateritized sandstone of Mesozoic mesa northwest of the Dugald river, Queensland.

the divide between the drainage to the Gulf of Carpentaria and that to the inland basin focusing on Lake Eyre. Elevation varies from 270 to 650 m. Near Mount Isa and Cloncurry rugged ranges with accordant summit levels are witness to the former extent of the peneplain (Figure 18.1). North of Cloncurry, northwest of the Dugald river and northeast of Lady Annie flat-topped mesas capped by lateritized flat-lying Mesozoic rocks represent further legacies of the Tertiary planation and also of the former greater extent of Mesozoic rocks.

As in the Windhoek area of South West Africa, the present drainage patterns bear little relationship either to the dominant relief features or to the underlying geology. The evidence indicates that they were initiated on the mid-Tertiary planation surface and have become superimposed on the present relief and geology. The acute features of the present relief and the extensive alluvial deposits along the major rivers are legacies of dissection following warping and uplift in Tertiary and Recent times and of excessive erosion and mass movement of weathered material during and following exceptionally heavy rains. Such rains occurred in 1971, 1972 and 1975, causing the main rivers to fill and overflow their normally dry river beds and become raging torrents, carrying large quantities of sediment and uprooted shrubs and trees.

In areas of outcropping and near surface bedrock, the relief features are closely related to lithology and geological structure. Rugged boulder-strewn terrain with prominent ridges characterizes areas underlain by quartzites and acid volcanic rocks, whereas lower level terrain occurs where residual soil mantles shales, slates, siltstones and schists. Minor ridges and valleys feature areas of dolomite and bedded limestone while subdued rugged terrain is characteristic of those underlain by calc silicate rocks. Open sandy plains studded with tors or whaleback hills distinguish areas underlain by granite, notably around Naraku. Prominent ridges of considerable linear extent either mark the position of major faults where silicification has accentuated contrasts in resistance to erosion between adjacent lithologies or are associated with exceptionally resistant ironstone horizons. Mount Remarkable, where Corella rocks abut Leichardt metamorphics, is in the former category; the knife edge ridges between Selwyn and Mount Cobalt in the latter. Contrasts in resistances to erosion between indurated relict laterite capping flat-lying Mesozoic rocks and less resistant strata in the tilted and folded underlying rocks are responsible for the rugged dissected plateau terrain south of Kuridala. By contrast the plains floored with colluvium, alluvium and residuum are remarkably level. Their river valleys are dry for most of the year and their beds encumbered with deep sand, the legacies cf deposition during the floods that follow heavy rains. Over the lower ground there is widespread evidence that pediplanation processes have fashioned the landscape, leaving coarse alluvium near stream courses and spreads of fine material in the level central areas of interfluves.

Soils   As in South West Africa and Botswana the characteristic soils are arid red earths, but grey and brown soils of heavy texture are found over level areas subject to flooding after rains and relict lateritic soils are associated with Mesozoic mesas.

Most soils are immature or even skeletal with little or no profile differentiation. The arid red earths are generally 60–120 cm deep and have a sandy to sandy clay loam texture becoming heavier with depth. Except over quartzites, where values are lower, the pH usually varies from 5.7–6.4 near surface and increases to 6.4–7.6 with depth. Calcrete nodules may occur at a depth of about one metre. Sometimes calcrete is exposed at surface but the great extents and thicknesses characteristic of much of southern Africa are absent from the low tree and shrub savanna zone, being largely confined to desert margins in Australia. The grey and brown soils of heavy texture are related to low-lying tracts near the creeks, notably those draining to Cabbage Tree Creek, the Cloncurry and Williams rivers north of Cloncurry, and to the Thorntonia and Inca Creek in the Lady Annie area. These soils generally comprise heavy clay loams with a layer of calcrete just above the abrupt change to calc silicate bedrock at the base of their profile. They become sticky after rains and develop deep vertical shrinkage cracks in the dry season.

Figure 18.4. Change from *Eucalyptus brevifolia-Enneapogon polyphyllus* low tree and shrub savanna over calc silicate bedrock (foreground) to *Acacia shirleyii* woodland over ferruginous siltstones (background), Lady Annie area, north of Mount Isa.

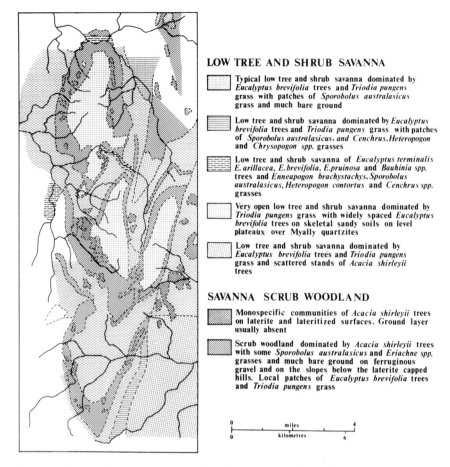

LOW TREE AND SHRUB SAVANNA

Typical low tree and shrub savanna dominated by *Eucalyptus brevifolia* trees and *Triodia pungens* grass with patches of *Sporobolus australasicus* grass and much bare ground

Low tree and shrub savanna dominated by *Eucalyptus brevifolia* trees and *Triodia pungens* grass with patches of *Sporobolus australasicus,* and *Cenchrus,Heteropogon* and *Chrysopogon spp.* grasses

Low tree and shrub savanna of *Eucalyptus terminalis* *E. arillacea, E.brevifolia, E.pruinosa* and *Bauhinia spp.* trees and *Enneapogon brachystachys,Sporobolus australasicus,Heteropogon contortus* and *Cenchrus spp.* grasses

Very open low tree and shrub savanna dominated by *Triodia pungens* grass with widely spaced *Eucalyptus brevifolia* trees on skeletal sandy soils on level plateaūx over Myally quartzites

Low tree and shrub savanna dominated by *Eucalyptus brevifolia* trees and *Triodia pungens* grass and scattered stands of *Acacia shirleyii* trees

SAVANNA SCRUB WOODLAND

Monospecific communities of *Acacia shirleyii* trees on laterite and lateritized surfaces. Ground layer usually absent

Scrub woodland dominated by *Acacia shirleyii* trees with some *Sporobolus australasicus* and *Eriachne spp.* grasses and much bare ground on ferruginous gravel and on the slopes below the laterite capped hills. Local patches of *Eucalyptus brevifolia* trees and *Triodia pungens* grass

```
0              miles           4
├──────────────┼──────────────┤
0            kilometres        6
```

Figure 18.5. Lady Annie area, vegetation. From Cole (1977) with permission.

The form, composition, and distribution of the vegetation associations and plant communities

In the rugged hilly terrain where, over outcropping or near surface Proterozoic rocks, the soils vary from skeletal stony sands to arid red earths, the typical vegetation is a low tree and shrub savanna characterized by small *Eucalyptus* trees, *Acacia* shrubs and *Triodia pungens* grass (Figure 18.2). This perennial grass has narrow rolled resinous leaves and forms widely spaced hummocks that grow outwards from the centre to produce rings. The *Triodia* genus which contains many different species is unlike any of the grass species in southern

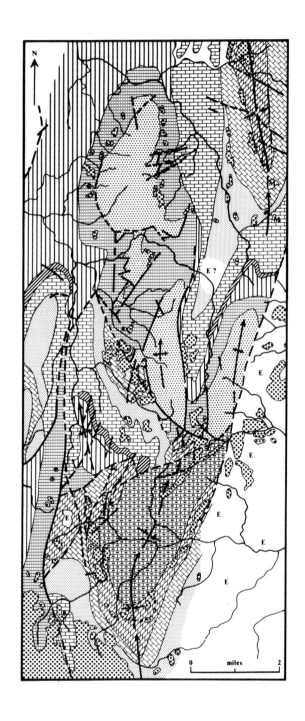

Figure 18.6. The Lady Annie–Lady Loretta area, geology. From Cole (1977) with permission after Alcock and Lee 1974. For key, see opposite.

Africa. Unlike the *Stipagrostis uniplumis*, characteristic of the low tree and shrub savannas bordering the Kalahari, it is not palatable. Throughout the greater part of the year there is much bare ground between the *Triodia pungens* hummocks, but after rains this may be covered by annual grasses like *Eriachne dominii* and *Sporobolus australasicus*. Over the level plains where arid red earths have developed from residuum overlying the Proterozoic rocks, *Aristida contorta* grass forms a sparse cover after rains between the widely scattered small trees and shrubs. This grass is also resinous, easily fired and burns so fiercely that it is commonly called kerosene grass. Over the grey and brown soils of heavy texture there is usually an abrupt change in the vegetation to one characterized by the flat bladed grasses *Astrebla squarrosa*, *A. pectinata*, *Iseilima macrotherum*, *Enneapogon arenaceus* and *Brachyachne convergens* associated with herbs after rains. The vegetation of the lateritic soils over the Mesozoic residuals is usually a scrub woodland of *Acacia cambagei* trees, *Eremophila* and *Myoporum* spp. shrubs and *Triodia pungens* grass in the area east of Mount Isa (Figure 18.3) and of *Acacia shirleyii* trees with a sparse cover of *Enneapogon brachystachys* grass northwest of that city (Figure 18.4). Stands of *Acacia cambagei* occupy areas of redistributed lateritic gravel mantling the surface of adjacent plains and between Mount Isa and Cloncurry also follow ferruginous horizons within the bedrock sequence, notably the Urquhart shales near Mount Isa. Throughout the area galleries of trees follow the stream courses with *Tristania grandiflora*, *Eucalyptus camuldulensis* and *Melaleuca leucadendron* in the

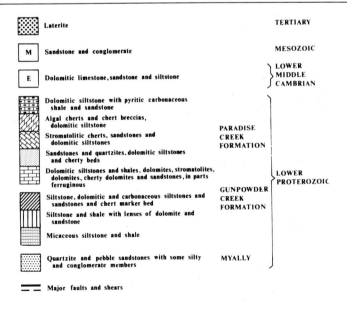

stream bed and *Bauhinia carronii, Eucalyptus papuana*, and *Terminalia aridicola* trees with *Enneapogon pennisetiformis* along the banks. Where there are wide spreads of alluvium the *Bauhinia carronii* trees extend outwards to form narrow belts of savanna parkland parallel to the valleys.

Within the typical low tree and shrub savannas different species of *Eucalyptus* and in some cases different species of grass occur over different types of bedrock. Usually *Eucalpytus brevifolia* and *Triodia pungens* are characteristic of sandy soils over siliceous rocks, whereas *E. argillacea* and *Enneapogon polyphyllus* are more common over calcareous rocks. *Acacia chisholmii* forms a well developed shrub layer along the dissected margins of the creeks. In the Dugald river area north of Cloncurry and in the Lady Annie area northwest of Mount Isa, where the vegetation has been mapped in detail, the relationship between the distributions of vegetation associations and bedrock lithology is so close that the vegetation maps virtually coincide with the geological maps (Figure 18.5 and 18.6). Thus in the Dugald river area an association of *Eucalyptus brevifolia, E. dichromophloia* and *Triodia pungens* covers the range produced by the Knapdale quartzite whereas one of *E. argillacea, E. terminalis, Acacia chisholmii* and *T. pungens* characterize areas underlain by calc silicate rocks. (See Nicholls *et al.* 1964–65). In the Lady Annie area an association of *E. brevifolia* and *T. pungens* occupies the skeletal sandy soils over the Myally quartzites whereas scrub woodlands of *Acacia shirleyii* trees delineate areas of laterite and of highly ferruginous Gunpowder Creek siltstones and shales (Cole 1977).

In the Dugald river area the typical low tree and shrub savanna cuts out completely over the belt of toxic ground underlain by the Dugald river lead–zinc lode where a lode assemblage comprising the indicator species *Polycarpaea glabra* and *Eriachne mucronata* associated in places with *Tephrosia* sp. nov., *Bulbostylis barbata* and a *Fimbristylis* sp. is present (Figure 18.7) (Nicholls *et al.* 1964–65). The actual distribution of species in this area shows a very close relationship to levels of lead, zinc and copper in the soils and bedrock. Overall *Eriachne mucronata* delineates the sub-outcrop of the lode, and *Polycarpaea glabra* occupies areas of very high lead, zinc and copper values—up to 10 000 ppm in the soils. *Tephrosia* sp. nov. occurs only where copper or lead values in the soils are between 50 and 2000 ppm.

In the Lady Annie area the background vegetation again cuts out and is replaced by *Eriachne mucronata, Polycarpaea glabra* and *Tephrosia* sp. nov. over the Lady Loretta lead–zinc deposit. Between Lady Annie and Mount Isa anomalous plant communities composed of the shrub *Jacksonia ramossissima*, in places accompanied by *Polycarpaea spirostylis*, occur over cupriferous ironstones formed over an extension of the Mount Kelly fault as a result of upward dispersion from concealed copper-bearing cherts and

Figure 18.7. Anomalous plant community of *Eriachne mucronata* and *Polycarpaea glabra*, over the Dugald river lead–zinc lode, replacing Eucalyptus brevifolia-Triodia pungens low tree and shrub savanna.

Figure 18.8. Anomalous plant community of *Jacksonia ramossissima* and *Polycarpaea spirostylis* (centre foreground) over cupriferous ironstone disclosing concealed copper deposits, Mount Kelly area, northwest of Mount Isa. *Eucalyptus brevifolia* low tree and shrub savanna in background.

Figure 18.9. Change from *Eucalyptus brevifolia-Triodia pungens* low tree and shrub savanna (left) to *Atalaya hemiglauca-Enneapogon polyphyllus* low tree savanna (right) over phosphate deposits in Cambrian siltstones, Lady Annie area northwest of Mount Isa.

dolomitic shales. Several areas of anomalous vegetation occur, each occupying sites too toxic for other species (Figure 18.8) (Cole 1980). Throughout the Mount Isa–Cloncurry area *Polycarpaea spirostylis* occurs wherever there are high levels of copper in soils and bedrock, occurring notably at Mount Isa mines, over the old Great Australia workings, in the Selwyn–Mount Elliot area and over many minor workings and prospects.

In the Lady Annie area the characteristic vegetation of *Eucalyptus brevifolia* and *Triodia pungens* is also absent from a large area where the Cambrian Beetle Creek siltstones contain phosphate deposits. Here small *Atalaya hemiglauca* trees in a grass layer of *Chrysopogon fallax* and *Enneapogon polyphyllus* form a distinctive low tree and shrub savanna association (Figure 18.9) (Cole 1980). Some 250 km farther south smaller *Atalaya hemiglauca* trees that are more widely spaced in the grass stratum disclose the presence of further phosphate deposits in comparable Cambrian rocks south of Duchess.

19 Mosaic distributions of savanna woodlands, parklands and grasslands in the Channel Country of southwest Queensland

In the Channel Country of southwest Queensland there are complex mosaic distributions of the major categories of savanna vegetation that are related both to the legacies of dissection of Tertiary planation surfaces and to the deposition of alluvium along the numerous river channels draining towards Lake Eyre. The complexity of the distributions of the plant communities results from the juxtaposition of areas of erosion and deposition which produce a variety of contrasting habitats over short distances (Figure 19.1).

Savanna woodlands characterized by *Eucalyptus melanophloia*, *E. populifolia* and *E. racemosa* trees occupy the laterite capped plateaux and mesas representing the relics of the Tertiary planation surface. (Figures 19.2 and 19.3). *E. populifolia* favours the slightly lower areas with red clay soils, whereas the other two species dominate in the slightly higher areas with sandy soils. Where deep buff coloured sands mantle the surface, *Callitris glauca* trees are also present (Figure 19.4). Below the breakaway edges of relict plateaux, this species dominates the vegetation over deep red sands representing the redistributed A horizon material of the old lateritic profile. Sometimes it is accompanied by *Eremophila mitchelli* and *Myoporum* spp. shrubs and sometimes by *Acacia aneura* trees. Over slight rises where the sand is particularly deep *Acacia aneura* forms pure stands. Where redistributed ferruginous lateritic gravel mantles the surface, *A. cambagei* or *A. georginae* (gidgea) trees form a scrub; the latter also forms a scrub over the 'gibber' plains in the very dry areas near Windorah. Throughout the area the above plant communities occur in repetitive sequence over relict

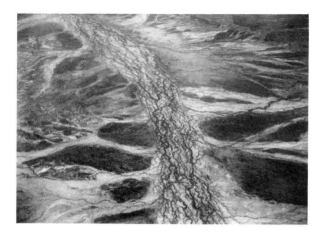

Figure 19.1. Aerial view over the Channel Country of southwest Queensland. The dark flat-topped plateaux relicts are capped with laterite and carry savanna woodlands.

Figure 19.2. Savanna woodland of *Eucalyptus* spp. trees over laterite capping of the Grey range near Quilpie. *Acacia aneura* trees on the slope below the breakaway.

Figure 19.3. Savanna woodland of *Eucalyptus melanophloia* trees and *Triodia* sp. grass on sandy soils between Cunnamulla and Charleville.

Figure 19.4. Stand of *Callitris glauca* trees on deep sands within the *Eucalyptus tessalaris* (left)–*Heteropogon contortus* savanna woodlands north of Charleville.

Figure 19.5. Broad bladed grasses and numerous herbs occupying an ephemeral channel after the passage of flood waters, Braidwood, Channel Country.

Figure 19.6. Clumps of *Triodia basedowi* on wind blown red sand between Braidwood and Retreat, Channel Country.

mesas and the marginal dissected terrain. However, where dissection has exposed shale or volcanic bedrock which has weathered to reddish brown or dark greyish brown soils of heavy texture, savanna grassland dominated respectively either by *Astrebla* spp. or by *Dichanthium sericeum* occurs. This is studded by *Acacia homalophylla* (boree) trees, forming savanna parkland, on similar soils with a slightly alkaline reaction and containing very high levels of nitrogen and potassium and high levels of phosphorus and chlorine (see Figure 2.13). These savanna parklands are characteristic of areas around residual lateritic mesas where the high base status of the soils may relate to precipitation of elements leached from the higher ground during lateritization. Different vegetational sequences occur along the channels draining towards Lake Eyre. Belts of trees, particularly *Eucalyptus microtheca, E. camuldulensis* and *Melaleuca saligna*, parallel the channels. On the adjoining alluvial soils a variety of broad bladed grasses, especially *Echinochloa turneriana* and *Panicum whiteii* and numerous herbs flourish after the passage of flood waters (Figure 19.5). On the low interfluves a sparse growth of ephemeral grasses, mainly *Aristida, Tragus* and *Enneapogon* spp. with *Portulaca* sp. and other pioneer species periodically occupy the generally bare clay pans where water stagnates after floods. Low tree and shrub savanna communities characterized by *Acacia tetragonophylla, Grevillea striata, Eremophila latrobei* and *Aristida* and *Enneapogon* spp. grasses form a sparse cover over stony patches of lateritic gravel while widely spaced hummocks of *Triodia basedowii* grass occupy low hills of wind blown red sand (Figure 19.6). The interdigitation of all categories of savanna and of the variety of plant communities within them produces an exceedingly complex mosaic in which there is a delicate balance between vegetation and edaphic conditions related fundamentally to landscape evolution since Tertiary times.

20   Savanna vegetation as
an environmental index

The vegetation of any area is the result of the spatial and temporal interplay of all the factors of the environment. Hence, provided that the relationships between the distribution of vegetation communities and the relative roles of these factors are understood, the nature and composition of the vegetation provides a valuable index of the potential of the land for wildlife, agriculture and silviculture, indicates terrain characteristics relevant for road and building constructions and for other engineering works, reveals the nature of superficial and bedrock geology, may disclose the presence of mineral orebodies and identify areas with health hazards. The applications of biogeographical/geobotanical investigations are particularly important in the savannas.

VEGETATION AS AN INDEX OF LAND POTENTIAL
FOR AGRICULTURE, AFFORESTATION
AND WILDLIFE CONSERVATION

Since the form and species composition of savanna vegetation reflect climatic and edaphic conditions, the vegetation of any given area provides a useful index of land potential for agriculture and afforestation.

Within the hierarchical framework of relationships between vegetation and environment the distribution of the major units, the vegetation formations and subformations is governed primarily by climate and soils at the Great Soils Group level but also by physiography and geomorphology.

The distribution of the vegetation associations is influenced mainly by soils at the Soil Series level with physiography, geomorphology and geology playing increasingly important roles, while the distribution of the smallest units of plant communities composed of individual species or assemblages of species is governed by extremes of relief, drainage and soils, as for example over precipitous slopes, rock outcrops or sand dunes, or by extreme conditions in the mineral status of the soils such as high concentrations of toxic elements emanating from mineral orebodies or deficiencies of major or trace elements caused either by extreme leaching or by mineral deficient parent material.

Savanna vegetation covers tropical areas with a marked dry season. It extends from the margins of the tropical forests where the rainfall averages 1500 mm with a short dry period in winter when temperatures are relatively low to the borders of the deserts where 500 mm of rainfall is sporadically concentrated in a few summer months. Changes in the form and composition of the vegetation from savanna woodlands to low tree and shrub savannas reflect the incidence, increasing duration and intensity of drought.

Within given climatic limits the distributions of each of the major categories of savanna vegetation are related to edaphic conditions. Characteristically the typical savanna woodlands occupy old planation surfaces that are characterized by poor drainage and by lateritic soils that are deficient in essential plant nutrients, have high concentrations of iron and aluminium and often a layer of indurated laterite in their profile. The natural vegetation is of limited value for grazing domestic stock and the soils present many difficulties and offer few opportunities for crop production. The natural grasses grow rapidly after the summer rains but soon become harsh and unpalatable. Cattle may be reared but not fattened on them; in summer they make reasonably good growth but in winter they normally lose half the summer gain in weight unless they are given supplementary feed or can be moved to better grazing afforded by other forms of savanna vegetation. In Brazil pastures of introduced grasses, notably *Hyparrhenia rufa, Panicum maximum* and *Melinis minutiflora* have been planted on campos cerrados land and in Australia research is directed to improving the grazing in areas where *Heteropogon contortus* forms the grass layer (Figure 20.1). The fundamental problem, however, is related to the nature of the soils. Unless its nutrient status can be improved by regular applications of manure and fertilizers over a long period, as has been achieved by Dutch immigrant farmers on cleared campos cerrados land north of Campinas, Brazil, pastures cannot be sustained, crops like rice now grown on a large scale give low yields and are deficient in mineral elements essential for health.

Within the savanna woodlands the individual vegetation associations and even particular tree species reflect differences in water relations and in the texture and mineral status in the soils that are related to relief and drainage, parent material and the degree of weathering that it has undergone (Webster 1965). The distribution of the associations may be governed primarily by soil conditions that are determined by geology and geomorphology, while the frequency of individual species and the spacing of individual plants may be related to the soil catena first recognized by Milne in the savanna woodlands of Tanzania as the sequence of soil profiles that are regularly

Figure 20.1. Cattle grazing *Heteropogon contortus* grasses within savanna woodlands dominated by *Eucalyptus crebra* south of Charters Towers, Queensland, Australia.

Figure 20.2. Overgrazing by cattle in the low tree and shrub savannas south of Lake Ngami, Botswana.

Figure 20.3. Plant community of *Goodenia scaevolina* (foreground), *Calythrix longiflora* and *Burtonia polyzyga* over canga (or recemented iron-rich scree) foreground; within the low tree and shrub savanna of *Eucalyptus brevifolia–Triodia pungens* (background left) in the Hamersley ranges area of Australia.

repeated over a regular succession of relief features developed over one rock type (Milne 1936, 1947).

Undoubtedly the poorest soil and drainage conditions within the savanna woodlands are those indicated by the stunted and contorted growth and the hard sclerophyllus leaves of campo cerrado tree species on the central Brazilian plateaux. The features exhibited particularly by *Salvertia convallariodora*, *Curatella americana*, *Kielmeyera* and *Qualea* spp. are due to the deposition of cellulose arising from surplus carbohydrates and the limited synthesis of proteins caused by deficiencies of nitrogen, calcium, phosphorus, sulphur, zinc and boron in the soil (Arens 1963). Additionally, recent evidence indicates that the same features are caused by and are indicative of aluminium toxicities in the soils (Goodland 1971b). In Africa *Uapaca*, *Protea* and *Faurea* spp. and in Australia *Banksia*, *Grevillea*, *Hakea*, *Calythrix* and certain *Eucalyptus* spp., occupying the oldest planation surfaces, exhibit similar features and are likewise indicative of extremely poor soils.

In Brazil, the cerradao form of savanna woodland is indicative of somewhat better soil and drainage conditions. Where this form of vegetation occupies lightly dissected terrain at the periphery of the old planation surfaces it may indicate the presence of near surface bedrock from which the relict lateritic capping has been largely removed. Under such conditions, as over basalt near Brasilia and Goiania in Goias and over limestone near Lagoa Santa in Minas Gerais, the cerradao indicates areas with some potential for agriculture provided that manure and fertilizers are used to build up and maintain soil nutrient status.

In Africa and Australia the individual vegetation associations indicate distinctive soils that have developed over particular geological bedrock units exposed by the removal of relict lateritic material. In Zambia *Brachystegia boehmii* woodlands denote shallow light textured sandy or stony soils derived from granite, gneiss or quartzite parent material that is most suitable for Virginia tobacco production or for afforestation with exotic pine trees (Cole 1965). *Brachystegia spiciformis* dominated woodlands indicate deeper well drained loams frequently derived from limestone and usually occurring at the periphery of the plateaux. These soils are suitable for most food crops and can sustain both commercial agriculture and thriving African peasant agriculture producing maize grown in rotation with a legume. The chipya form of vegetation that is characterized by *B. spiciformis*, *Pterocarpus angolensis*, *Erythrophloeum africanum* and *Parinari mobola* in the Chafakuma area along the Congo–Zambezi watershed is also indicative of deep chocolate loams derived from limestone in the dissected belt separating the mid-Tertiary and end-Tertiary planation surfaces and is also capable of sustaining permanent agriculture.

Savanna woodlands dominated by *Julbernardia paniculata* trees usually range over intermediate soil types while *B. floribunda* woodlands are usually indicative of heavy, poorly drained yellowish red clay soils derived from gabbro on the lower lying parts of the plateau. In some areas one species of *Brachystegia* or *Julbernardia* dominates the vegetation over large areas; in others, as between Ngomo and Kalomo, zones dominated in turn by *B. boehmii*, *J. paniculata* and *B. spiciformis* and related to the soil catena are repeated in regular succession from plateau summit to valley bottom and outline areas of differing potential for different crops.

In the Northern Territory of Australia distinctive vegetation associations within the savanna woodlands again indicate the agricultural potential in an area currently used mainly for cattle grazing. The tall *Eucalyptus tetrodonta-E. miniata* woodlands that cover the level Tertiary peneplain occupy highly leached lateritic red earths that offer few opportunities for agriculture. Between Darwin and Katherine, around Mount Litchfield and south of the Daly and Finniss rivers, where by virtue of dissection of the Tertiary peneplain granite bedrock is exposed at or near surface, woodlands of *E. grandifolia* associated with *Grevillea heliosperma*, *Persoonia falcata*, *Owenia vernicosa*, *Livistona* and *Pandanus* palms occupy and indicate light sandy soils that given more favourable economic circumstances would be suitable for Virginia tobacco production. Around Katherine the open woodlands of *Eucalyptus foelscheana* and *Erythrophloeum chlorostachys*, like those of *B. spiciformis* and *E. africanum* in Zambia, denote dark reddish brown krasnozem soils derived from limestone that given markets and transport facilities could support commercial maize production.

The poorer sandy soils of savanna woodland areas offer some potential for silviculture and for agroforestry. The latter could form a variant of the chitamene system of shifting cultivation practised over a long period in Zambia. Under this system the savanna woodland trees are cut to breast height and the brushwood is piled around the cut trees and burnt; crops are sown in the ashes and cultivation first of maize, millets and other food crops and later of cassava continues for some three to seven years until the soils become impoverished and weeds take over, whereupon the land is abandoned to revert to woodland for a period of between thirty and fifty years, depending on site conditions, after which the process is repeated. By the retention of some trees or the planting of others the woodlands could be better sustained to provide timber for houses and wood for fuel in a cultivation system that under current economic and social circumstances is best suited to the environment.

With declining markets for tobacco the sandy soils offer some promises for silviculture. In Zambia some success has been achieved with *Pinus douglasiana* (from Mexico) and *P. insularis* (from the Philippines) in experiments near Ndola and with *Callitris cupressiformis*, *Cupressus lusitanica* and *Maesopsis eminis* near Kasama, but plantings of *Eucalyptus* spp. have not been successful. Whereas *Eucalyptus* plantations have been successfully established in eastern Zimbabwe, South Africa and Brazil, site conditions within the typical savanna woodlands of Zambia appear to be unfavourable. In Australia there are extensive natural stands of *Callitris glauca* on the sandy soils within the savanna woodlands of southwest Queensland and under current economic circumstances silviculture would be neither practical nor necessary.

Within the typical savanna woodlands of Africa and Australia there are many vegetation associations additional to those cited above. Each occupies a distinctive habitat with specific agricultural, or in some cases silvicultural or agroforestry, potential. In many cases those sites indicated by the vegetation to be favourable for agriculture are also suitable for silviculture while some sites that are unfavourable for agriculture may be suitable for afforestation.

In contrast to the typical savanna woodlands those dominated respectively by *Colophospernum mopane* trees in Africa and by *Acacia harpophylla* in Australia occupy highly alkaline heavy textured soils that tend to gilgai or crab-hole after rains. These soils pose serious problems for agriculture being virtually impossible to cultivate. In Australia since 1945 large areas have been cleared by bulldozer and anchor chain and sown to wheat and pasture grasses from low-flying aircraft. In Africa experimental work was undertaken in the 1950s in order to assess the potential of areas of *Colophospernum mopane* woodland for the resettlement of people displaced by the building of the Kariba dam. In both continents problems remain for both species sucker vigorously after the land is cleared and the alkaline soils are very difficult to work. Indeed the presence of the species indicates limiting conditions for agriculture. In Australia, by persistent effort to combat suckering, success in pasture establishment has been achieved, notably in the Arcadia valley where the best results are in alluvial soils revealed by the residual presence of *Bauhinia* spp. trees (See Figure 17.8). Likewise within the *Colophospernum mopane* woodlands in the Zambezi valley the areas with *Acacia* thicket that occupy alluvial soils provide the best sites for agriculture and were selected for resettlement of people displaced by the creation of the Kariba dam.

In contrast to the savanna woodlands, the savanna parklands are indicative of land of agricultural promise. The grass layer is composed of species that remain sweet and nutritious throughout the dry season and provide excellent all year grazing for beef cattle. The soils generally have a good mineral nutrient status but they tend to be heavy textured and, depending on parent material, may be difficult to work. Much of the original parkland that occupied the krasnozem soils derived from limestone bedrock in the Mazabuka, Monze and Broken Hill areas of Zambia and the reddish brown loams derived from basic igneous rocks in the Mazoe and Marandellas areas of Zimbabwe have been cleared largely for maize production that has achieved some of the highest yields in the world. In Queensland, Australia, sorghum, originally tried by the British Food Corporation at Peak Downs immediately after the Second World War, is now successfully grown on the black earth soils derived from basalt in the Peak Downs–Rolleston area where it is used to fatten beef cattle raised both on the adjacent natural grassland of the savanna parkland and on the savanna grasslands of the Barkly Tableland and western Queensland.

The savanna parklands occupy the drier areas of the savanna belts and, as was demonstrated during the East African groundnut venture, the availability of moisture may be critical for agriculture. In this context individual species of *Acacia* and *Combretum* have specific moisture requirements that are a function of rainfall and soil texture (Vincent *et al.* 1960). The distribution of these species may be used to assess moisture availability for crop production in a given area.

Some areas of savanna parkland that have lighter soils derived from granite bedrock have been brought into cultivation for fruit, vegetable and field crops. The outstanding example is the South African Lowveld where differences in the vegetation outlined different qualities of land and where irrigation water, available both from reservoirs and from the major rivers crossing the area (Cole 1956, 1961) supports large orchards of citrus and other subtropical fruits, sugar cane and a variety of other crops. Similarly favourable conditions of water availability occur in the Lowveld of Zimbabwe, notably along the Sabi and Lundi valleys and in the Transvaal Bushveld where in each area the vegetation cover reflects soil characteristics and indicates the potential for specific crops.

The low tree and shrub savannas delineate semi-arid terrain that in most areas can be used only as grazing of low carrying capacity for domestic stock or as wildlife reserves. In the Sudan relationships between the distributions of vegetation associations and individual species and the moisture regimes, physical and chemical properties of the soils and the micro-relief features have been demonstrated; the need for an elucidation of the Quaternary geomorphology to explain the complex mosaics of vegetation and soils has been acknowledged (Morrison *et al.* 1948). The *Acacia seyal–A. fistula–Balanites aegyptica* association outlines areas of dark and very dark grey brown soils and like its ecotone with the *Acacia mellifera–Cadaba rotundifolia* association offers opportunities for crop production, provided the heavier soils and the depressions slightly below the general level which are either excessively wet or seasonally flooded, are avoided (Smith 1949, Gunn and Brewer 1951–53, Bunting and Lea 1962). Here an understanding of the vegetation/soil/geomorphology relationships is critical.

In Australia reconnaissance studies by the Commonwealth Scientific and Industrial Research Organization in the Alice Springs area (Perry *et al.* 1962) have identified numerous land systems within which the composition of the vegetation is indicative of soil and physiography. Thus whereas a low tree and shrub savanna of *Triodia* spp. grass with scattered small *Eucalyptus brevifolia* or *Acacia aneura* trees occupies red sands, red clayey sands or red earths of erosional land surfaces still mantled with lateritic material, a vegetation of *Acacia aneura* trees (mulga) with a ground layer of short flat bladed grasses, mainly *Eragrostis eriopoda* or *Chloris acicularis*, and forbs occupies the red earths of the gently undulating plains where Quaternary deposits mantle much of the erosional land surface. Variations in the composition of the ground layer reflect variations in the soil and moisture retention after rains. Communities of *Atriplex* spp. (salt bush) outline areas of saline and texture contrast soils whereas those of grasses and forbs favour alluvial soils. Lack of water precludes crop production in this area but should irrigation become possible the vegetation provides a guide to the most favourable areas.

In the low tree and shrub savannas of northwest Queensland the form and composition of the vegetation again provides an index of environmental conditions and of agricultural potential. Only those areas of broad bladed grasses that are largely confined to plains where dark brown loams or deep red earths overlie Mesozoic and later sediments provide palatable grazing for cattle. The large areas dominated by *Eucalyptus brevifolia* trees and *Triodia pungens* trees are virtually useless, providing grazing only after rains when annual grasses occupy the spaces between the *Triodia* clumps.

The low tree and shrub savannas of South West Africa and Botswana differ from those of Australia for the characteristic grasses, notably *Stipagrostis uniplumis*, afford palatable grazing throughout the year. Additionally, many of the trees and shrubs, notably species of *Acacia* and *Grewia*, afford valuable browse (see Chapter 10). These features doubtless explain why these areas have sustained large herds of wild game and why currently some of them raise excellent beef cattle. Some vegetation associations whose distribution is influenced largely by soils and geology are more favourable than others (see Chapter 10). Most favourable are those dominated by *Acacia mellifera* trees associated with other small *Acacia* trees, *Grewia flava* and other shrubs that outline areas of near surface Proterozoic sedimentary rocks near Witvlei in South West Africa and near Ghanzi in western Botswana where there are established farming blocks. Least favourable are those dominated by *Terminalia sericea* trees and *Combretum collinum* shrubs that occupy areas of deep Kalahari Sand. Communities of *Catophractes alexandrii* that indicate areas of near surface calcrete are significant because water can usually be obtained beneath the calcrete capping. Areas where water cannot be readily obtained and where the stock-carrying capacity of the vegetation is low are best conserved as wildlife reserves.

The low tree and shrub vegetation of the Agreste and Sertao of Brazil, under acute population pressure relative to their agricultural capacity, has supported uncertain subsistence agriculture and cattle raising for a long period. Opportunities for irrigation are limited to small areas along some of the major rivers, notably the Sao Francisco, but water shortages are acute and periodic droughts severe. A variety of food and commercial crops including maize, cassava, cotton and tobacco are often grown in the same field in the hope that if one fails another will succeed. The taller, denser vegetation of the Agreste indicates more favourable conditions than the low shrub vegetation of the Sertao but the characteristic drought resisting features of the thorny cacti (*Cereus* and *Pilocereus* spp.) opuntias and bromeliads carry the warning that unless the land can be irrigated it is too dry for most crops. In the Agreste around Pesqueira, under a mixed crop/dairy cattle economy, tomatoes have been successfully grown on a large scale using methods of land rotation and mulching to conserve moisture and heavy applications of manure to maintain fertility. In the Sertao the production of long stapled tree cotton in the Valley of Serido and of onions under irrigation along the Sao Francisco river represent pockets of successful commercial agriculture in a large area of cattle rearing and struggling subsistence agriculture (Cole 1960b).

The agricultural value of savanna grasslands depends on whether they are related to the savanna woodlands and occupy relatively small watershed areas in the centres of the plateaux, follow restricted areas of periodically inundated alluvium along valleys adjoining parklands or cover extensive plains as in the case of the Llanos of the Orinoco basin and the Mitchell–Flinders grasslands of the Barkly Tableland and Great Artesian Basin of Australia.

In all three southern continents, due to the poverty of the soils they occupy, the watershed grasslands have a low nutritive status. They provide reasonable grazing for a short period following rains in early summer but subsequent rank growth and the development of cellulose, caused by the deficiency of essential nutrients in the soil, makes them harsh and unpalatable. The valley grasslands, due to the favourable nutrient status and superior water retaining properties of the soils they occupy, provide good grazing which remains palatable throughout the dry season. Hitherto differences in the qualities of the watershed and valley grasslands have governed the movements of wild game in Africa and have formed the basis for the system whereby domestic cattle are grazed on the watershed grasslands during the summer rainy period when the valley grasslands are excessively wet or even flooded and moved onto the valley grasslands in the winter half year.

Within each category of grassland there are discrete associations whose distributions reflect particular habitat conditions. In Zambia and Tanzania the distribution of the associations within the valley grasslands is related to drainage features (Vesey-Fitzgerald 1963) and drainage evolution (Cole 1963a) whereas on the Serengeti plains they have been correlated directly with soils and in turn with the east to west climatic and lithological sequence that occurs in this part of Tanzania (Anderson and Talbot, 1965). At present remoteness and difficulties of movement during the wet season hinder the utilization of many of the valley grasslands by domestic herds while the poverty of the grazing restricts the use of watershed grasslands. Nevertheless, conflict between man and wildlife has arisen in some areas. The decline in the numbers of lechwe that inhabit the seasonally inundated grasslands in Zambia, for example, is due not only to excessive slaughter but also to competition of the cattle grazing the Kafue Flats in winter. Knowledge of the grass assocations and of the factors influencing their distribution, including landscape evolution, would provide the basis for a rational allocation of land between domestic and wild beast and permit a wiser use of available grazing.

The savanna grasslands dominated by *Astrebla* and *Iseilima* spp. that cover the vast tracts of country on the Barkly Tableland and over the plains of central Queensland, respectively, constitute the most valuable cattle rearing and cattle and sheep rearing areas of Australia. Formerly handicapped by remoteness and inadequate water supplies which respectively necessitated overland trekking and led to considerable stock losses, the grasslands of the Barkly Tableland have increased in importance with the coming of road cattle trains that provide rapid transport to fattening grounds and slaughter houses on the east coast. The grassland plains of central Queensland have likewise benefitted from this development. Both areas have also benefitted from the growing of sorghum for fattening on the savanna parklands of the Peak Downs–Rolleston area. In Australia the carrying capacity and nutritive properties of the *Astrebla–Iseilima* grasslands depend on adequate rainfall. In good seasons they provide good summer grazing and standing hay through the dry winter months but in years of drought they may be eaten to the ground and there are no browse plants to provide alternative feed.

The savanna grasslands of the Llanos of the Orinoco Basin in Venezuela likewise constitute important cattle rearing areas. Because of more reliable rainfall and the regular inundation of areas adjoining the rivers in the lower Llanos, these areas are not handicapped by drought and, according to the state of the vegetation cover, cattle can be moved between the upper and lower Llanos in a similar way to that practised between the watershed and valley grasslands in Africa.

Finally, the periodically inundated areas of the Pantanal of Brazil and the Channel Country of Australia provide rich fattening pastures for cattle. The potential of the Okavango is different. In years of good rainfall and grass growth large herds of cattle move into the area around Lake Ngami which becomes overgrazed (Figure 20.2). In the Okavango delta periodic inundation, inaccessibility and the prevalence of the tse-tse fly impose restraints and most of the area northwards to the Caprivi Strip appropriately remains the preserve of wild game. Periodically consideration is given to using the waters of the Okavango streams for irrigation but only limited areas of levee soils marked by narrow belts of *Acacia* trees would be suitable and the larger areas of *Colophospernum mopane* woodland occupying riverine silts suffer from high alkalinity and pose cultural problems.

THE USE OF VEGETATION FOR GEOLOGICAL MAPPING AND MINERAL EXPLORATION

Provided that the relationships between the distribution of vegetation units at all levels of classification and environmental factors is understood the vegetation may be used to assist geological mapping and mineral exploration in several ways. Firstly, because in areas of near surface bedrock the distribution of plant communities is clearly related to soils and lithologies (see Chapters 8–10, 15 and 18), the vegetation may assist the recognition and mapping of geological units both in the field and on satellite imagery and aerial photographs. Secondly, because plant distributions are sensitive to moisture relationships, species distribution patterns may reveal the presence of structural features. Thirdly, relationships between vegetation formations and associations and geomorphological features may assist the identification of areas with a potential for those minerals whose occurrence is influenced by geomorphology. Fourthly, and perhaps most importantly, mineral indicator species and biogeochemical analyses of plant samples may be used in the detection and location of orebodies.

On the Zambian Copperbelt, from which most of the lateritic mantle has been eroded, differences in the form and composition of the savanna woodlands distinguish the different bedrock types that make up the geological groups and series of the Katanga System that, in the Lower Roan Group, contains important copper orebodies (Horscroft 1961) (see Chapter 8, pp. 135–136). These relationships assisted the geological mapping of the area and, in the early days of exploration, the common occurrence of a small creeper bush of the *Llandorphia genus* provided a guide to the Ore formations. Natural clearings where the open savanna woodlands that covered the Lower Roan series of rocks gave way to low shrub communities composed of *Becium homblei* and a *Cryptosepalum* sp. delineated areas where toxic levels of copper in the soils emanating from the copper orebodies precluded tree growth. In some cases the anomalous vegetation occurred directly over the orebodies, in others it occupied dambos where subsurface copper bearing drainage waters circulated within the rooting depth of plants—a reminder that relationships between vegetation, geochemistry, geomorphology and geology must be elucidated when vegetation is used in mineral exploration. *Becium homblei*, which germinates only when the copper content of the growth medium exceeds 50 ppm, has proved a reliable copper indicator plant growing over cupriferous ground not only within the savanna woodlands of the Copperbelt but also within savanna parkland east of Lusaka and over the Mangula orebodies in Zimbabwe. Correct identification of species, however, is essential for the related species *Becium obovatum* is widely distributed.

On the Katanga the savanna woodland vegetation likewise cuts out over mineralized ground where zonal patterns of plant species distribution that are related to differing levels of toxicity obtain (Duvigneaud 1958, 1959, Duvigneaud and Denaeyer de Smet 1960, 1963). Thus *Bulbostylis mucronata* and *Acrocephalus robertii* occupy the outcrops of the ore-bearing beds and the workings and are succeeded in turn downslope by species of *Becium*, *Ascolepis*, *Commelina* and *Pandiaka* over highly cupriferous colluvial material derived from the workings and by *Cryptosepalum* sp., *Loudetia simplex* and *Bulbostylis* spp. and by grassland dominated by *Hyparrhenia* spp. and studded with *Uapaca robynsii* and *Parinari mobola* trees on the lower values. As in Zambia the presence of the *Cryptosepalum* sp. on an adjacent dambo where the subsurface drainage from the ore-bearing ridge approached the surface provided a reminder of the need for cognisance of geomorphology.

In recent years the vegetation has been used alongside other exploration techniques to locate the continuation of the Katanga System of rocks in Botswana and South West Africa where they are masked by calcrete and Kalahari Sand (see Chapter 10). There, in areas of near surface bedrock, distinctive vegetation associations within the low tree and shrub savannas distinguished the different lithological units within the Proterozoic sequence while two new indicator plant species, *Helichrysum leptolepis* and *Ecbolium lugardae*, were identified and used to locate copper deposits in South West Africa and Botswana respectively (Figures 10.11 and 10.22) (Cole and le Roex 1978).

In the savanna woodlands of northern Australia different vegetation associations cover different geological units in those areas from which the Tertiary lateritic cover has been largely removed (see Chapter 15). In the Rum Jungle area the shale formation, which was the host rock for the uranium orebodies, is characterized by a woodland of *Eucalpytus papuana*, *Terminalia pterocarya* and *Xanthostemon paradoxus* (believed to be an uranium indicator) whereas one of *E. grandifolia*, *Owenia vernicosa*, *Grevillea parallela* and abundant *Livistona* and *Pandanus* palms occupy areas underlain by granite and a more open one of *E. foelscheana* and *Erythrophloeum chlorostachys* covers areas underlain by limestone. In Arnhem land the two last named species together with *Eucalyptus tectifica* and *Gardenia megasperma* distinguish the Upper Proterozoic or Lower Cambrian limestones of the Bulman formation which host lead–zinc deposits, whereas sparsely distributed small *Cochlospermum fraseri* and *Acacia pallida* trees occupy areas of outcropping dolerite and grasslands with scattered *Terminalia platyphylla* and *Tristania grandiflora* trees cover areas of alluvium. Anomalous plant communities of *Gomphrena canescens*, *Polycarpaea synandra* var. *gracilis* and *Tephrosia* affino *polyzyga*, the last two being lead indicators, mark the site of the lead–zinc deposits, while *Bulbostylis barbata* and *Aristida browniana* occur over ground receiving drainage from the mineralized crust capping the lead–zinc deposits (Cole *et al.* 1968).

In the savanna woodlands around Chillagoe and Mungana in eastern Queensland the well known copper indicator *Polycarpaea spirostylis* accompanied by *Bulbostylis barbata* and the grass *Eriachne mucronata* delineate areas of copper mineralization and also cover old workings (Cole 1965).

In the low tree and shrub savannas of northwest Queensland different vegetation associations outline distinctive lithological units within the Precambrian rock sequence (see Chapter 18) while anomalous plant communities delineate mineralized areas in the Lady Annie, Mount Isa and Cloncurry areas. The largest anomalies are those over the Lady Annie phosphate deposits (Cole 1977, 1980) and the Dugald river lead–zinc load (Nicholls *et al.* 1964–65). The first comprises an open woodland of small *Atalaya hemiglauca* trees regularly distributed through a grassland composed of broad bladed grasses, notably *Enneapogon polyphyllus*, which replaces the characteristic *Eucalyptus brevifolia* dominated communities (Figure 18.9). Where present in stands *Atalaya hemiglauca* is a phosphate indicator, occurring again over deposits south of Duchess. The geobotanical anomaly over the Dugald river lead–zinc lode occurs where high concentrations in the soils of lead and zinc, and in places of copper, preclude the growth of trees or of the widely distributed *Triodia pungens* grass. The anomalous vegetation comprises small *Polycarpaea glabra* plants, *Eriachne mucronata* grass and the taller *Tephrosia* sp. nov. shrub, with the first named occupying the most toxic ground and the last occurring over lower metal concentrations at the periphery (Figures 18.7).

Throughout northern Australia *Polycarpaea spirostylis* is a copper indicator in areas of savanna woodland and low tree and shrub savanna. *Polycarpaea glabra* is a lead–zinc indicator that occurs over the Dugald River Lode and also over the Lady Loretta deposit discovered in 1971. In that year serious erosion that accompanied the exceptionally heavy rains was followed by the development of new communities of *P. spirostylis* over hitherto unknown areas of cupriferous bedrock from which much of the overlying mantle of residual soil had been removed—a reminder of the importance of the dynamic nature of vegetation/geomorphology/bedrock geology and relationships.

The relevance of identification of broad-scale relationships between vegetation and geomorphology as guides in mineral exploration may be assessed by reference to the Hamersley ranges of Australia and the Cerro Bolivar and San Isidro area of Venezuela where Proterozoic rocks of comparable age host important iron orebodies.

The low tree and shrub savanna of the Hamersley ranges is composed of species belonging to the Palaeotropic and Antarctic floral elements of the Northern and Southwestern phytogeographical provinces of Australia, whereas the vegetation of the surrounding areas is largely composed of endemic Australian floral elements of the Eremean province. These contrasts are related to the geomorphological evolution of the landscape. The vegetation over the Hamersley ranges is related to the mid-Tertiary planation surface whose last vestiges are represented in the accordant summit levels of the ranges. That of the surrounding area is composed of species that evolved to occupy the new habitats that were created when, following uplift and under an increasingly arid climate, the Tertiary landscape was destroyed and vast quantities of sediments were deposited as alluvium or piled into sand dunes in the present valleys. During the period of the mid-Tertiary planation intense weathering was associated with the development of deep lateritic soils while the minerals in the rocks below were mobilized and either carried away in stream water or precipitated in favourable structures. The high grade haematite deposits of the Hamersley ranges were probably formed at this time by enrichment from the banded ironstones of the Brockman formation where the latter were exposed and where synclinal structures favoured precipitation at the contact with the underlying McCrae shales. The present anomalous vegetation of the Hammersley ranges identifies the region where these processes operated over the Proterozoic rocks. During the subsequent erosion cycles and under fluctuating climatic conditions screes formed below the newly created scarp faces. Those composed of fragments of the iron orebodies were subsequently cemented by precipitation from iron-rich waters to form canga. At the same time groundwater laterite formed along the valleys which have since been eroded leaving the laterite to form the limonite capping of strings of mesas.

While the recognition of the relationships between the Tertiary floral element in the vegetation and relicts of the Tertiary planation surface over the Proterozoic banded ironstone formations targets on potential areas for the location of the iron orebodies, different vegetation associations distinguish different lithological units within the Brockman iron formation and distinctive plant assemblages discriminate the iron orebodies and the canga. Thus whereas *Eucalyptus brevifolia* trees distinguish the skeletal soils of the

Brockman iron formation capping most of the ranges, *Acacia–Cassia–Eremophila* associations occupy the lower slopes and adjacent plains. The *Ptilotus* genus is widespread with different species favouring different lithologies. *P. astrolasius* favours the Wittenoom dolomite, and *P. candelabrum* and *P. gomphrenoides* the alluvial flood plains, while in a quite remarkable way, *P. auriculifolium* delineates a dolerite dyke that cuts through the Brockman iron formation and at the contact creates favourable conditions for the accumulation of water (Cole 1965).

The iron orebodies and the canga carry a distinctive plant assemblage of *Acacia patens, Goodenia* sp. nov., *G. scaevolina, Burtonia polyzyga, Calythrix longiflora, Polycarpaea holtzei* and *Dampiera candicans*, that occur in varying combinations at different sites according to the prevailing iron and phosphorus levels (Figure 20.3).

In Venezuela the iron orebodies at Cerro Bolivar, Cerro Altimira and San Isidro have similarly been formed by enrichment of banded ironstones of Proterozoic age, in this case in synclines within either anticlinoria or synchlinoria. Here the mid-Tertiary surface is represented in the accordant summit levels of the ranges and the end-Tertiary surface by the floor of the surrounding area. Intermediate surfaces may also be recognized. Vegetation/geomorphology relationships show some contrasts with those in the Hamersley ranges because the lower Orinoco region experiences a hot humid climate that favours intense leaching which is still active.

The climate can sustain tropical forests but either an open type of savanna woodland or campo cerrado with *Curatella americana* and *Byrsomima* spp. trees or savanna grassland prevails over the ill-drained end-Tertiary surface characterized by sandy lateritic soils (Figures 6.10 and 6.11). Tropical forests clothe the slopes of the ranges with deep red to chocolate clay loams but over the iron orebodies on Cerro Bolivar, Cerro Altimira and San Isidro gives way abruptly to a dry scrub community of *Clusia* and *Myrcia* spp. accompanied by cacti and bromelias (Cole 1965, 1980). The distribution of this community of species exhibiting drought resistant features appears to be controlled primarily by conditions of edaphic aridity over the iron orebodies. These arid conditions result from the fact that intense leaching over the orebodies produced an indurated ironstone crust — locally called canga — that, being underlain by haematite fines, collapsed to create cavernous ground. In Venezuela the term canga is used for a different product giving rise to a different type of terrain from that in Australia, but in both countries the canga has a distinctive vegetation. In Venezuela there are nearby areas of indurated lateritic crust with a campo cerrado vegetation that forms tongues running downslope through the tropical forests.

Thus in Venezuela and in Australia the relationship between vegetation and geomorphology provides the guides to areas underlain by the Proterozoic banded ironstone formations that host the commercial iron orebodies which themselves are distinguished by their distinctive vegetation of drought resistant communities within an area climatically capable of sustaining tropical forest.

The above cited provide a few examples of the many cases in which differences in the vegetation within the savannas has assisted geological mapping and mineral exploration. The recently discovered diamond bearing kimberlite pipes in the Orapa and Kimberley areas of Botswana and Australia respectively also had vegetational expression, as did the nickel–copper deposit at Empress in Zimbabwe (Cole 1971b) and numerous other less well documented mineral occurrences. In some cases the anomalies are obvious, in others they are subtle. In all cases their recognition requires a full understanding of the relationships between vegetation and environment.

VEGETATION AS AN INDICATOR OF ENVIRONMENTAL HEALTH HAZARDS

The plant communities that indicate either concentrations or deficiencies of mineral elements in the soils delineate areas that may be hazardous for grazing animals and also for man when he consumes the pastoral products and food crops raised on them. In undisturbed natural terrain stock normally avoid the anomalous plant communities including those composed largely of grasses. Over the Dugald River Lode in northwest Queensland the avoidance of *Eriachne mucronata* grass is remarkable when all other grasses are eaten down. On the other hand the presence of an unfamiliar species, likewise indicative of a hazard, may cause problems. A documented example is that of *Neptunia amplexicaulis* that spread into a well watered pasture in Queensland, where horses were on agistment from neighbouring drought-stricken cattle and sheep stations. The plant accumulated selenium from low concentrations in the soils emanating from limestone bedrock and the horses that ingested the plant died.

Anomalous plant communities usually occupy old mine dumps and waste heaps and may provide valuable indicators of contaminated grounds centuries after the workings have been abandoned. Within the low tree and shrub savanna and low savanna woodland zone of Botswana the occurrences of *Helichrysum leptolepsis* over old copper workings near Matzitamma and Thakadu reveal the contaminated ground. Anomalous plant communities may also indicate areas contaminated by emissions from smelters, the occurrence of *Bulbostylis barbata* over ground contaminated by the Mount Morgan copper smelter within the savanna woodland zone of eastern Queensland, Australia, providing a good example.

Within the savanna woodlands of Africa the distribution of a particular form of cancer which develops in children of African, Indian, British, Syrian and Lebanese parentage, particularly between the ages of two and twelve with a pronounced peak at six years, has been shown to occur only in those areas where the rainfall exceeds 760 mm annually and the temperature does not fall below 15°C. The area of incidence coincides with the tse-tse fly belt and it has been suggested that the tumours result from a virus borne infection carried by some arthropod. The anatomical distribution of the tumour supports this suggestion. The distribution of the cancer, however, coincides with areas of highly leached lateritic soils that are deficient in essential mineral nutrients. This suggests that mineral deficiencies during the vital years of child growth caused by deficiencies in food crops grown on the poor soils may result in susceptibility to disease (Cole 1965). In any area within the savanna woodlands the species composition of the vegetation reflects the texture and mineral status of the soils and the character of the leaves of some trees, notably *Uapaca* spp. indicates acute mineral deficiencies. The vegetation may thus not only indicate the agricultural potential of the land but also the hazards of poor soils for human health.

VEGETATION AS AN INDICATOR OF ENVIRONMENTAL CONSTRAINTS AND HAZARDS RELEVANT FOR ENGINEERING CONSTRUCTION

Since the form and composition of the savanna vegetation reflect the interplay of environmental factors it follows that discrete categories of savanna, individual vegetation associations and plant communities whose distribution is influenced by one or more dominant factors, may indicate particular environmental constraints and hazards relevant for engineering construction.

The savanna grasslands, notably in Australia and Africa, occupy areas of black cracking montmorillonitic clays that swell and become sticky after rains, crack deeply on drying out and develop gilgai or crab-hole features. The last mentioned features are clearly outlined as lozenge or almond shaped areas with concentric belts of discrete plant communities that, for example, are clearly revealed on aerial photographs of the Cloncurry plains and can be identified by their brilliant red colours on colour composites generated from satellite imagery acquired after rains (see Chapter 16). Such areas pose particular problems for road construction; unsurfaced roads become impassable guagmires after rains and on drying out become cracked, uneven and exceedingly bumpy. Unless provided with adequate stone and gravel foundations roads surfaced with bitumen suffer from the alternating expansion and contraction of the subsurface and become uneven and broken.

Where possible roads are aligned to avoid such areas, and to take advantage of areas of relict lateritic material outlined by the savanna woodlands they support. These can be readily identified on aerial photographs and satellite imagery. Thus cognisance of the distribution of vegetation associations and plant communities that indicate soil and drainage conditions can both target and assist the solution of the problems that confront road construction and likewise the construction of buildings. In the Australian savannas the cattle stations and farm homesteads are invariably located on areas of relict lateritic material.

The savanna parklands pose lesser hazards than the savanna grasslands but there too the surface becomes sticky after rains and cracks on drying. Calcrete, however, may be present at shallow depth and offers a suitable and widely used surfacing material for dirt roads. In the drier parts of Africa its presence is usually revealed by grey leaved shrubs notably *Catophractes alexandri* or suffructices like *Petalidium englerianum*, *Hermannia damarana* or *Leucas pechelli*. In Australia the grey leaved *Cassia pruinosa* may disclose its presence.

Within the low tree and shrub savannas the areas of firm ground with residual gravelly or sandy red earth soils most suitable for roads are revealed by the most typical low tree and shrub savanna form of vegetation in which distinctive banding may reveal near surface bedrock, whereas locally grasslands usually denote areas of dark brown or black cracking soils posing the same problems for road or building construction as the extensive savanna grasslands and parklands. Stands of *Terminalia sericea* or *Acacia giraffae* trees in Africa or of *Callitris glauca* trees in Australia usually indicate areas of deep sand to be avoided in road or building construction.

Within the outline framework the actual form and composition of the vegetation reflects the precise conditions of the physical environment and provides the detailed guide to conditions for road and building construction in any given area.

CONCLUSIONS

In the foregoing examples of the ways in which the various categories of savanna vegetation and the vegetation associations and plant communities within them may provide an index of agricultural potential, an indicator of geological bedrock and mineral orebodies and a guide to environmental hazards have been cited. Such examples afford only an outline review of the applications that may stem from a full understanding of the relationships between vegetation and environment within the savannas.

21 Conclusions: savanna stability, dynamics and tension zones

In the foregoing chapters the form, composition and distribution of the major categories of savanna vegetation and of the vegetation associations and plant communities within them are shown to result from the responses of plant species to the interplay of changing environmental factors over both space and time. Climate and the legacies of landscape evolution largely control the distributions of the major categories of savanna vegetation, whereas soils and bedrock geology determine the composition of vegetation associations and plant communities within them. Everywhere the form and composition of the vegetation have been influenced by long-term climatic changes and geological events and by the short-term activities of grazing animals and man.

The distribution of vegetation types, the spread and retreat of plant species, the evolution of new species and extinction of others have been influenced by the climatic, edaphic and geomorphological changes that attended the break-up of Gondwanaland and continental drifting from the Cretaceous onwards, the Tertiary earth building movements and the Pleistocene glaciation. In the southern continents palynological studies indicate that there have been major changes in the distributions of savannas and forest since the Tertiary period. In the past the savanna grasslands and savanna woodlands have occupied areas that today carry forest in South America. In both Africa and South America the dry types of savanna have also been more widespread in the past, with evidence of linking corridors between the low tree and shrub savannas of South West Africa and Botswana and those of Tanzania, Kenya and Somaliland and between the caatinga of the Pantanal and of northeast Brazil. In Africa and Australia sand plains that are now vegetated bear witness to drier conditions at some stage in the Pleistocene. In each continent there are core areas of savanna woodland distribution beyond which there are isolated outliers of this form of vegetation. Likewise there are core areas of low tree and shrub savannas with corridors or 'stepping stones' linking them to their outliers.

Today in the core areas of their distribution the savanna woodlands occupy the lateritic soils of the older planation surfaces whereas savanna grasslands, parklands and low tree and shrub savannas respectively occupy the black clay soils, brown loams and arid red earths associated with level, lightly dissected and rugged terrain of the younger surfaces. Upon this broad canvas, however, the actual vegetation associations or plant communities depend on the degree of preservation of the planation surface and the extent to which the bedrock is exposed, since together these influence the development of specific soil types.

The various categories of savanna are in a state of dynamic equilibrium with the environment in the core areas of their distribution and unless disturbed by man the plant cover is relatively stable. At the periphery of their distributions the individual categories interact and compete with one another in tension zones. Here slight changes of climate and the continuous processes of landscape evolution result in the advance of one category of vegetation at the expense of another. Here the cover is unstable and highly vulnerable to prolonged drought or exceptional rains, to erosion, to heavy grazing and to changes brought about by man's activities.

Because of the relationships between the form, composition and distribution of the savanna vegetation and the interplay of environmental parameters the vegetation provides an index of land potential for agriculture and forestry, yields information on superficial and bedrock geology, on the nature and depth of subsurface water supplies and on mineralization, and distinguishes areas that pose problems for highway and building construction.

The impact of man on savanna vegetation is manifest in his use of fire, in his management of wildlife resources and in his use of the land for grazing domestic stock and for cultivation.

Fire is a factor of the savanna woodland and savanna grassland environment. In both its major function is to remove dead material and promote a regrowth of the grasses. The morphological and physiological characteristics of the trees that enable them to withstand seasonal drought also enable them to survive fire. An outstanding feature of the trees in the savanna woodlands, particularly in Australia and in central and southern Africa, is their resilience. In Australia this is marked by the regrowth and suckering of *Eucalyptus* trees, especially *E. populnea*, following clearing and burning to encourage pasture grasses and in Africa by the regrowth of the *Brachystegia*, *Isoberlinia* and *Julbernardia* trees after lopping and burning in preparation for cultivation. The species characteristic of soils with very high pH values, *Colophospermum mopane* in Africa and *Acacia harpophylla* in Australia, are both aggressive and spread rapidly from suckers after clearing for cultivation or pasture.

The impact of man's cultural practices on savanna vegetation takes various forms depending on the type of vegetation. Under natural conditions the differing grazing and browsing habits of wild animals maintain the relative proportions of trees, shrubs and grasses and other herbs. Where the savanna parklands, grasslands and low tree and shrub savannas are reserved for the conservation of wildlife this long-term vegetational stability is maintained. In some areas elephants may destroy trees and thereby promote grass growth but as this is preferentially grazed by zebra and antelopes seedling trees are established and the vegetation gradually returns to its former state.

In central and southern Africa, tropical South America and northern and eastern Australia the grazing of domestic stock is widespread in all types of savanna. Apart from opening up the savanna woodlands to encourage grass growth cattle grazing has had relatively little impact on the form or composition of this type of vegetation. In the low tree and shrub savannas of central and southern Africa where cattle are grazed at low densities in coexistence with the wild fauna the stability of the vegetation is maintained. Under high densities causing overgrazing in West Africa, however, the vegetation deteriorates and desertification ensues. In some areas, notably the savanna grasslands and parklands where cattle replace wild game, browsing ceases and the increase of shrubs leads to 'bush encroachment'. In areas of sloping terrain at the periphery of savanna grasslands, as dissection promotes better drainage and soil renewal, conditions become more favourable for trees and shrubs and there is a natural tendency for the vegetation to change to parkland, woodland or thicket. Here grassland is maintained only by the introduction of browsing animals such as goats and/or the judicious use of fire.

Except in West Africa and India, and more recently in Brazil, cultivation is restricted to relatively small areas. In recent decades large areas of the campos cerrados of Brazil have been cleared for rice production and in southern Africa well watered and irrigable areas of fertile soils in the dry savanna woodland and parkland zones have been planted with sugar cane and horticultural crops. Here the land potential has been fulfilled and agricultural stability has been achieved. In West Africa and India, on the other hand, acute population pressures, subsistence cultivation and excessive grazing from stock numbers far in excess of the carrying capacity of the grass cover of the savanna woodlands and the low tree and shrub savannas has radically changed or even totally destroyed the vegetation, leading ultimately to the desertification of the Sahel zone. While prolonged drought has exacerbated the problem in Africa and led to widespread stock losses and human starvation, the basic problem is that of overutilization of a fragile resource. Other areas are vulnerable, notably the tension zones of the Okavango in Botswana and the Channel Country of southwest Queensland and the borders of the Kalahari in Botswana and South West Africa, where good grass growth following above average rains encourages overstocking and subsequent losses in drought years.

The nature and composition of savanna vegetation reflect the environmental conditions and provide a reliable index of its potential for agricultural and other uses. While the savannas and particularly the savanna woodlands constitute the major part of the world's undeveloped or underdeveloped lands, it is important to emphasize that their potential is constrained by the environmental conditions they reflect. Successful land use has been achieved only when this has been recognized. The lessons of the failures of the East African groundnut scheme and the Queensland sorghum scheme in the 1950s are relevant today. The tragedy of human starvation in the Sahelian zones of the Sudan and Ethiopia are reminders that the overprovision

Figure 21.1. Bare area due to overgrazing around a borehole where stock are watered, east of Dodoma, Tanzania.

of wells and boreholes that encourage overstocking and overpopulation relative to the vegetational resources can lead to disaster in years of drought (Figure 21.1). The years of drought in West Africa have been parallelled by years of good rains in Botswana and South West Africa but as the pressure and wind systems move northward to bring rains to West Africa these areas could suffer comparable prolonged droughts. In all areas the vegetation indicates the potential and should be understood, not disregarded.

Appendix: list of plant species

ACANTHACEAE
Barleria affinis C. B. Clarke
  B. bremekampii Oberm.
  B. galpinii C. B. Clarke
  B. senensis Klotzsch
Blepharis innocua C. B. Clarke
Ecbolium lugardae B. E. Br.
  E. revolutum C. B. Clarke
Glossochilous parviflorus Nees
Justicia betonicoides C. B. Clarke
Peristrophe cernua Nees
Petalidium englerianum (Schinz) C. B. Clarke
  P. parvifolium Schinz
AMARANTACEAE
Gomphrena canescens R. Br.
Leucosphaera bainesii (Hook. F.) Gilg.
Ptilotus astrolasius F. Muell.
  P. auriculifolium F. Muell.
  P. candelabrum
  P. gomphrenoides F. Muell.
  P. spicatus F. Muell.
AMARYLLIDACEAE
Copernicia tectorum Mart.
Crinum charnsii Bak.
Nerine laticome (Ker) Dur. & Shinz.
Vellozia humilis Baker
ANACARDIACEAE
Astronium urundeuva Engl.
Lannea kerstingii Engl. & K. Kraus
  L. schimperi Engl.
  L. stuhlmanni
Ozoroa paniculosa (Song.) R. & A. Fernandes
  O. reticulata (E. G. Baker) R. & A. Fernandes
Quebrachia brasiliensis
Rhus ciliata Licht.
  R. lancea L.f.
  R. leptodictya Diels
  R. pyroides Burch.
  R. tenuinervis Engl.
Sclerocarya birrea (A. Rich.) Hochst.
  S. caffra Sond.
Spondias tuberosa Arruda
ANONACEAE
Anaxagorea brevipes Benth.

Annona senegalensis Pers.
APOCYNACEAE
Aspidosperma tomentosum Mart.
Carissa bispinosa (L.) Desf. ex Brenan.
  C. lanceolata R. Br.
Diplorhynchus condylocarpon (Mull. Arg.)
  Pichon
Hancornia speciosa Gomez
ARALIACEAE
Cussonia barteri Seeman
BIGNONIACEAE
Catopractes alexandrii D. Don.
Markhamia acuminata K. Schum.
  M. tomentosa K. Schum. ex Engl.
Marquesia macroura Gilg. R.E. Fr.
Rhigozum brevispinosum Kuntze
  R. trichotomum Burch.
Stereospermum kunthianum Cham.
Tabebuia caraiba (Mart.) Bur.
  T. chrysantha Nichols
Tecoma aurea DC
  T. caraiba Mart.
BIXACEAE
Cochlospermum fraseri Planch.
  C. planchoni Hook ex Planch.
BOMBACACEAE
Adansonia digitata L.
Bombax costatum Pellegrin & Vuillet
Boswellia dalziellii Hutchinson
  B. serrata Roxb. ex Colebr.
BURSERACEAE
Commiphora africana (A. Rich) Engl.
  C. karibenis Wild
  C. pendunculata Engl.
  C. pyracanthoides Engl.
Trattinickia burserifolia Mart.
CACTACEAE
Cereus jamacuaru DC
  C. squamulosus DC
Leimaireocereus sessius
Pereskia guamacho Weber
Pilocereus gounellei Weber
CAPPARIDACEAE
Boscia albitrunca (Burch.) Gilg. & Bened.
  B. foetida Schinz

Cadaba rotundifolia Forsk
Capparis aphylla Roth
  C. odorotissima Jacq.
Cleome viscosa L.
Maerua angolensis DC
CARYOCARACEAE
Caryocar brasiliensis Camb.
CARYOPYLLACEAE
Polycarpaea corymbosa (L.) Lam.
  P. glabra C. T. White & Francis
  P. holtzei Maiden
  P. spirostylis F. Muell.
  P. synandra F. Muell. var. gracilis Benth.
CELASTRACEAE
Maytenus senegalensis (Lam.) Exell
  M. tenuispina (Sond.) Marais
COMMELINACEAE
Commelina erecta L.
COMBRETACEAE
Anogeissus latifolia Wace
  A. leiocarpus (DC) Guill. & Perr.
  A. schimperi Wall.
Combretum albopunctatum Suesseng
  C. apiculatum Sond.
  C. binderianum Kotschy
  C. collinum Fresen.
  C. engleri Schinz
  C. erythrophyllum Sond.
  C. ghasalense Engl. & Diels
  C. glutinosum Guill. & Perr.
  C. gueinzii Sond.
  C. hereroense Schinz
  C. imberbe Wawra
  C. mechowianum O. Hoffin.
  C. molle R. Br. ex G. Don
  C. mossambicense (Klotzsch) Engl.
  C. negricans Leprieur ex Guill. & Perr.
  C. zeyheri Sond.
Terminalia avicenniodes Guill. & Perr.
  T. canescens (DC) Radlk.
  T. glaucescens Planch. ex Benth.
  T. laxiflora Engl.
  T. macropter Mart.
  T. platyphylla F. Muell.
  T. mollis Laws
  T. prunioides Laws
  T. pterocarya F. Muell.
  T. sericea Burch. ex DC
  T. sericea Cambess.
  T. volucris R. Br. ex Benth.
COMPOSITAE
Dicoma niccolifera Wild.
Flaveria australisica Hook
Helichrysum leptolepis DC
Pegolettia pinnatiloba
Tarchonanthus camphoratus L.

CONIFERAE
Callitris cupressiformis Vent.
  C. glauca R. Br. ex Mirb.
  C. intratropica R. T. Baker & H. G. Sm.
Cupressus lusitanica Lind. ex Parl.
CYPERACEAE
Cyperus longus L.
  C. margaritaceus Vahl.
Bulbostylis barbata (Rottb.) C. B. Clarke
  B. conifera (Kunth.) A. A. Beetle
  B. mucronata C. B. Clarke
Fimbristylis exilis Roem & Schult.
  F. ferruginea (L.) Vahl.
  F. schultzii Boeck.
Kylinga alba Nees
Scleria hirtella Boeck.
Trilepis pilosa Boeck.
DILLENIACEAE
Curatella americana L.
DIPTEROCARPACEAE
Dipterocarpus intricatus Dyer
  D. obstusifolius Teysm.
  D. tuberculatus Roxb.
Monotes glaber Sprague
  M. kerstingii Gilg.
Pentacme suavis A. DC
Shorea obtusa Wall.
  S. robusta Roxb.
EBENACEAE
Diospyros acida
  D. lysioides Desf.
  D. melanoxylon Roxb.
  D. mesmiliformis Hochst. ex A. DC
Euclea undulata Thunb.
EUPHORBIACEAE
Acalypha indica Linn.
Bridelia ferruginea Benth.
Croton gratissimus Burch.
  C. menyhartii Pax
Euphorbia ingens E. May
Excoecaria parivfolia Muell. Arg.
Hymenocardia acida Tvl.
Petalostigma banksii Britten & S. Moore
  P. pubescens Domin.
  P. quadriloculare F. Muell.
Pseudolachnostylis maprounefolia Pax.
Spirostachys africana Sond.
Uapaca kirkiana Muell. Arg.
  U. nitida Muell. Arg.
  U. robynsii de Wild
  U. togoensis Pax.
FABIACEAE
Livistona humilis R. Br.
GOODENIACEAE
Dampiera condicans F. Muell.
Goodenia scaevolina F. Muell.

GRAMINAE
Andropogon bicornis Forsk
   A. gayanus Kunth.
   A. linearis Staph.
   A. tectorum Schum. & Thonn.
Anthephora pubescens Nees
Aristida bipartita (Nees) Trin ex Rupr.
   A. browniana Henrard
   A. canescens Henrard
   A. capillacea Lam.
   A. congesta Roem. & Schult.
   A. contorta F.v.M.
   A. graciflora Pilger
   A. hordeacea Kunth.
   A. kalahariensis
   A. meridionalis Henr.
   A. pallens Cav.
   A. scabrivalvis Hackel
   A. unaequiglumis Domin.
Arundinaria falcata Nees
   A. setosa Trin.
Astrebla elymoides F. Muell.
   A. lappacea Domin.
   A. pectinata (Lindl.) F. Muell. ex Benth.
   A. squarrosa C. E. Hubbard
Axonopus areus Beauv.
   A. caulescens (Mez.) Henrard
Bothriochloa intermedia (R.Br.) A. Camus
   B. pertusa (Willd.) Maire
   B. radicans (Lehm.) A. Camus
Brachiaria cruciformis Griseb.
   B. negropedata Stapf.
Brachyachne convergens Stapf.
Cenchrus ciliaris L.
Chloris acicularis Lindl.
   C. gayana Kunth.
Chionachne cyathopoda F. Muell.
Chrysopogon fallax S. T. Blake
   C. pallidus Domin.
   C. serrulatus Trin.
Cymbopogon excavatus (Hochst.) Stapf.
   C. plurinodis (Stapf.) Stapf. ex Burtt Davy
Cynodon dactylon (L.) Pens.
Dichanthium fecundum S. T. Blake
   D. sericeum (R. Br.) Guillaumin
Digitaria capense
   D. eriatha Steud
   D. monodactyla Stapf.
   D. monostachya Willd. ex. Steud.
Diplachne fusca Beauv.
Echinochloa pyramidalis Hitchc. & Chase
   E. stagnina Beauv.
   E. turnerana (Domin.) J. M. Black
Elionurus argenteus Nees.
Enneapogon arenaceous (Lindl.) C. E.
   Hubbard

   E. brachystachys (Jaub. & Spach.) Stapf.
   E. cenchroides (Licht. ex Roem & Schult.)
      C. E. Hubbard
   E. cenchroides (Licht.) C. E. Hubbard
   E. pennisetiformis
   E. polyphyllus (Domin.) Burbidge
   E. scoparius Stapf.
Eragrostis barbinodis Hack.
   E. biflora Hack.
   E. chalcantha Trin.
   E. curvula (Schrad.) Nees
   E. echinochloides Stapf.
   E. horizontalis Peter
   E. japonica Trin.
   E. lehmanniana Nees
   E. maypurensis (H.B.K.) Steud.
   E. pallens Hack.
   E. porosa Nees
   E. pseudo-obtusa Trin.
   E. racemosa (Thunb.) Steud.
   E. rigida Scrib.
   E. rigidior Pilg.
Eriachne avenacea R. Br.
   E. dominii Hartley
   E. mucronata R. Br.
   E. obtusa R. Br.
   E. trisecta Nees
Eulalia cumingii A. Camus
   E. fulva (R. Br.) Kuntze
   E. tristachya Kuntze
Fingerhuthia africana Lehm.
Heteropogon contortus (L.) Beav. ex Roem.
   & Schultz
   H. triticeus (R. Br.) Stapf. ex Craib.
Hyparrhenia dissoluta (Nees ex Steud) C. E.
   Hubbard
   H. filipendula (Hochst.) Stapf.
   H. rufa (Nees) Stapf.
Imperata cylindrica (L.) Beauv.
Ischaemum afrum (J. C. Gmel) Dandy
   I. brachyantherum Fenzl. ex Hack
Iseilima macrathera Domin.
   I. macratherum Domin.
   I. vaginiflorum Domin.
Leptocoryphium lanatum (H.B.K.) Nees
Loudetia flavida (Stapf.)
   L. simplex Nees (C. E. Hubb)
Melinis minutiflora Beauv.
Monocymbium ceressilorme (Nees) Stapf.
Oropetium capense (Stapf.)
Oryza barthii A. Chgev.
Panicum caricoides Nees ex Trin.
   P. coloratum L.
   P. decompositum R. Br.
   P. maximum Jacq.
   P. spectabile Nees ex Trin.

P. whitei J. M. Black
Paratheria prostrata Griseb.
Paspalum carinatum Flagge
 P. fasciculatum Willd. ex Flagge
 P. plicatum Michx.
 P. repens Berg
Phragmites karka (Retz.) Trin. ex Steud.
Plectrachne pungens (R. Br.) C. E. Hubbard
Pogonarthria squarroa (Licht.) Pilg.
Pseudoraphis spinescens R. Br. Vickery
Rhynchelytrum villosum (Parl.) Chiov.
Rhynchospora barbata Kunth.
 R. globosa Roem. & Sch.
Saccharum nargena Wall.
Schizachyrium brevifolium Stapf.
 S. jeffreysii Stapf.
 S. sanguineum (Retz.) Alston
Schmidtia bulbosa Stapf.
 S. pappophoroides Steud.
Sehima galpinii Stent.
 S. nervosum (Rottler) Stapf.
Setaria geniculata (Lam.) Beauv.
 S. lindenbergiana Stapf.
 S. perennis Hack. ex. Schinz.
 S. woodii Hack.
Sorghum intrans F. Muell.
 S. plumosum (R. Br.) Beauv.
 S. serratum Stapf.
Sporobolus australasicus Domin.
 S. ioclados Nees
 S. robustus Kunth.
Stipagrostis uniplumis (Licht.) de Wint.
Themeda arguens (L.) Hack.
 T. australis (R. Br.) Stapf.
 T. triandra Forsk.
Trachypogon capensis Trin.
 T. montufari Nees
 T. plumosus (H.B.K.) Nees
 T. lspicatus (L.f.) Kuntze
 T. vestitus Anders
Tricolaena monachne Stapf.
Triodia basedowii Pritzel
 T. microstachya R. Br.
Tristachya chrysothrix Nees
 T. hispida (L.f.) K. Schum.
 T. rehmanii Hack ex. Schinz.
Urochoa brachyura (Hack.) Stapf.
Vetiveria elongata (R. Br.) Stapf. ex C. E.
  Hubbard
 V. nigritana Stapf.
 V. pauciflora S. T. Blake
Vossia cuspidata (Roxb.) Griff.
GUTTERIFERAE
Kielmeyera coriacea (Spr.) Mart.
Psorospermum revolutum Drake

IRIDACEAE
Lapeirousia caerulea Schinz.
LABIATAE
Acrocephalus robertii Robyns
Becium bomblei de Wild
 B. obovatum (E. Mey ex. Benth.) N. E. Br.
Hemizyga bracteosa (Benth.) Brig.
Leucas pechelli (O. Kunze) Guerke
Ocimum americanum L.
 O. sanctum L.
LEGUMINOSAE
Acacia acuminata Benth.
 A. albida Del.
 A. aneura F. Muell. ex Benth.
 A. arabica Willd.
 A. cafra (Thunb.) Willd.
 A. cambagei R. T. Baker
 A. campylacantha (Hochst ex A. Rich.)
  Brenan
 A. catechu Willd.
 A. chisholmii F. M. Bailey
 A. coriacea DC
 A. difficilis Maiden
 A. eriocarpa Brenan
 A. erioloba E. Mey
 A. erubescens Welw. ex Oliv.
 A. exuvialis Verdoorn
 A. farnesiana (L.) Willd.
 A. fleckii Schinz
 A. galpinii Burtt Davy
 A. georginae F. M. Bailey
 A. gerrardii Benth.
 A. giraffae Willd.
 A. harpophylla F. Muell. ex Benth.
 A. hebechlada DC
 A. homalophylla A. Cunn.
 A. karroo Hayne
 A. leucophloia Willd.
 A. leuderitzii Engl.
 A. lysiphloia F. Muell.
 A. mellifera Benth.
 A. nigrescens Oliver
 A. nilotica (L.) Willd. ex Del.
 A. pallida F. Muell.
 A. raddiana Savi.
 A. reficiens Wawra
 A. senegal (L.) Willd.
 A. seyal Delile
 A. shirleyii F. Muell.
 A. sieberiana Scheele
 A. tetragonophylla F. Muell.
 A. tortilis (Forsk.) Hayne
 A. welwitschi Oliver
 A. xylocarpa A. Cunn.
Afrormosia angolensis Harms.
 A. laxiflora Harms.

Afzelia cuanensis Oliver
  A. quanzensis Welw.
Albizzia anthelmintica Brongw.
  A. antunesiana Harms.
  A. harveyi Fourn.
  A. petersiana Oliver
Andira humilis Benth.
Baidiaea plurijuga Harms.
Bauhinia carronii F. Muell.
  B. cunninghamii (Benth.) Benth.
  B. hookeri F. v. M.
  B. macrantha Oliver
Bowdichia virgiloides H.B.K.
Brachystegia alenii Hutchinson & Burtt Davy
  B. boehmii Taub.
  B. floribunda Benth.
  B. longifolia Benth.
  B. speciformis Benth.
  B. tamarindoides Welw. ex Benth.
  B. taxifolia Harms.
  B. utilis Hutchinson & Burtt Davy
Burkea africana Hook
Burtonia polzyga Benth.
Caesalpinia coriaria Willd.
  C. grnadillio Pittier
  c. pyramidalis Tul.
Cassia moschata Benth.
  C. pruinosa F. Muell.
Colophospermum mopane (Kirk ex Benth.)
  Kirk ex J. Leonard
Crotalaria trifoliastrum
Cryptosepalum pseudotaxis Bak.
Dalbergia melanoxylon Guill. & Perr.
Daniella oliverii (Rolfe) Hutch & Dalz.
Detarium microcarpum Guill. & Perr.
Dichrostachys cinerea (L.) Wight & Arn.
Dimorphandra mollis Benth.
Entada africana Guill. & Perr.
Erythrina senegalensis A. Rich.
Erythrophloeum africanmum Harms.
  E. chlorostachys (F. Muell.) Baillon
  E. intermedia
Guibourtia coleosperma (Benth.) J. Leon.
  G. conjugate (Bolle) J. Lear
Hymenaea courbaril L.
Isoberlinia doka Craib & Stapf.
  I. globiflora Hutchinson apude Greenway
  I. tomentosa Hutchinson apude Greenway
Jacksonia odontoclada F. Muell. ex Benth.
  J. ramossissima Benth.
Julbernardia paniculata Hutchinson apude
  Greenway
Lonchocarpus capassa Rolfe
  L. nelsii Schninz ex Heering & Grimme
Mundulea sericea (Willd.) A. Cher.
Neptunia amplexicaulis Domin.

Ormocarpum trichocarpum (Taub.) Harms.
Parkia clappertoniana Keay.
Peltophorum africanum Sond.
Piliostigma thongii (K. Schumm.) Milne
  Redhead
Piptadenia macrocarpa Benth.
Prosopis africana Taub.
  P. juliflora DC
  P. spicigera L.
Pterocarpus angolensis DC
  P. antunesii Harms.
  P. brenanii L. Barb. & Toore
  P. erinaceua Poir.
  P. marsupium Roxb.
  P. pedatus Pierre
  P. rotunfidolius (Sond.) Druce
  P. vernalis Pittier
Schotia brachypetala Sond.
Sesbania benthamiana Domin.
Sindora cochinchinensis Baill.
Stryphnodendron barbatimao Mart.
Tamarindus indicus L.
Tephrosia tenella A. Gray
Tyosema esculentum (Burch) A. Schreiber
Xylia xylocarpa Taub.
LONGANIACEAE
Strynos spinosa Lam.
LILIACEAE
Dipcadi gracillimum Baker
Aloe littoralis Koen. ex Baker
  A. marlothii Berger
Pseudagaltonia clavata (Mast. ex Baker)
  Phillips
Sanseveria ethiopica
Smilax kraussiana Meissner.
MALPIGHIACEAE
Brysonima coccolobifolia (Spr.) Kunth.
  B. crassifolia (L.) Kunth.
Triaspis glaucophylla Engl.
Byrsonima verbascifolia Rich. ex Juss.
MALVACEAE
Ceiba pentandra Gaertor
Sida acuta Surm. f.
MELIACEAE
Cedrela fissilis Vell.
Entandrophragma delevoyi de Wild
Khaya nyasica Staph. ex E. G. Baker
  K. senegalensis A. Juss.
Owenia vernicosa F. Muell.
Trichelia emetica Vahl.
MONTINIACCAE
Montinia caryophyllacea Thunb.
MYOPRACEAE
Eremophila latrobei F. Muell.
  E. mitchellii Benth.
Myoporum platycarpum R. Br.

MYRTACEAE
Calythrix archaeta F. Muell.
  C. longiflora F. v. M.
  C. microphylla A. Cunn.
Eucalyptus alba Reinw. ex Blume
  E. apodophylla Blakely & Jacobs
  E. argillacea W. V. Fitzg.
  E. bigalerita F. Muell.
  E. bleeseri Blakely
  E. camaldulensis Dehn.
  E. citriodora Hook.
  E. clavigera A. Cunn. ex Schauer
  E. confertiflora F. Muell.
  E. crebra F. Muell.
  E. dichromophloia F. Muell.
  E. drepanophylla F. Muell. ex Benth.
  E. ferruginea Schauer
  E. foelscheana F. Muell.
  E. grandifolia R. Br. ex Benth.
  E. hemiphloia F. v M. ex Benth.
  E. jensenii Maiden
  E. latifolia F. Muell.
  E. leptophleba F. Muell.
  E. melanophloia F. Muell.
  E. microtheca F. Muell.
  E. miniata A. Cunn. ex Schauer
  E. nesophila Blakely
  E. papuana F. Muell.
  E. phoenicea F. Muell.
  E. polycarpa F. Muell.
  E. populifolia Blakely
  E. populnea F. Muell.
  E. porrecta S. T. Blake
  E. pruinosa Schauer
  E. racemosa Cav.
  E. setosa Schauer
  E. shirleyi Maiden
  E. siderophloia Benth.
  E. tectifica F. Muell.
  E. terminalis F. Muell.
  E. tessellaris F. Muell.
  E. tetrodonta F. Muell.
Eugenia bleeseri Schwarz
Eugenia suborbicularis Benth.
Melaleuca acacioides F. Muell.
Melaleuca leucadendron (L.) L.
Melalauca saligna Schauer
Melaleuca symphyocarya F. Muell.
Melaleuca viridiflora Sol. ex Gaertn.
Planchonia careya (F. Muell.) R. Knuth
Syzygium guineense (Willd.) DC
Tristania grandiflora Cheel
Xanthostemon paradoxus F. Muell.
NYCTAGINACEAE
Phaeoptilum spinosum Radlk.

OCHNACEAE
Lophira lanceolata Van Tiegh. ex Keay
Ochna pulchra Hook.
OCHYSIACEAE
Salvertia convallariodora St. Hil.
OLACINEAE
Ximenia americana L.
OLINACEAE
Desmostachya bipinnata Stapf.
PALMACEAE
Borassus aethiopum Mart.
Copernicia cerifera Mart.
  C. tectorum Mart.
Hyphaene thebaica (L.) Mart.
  H. ventricosa Kirk.
Mauritia minor Burr.
  M. vinifera L.f.
PEDALIACEAE
Dicerocaryum zanguibarium (Lour.) Merrill
PINACEAE
Pinus douglasiana Lamb
  P. insularis Ehdl.
POACEAE
Dactyloctenium aegypticum (L.) P. Beauv.
POLYGALACEAE
Polygala amatymbica Eckl & Zey.
PROTEACEAE
Faurea saligna Harv.
  F. speciosa Welw.
Grevillea dimidiata F. Muell.
  G. dryandri R. Br.
  G. glauca Knight
  G. heliosperma R. Br.
  G. parallella Knight
  G. pteridofolia Knight
  G. striata R. Br.
  G. wickhamii Meissner
Persoonia falcata R. Br.
Protea caffra Meissner
Protea elliottii C. H. Wright
Roupala acuminata Glaziou
RHAMMACEAE
Aizyphus zeyheriana (Sond.)
Alphitonia excelsa (Fenzl.) Benth.
Maesopsis eminis Engl.
Ventilago viminalis Hook.
Zizyphus joazeiro Mart.
  Z. jujuba Lamk.
  Z. mucronata Willd.
ROSACEAE
Licania rigidath.
Parinari curatellifolia Planch. ex Benth.
  P. excelsa Sabine
  P. mobola Oliv.
RUBIACEAE
Crossopteryx febrifuga Th.

Gardenia megasperma F. Muell.
Mitragyna inermis Kuntze
Pavetia zeyheri Sond.
Platycarpum orinocense Humb. & Bonpl.
Randia aculeata L.
Timonius timon (Spreng.) Merr.
SAPINDACEAE
Atalaya hemiglauca (F. Muell.) F. Muell. ex
  Benth.
SAPOTACEAE
Butyrospermum paradoxum (Gaertn. f.)
  Hepper
Mimusops zeyheri Sond.
SCHROPHULARIACEAE
Aptosimum leucorrhizum (E. Mey.) Phill.
SIMARABACEAE
Kirkia acuminata Oliver
  K. africana
STERCULIACEAE
Dombeya rotundifolia (Hochst.) Harv.
Hermannia angolensis K. Schum.
  H. damarana Bak. f.
STERCULIACOAE
Sterculia setisera Delile

TILIACEAE
Grewia avellana Hiern.
  G. bicolor Juss.
  G. flava DC
  G. hexamita Burret
  G. flavescens Juss.
  G. retinervis Burret
UMBELLIFERAE
Steganotaenia araliacea Hochst.
URTICACEAE
Pipturus argenteus Wedd.
VERBENACEAE
Chascanum heredaceum (Sond.) Moldenke
Clerodendrum myricoides (Hochst.) Vatke.
  C. ternuatum Schinz
Holmskioldia tellensis (Klotzsch) Vatke
Tectoma grandis L.f.
Vitex rehmannii Gurke
  V. zeyheri Sond.
ZINGIBERACEAE
Afromomum biauriculatum K. Schum.
ZYGOPHYLLACEAE
Balanites aegyptiaca Delile
Guiera senegalensis J. F. Gmel.
Spathia nervosa

Bibliography

Acocks, J. P. H. (1975). *In* Killick, D. J. B. (ed.) "Veld types of South Africa", 2nd edn. Mem. Bot. Survey, South Africa.

Adejuwan, J. O. (1971). Savanna patches within forest areas in Western Nigeria: a study of the dynamics of forest boundary. *Bull. Inst. Fr. Afr. Noire Ser. A* **33**, 327–344.

Alcock, P. and Lee, M. F. (1974). Aspects of the geology and exploration of the Lady Loretta lead-zinc-silver deposit, northwest Queensland. "Recent technical and social advances in the north Australian minerals industry": paper presented at the regional meeting August 1974. (Mount Isa: Australian IMM, Queensland branch). *Symposium Series* No. 6, 207–315.

Alvin, P. de T. and Araujo, W. A. (1952). El suelo como o factor ecologico en el desarrolle de la vegetacion en el centrooeste del Brasil. *Revista Interamericana de Ciencias Agricolas* **2**, 153–160.

Anderson, G. D. and Talbot, L. M. (1965). Soil factors affecting the distribution of the grassland types and their utilization by wild animals on the Serengeti Plains, Tanganyika. *J. Ecol.* **53** (1), 33–56.

Anderson, G. D. and Herlocker, D. J. (1973). Some factors affecting the distribution of the vegetation types and their utilization by wild animals in Ngorongoro Crater, Tanzania. *J. Ecol.* **61** (3), 627–652.

Arens, K. (1958). O cerrado como vegetacao oligotrofica. *Bol. Fac. Filos. Cienc. Letras, Univ. Sao Paulo* **224** (154), 59–77.

Arens, K. (1963). As plantas lenhosas dos campos cerrados como flora adaptada as deficiencias minerais do solo. *In* Ferri, M. G. (ed.) *Simposio sobre o cerrado*, pp. 285–289. University of Sao Paulo, Sao Paulo.

Askew, G. P., Moffatt, D. J., Montgomery, R. F. and Searl, P. (1970a). Soil landscapes in N.E. Mato Grosso. *Geogr. J.* **136** (2), 211–226.

Askew, G. P., Moffatt, D. J., Montgomery, R. F. and Searl, P. L. (1970b). Interrelationships of soil and vegetation in the savanna–forest boundary zone of north eastern Mato Grosso. *Geogr. J.* **136**, 370–376.

Aubreville, A. (1938). La foret coloniale. "Les Forets de l'Afrique Tropicale", 352 pp.

Aweto, A. O. (1981). Secondary succession and soil fertility restoration in south western Nigera. *J. Ecol.* **69**, 957–963.

Barbault, R. (1983). Reptiles in savanna ecosystems. *In* Bourliere, F. (ed.) "Ecosystems of the World" Vol. 13, Tropical Savannas, pp. 325–336. Elsevier, Amsterdam, Oxford and New York.

Beard, J. S. (1949). Brazilian Campo Cerrado: fire climax or edaphic climax? *Geogr. Rev.* **39**, 664–666.

Beard, J. S. (1953). The savanna vegetation of northern tropical Amazonas. *Ecol. Manag.* **23**, 149–215.

Beard, J. S. (1967). Some vegetation types of tropical Australia in relation to those of Africa or Amazonas. *J. Ecol.* **55** (2), 271–290.

Beard, J. S. (1969). The natural regimes of the deserts of Western Australia. *J. Ecol.* **57** (3), 677–712.

Bell, R. H. V. (1970). The use of the herb layer by grazing ungulates in the Serengeti. *In* Watson, A. (ed.) "Animal Populations in Relation to their Food Resources", pp. 111–123. Blackwell Scientific, Oxford and Edinburgh.

Bell, R. H. V. (1971). A grazing system in the Serengeti. *Sci. Amer.* **224**, 86–93.

Bennett, H. H. and Allison, R. V. (1928). "The Soils of Cuba". Washington Tropical Plant Research Foundation.

Beuchner, H. K. and Dawkins, H. C. (1961). Vegetation change induced by elephants and fire in Murchison Falls National Park, Uganda. *Ecology* **42**, 752–776.

Bews, J. W. (1929). "The World's Grasses". Longmans Green, London.

Bigalke, R. C. (1961). Some observations on the ecology of the Etosha Game Park, South West Africa. *Ann. Cape Prov. Mus.* **1**, 49–67.

Blair Rains, A. and Yalala, A. M. (1970). "The Central and Southern State Lands, Botswana". Report, Ministry of Overseas State Lands, Botswana". Report, Ministry of Overseas Development, Tolworth, Surrey, UK.

Blake, S. T. (1938). The plant communities of western Queensland and their relationship with special reference to the grazing industry. *Proc. Roy. Soc. Queensland* **49**, No. 16, 156–204. University of Queensland Department of Biology Papers 1, No. 8.

Blasco, F. (1983). The transition from open forest to savanna in continental southeast Asia. *In* Bouliere, F. (ed.) "Ecosystems of the World" Vol. 13, Tropical Savanna, pp. 167–182. Elsevier, Amsterdam, Oxford and New York.

Bleackley, D. (1962). The northern savannas of the Rupununi district. *Geol. Surv. British Guiana, Records* **1**, 7–19.

Boaler, S. B. (1963). The annual cycle of stem growth increment in trees of *Pterocarpus angolensis DC* at Kabungu, Tanganyika. *Commonw. For. Rev.* **42**, 232–236.

Boshoff, A. F. (1978). *Geobotany, biogeochemistry and geochemistry in mineral exploration on the western fringes of the Kalahari desert with specific reference to the detection of copper mineralization beneath transported overburden.* Ph.D. Thesis, University of London.

Boughey, A. S. (1961). The vegetation types of Southern Rhodesia—a reassessment. *Proc. Trans. Rhodesian Sci. Assoc.* **49**, 54–98. *Rhodesian Sci. Assoc.* **49**, 54–98.

Boulbet, J. (1979). Le Phnom Koulen et sa region. *Bull. EFEO* **12**, 1–36.

Bourliere, F. (ed.) (1983). "Ecosystems of the World" Vol. 13, Tropical Savannas. Elsevier, Amsterdam, Oxford and New York.

Brenan, J. P. (1978). Some aspects of the phytogeography of tropical Africa. *Ann. Mo. Bot. Gard.* **65**, 437–478.

Brenan, J. P. M. *et al.* (1978). The Sahel Symposium. *Geogr. J.* **144** (3), 404–415.

Brown, E. H. (1970). The Geomorphology of the 20 km square. *In* Brown, E. H., Askew, G. P., Thornes, J. B., Young, A., Townshend, J. R. G. and Daultrey, S. C. (eds) "Geographical Research on the RS/RGS Expedition to the Northeastern Mato Grosso, Brazil", pp. 367–370. GJ 136(3) Sept. 365–409.

Brown, E. H., Askew, G. P., Thornes, J. B., Young, A., Townshend, J. R. G. and Daultrey, S. G. (1970). Geographical research on the R.S./RGS Expedition to the north eastern Mato Grosso, Brazil. *Geogr. J.* **136** (3), 365–409.

Budowski, G. (1956). Tropical savannas a sequence of forest felling and repeated burning. *Turrialba* **6**(1–2), 23–3.

Buerger, A. D. (1976). *Geobotanical, biogeochemical and geochemical studies in the mosaic of savanna types in southern Ngamiland with special reference to their use in mineral exploration in calcrete and sand covered areas.* M. Phil. Thesis, University of London.

Bunting, A. H. and Lea, J. D. (1962). The soils and vegetation of the Fung, east central Sudan. *J. Ecol.* **50** (3), 529–558.

Butler, B. E. (1959). Periodic phenomena in landscapes as a basis for soil studies. *CSIRO Aust. Soil Pub.* **14**.

Cahen, L. (1954). "Geologie du Congo Belge". Liege, Vaillant-Carmanne.

Cahen, L. and Lepersonne, J. (1952). Equivalence entre le systeme du Kalahari du Congo Belge et les Kalahari beds de l'Afrique australe. *Mem. Soc. Belge Geol.* **8**, 4.

Champion, H. G. (1936). A preliminary survey of the forest types of India and Burma. Indian Forest Records Vol. 1, No. 1, "Silviculture". Manager of Publications, Delhi.

Charter, C. G. (1941). Reconnaissance survey of the soils of British Honduras. *Trinidad Govt Printer.*

Chevalier, A. (1900). Les zones et les provinces botaniques de l'A.O.F. *C.R. Acad. Sci. Paris CXXX*, 1205–1208.

Chevalier, A. (1929). Sur le degredation des sols tropicaux causee par les feux. *C.R. Acad. Sci. Paris* **188**, 84–85.

Christian, C. S. and Stewart, G. A. (1952). Survey of the Katherine–Darwin region, 1946. *CSIRO Land Res. Series No. 1.*

Christian, C. S., Paterson, S. J., Perry R. A., Slatyer, R. O., Stewart, G. A. and Traves, D. M. (1953). Survey of the Townsville–Bowen region, 1950. *CSIRO Land res. Series No. 2.*

Christian, C. S., Noakes, L. C., Perry, R. A., Slatyer, R. O., Stewart, G. A. and Traves, D. M. (1954). Survey of the Barkley region, Northern Territory and Queensland, 1947–48. *CSIRO Aust. Land. Res. Series No. 3.*

Christoffel, H. M. (1939). Informe definitivo sobre los suelos e las posibilidades agricolas en la gran Sabano. *In* Aguerrevere *et al.* (eds) *Rev. Fom Caracas* **19**, 598–631.

Clayton, W. D. (1957). The swamps and sand dunes of Hadejia. *Nigerian Geographical Journal.* **1**, 31–37.

Clayton, W. D. (1958a). Secondary vegetation and the transition to savanna near Ibadan Nigeria. *J. Ecol.* **46** (2), 217–229.

Clayton, W. D. (1958b). Erosion surface in Kabba province, Nigeria. *J. West African Sci. Assoc.* **4**, 141–149.

Clayton, W. D. (1961). Derived savanna in Kabba Province, Nigeria. *J. Ecol.* **49**, 595–604.

Clayton, W. D. (1963). The vegetation of Katsina province, Nigeria. *J. Ecol.* **49**, **51** (2), 345–352.

Clos-Arceduc, M. (1956). Etude sur photographies aeriennes d'une formation vegetale Sahelienne; la Brousse Tigree. *Bull. Inst. Fr. Afr. Noire Ser. A* **18**, 677–684.

Coaldrake, J. E., Tothill, J. C., McHarg, G. W. and Hargreaves, J. N. G. (1972). Vegetation map of Narayen Research Station, Southeast Queensland. CSIRO, Australia Dir. Trop. Pastures. Tech. Paper No. 12, 9 pp.

Codd, L. E. W. (1951). Trees and shrubs of the Kruger National Park. *Union of S. Africa Bot. Surv. Mem.* **26**.

Coetzee, B. J. (1974). A phytosociological classification of the Jack Scott Nature Reserve. *Bothalia* **11**, 329–347.

Coetzee, B. J. (1975). A phytosociological classification of the Rustenburg Nature Reserve. *Bothalia* **11**, 561–586.

Coetzee, B. J., van der Meulen, F., Zwanziger, S. Gonsalves, P. and Weisser, P. J., (1976). A phytosociological classification of the Nylsvlei Nature Reserve. *Bothalia* **12**, 137–160.

Cole, M. M. (1956). "The South African Lowveld". Bude, England, Geographical Publications Limited.

Cole, M. M. (1959). The distribution and origin of the Savanna vegetation with particular reference to the campos cerrados of Brazil. *Comptes Rendus du XVIII Congress International de Geographie.* Rio de Janerio, 1956. Tome Premier Actes du Congres, pp. 339–345.

Cole, M. M. (1960a). Cerrado caatinga and pantanal: distribution and origin of the savanna vegetation of Brazil. *Geogr. J.* **126** (2), 168–179.

Cole, M. M. (1960b). "The Brazilian Savanna". Instituto Pan-Americano de Geographia e Historia, Commissao de Geografia, Revista Geographica **26** (52), 5–40.

Cole, M. M. (1961). "South Africa". Methuen and Co. Ltd., London.

Cole, M. M. (1962). The Rhodesian economy in transition and the role of Kariba. *Geography XIVII*, 15–40.

Cole, M. M. (1963a). Vegetation and geomorphology in Northern Rhodesia: an aspect of the distribution of the savanna of central Africa. *Geogr. J.* **129** (3), 290–310.

Cole, M. M. (1963b). Vegetation nomenclature and classification with particular reference to the savannas, *South African Geogr. J.* **55**, 3–14 (Pres. Address).

Cole, M. M. (1965). *Biogeography in the service of man.* Inaugural Lecture, Bedford College, University of London 1964.

Cole, M. M. (1967). The use of vegetation in mineral exploration in Australia, *Proc. 8th Commonw. Min. and Metall. Congress* **6**, 1429–1458.

Cole, M. M. (1971a). The importance of environment in biogeographical/geobotanical and biogeochemical investigations, *Can Inst. Mon. Metall., special volume* **11**, 414–425.

Cole, M. M. (1971b). Biogeographical/geobotanical and biochemical investigations connected with exploration for nickel–copper ores in the hot, wet summer/dry winter savanna woodland environment. *J. S. African Inst. Min. and Metall.* **1971**, 199–214.

Cole, M. M. (1973). Geobotanical and biogeochemical investigations in the sclerophyllus woodland and shrub associations of the Eastern Goldfields area of Western Australia with particular reference to the role of *Hybanthus floribundus* (Lindl.) F. Muell as a nickel indicator and accumulator plant. *J. Appl. Ecol.* **10**, 269–320.

Cole, M. M. (1977). Landsat and airborne multi-spectral imagery in geological mapping and identification of ore horizons in Lady Annie/Lady Loretta and Dugald River areas, Queensland, Australia. *Trans. Inst. Min. and Metall. (Section B: Appl. Earth Sci.)* **86**, B195–215.

Cole, M. M. (1980). Geobotanical expressions of orebodies. *Trans. Inst. Min. and Metall. (Section B: Appl. Earth Sci.)* **89**, B73–143.

Cole, M. M. (1982a). The influence of soils, geomorphology, and geology on the distribution of plant communities in savanna ecosystems. *In* Huntley, B. J. and Walker, B. H. (eds) "Ecology of Tropical Savannas", pp. 145–174. Springer-Verlag, Berlin, Heidelberg and New York.

Cole, M. M. (1982b). Integrated use of remote sensing imagery and geobotany in mineral exploration. *Trans. Geol. Soc. S. Africa* **85** (1), 13–28.

Cole, M. M. (1982c). Multispectral and thermal imagery, geobotany and geomorphology in mineral exploration. *In* Glen, H. W. (ed.) *Proc. 12th C.M.M.I. Congress*, Vol. 2, pp. 935–944. South Africa Institute of Mining and Metallurgy and the Geological Society of South Africa.

Cole, M. M. (1983). Enhanced Landsat and HCMM imagery for mineral exploration in contrasting areas of subtropical humid and semi-arid terrain. *Adv. Space Res.* **3**, 181–185.

Cole, M. M. (1984). Geobotany in geological mapping and mineral exploration. *In* Teleki, P. and Weber, C. (eds) "Remote Sensing for Geological Mapping". BRGM No. 82, IUGS No. 18, pp. 267–286.

Cole, M. M. (1985). Simple remote sensing in prospecting for gold, uranium and base metals in desert areas in Australia and Africa—some case studies. *In* M. J. Jones (ed.) "Prospecting in Areas of Desert Terrain". Institute of Mining and Metallurgy, London.

Cole, M. M. and Brown, R. C. (1976). The vegetation of the Ghanzi area of Western Botswana. *J. Biogeog.* **3**, 169–196.

Cole, M. M. and Edmiston, D. J. (1980). HCMM and Landsat imagery for geological mapping in northwest Queensland Australia. *Proc. Remote Sensing of Environment Symposium, Costa Rica.*

Cole, M. M. and le Roex, H. D. (1978). The role of geobotany, biogeochemistry and geochemistry in mineral exploration in South West Africa and Botswana— a case history. *Trans. Geol. Soc. S. Africa* **81**, 277–317.

Cole, M. M. and Owen-Jones, E. S. (1977). "The Use of Landsat Imagery for Terrain Analysis in Northwest Queensland", 3 vols. E.R.T.S. follow-on programme study No. 26928 (29650) Final Report, Department of Industry, London.

Cole, M. M., Provan, D. M. J. and Tooms, J. S. (1968). Geobotany biogeochemistry and geochemistry in mineral exploration in the Bulman–Waimuna Springs area, Northern Territory, Australia. *Trans. Inst. Min. and Metall. (Section B: Appl. Earth Sci.)* **77**, B81–104.

Cole, M. M., Owen-Jones, E. S., Beaumont, T. E. and Custance, N. E. D. (1974). Recognition and interpretation of spectal signatures of vegetation from aircraft and satellite imagery in western Queensland, Australia. *European Earth Resources Satellite Experiments: Proceedings of a Symposium, Frascati, Italy.* ESRO SP 100, pp. 243–87.

Crockett, R. N. and Jennings, C. M. H. (1965). Geology of part of the Okwa valley, western Bechnanaland. *Rec. Geol. Surv. Bechuanaland, Protectorate* **1961–62**, 101–113.

Crook, A. E. (1956). A preliminary vegetation map of the Melsetter Intensive Conservation Area, Southern Rhodesia. *Rhod. Agric. J.* **53**, 3–25.

CSIRO (1960). "The Australian Environment", 3rd edn.

Cummings, D. H. M. (1982). The influence of large herbivores on savanna structure in Africa. *In* Huntley, B. J. and Walker, B. H. (eds) "Ecology of Tropical Savannas", pp. 217–245. Springer-Verlag, Berlin, Heidelberg and New York.

da Cunha, E. (1940). "Os Sertoes", 15th edn. Rio de Janeiro.

Dansereau, P. (1951). Description and recording of vegetation upon a structural basis. *Ecology* **32**, 172–229.

Dansereau, P. (1957). "Biogeography: An Ecological Perspective". Ronald Press, New York.

Dansereau, P. (1958). A universal system for recording vegetation. *Contr. Bot. Inst. Univ. Montreal*, No. 72, pp. 1–52.

Dansereau, P. and Arros, J. (1959). Essais d'application de la dimension structural en phytosociologie, 1. Quelques examples europeens. *Vegetatio* **9**, 48–99.

Darling, F. F. (1960). "Wildlife in an African Territory". Oxford University Press, London.

Dean, G. J. W. (1967). Grasslands of the Rukwa valley. *J. Appl. Ecol.* **4** (1), 45–58.

de Beer, J. S. (1962). Provisional vegetation map of the Bechuanaland Protectorate. Internal Report, Department of Agriculture, Bechuanaland Protectorate.

d'Hoore, J. L. (1964). "Soil map of Africa Scale 1 to 5,000,000 Explanatory Monograph, 250 pp. C.C.T.A., Lagos.

Dixey, F. (1938). Some observations on the physiographic development of central and southern Africa. *Trans. Geol. Soc. S. Afr.* **41**, 114–170.

Dixey, F. (1942). Erosion surfaces in central and southern Africa. *Trans. Geol. Soc. S. Afr.* **45**, 151–181.

Dixey, F. (1943). Morphology of the Congo–Zambezi watershed. *S. Afr. Geog. J.* **25**, 20–41.

Dixey, F. (1944). The geomorphology of Southern Rhodesia, *Trans. Geol. Soc. S. Afr.* **48**, 9–46.

Dixey, F. (1955). Some aspects of the geomorphology of central and southern Africa. Alex. du Toit Memorial Lecture No. 4. *Trans. Geol. Soc. S. Afr.* **58**.

Drude, O. (1890). "Handbuch der Pflanzengeographie", 582 pp. Engelhorn, Stuttgart.

Dury, G. H. (1971). Relict deep weathering and duricrusting in relation to the palaeo-environments of middle latitudes. *Geogr. J. G.J.* **137** (4), 511–521.

Duvigneaud, P. (1955). Etude ecologiques de la vegetation en Afrique tropicale. *Coll. Reg. Ecol. Globe, Paris, Ann. Biol.* **31**, 375–392.

Duvigneaud, P. (1958). La vegetation du Katanga et de ses sols metalliferes. *Bull. R. Soc. Bot. Belg.* **90**, 127–186.

Duvigneaud, P. (1959). Plantes "cobaltophytes" dans le Haut-Katanga. *Bull. R. Soc. Bot. Belg.* **91**, 111–134.

Duvigneaud, P. and Denaeyer de Smet, S. (1960). Influence des sols toxiques sur la vegetation. Action de certain metaux lourds du sol (cuivre, cobalt, manganese, uranium) sur la vegetation dans le Haut Katanga. *In* "Rapport de sol et la vegetation", pp. 121–139. Masson, Paris.

Duvigneaud, P. and Denaeyer de Smet, S. (1963). Cuivre et vegetation au Katanga. *Bull. R. Soc. Bot. Belg.* **93**, 93–231.

Dye, P. J. and Walker, B. H. (1980). Vegetation–environment relations on sodic soils of Zimbabwe Rhodesia. *J. Ecol.* **68** (2), 599–606.

Eden, M. J. (1964). The savanna ecosystem — Northern Rupununi, British Guyana. *McGill Univ. Savanna Res. Project. Savanna Research Series No. 1*, pp. 1–216.

Eden, M. J. (1967). The effect of changing fire conditions on the vegetation of the Estacion Biologica de los Llanos Calabozo. *Biol. Soc. Ven Cs Nat.* **111**, 104–113.

Eden, M. J. (1970). Savanna vegetation in the northern Rupununi, Guyana. *J. Trop. Geog.* **30**, 17–28.

Eden, M. J. (1971). Scientific exploration in Venezuelan Amazonas. *Geogr. J.* **137**, (2) 149–156.

Eden, M. J. (1973). The savanna environment, Guyana: II. Savanna vegetation in the northern Rupununi. *McGill Univ. Savanna Res. Project. Savanna Res. Ser. No. 17* 14 pp.

Eden, M. J. (1974). Palaeoclimatic influences and the development of savanna in southern Venezuela. *J. Biogeog.* **1**, 95–109.

Eiten, G. (1963). Habitat flora of Fazenda Campininha, Sao Paulo, Brazil. *In* Ferri, M. G. (ed.) *Simposio sobre o cerrado*, pp. 181–231. University of Sao Paulo, Sao Paulo.

Eiten, G. (1972). The cerrado vegetation of Brazil, *Bot. Rev.* **38**, 201–341.

Eiten, G. (1975). The vegetation of the Serra do Roncador. *Biotropica* **7**, 112–135.

Eiten, G. (1978). Delimitation of the cerrado concept. *Vegetatio* **36**, 169–178.

Eiten, G. (1982). Brazilian savannas. *In* Huntley, B. J. (ed.) "Ecology of Tropical Savannas", pp. 25–47. Springer-Verlag, Berlin, Heidelberg and New York.

Ernst, W. (1972). Ecophysiological studies of heavy metal plants in South Central Africa. *Kirkia* **8**, 125–145.

Ernst, W. (1975). Variations in the mineral contents of leaves of trees in miombo woodland in South Central Africa. *J. Ecol.* **63** (3), 801–808.

Ernst, W. and Walker, B. H. (1973). Studies on the hydrature of trees in miombo woodland in South Central Africa. *J. Ecol.* **61** (3), 667–674.

Exell, A. W. and Wild, H. (1961, 62). "Flora Zambesiaca", Vol. 1, Parts 1 and 2. Crown Agents, London.

Exell, A. W., Fernandes, A. and Wild, H. (1963, 66). "Flora Zambesicaca", Vol. 2, Parts 1 and 2. Crown Agents, London.

Faissol, S. (1952). "O Mato Grosso de Goias". Conselho Nacional de Geografiar, Rio de Janeiro.

Fanshawe, D. B. (1968). The vegetation of Zambian termitaria. *Kirkia* **6**, 169–180.

Fanshawe, D. B. (1969). The vegetation of Zambia. *For. Res. Bull.* **7**, 1–67.

Ferri, M. G. (1944). Transpiracao de plantas permanentes dos cerrados. *Bot. Fac. Filos Cienc. Sao Paulo XLI, Botanica* **4**, 159–224.

Ferri, M. G. (1953a). Balanco da agua das plantas da caatinga. *Ann. IV Congr. Nac. Soc. Bot. Brasil*, Recife, 314–332.

Ferri, M. G. (1953b). Water balance of plants from the caatinga. 2. Further information on transportation and structural behaviour. *Rev. Biol. Brasil* **13** (3), 237–244.

Ferri, M. G. (1955). Contribucao ao conhecimento da ecologia do cerrado e da caatinga. *Bot. Fac. Filos. Cienc. Sao Paulo. Letr.* No. 195 (Botanica No. 12).

Ferri, M. G. (1961a). Problemas de economia d'agua na vegetacao de caatinga e cerrados brasileiros. Fundamentos de manejo de pastagens. *Inst. Interamer. Gen. Agric. (Zona Sul) e Depto. Med. Anim. Sect. Agric. Sao Paulo* 189–199.

Ferri, M. G. (1961b). Problems of water relations of some Brazilian vegetation types, with special consideration of the concepts of xeromorphy and xerophytism. Plant water relationships in arid and semi-arid conditions. *Madrid Symposium 1959 UNESCO*, 191–197.

Ferri, M. G. (1961c). Aspects of the soil-water-plant relationships in connection with some Brazilian types of vegetation. Tropical soils and vegetation. *Proc. Abidjan Symposium 1959 UNESCO*, 103–109.

Ferri, M. G. (1964). *Simposio sobre o cerrado*, 423 pp. University of Sao Paulo, Sao Paulo.

Ferri, M. G. (ed.) (1971). *III Simposio sobre o cerrado*, 239 pp. University of Sao Paulo, Sao Paulo.

Ferri, M. G. (1973). Sobre a origem, a manutencao e a transformacao dos cerrados tipos de savanna de Brasil. *Revista de Biologia, (Lisbon)* **9**, 1–13.

Ferri, M. A. (ed.) (1977). *IV Simposio sobre o cerrado. Bases para utilizacao Agropecuaria*, 450 pp. University of Sao Paulo, Sao Paulo.

Ferri, M. G. and Coutinho, L. M. (1958). Contribuicao ao conhecimento da ecologia do cerrado. Estudo comparativo da economia d'agua de sua vegetacao, em

Emas (Est. Sao Paulo), Campo Grande (Est. Mato Grosso) e Goiania (Est. Goias). *Bol. Fac. Fil. Cienc. Letr. Univ. Sao Paulo* No. 224 (Botanica No. 15), 103–150.

Ferri, M. G. and Labouriau, L. G. (1952). Water balance of plants from the caatinga. 1. Transpiration of some of the most frequent species of the caatingas of Paulo Afonso (Bahia) in the rainy season. *Rev. Biol. Brasil* **12** (3), 301–312.

Ferri, M. G. and Lamberti, A. (1960). Informacoes sobre a economia d'agua de plantas de um Taboleiro no Municipio de Goiana (Pernambuco). *Bol. Fac. Fil. Cienc. Letr. Univ. Sao Paulo* No. 247 (Botanica No. 17), 133–145.

Fitzpatrick, E. A. and Nix, H. A. (1970). The climatic factor in Australian grassland ecology. *In* Moore, R. M. (ed.), "Australian Grasslands". A.N.U. Press, Canberra A.C.T.

Foldats, E. and Rutkiss, E. (1969). Suelo y agua como factores determinantes en la seleccion de algunas especies de arboles que en furma aislada acompanan nuestros pastizales. *Bot. Soc. Venez. Cienc. Nat.* **115–116**, 9–30.

FAO-UNESCO (1974). "Soil Map of the World 1:5000,000", Vol. 1 Legend, 59 pp. FAO-UNESCO, Paris.

Fosberg, F. R. (1967). Classification of vegetation for general purposes. *In* Peterken, G. F. (ed.) "International Biological Programme Handbook No. 4", pp. 73–120. Blackwell Scientific, Oxford.

Fry, C. H. (1983). Birds in savanna ecosystems. *In* Bourliere, F. (ed.) "Ecosystems of the World", Vol. 13, Tropical Savannas, pp. 337–358. Elsevier, Amsterdam, Oxford and New York.

Gibbons, C. L. M. (1981). Tors in Swaziland. *Geogr. J.* **147**, 72–8.

Gillman, C. A. (1949). Vegetation types map of Tanganyika Territory. *Geogr. Rev.* **39**, 7–37.

Glover, J. (1963). The elephant problem at Tsavo. *E. Afr. Wildl. J.* **1**, 30–39.

Gonzalez, E., van der Hammen, T. and Flint, R. F. (1965). Late Quaternary glacial and vegetational sequence in Valle de Lagunillas, Sierra Nevada del Cocuy, Colombia. *Leidse. Geol. Meded.* **32**.

Goodland, R. (1964). *The phytosociological study of the Northern Rupununi Savanna, British Guyana.* Thesis, McGill University, Montreal, Quebec, 156 pp.

Goodland, R. (1966a). On the savanna vegetation of Calabozo, Venezuela and Rupununi, British Guyana. *Separata Boletin de la Sociedad Venezolana de Ciencas Naturales*, **26**, 341–359.

Goodland, R. (1966b). South American savannas. Comparative studies, Llanos and Guyana. *McGill Univ. Savanna Res. Project. Savanna Res. Series No. 5*, 56 pp.

Goodland, R. (1971a). A physiognomic analysis of the cerrado vegetation of central Brazil. *J. Ecol.* **59**, 411–419.

Goodland, R. (1971b). Oligotropismo e aluminio no cerrado. *In* Ferri, M. G. (ed.) *III Simposio sobre o cerrado*, pp. 44–60. University of Sao Paulo, Sao Paulo.

Goodland, R. and Pollard, R. (1973). The Brazilian cerrado vegetation: a fertility gradient. *Ecology* **61**, 219–224.

Gossweiler, J. and Mendonca, F. A. (1939). *Carta fitogeografica de Angola*, Gov. Geral de Angola, Lisboa.

Greenway, P. J. (1973). A classification of the vegetation of East Africa. *Kirkia* **9** (1), 1–68.

Grisebach, A. H. R. (1872). "Die vegetation der Erde nach ihrer klimatischen Anordnung. Leipzig.

Grove, A. T. (1957). Patterned ground in northern Nigeria. *Geog. J.* **123**, 271–274.

Grove, A. T. (1958). The ancient erg of Hausaland and similar formations on the southern side of the Sahara. *Geogr. J.* **124**, 526–533.

Grove, A. T. (1969). Landforms and climatic changes in the Kalahari and Ngamiland. *Geogr. J.* **135** (2), 191–212.

Grunow, J. O., Groeneveld, M. T. and du Toit, S. H. C. (1980). Above ground dry matter dynamics of the green layer of a South African tree savanna. *J. Ecol.* **68** (3), 877–890.

Gunn, R. and Brewer, E. (1951–1953). Report on estimation of irrigable areas in the Sudan 1951–53. Sir Alexander Gibb and Partners, London and Khartoum. Report for the Sudan Government.

Gwynne, M. D. and Bell, R. H. V. (1968). Selection of vegetation components by grazing ungulates in the Serengeti National Park. *Nature* **220**, 390–393.

Hallsworth, E. G. and Robertson, Gwen, K. (1951). The nature of gilgai and melonhole soils. *Aust. J. Sci.* **13**, 181.

Hambler, D. J. (1964). The vegetation of granitic outcrops in Western Nigeria. *J. Ecol.* **52** (3), 573–594.

Harrison Church, R. J. (1957). "West Africa. A study of the Environment and Man's Use of it", pp. 1–547. Longmans Green and Co., London, New York and Toronto.

Hayek, F. (1926). "Allgemeine Pflanzen-geographie". Borntrager, Berlin.

Hatch, M. D. and Slack, C. R. (1966). Photosynthesis of sugar cane leaves. *Biochem J.* **101**, 103–111.

Henkel, J. S. (1931). Types of vegetation of Southern Rhodesia. *Proc. Rhod. Sci. Assoc.* **30**, 1–24.

Hill, D. and Denmead, A. K. (1960). "The Geology of Queensland". Melbourne University Press.

Hills, E. S. and Randall, R. E. (eds) (1968). "The Ecology of the Forest/Savanna Boundary". *Proc. I.G.U. Humid Tropics Commission Symposium*, Venezuela 1964. *McGill Univ. Savanna Res. Project. Savanna Res. Series* No. 13.

Hills, T. L. (1965). Savannas. A review of major research problems in tropical geography. *Canadian Geographer* **ix**(4), 216–228.

Hopkins, B. (1962). Vegetation of the Olokemeji Forest Reserve, Nigeria. 1. General features of the reserve and the reserve site. *J. Ecol.* **50** (3), 559–598.

Hopkins, B. (1965a). Observations on savanna burning in the Olokemeji Forest Reserve. *J. Appl. Ecol.* **2**, 367–382.

Hopkins, B. (1965b). Vegetation of the Olokemeji Forest Reserve. II. The climate with special reference to the seasonal changes. *J. Ecol.* **53** (1), 109–124, 125–138.

Hopkins, B. (1965c). "Forest and Savanna: An Introduction to Tropical Plant Ecology with Special Reference to West Africa". Heinemann, London.

Hopkins, B. (1970a). Vegetation of the Olokemeji Forest Reserve. VI. The plants on the forest site with special reference to their seasonal growth. *J. Ecol.* **58** (3), 765–93.

Hopkins, B. (1970b). The vegetation of the Olokemeji Forest Reserve. VII. The plants of the savanna site with special reference to their seasonal growth. *J. Ecol.* **58** (3), 795–826.

Horscroft, F. D. M. (1961). Vegetation. *In* Mendelsohn, F. (ed.) "The geology of the Northern Rhodesian Copper Belt, pp. 73–80. Macdonald, London.

Howard-Williams, C. (1969). *The ecology of Becium homblei* Duvign and Planck. M.Phil Thesis, University of London.

Howard-Williams, C. (1970). The ecology of *Becium homblei* in Central Africa with special reference to metalliferous soils. *J. Ecol.* **58**, 741–763.

Howard-Williams, C. (1971a). Morphological variation between isolated populations of *Becium homblei* growing on heavy metal soils. *Vegetatio* **23**, 141–151.

Howard-Williams, C. (1971b). Environmental factors controlling the growth of plants on heavy metal soils. *Kirkia* **8**, 91–102.

Huntley, B. J. (1982). Southern African savannas. *In* Huntley, B. J. and Walker, B. H. (eds) "Ecology of Tropical Savannas". Springer-Verlag, Berlin, Heidelberg and New York.

Huntley, B. J. and Walker, B. H. (eds) (1982). "Ecology of Tropical Savannas", Vol. 42 in Ecological Studies Series. Springer-Verlag, Berlin, Heidelberg and New York.

Ijzerman, R. (1931). "Outline of the Geology and Petrology of Surinam". Kemink, Utrecht.

Isbell, R. F. (1957). The soils of the Inglewood–Talwood–Tara–Glenmorgan region, Queensland. *Qld. Bur. Investigations Tech. Bull.* **5**.

Isbell, R. F. (1958). The occurrence of an highly alkaline solonetz soil in Southern Queensland. *Qld. J. Agr. Sci.* **15**, 15–23.

Isbell, R. F. (1962). Soils and vegetation of the Brigalow Lands, Eastern Australia. CSIRO, Aust. Div. Soils and Land use Series No. 43. 59 pp. CSIRO, Melbourne.

Isbell, R. F., Thompson, C. H., Hubble, G. D., Beckman, G. G. and Paton, T. R. (1967). "Atlas of Australian Soils", Sheet 4, Brisbane–Charleville–Rockhampton–Clermont Area (with explanatory data). CSIRO, Melbourne.

Isbell, R. F., Webb, A. A. and Murtha, G. G. (1968). "Atlas of Australian Soils", Sheet No. 7, Northern Queensland (with explanatory data). CSIRO, Melbourne.

Jarman, P. J. (1972). Seasonal distribution of large mammal populations in the unflooded middle Zambezi valley. *J. Appl. Ecol.* **9**, 283–299.

Jeans, D. N. (ed.) (1978). "Australia — a Geography". Routledge and Kegan Paul, London.

Jenik, J. and Hall, J. B. (1966). The ecological effects of the Harmattan winds in the Djebobo massif (Togo Mts, Ghana). *J. Ecol.* **54** (3), 767–780.

Johannessen, C. (1963). Savannas of interior Honduras. Ibero Americana 46, p. 173. Berkeley, University of California.

Jones, C. F. (1930). Agricultural regions of South America III. *Econ. Geog.* **6**, 1–36.

Jones, E. W. (1956). Ecological studies in the rain forest of Southern Nigeria. IV. The plateau forest of the Okomu forest reserve. *J. Ecol.* **44** (1), 83–117.

Jones, E. W. (1963). The forest outliers in the Guinea zone of Northern Nigeria. *J. Ecol.* **51** (2), 415–434.

Keay, R. W. J. (1949). An example of Sudan zone vegetation in Nigeria. *J. Ecol.* **37**, 335–364.

Keay, R. W. J. (1951). Ecological status of savanna vegetation in Nigeria. *In* "Management and Conservation of Vegetation in Africa". *Commonwealth Bureau of Pastures and Field Crops, Bull. 41*, Aberystwyth.

Keay, R. W. J. (1952). *Isoberlinia* woodlands in Nigeria and their flora. *Lejeunia* **16**, 17–26.

Keay, R. W. J. (1953). "An Outline of Nigerian Vegetation". Government Press, Lagos.

Keay, R. W. J. (1957). Wind dispersed species in a Nigerian forest. *J. Ecol.* **45** (2), 471–478.

Keay, R. W. J. (1959). Derived savanna—derived from what? *Bull. IFAN Ser. A* **21**, 28–39.

Keay, R. W. J., *et al.* (1959). "Vegetation Map of Africa South of the Tropic of Cancer". Oxford University Press, Oxford.

Kellman, M. (1979). Soil enrichment by neotropical savanna trees. *J. Ecol.* **67**, 565–578.

Kelly, R. D. and Walker, B. H. (1979). The effects of different forms of land use on the ecology of a semi arid region in S.E. Rhodesia. *J. Ecol.* **64** (2), 553–576.

Kemp, R. H. (1963). Growth and regeneration of open savanna woodland in Northern Nigeria. *Commonw. For. Rev.* **42**, 200–206.

Kershaw, K. A. (1968). Classifications and ordinations of Nigerian savanna vegetation. *J. Ecol.* **56** (2), 467–482.

Killick, H. J. (1959). The ecological relationships of certain plants in the forest and savanna of central Nigeria. *J. Ecol.* **47** (1), 115–128.

King, L. C. (1947). Landscape study in Southern Africa. *Proc. Geol. Soc. S. Afr.* **50**, 23–52.

King, L. C. (1948). A theory of bornhardts. *Geogr. J.* **112**, 83–87.

King, L. C. (1951). The geomorphology of the eastern and southern districts of Southern Rhodesia. *Trans. Geol. Soc. S. Africa.* **54**, 33–64.

King, L. C. (1953). Causes of landscape evolution. *Bull. Geol. Soc. Am.* **64**, 721–752.

King, L. C. (1957). O geomorfologia do Brasil oriental *Rev. Bras Geogr.* **18**, 147–265.

King, L. C. (1962). "The Morphology of the Earth". Oliver and Boyd, Edinburgh and London.

King, L. C. (1967). "South African Scenery", 3rd ed. Oliver and Boyd, Edinburgh and London.

Kortshack, H. P., Hartt, C. E. and Burr, G. O. (1965). Carbon dioxide fixations in sugar cane leaves. *Plant Physiol.* **40**, 209–213.

Kuchler, A. W. (1949). A physiognomic classification of vegetation. *Ann. Assoc. Amer. Geographers* **39**, 201–210.

Kuchler, A. W. (1972). On the structure of vegetation. *Ecology* **53**, 196–198.

Laboriau, L. G. (ed.) (1966). *Segundo Simposio Sobre o Cerrado. An Acad. Bras Cienc.* **38** (supplement), 346 pp.

Laboriau, L. G., Marques Valio, I. F. and Heringer, E. P. (1964). Sobre o sistema reproductivo de plantas dos cerrados. *An. Acad. Bras. Cienc* **36**, 449–464.

Lamprey, H. F. (1963). Ecological separation of the larger mammal species in the Tarangire Game Reserve, Tanganyika. *E. Afr. Wildlife J.* **1**, 63–92.

Lanjouw, J. (1936). Studies of the vegetation of the Surinam savannas and swamps. *Ned. Kruidk Arch.* **46**, 823–851.

Lawton, R. M. (1964). *Marquesia acuminata* (Gilg.) R. E. Fr. evergreen forests and related chipya vegetation types of north eastern Rhodesia. *J. Ecol.* **52** (3), 467–480.

Lawton, R. M. (1978). A study of the dynamic ecology of Zambian vegetation. *J. Ecol.* **66** (1), 175–198.

Legris, P. and Blasco, F. (1972). Carte internationale du Tapis vegetal, Cambodge. 1:1,000,000. *Trav. Sec. Sci. Tech. Inst. Fr. Pondichery* H.S. No. 11, 240 pp.

Leiberman, D. (1982). Seasonality and phenology in a dry tropical forest in Ghana. *J. Ecol.* **70** (3), 791–806.

Leistner, O. A. (1967). The plant ecology of the southern Kalahari. *Mem. Bot. Surv. S. Africa* **58**.

Lind, E. M. and Morrison, M. E. (1974). "East Africa Vegetation". Longman, London.

Lopes, A. S. and Cox, F. R. (1971). Cerrado vegetation in Brazil: an edapthic gradient. *Agronomy J.* **69**, 828–831.

Lopes, A. S. and Cox, F. R. (1977). A survey of the fertility status of surface soils under cerrado vegetation of Brazil. *J. Soil Sci. Am.* **41**, 742–747.

MacVicar, C. N. (1977). *Soil classification: a binomial system for South Africa.* Dept. Agric. — Tech. Services, Pretoria. 150 pp.

Malaisse, F. (1974). Phenology of the Zambezian woodland area, with emphasis on the miombo ecosystem. *In* Leith, H. (ed.) "Phenology and Seasonality Modelling", vol. 8 in Studies Series, pp. 269–286. Springer-Verlag, Berlin and New York.

Malaisse, F. (1978). High termitaria. *In* Werger, M. J. A. (ed.) "Biogeography and Ecology of Southern Africa", pp. 1279–1300.

Malaisse, F., Freson, R., Goffinet, G. and Malaisse-Mousset, M. (1975). Litter fall and litter breakdown in miombo. *In* Golley, F. and Medina, E. (eds) "Tropical Ecological Systems, and Trends in Terrestrial and Aquatic Research, vol. 11 in Ecological Studies Series, pp. 137–152. Springer-Verlag, Berlin and New York.

Mason, M. (1975). *Geobotany, biochemistry and geochemistry in exploration for stratiform copper deposits in the low tree and shrub savanna of central South West Africa.* Ph.D. Thesis, University of London.

McConnell, R. B. (1959). The Takutu Formation in British Guyana and the probable age of the Roraima Formation. 2nd Caribbean Geological Conference Puerto Rico, pp. 163–170.

McConnell, R. B. (1962). *Notes on the erosion levels and geomorphology of British Guyana.* Geol. Survey British Guyana, Georgetown.

McConnell, R. B. (1968). Planation surfaces in Guyana. *Geogr. J.* **134** (4), 506–520.

Medina, E. (1982). Physiological ecology of Neotropical savanna plants. *In* Huntley, B. J. and Walker, B. H. (eds) "Ecology of Tropical Savannas", pp. 305–335. Springer-Verlag, Berlin, Heidelberg and New York.

Medina, E. (1982b). Nitrogen balance in the Trachypogon grasslands of central Venezuela. *Plant and Soil* **67**, 305–314.

Menaut, C. and Cesar, J. (1979). Structure and primary functions of Lamto savanna (Ivory Coast). *Ecology* **60**, 1197–1210.

Menaut, C. and Cesar, J. (1982). The structure and dynamics of a West African savanna. *In* Huntley, B. J. and Walker, B. H. (eds) "Ecology of Tropical Savannas". Springer-Verlag, Berlin, Heidelberg and New York.

Milne, G. (1936). A provisional soil map of East Africa (Kenya, Uganda, Tanganyika and Zanzibar) with explanatory memoir. *Amani Memoirs*, 34 pp.

Milne, G. (1947). A soil reconnaissance journey through parts of Tanganyika Territory, December 1935-February 1936. *J. Ecol.* **35**, 192–265.

Milne, G., Beckley, V. A., Gethin Jones, G. H., Martin, W. S., Griffith, G. and Raymond, L. W. (1936). "A Provisional Soil Map of East Africa" (Kenya, Uganda, Tanganyika and Zanzibar) with explanatory notes. *Amani Memoirs*, 34 pp.

Misra, R. (1983). Indian savannas. *In* Bourliere, F. (ed.) "Ecosystems of the World" vol. 13, Tropical Savannas, pp. 151–166. Elsevier, Amsterdam, Oxford and New York.

Mohr, E. C. J., and van Baren, F. A. (1954). "Tropical Soils". N. V. Uitgeverij W. Van Hoeve, The Hague and Bandung.

Monasterio, M. and Sarmiento, G. (1976). Phenological strategies of plant species in the tropical savanna and the semi-deciduous forest of the Venezuelan Llanos. *J. Biogeog.* **3**, 325–356.

Monteiro, R. F. R. (1970). Estudo da flora e da vegetacao das florestas abertas do planalto do Bie. Instituto de Investigacao Cientifica de Angola, Luanda, 352 pp.

Montgomery, R. F. and Askew, G. P. (1983). Soils of tropical savannas. *In* Bourliere, F. (ed.) "Ecosystems of the World" vol. 13, Tropical Savannas. Elsevier, Amsterdam, Oxford and New York.

Morgan, W. B., and Moss, R. P. (1965). Savannas and forests in western Nigeria. *Africa* **35** (3), 286–294.

Morgan, W. B. and Pugh, J. C. (1969). "West Africa". Methuen, London.

Morrison, C. G. T., Hoyle, A. D. and Hope-Simpson, J. F. (1948). Tropical soil vegetation catenas and mosaics. A study of the Anglo-Egyptian Sudan. *J. Ecol.* **36**, 1–84.

Moss, R. P. (1963). Soils slopes and land use in south western Nigeria. *Trans. Inst. Br. Geog.* **32**, 143–168.

Moss, R. P. and Morgan, W. B. (1970). Soils, plants and farmers in West Africa. *In* Garlick, J. P. (ed.) "Human Ecology in the Tropics", pp. 1–31. Pergamon Press, London.

Newsome, A. E. (1983). The grazing Australian marsupials. *In* Bourliere, F. (ed.) "Ecosystems of the World" vol. 13, Tropical Savannas, pp. 441–462. Elsevier, Amsterdam, Oxford and New York.

Nicholls, O. W., Provan, D. M. J., Cole, M. M. and Tooms, J. S., 1964–65. Geobotany and geochemistry in mineral exploration in the Dugald river area, Cloncurry district, Australia. *Trans. Inst. Min. Metall.* **74**, 695–799.

Nix, H. A. (1983). Climate of tropical savannas. *In* Bourliere, F. (ed.) "Ecosystems of the World" vol. 13, Tropical Savannas, pp. 37–62. Elsevier, Amsterdam, Oxford and New York.

Northcote, K. H. (1965). A factual key for the recognition of Australian soils, 2nd ed. *CSIRO Aust. Div. Soils Divl. Report 2/65.*

Northcote, K. H. (1968). "Atlas of Australian Soils". Sheet 8. Northern part of the Northern Territory with explanatory data. CSIRO, Melbourne.

Oppenheimer, H. R. (1960). Adaptions to drought: xerophytism. *In* "Plant Water Relationships in Arid and Semi-Arid Conditions. *Rev. of Res. UNESCO Arid Zone Res.* **15**, 105–138.

Oviedo y Valdes, G. F. (1535). "Historia general y natural de las Indias" vol. 1 (edition by F. A. de los Rios, 1851).

Papadakis, J. (1961). "Climatic Tables for the World". Published by the author, Buenos Aires.

Perry, R. A., Mabbutt, J. A., Litchfield, W. H., Quinlan, T., Lazarides, M., Jones, N. O., Slatyer, R. O., Stewart, G. A., Bateman, W. and Ryan, G. R. (1962). General report on the lands of the Alice Springs area, Northern Territory, Australia, 1956–57. *CSIRO, Land Res. Series* No. 6.

Phipps, J. B. and Goodier, R. (1962). A preliminary account of the plant ecology of the Chimanimani Mountains. *J. Ecol.* **50** (2), 291–320.

Phillips, J. F. V. (1930). Fire. Its influences on biotic communities and physical factors in South and East Africa. *S. Afr. J. Sci.* **27**, 352–367.

Plumstead, E. P. (1962). Possible angiosperms from Lower Permian coal of the Transvaal. *Nature* **194** (4828), 594–595.

Plumstead, E. P. (1966). Recent palaeobotanical advances and problems in Africa. *Symposium on florestics and stratigraphy of Gondwanaland* 1–2.

Prescott, J. A. (1931). The soils of Australia in relation to vegetation and climate. *Sci. Industrial Res. Aust. Coun. Bull.* **52**.

Prescott, J. A. (1944). *A soil map of Australia*. CSIR. *Aust. Bull.* **177**.

Prescott, J. A. and Pendleton, R. L. (1952). Laterite and lateritic soils. *Comm. Soil. Sci. Tech. Comm.* **47**, 51 pp.

Pugh, J. C. (1954). High level surfaces in the Eastern Highlands of Nigeria. *S. Afr. Geog. J.* **36**, 31–42.

Pugh, J. C. (1956). Fringing pediments and marginal depressions in the inselberge landscape of Nigeria. *Trans. Inst. Br. Geog.* **22**, 15–31.

Pugh, J. C. and King, L. C. (1952). Outlines of the geomorphology of Nigeria. *S. Afr. Geog. J.* **34**, 30–36.

Pulle, A. A. (1906). "Enumeration of the Vascular Plants known from Suriname". Leyden.

Pulle, A. A., 1938. Exploracoes botanicas de Suriname. *An. Reun. Sul. American Bot.* **1**, 239–248.

Puri, G. S. (1960). "Indian Forest Ecology". Oxford Bk. New Delhi.

Rachid, M. (1947). Transpiracao e sistemas subterraneous de vegetacao de verao nas campos cerrados de Emas. *Bot. Fac. Filos Cienc. Sao Paulo Letr. LXXX* Botanica No. 5.

Ramsay, D. McC. (1964). An analysis of Nigerian savanna. II. An alternative analysis and its application to the Gombe sandstone vegetation. *J. Ecol.* **52** (3), 457–466.

Ramsay, D. McC. and de Leeuw, P. N. (1964). An analysis of Nigerian savanna. I. The survey area and the vegetation developed over Bima sandstone. *J. Ecol.* **52** (2), 233–254.

Ramsay, D. McC. and de Leeuw, P. N. (1965). An analysis of Nigerian savanna. III. The vegetation of the Middle Gongola region and soil parent materials. *J. Ecol.* **53** (3), 643–660.

Ratter, J. A., Richards, P. W., Argent, G. and Gifford, D. R. (1973). Observations on the vegetation of northeastern Mato Grosso. I. The woody vegetation types of the Xavantina-Cachimbo Expedition area. *Phil. Trans. R. Soc. London.* **B266**, 449–492.

Rattray, J. M. (1960). "The Grass Cover of Africa". F. A. O., Rome.

Raunkiaer, C. (1907). The life forms of plants and their bearing on geography. *In* "Collected Essays", pp. 2–104. Clarendon Press, Oxford, 1934.

Raunkiaer, C. (1916). The use of leaf size in biological plant geography. *In* "Collected Essays", pp. 368–378. Clarendon Press, Oxford, 1934.

Raunkiaer, C. (1934). "The Life Forms of Plants and Statistical Plant Geography". Clarendon Press, Oxford.

Rawitscher, F. (1942). Problemas de fitoecologia como consideracoes especiais sobre o Brasil Meridional 1 a parte. *Bot. Fac. Filos Cienc. Sao Paulo Letr. XXVIII* Botanica 3.

Rawitscher, F. (1944). Problemas de Fitoecologia como consideracoes especiais sobre o Brazil Meridional 2a parte. *Bot. Fac. Filos Cienc. Sao Paulo. Letr. XLI* Botanica 4.

Rawitscher, F. (1948). The water economy of the vegetation of the campos cerrados in southern Brazil. *J. Ecol.* **36**, 237–263.

Rawitscher, F. (1949). El balanco de agua de la vegetacion de los campos secos del Brasil meridional y su significacion. *Cienc e Invest.* **5**, (384).

Rawitscher, F. K. and Rachid, M. (1946). Troncos subterraneos de plantas brasileiras. *An. Acad. Bras. Cienc.* **18**, 261–280.

Rawitscher, F., Ferri, M. G. and Rachid, M. (1943). Profundidade dos solos e vegetacao em Campos Cerrados do Brasil Meridional. *Ann. Acad. Bras. Sci.* **15** (4) 267–296.

Richards, P. W. (1957). Ecological notes on West African vegetation. 1. The plant communities of the Idlanre Hill, Nigeria. *J. Ecol.* **45** (2), 563–78.

Richter-Zwanziger, S. M. (1977). *Geobotanical and biogeochemical investigations in the Otavi Mountainland, South West Africa.* Ph.D. Thesis, University of London.

Rollet, B. (1962). *Inventaire forestier de l'Est Mekong*, Rapport FAO No. 1500, Rome, 184 pp.

Rollet, B. (1972). La vegetation du Cambodge. *Bois For. Trop.* **145**, 23–38; **146**, 3–20.

Ross Cochrane, G. (1963). A physiographic vegetation map of Australia. *J. Ecol.* **51** (3), 639–656.

Rutherford, G. R. (1962). Chemical and neotropical data and some observations on the pedogenesis of the soils of north west Kimberley area, Western Australia. *CSIRO Aust. Div. Land Res. and Reg. Surv. Divl. Rept. 62/3.*

Rutherford, M. C. (1972). Notes on the flora and vegetation of the Omuverume Plateau and Mountain, Waterberg, S.W. Africa. *Dinteria*, 3–55.

Sarmiento, G. (1983). The savannas of tropical America. *In* Bourliere, F. (ed.) "Ecosystems of the World" vol. 13, "Tropical Savannas". Elsevier, Amsterdam, Oxford and New York.

Sarmiento, G. and Monasterio, M. (1969). Studies on the savanna vegetation of the Venezuelan Llanos. 1. The use of association analysis. *J. Ecol.* **57**, 579–598.

Sarmiento, G. and Monasterio, M. (1975). A critical consideration of the environmental conditions associated with the occurrence of savanna ecosystems in Tropical America. *In* Golley, F. and Medina, E. (eds) "Tropical Ecological Systems", pp. 223–250. Springer-Verlag, Berlin.

Sarmiento, G. and Monasterio, M. (1983). Life forms and phenology. *In* Bourliere, F. (ed.) "Ecosystems of the world" vol. 13, Tropical Savannas, pp. 79–108. Elsevier, Amsterdam, Oxford and New York.

Schimper, A. F. W. (1903). "Plant Geography Under a Physiological Basis". Clarendon Press, Oxford.

Schmid, M. (1958). Flora agrostologique de l'Indochine. *Agron. Trop.* **13**, 1–320.

Schmid, M. (1974). Vegetation du Vietnam. Le massif sud-Annamitique et les regions limitrophes. *Mem. ORSTOM* No. 74, 1–243.

Sinclair, A. R. E. (1983). The adaptions of African ungulates and their effects on community functions. *In* Bourliere, F (ed.) "Ecosystems of the World" vol. 13, Tropical Savannas", pp. 401–426. Elsevier, Amsterdam, Oxford and New York.

Sleeman, J. R. (1963). The soils of the Leichardt Gilbert area, northwest Queensland. Morphology and laboratory data. *CSIRO Aust. Div. Land Res. and Regional Survey Divl. Rept. 63/1.*

Smith, A. C. (1973). Angiosperm evolution and the relationship of the floras of Africa and America. *In* Meggers, B. J., Ayensu, E. S. and Duckworth, W. D. (eds) "Tropical Forest Ecosystems in Africa and South America: A comparative Review" pp. 49–61. Smithsonian Institute, Washington, D.C.

Smith, J. (1949). Distribution of the species in the Sudan in relation to rainfall and soil texture. *Bull. 4,* Sudan Ministry of Agriculture, Khartoum.

Spate, O. H. K. and Learmouth, A. T. A. (1967). "India and Pakistan — A General and Regional Geography", 3rd edn. London, Methuen.

Spech, N. H., Wright, R. L., van der Graaff, R. H. M., Fitzpatrick, E. A., Mabbutt, J. A. and Stewart, G. A. (1965). General report on lands of the Tipperary area, Northern Territory, 1961. *CSIRO, Aust. Land. Reg. Surv. 13.*

Stace, H. C. T., Hubble, G. D., Brewer, R., Northcote, K. H., Sleeman, J. R., Mulcahy, M. J. and Hallsworth, E. G. (1968). "A Handbook of Australian Soils". Rellim Technical Publications, Glenside, South Australia for CSIRO and International Society for Soil Science.

Stebbing, E. P. (1922–26). "Forests of India". John Lane, London.

Stebbing, E. P. (1935). The encroaching Sahara. The threat to the West African colonies. *Geogr. J.* **85,** 506–524.

Stebbing, E. P. (1937). "The Forests of West Africa and the Sahara". Chambers, London.

Stephens, C. G. (1950). Comparative morphology and genetic relationships of central Australian, North American and European soils. *J. Soil Sci.* **1,** 123–149.

Stephens, C. G. (1958). Phenology of Australian soils. *Trans. R. Soc. S. Australia* **81,** 1–12.

Stephens, C. G. (1961). The soil landscapes of Australia. *CSIRO Aust. Soil. Publ.* 18.

Stephens, C. G. (1962). "A Manual of Australian Soils", 3rd edn. CSIRO Melbourne.

Stewart, G. A. (1956). The soils of the Katherine–Darwin region, Northern Territory. *CSIRO Aust. Soil Publ.* 6.

Sturmfels, F. K. (1952). *Preliminary report on the geology of the Bulman lead-zinc prospect.* Unpublished Report, Enterprise Exploration Co. Ltd.

Tarling, D. H. and Runcorn, S. K. (eds) (1973). "Implications of Continental Drift to the Earth Sciences". Academic Press, London and New York.

Tate, G. H. H. and Hitchcock, C. B. (1930). The Cerro Duida region of Venezuela. *Geogr. Rev.* **20,** 31–52.

Taylor, B. W. (1963). An outline of the vegetation of Nicaragua. *J. Ecol.* **51,** 27–54.

Theron, G. K. (1973). *n Ekologiere studie van die plantegroet van die Loskopdam-natuurrestvaat.* D. Sc. Thesis, University of Pretoria.

Theron, G. K. (1975). The distribution of summer rainfall zone *Protea* species in South Africa with special reference to the ecology of *Protea caffra. Boissiera* **24,** 233–244.

Thomas, M. F. (1971). Savanna lands between desert and forest. *Geog. Mag. London* **44,** 185–89.

Thomas, M. F. (1974). "Tropical geomorphology". Macmillan, London.

Thornes, J. B. (1970). The hydraulic geometry of stream channels in the Xingu-Araguaia headwaters. *In* Brown, E. H., Askew, G. P., Thomas, J. B., Young, A., Townshend, J. R. G. and Daultrey, S. G. (eds), "Geographical Research on the Royal Society/Royal Geographical Society Exploration to Northeastern Mato Grosso, Brazil" pp. 376–381. *Geogr. J.* **136**(3), 365–409.

Thornthwaite, C. W. (1948). An approach towards a rational classification of climate. *Geogr. Rev.* **38,** 55–94.

Tinley, K. L. (1966). *An ecological reconnaissance of the Moremi Wildlife Reserve.* Botswana Okavango Wildlife Society, Johannesburg.

Trapnell, C. G. (1943). "The Soils, Vegetation and Agriculture of Northeastern Rhodesia". Government Printer, Lusaka; 2nd edition 1953.

Trapnell, C. G. (1953). "The Soils, Vegetation and Agriculture of Northeastern Rhodesia". Lusaka; 2nd edn. Government Printer, Lusaka.

Trapnell, C. G. (1959). Ecological results of woodland burning experiments in Northern Rhodesia. *J. Ecol.* **47**, 129–168.

Trapnell, C. G. and Clothier, J. N. (1937). "The Soils, Vegetation and Agricultural Systems of Northwestern Rhodesia". 1st edn. Government Printer, Lusaka.

Trapnell, C. G. and Clothier, J. N. (1957). "The Soils, Vegetation and Agricultural Systems of Northwestern Rhodesia, 2nd edn. Government Printer, Lusaka.

Trapnell, C. G., Martin, J. D. and Allan, W. (1950). "A Vegetation Soil Map of Northern Rhodesia". Government Printer, Lusaka.

Trapnell, C. G., Friend, M. T., Chamberlain, G. T. and Birch, H. F. (1976). The effects of fire and termites on a Zambian woodland soil. *J. Ecol.* **64** (2), 577–588.

Twidale, C. R. (1981). Granitic inselbergs, domed, block-strewn and castellated. *Geogr. J.* **147**, 54–71.

USDA Soil Survey Staff. (1960). Soil classification, a comprehensive system. 7th approximation.

USDA Soil Survey Staff (1975). "Soil taxomony" 754 pp. USDA, Washington, D.C.

van der Hammen, T. (1961). The Quaternary climate changes of northern South America. *Annals New York Acad. Sci* **95**, 676–683.

van der Hammen, T. (1963). A palynological study on the Quaternary of British Guyana. *Leidse. Geol. Meded* **29**, 125–180.

van der Hammen, T. (1972). Changes in vegetation and climate in the Amazon basin and surrounding areas during the Pleistocene. *Geol. Mijnb.* **51**, 641–643.

van der Hammen, T. (1974). The Pleistocene change of vegetation and climate in tropical South America. *J. Biogeog.* **1**, 3–26.

van der Hammen, T. (1983). The palaeoecology and palaeogeography of savannas. *In* Bourliere, F. (ed.) "Ecosystems of the World" vol. 13, Tropical Savannas, pp. 19–36. Elsevier, Amsterdam, Oxford and New York.

van der Hammen, T. and Gonzalez, E. (1960). Upper Pleistocene and Holocene climate and vegetation of the Sabana de Bogota (Colombia, South America). *Leidse. Geol. Meded.* **25**, 261–315.

van der Hammen, T. and Gonzalez, E. (1965). A pollen diagram from Laguna de la Herrera (Sabana de Bogota). *Leidse Geol. Meded.* **32**, 183–191.

van der Meulen, F. (1979). *Plant sociology of the western Transvaal Bushveld: a syntaxonomic and synecological study*. Dr. thesis, University of Nijmegen. (Also as *Diss. Bot.* **49**, Cramer Lehre.)

van der Meulen, F. and Westfall, R. H. (1980). Structural analysis of Bushveld vegetation in Transvaal, South Africa. *J. Biogeog.* **7** (4), 337–348.

van Wyk, P. and Fairall, N. (1969). The influence of the African elephant on the vegetation of the Kruger National Park. *Koedoe* **12**, 57–89.

Veryard, R. G. (1962). The changing climate. *Discovery* **23** (1).

Vesey-Fitzgerald, D. F. (1963). Central African grassland. *J. Ecol.* **51** (2), 243–274.

Vesey-Fitzgerald, D. F. (1970). The origin and distribution of valley grasslands in East Africa. *J. Ecol.* **58** (1), 51–76.

Vincent, V., Thomas, R. G. and Staples, R. R. (1960). *An Agricultural Survey of Southern Rhodesia. Part 1. Agro-ecological survey*. Fed. of Rhodesian and Nyasaland, Salisbury.

Waibel, L. (1948). Vegetation and land use in the Planalto central of Brazil. *Geogr. Rev.* **38** (4), 529–554.

Walker, B. H., Ludwig, D., Holling, C. S. and Peterman, R. M. (1981). Stability of semi-arid savanna grazing systems. *J. Ecol.* **69** (2), 473–498.

Warming, E. (1892). "Lagoa Santa", 386 pp. University of Sao Paulo, Sao Paulo. (Portuguese edition 1973.)

Watson, J. P. (1964). A soil catena on granite in Southern Rhodesia. I. Field observations. II. Analytical data. *J. Soil Sci.* **15**, 238–257.

Watson, J. P. (1965). A soil catena on granite in Southern Rhodesia. III. Clay minerals. IV. Heavy minerals. V. Soil evolution. *J. Soil Sci.* **16** (1), 158–169.

Weare, P. R. and Yalala, A. M. (1971). Provisional vegetation map of Botswana. *Botswana Notes and Records* **3**, 131–148. (The Botswana Society, Gaberone.)

Webster, R. (1965). A catena of soils on the Northern Rhodesian plateau. *J. Soil Sci.* **16** (1), 31–43.

Wellington, J. H. (1940). Stages in the process or river-superimpositionn in the Southern Transvaal. *S. Afr. J. Sci.* **37**, 78–96.

Wellington, J. H. (1949). A new development scheme for the Okavango Delta, northern Kalahari. *Geogr. J.* **108**, 62–69.

Wellington, J. H. (1955). "Southern Africa. A Geographical Study" Vol. 1, Physical Geography. University Press, Cambridge.

Werger, M. J. A. (1978). Vegetation structures in the southern Kalahari. *J. Ecol.* **66** (3), 933–942.

White, F. (1965). The savanna woodlands of the Zambezian and Sudanese Domains. *Webbia* **19**, 651–681.

White, L. P. (1970). Brousse tigree patterns in Southern Niger. *J. Ecol.* **58** (2), 549–554.

Whitehouse, F. W. (1940). Studies in the late geological history of Queensland. *Papers Univ. Queensland, Dept. Geology* **2** (1), 1–74.

Whitehouse, F. W. (1948). The geology of the Channel country of southwestern Queensland. *Bureau of Investigation Tech. Bull. No. 1, Univ. of Queensland, Dept. of Geology New Series No. 34*, 1–29.

Wijmstra, T. A. and van der Hammen, T. (1966). Palynological data on the history of tropical savannas in northern South America. *Leid. Geol. Meded.* **38**, 71–90.

Wild, H. (1952). The vegetation of Southern Rhodesia termitaria. *Rhod. Agric. J.* **49**, 280–292.

Wild, H. (1953). Vegetation survey of the Changara Mtoko Reserve area. *Rhod. Agric. J.* **50**, 401–546.

Wild, H. (1955). Observations on the vegetation of the Sabi-Lundi Junction area. *Rhod. Agric. J.* **52**, 533–546.

Wild, H. (1968). Phytogeography in South Central Africa. *Kirkia* **6**, 197–222.

Wild, H. (1975). Termites and the serpentines of the Great Dyke of Rhodesia. *Trans. Rhod. Sci. Assoc.* **57**, 1–11.

Wild, H. and Fernandes, A. (eds) (1967–68). Vegetation map of the Flora Zambesiaca area. M.O. Collins (Pvt.) Ltd., Salisbury, Rhodesia.

Williams, O. B. (1970). Population dynamics of two perennial grasslands in Australia semi-arid grassland. *J. Ecol.* **58** (3), 869–876.

Williams, R. J. (1955). Vegetation regions. *In* "Atlas of Australian Resources" (map and explanatory notes). CSIRO.

Wood, J. G. and Williams, R. J. (1960). "Vegetation in the Australian Environment". CSIRO 1949: 3rd edition (revised) 1960.

Worrall, G. A. (1960). Patchiness in vegetation in the northern Sudan. *J. Ecol.* **48** (1), 107–116.

Wright, E. P. (1978). Geological studies of the northern Kalahari. *Geogr. J.* **144**, 235–249.

UNESCO (1959). "Vegetation Map of Africa". L'Association pour l'Etude Taxonomique de la Flore d'Africa Tropicale and Oxford University Press.

Young, A. (1976). "Tropical Soils and Soil Surveys", Cambridge Geographical Studies Vol. 9. Cambridge University Press, Cambridge.

Index